Transcultural Ecocriticism

Transcultural Ecocriticism

Global, Romantic and Decolonial Perspectives

Edited by
Stuart Cooke and Peter Denney

BLOOMSBURY ACADEMIC
LONDON • NEW YORK • OXFORD • NEW DELHI • SYDNEY

BLOOMSBURY ACADEMIC
Bloomsbury Publishing Plc
50 Bedford Square, London, WC1B 3DP, UK
1385 Broadway, New York, NY 10018, USA
29 Earlsfort Terrace, Dublin 2, Ireland

BLOOMSBURY, BLOOMSBURY ACADEMIC and the Diana logo are trademarks of
Bloomsbury Publishing Plc

First published in Great Britain 2021
This paperback edition published 2022

Copyright © Stuart Cooke, Peter Denney and contributors, 2021

Stuart Cooke, Peter Denney and contributors have asserted their right under the Copyright, Designs and Patents Act, 1988, to be identified as Authors of this work.

For legal purposes the Acknowledgements on p. xii constitute an extension
of this copyright page.

Cover design: Eleanor Rose
Cover image: Ocean currents map, 1876 © Getty Images

All rights reserved. No part of this publication may be reproduced or transmitted in any form or by any means, electronic or mechanical, including photocopying, recording, or any information storage or retrieval system, without prior permission in writing from the publishers.

Bloomsbury Publishing Plc does not have any control over, or responsibility for, any third-party websites referred to or in this book. All internet addresses given in this book were correct at the time of going to press. The author and publisher regret any inconvenience caused if addresses have changed or sites have ceased to exist, but can accept no responsibility for any such changes.

A catalogue record for this book is available from the British Library.

A catalog record for this book is available from the Library of Congress.

ISBN: HB: 978-1-3501-2163-8
PB: 978-1-3502-1382-1
ePDF: 978-1-3501-2164-5
eBook: 978-1-3501-2165-2

Typeset by Deanta Global Publishing Services, Chennai, India

To find out more about our authors and books visit www.bloomsbury.com and sign up for our newsletters.

Contents

List of figures		vii
Notes on contributors		viii
Acknowledgements		xii

1 Thinking about transcultural ecocriticism: Space, scale and translation *Stuart Cooke and Peter Denney* 1

Part I Planetary localities

2 Urban narrative and climate change *Ursula K. Heise* 21

3 Scaling down our imagination of the human: Ted Chiang and the fable of extinction *Chris Danta* 41

4 'Re-enchanting the world' from Mozambique: The African Anthropocene and Mia Couto's poetics of the planet *Meg Samuelson* 63

5 Ecological imaginations in contemporary Chinese science fiction *Mengtian Sun* 82

Part II Beyond the romantic frontier

6 The colonial translation of natures *Alan Bewell* 103

7 Sensing empire: Travel writing, picturesque taste and British perceptions of the Indian sensory environment *Peter Denney* 124

8 The dark side of romantic dendrophilia *Ve-Yin Tee* 148

9 Shaping selves and spaces: Romanticism, botany and south-west Western Australia *Jessica White* 169

Part III Decolonial poetics

10 Transcultural ecopoetics and decoloniality in *meenamatta lena narla puellakanny: Meenamatta Water Country Discussion* *Peter Minter* 191

11 Theorizing decolonized literary environments *Stephen Muecke*   221

12 Placing invisible women: Environment, space and power in two
    works by Ana Patricia Martínez Huchim *Maia Gunn Watkinson*   238

13 Geoterritorial island poetics, or transcultural composition with
    a wetland in southern Chile *Stuart Cooke, with Juan Paulo
    Huirimilla Oyarzo*   262

Index   283

Figures

6.1	Title page from Thomas Pennant's *Arctic Zoology* (1784)	104
6.2	Engraving of George Stubb's *The Duke of Richmond's First Bull Moose* in Thomas Pennant's *Arctic Zoology* (1784)	105
6.3	From Edward Topsell's *History of Four-Footed Beasts* (1607)	106
8.1	'The Pleystow, vulg: The Plestor', in Gilbert White, *The Natural History and Antiquities of Selborne* (London: Bensley, 1789)	150
8.2	*Swilcar Oak (in Needwood Forest) Staffordshire*	160
8.3	'Bleeding Heart' is not only a pejorative label that can be applied to an environmentalist, it is also the name of a tree with red, heart-shaped leaves that is indigenous to Australia	161
10.1	Jonathan Kimberley and puralia meenamatta (Jim Everett), *beyond the colonial construct: meenamatta map of unlandscape* [2006, synthetic polymer, charcoal and text on linen, 240 x 240 cm (four panels)] and *meenamatta lena walantanalinany (meenamatta water country)* (2006, synthetic polymer and charcoal on linen, 240 x 240 cm (four panels))	199
10.2	Jonathan Kimberley and puralia meenamatta (Jim Everett), *balouina miengalina bagota: blood juice cloud (meenamatta tomato)* (2006, synthetic polymer, charcoal and text on linen, 182 x 182 cm (four panels))	210
10.3	Jonathan Kimberley and puralia meenamatta (Jim Everett), *Key to writing: beyond the colonial construct: meenamatta map of unlandscape* (2006, from Puralia (Jim Everett) Meenamatta and Jonathan Kimberley, *Meenamatta Lena Narla Puellakanny: Meenamatta Water Country Discussion. A Writing and Painting Collaboration* (Hobart: Bett Gallery and Devonport Gallery, 2006), p. 41)	212

Contributors

Alan Bewell is Professor of English at the University of Toronto. His primary research field is British Romanticism, focusing on colonialism, ecopoetics, science, medicine and literature. His most recent monograph, *Natures in Translation: Romanticism and Colonial Natural History* (2017), examines the ways in which the global transport and exchange of plants, animals and natural commodities transformed global natures and shaped how British writers and Indigenous peoples came to understand themselves and their natures. He is currently working on a book entitled *Romanticism and Mobility*, which studies how Romantics reacted to a world of moving people, things and ideas.

Stuart Cooke is Senior Lecturer in Creative Writing and Literary Studies at Griffith University. He has authored the book *Speaking the Earth's Languages: A Theory for Australian-Chilean Postcolonial Poetics* (2013) and the poetry collections *Lyre* (2019), *Opera* (2016) and *Edge Music* (2011). He writes on eco-, etho- and ethno-poetics, with particular interests in non-human art and transcultural theory. He has also translated a variety of Indigenous and non-Indigenous poets from Spanish and Portuguese.

Chris Danta is Associate Professor of English at the University of New South Wales, Sydney. His research operates at the intersection of literary theory, philosophy, science and theology. He is the author of *Literature Suspends Death: Sacrifice and Storytelling in Kierkegaard, Kafka and Blanchot* (Bloomsbury, 2011) and, more recently, *Animal Fables after Darwin: Literature, Speciesism, and Metaphor* (2018).

Peter Denney is Senior Lecturer in History at Griffith University. His research focuses on the literature and history of Britain in the long eighteenth century, paying particular attention to landscape, poverty, the senses, popular culture and political radicalism. He has recently co-edited *Sound, Space and Civility in the British World, 1700-1850* (2019) and *Politics and Emotions in Romantic Periodicals* (2019). He is also completing a monograph on landscape and soundscape in Britain from Defoe to Cobbett.

Ursula K. Heise is Chair of the English Department at UCLA. She also holds the Marcia H. Howard Chair in Literary Studies at the Department of English and is co-founder of the Lab for Environmental Narrative Strategies (LENS) at UCLA's Institute of the Environment and Sustainability. Her research and teaching focus on contemporary literature and the environmental humanities; environmental literature, arts and cultures in the Americas, Western Europe and Japan; literature and science; science fiction; and narrative theory. Her books include *Chronoschisms: Time, Narrative, and Postmodernism* (1997), *Sense of Place and Sense of Planet: The Environmental Imagination of the Global* (2008) and *Imagining Extinction: The Cultural Meanings of Endangered Species* (2016), which won the 2017 book prize of the British Society for Literature and Science. She is editor of the series *Natures, Cultures, and the Environment*, and producer and writer of the documentary *Urban Ark Los Angeles* (2018).

Juan Paulo Huirimilla Oyarzo was born on the island of Calbuco, Chile, in 1973. Widely published and anthologized, his poems have been translated into Catalán, Dutch, English, Galician and German. His books include *El ojo de vidrio* (2001), *Canto para niños de Chile* (2005) and *Palimpsesto* (2005), and he is the editor of the anthology *Cantos de guerrero* (2012). He has also written various essays on Huilliche culture and poetics. Huirimilla works as a supervisor of Indigenous language (Mapudungun) education and as a lecturer in arts education at La Universidad de Los Lagos, Puerto Montt.

Peter Minter is a poet, poetry editor and writer on poetry and poetics. He teaches Indigenous Studies, Creative Writing and Australian Literature at the University of Sydney. His books include the poetry collections *blue grass* (2016) and *Empty Texas* (1999), and with Anita Heiss he edited *The Macquarie PEN Anthology of Aboriginal Literature* (2008).

Stephen Muecke is Professor of Creative Writing in the College of Humanities, Arts and Social Sciences at Flinders University, South Australia, and is a Fellow of the Australian Academy of the Humanities. His recent books are *Latour and the Humanities*, edited with Rita Felski (2020) and *The Children's Country: Creation of a Goolarabooloo Future in North-West Australia*, co-authored with Paddy Roe (2020).

Meg Samuelson is Associate Professor in the Department of English and Creative Writing at the University of Adelaide, Australia, and Associate Professor Extraordinary at Stellenbosch University, South Africa. She has published widely in Southern African and Indian Ocean literary and cultural studies. Her recent research engages with narrative fiction from the African Indian Ocean littoral, photography in Zanzibar, surfing cultures of the Indian Ocean shore-break, sharks as uncanny figures of racial terror in the Anthropocene, the southern orientations of J. M. Coetzee's writing, the oceanic south and world maritime literatures and the practice and poetics of care in fiction from Southern Africa.

Mengtian Sun received her PhD degree in English Literature from the University of Melbourne. Her research interests mainly include comparative literature, modern and contemporary literature, fantasy and science fiction, critical theory, gender studies. Her research has appeared in several journals such as *Science Fiction Studies* and *Frontiers of Literary Studies in China*.

Ve-Yin Tee is Assistant Professor in the Department of British and American Studies, Nanzan University, Japan. He is the author of *Coleridge, Revision and Romanticism* (2009) as well as the teen novel *On Donuts and Telekinesis* (2014). Though he has also published on British painting and Singaporean war history, he is principally interested now in British representations of nature. He is putting together a collection of essays entitled *Romantic Environmental Sensibility: Nature, Class and Empire*.

Jessica White is the author of the novels *A Curious Intimacy* (2007) and *Entitlement* (2012) and a hybrid memoir about deafness, *Hearing Maud* (2019). Her short stories, essays and poems have appeared widely in Australian and international literary journals, and she has won awards, funding and residencies. Jessica is a researcher and lecturer at the University of Queensland, where she is writing an ecobiography of Western Australia's first female scientist, nineteenth-century botanist Georgiana Molloy. In 2020 she will be a fellow at the Rachel Carson Center for the Environment in Munich and at the University of Edinburgh Environmental Humanities Network.

Maia Gunn Watkinson recently completed her doctorate in Spanish and Latin American Studies at the University of New South Wales, Australia, and has taught at the University of Technology, Sydney. Her postgraduate research focused on the politics of Indigenous literary production in Mexico, in particular bilingual literature in the Maya and Spanish languages in the southern region of the Yucatán Peninsula. In her work she analysed the links between: cultural production; social, political and material conditions; and representation. Her research belongs to the broad field of Latin American literary and cultural studies. In this field her investigations centre on three key considerations: (1) the processes and mechanisms of legitimization of writers in Indigenous languages; (2) the politics of gender and representation and (3) representations of space and place.

Acknowledgements

We are enormously grateful to the Griffith Centre for Social and Cultural Research, and in particular its enlightened and energetic director, Professor Susan Forde, for funding our research over many years, including the conference which generated the idea for this book. We thank the large number of scholars who participated in that stimulating event on the Gold Coast, Queensland. We are also deeply indebted to David Avital for commissioning this collection, and to Ben Doyle, Lucy Brown and the editorial team at Bloomsbury for providing such superlative and highly efficient assistance throughout the publication process.

Acknowledgements for Chapter 13

This research was supported by Griffith University under the grant 'Working with the Humedal Antiñir: Transcultural, Poetic Ethnography in Southern Chile'.

1

Thinking about transcultural ecocriticism
Space, scale and translation
Stuart Cooke and Peter Denney

We present the following collection of chapters at a critical juncture in the Anthropocene. Urgently, planetary responsibility and situated knowledges need to be entwined in propositions for social and environmental justice. All around us, bodies, texts and artworks are converging in old and new forms of politics and earthly accountabilities. Never before has the world been smaller, but never has it been so overwhelming in its complexity, either. Suddenly, the critical project has become planetary, biological, even geological. As Timothy Morton puts it, 'ecological science, with its three-kilometer ice cores and its close reading of the weather, has transformed the environment into a gigantic library, a palimpsest of texts waiting to be read.'[1] Life in all of its manifestations – from DNA to forests – has textual qualities; what does it mean to 'read' such a staggering variety of data? The use of imaginative, synthetic scholarship has never been more important; reading, interpretation and translation have become not just critical but essential skills. Transcultural ecocriticism emerges in response to these concerns.

Next to alarm at the looming planetary emergency, we are inspired by the trajectory of a century or more of avant-garde poetics and criticism, particularly as it has crystallized in revised formulations of 'English', 'American' and 'New World' poetics. Here the path was lit by those like Jerome Rothenberg, who, from the 1960s onward, helped to inaugurate a radically new conception of poetry, which 'drew in whole worlds we hadn't previously imagined', and demanded 'new forms of writing & thinking' – all in order to effect 'an expansion of what we could now recognize as poetry'.[2] Crucially, combining myriad traditions of global poetics along with a bold, neo-romantic fervour, the new poetry was no longer literature per se but rather a means 'for experiencing & comprehending the world', through which 'the visions of the individual' doubled as what

Mallarmé had called 'the words of the tribe'.[3] Poetry had become a means for both ecological *and* transcultural, transcorporeal relation. More recently, dismayed by 'an upsurge of new nationalisms & racisms', Rothenberg has proposed an *omnipoetics* in order to seek out 'an ever greater assemblage of words & thoughts as a singular buttress against those forces that would divide and diminish us'.[4]

If an omnipoetic assemblage that reaches towards the infinite strays too far from the bounds of analytical precision, then a transcultural ecocriticism might nevertheless retain its germinal impulses. Such an approach recognizes not only that Western literatures are but a minority portion in a much larger compendium of global literatures, but also that there are vital exchanges and parallels between and across many of these literatures. We don't want to stop here, either; the whole world is out there. Accordingly, we are interested in pursuing the opportunities proposed by the ecological text for more-than-human relation. One aim in this context might be to theorize how the creative formations of other animals, plants, insects and forces can be drawn into relation with some of the discourses surrounding human art.[5] As much as possible, we seek here to abandon what Marcella Durand calls the 'idea of the center', venturing instead into a dynamic system where the values of all living and non-living things are contextually integrated, and the myriad perspectives of all things are explored 'as an attempt to subvert the dominant paradigms of mono-perception, consumption and hierarchy'.[6] Implicit to transcultural ecocriticism is a radical, decolonial theorization, where Western modes of conquest, categorization and extraction are checked in order to embrace a multi-vocal array of complex expressions. There is potentially an infinite variety in such an array; therefore, a transcultural ecocriticism attempts to embrace the myriad ways in which an ecological system might articulate both itself and the connections between its various parts.

If there is a 'traditional' ecocriticism, it relies upon romanticism. Often inflected through Heideggerian and phenomenological accounts of unitary, coherent subjects, the first waves of ecocriticism often focused on how texts might cultivate deep and lasting attachments to particular, cherished places. By and large, in traditional ecocriticism 'the assumption is that identity, whether individual or communitarian, is constituted by the local'.[7] As Lynn Keller outlines, the 'tenacity' of romanticism in ecocriticism is evidenced by the fact that, until the early years of the new century, many environmental critics continued to lament what they perceived to be the increasing separation of industrialized humans from the natural world, 'much as the romantic poets themselves did nearly two centuries earlier'. Simply, the ecocritics lamented that split, and treated poetry 'as a means of transcending it'. In the New World, too, settlers had imported from Western Europe a sense of nature as something apart from human civilization, 'a sacred and vanishing space offering escape from industrialized modernity, a treasured refuge for human and non-human species alike'.[8] In ecocriticism so conceptualized, nature poems were of value because they returned readers to 'a sense of being at home on earth', and allowed at least momentary solace from city life.[9] Like the literature it privileged, early ecocriticism sought an experiential immediacy in nonurban environments.

However, more recent ecocritical work has sought out poetry and fiction that, in Keller's words, 'are more analogous to landfills scavenged by gulls or city boulevards awash in diesel fumes'. Instead of trying to escape the problems of 'a warming, toxified world', ecocriticism has embraced them.[10] Indigenous ecological knowledges have also played a significant part in interrogating the split between urban and nonurban spaces; in Australia, for example, many have adopted 'country' instead of 'nature' to foreground the priority of Indigenous sovereignty and the continent's material-semiotic-spiritual complex, which includes human and non-human societies in an entangled, polyvocal network. In this context, much of the anxiety of early ecocriticism about a 'vanishing nature' is inseparable from the cultural heritage of those ecocritics themselves: until recently, ecocriticism has been predominantly the concern of white, European scholars who, much as they might lament the fact, were beneficiaries of European invasion, colonization and theft of Indigenous peoples' lands, labour and resources. In all, ecocritical scholarship has increasingly understood 'nature' as thoroughly inextricable from 'culture(s)'; resisting focus on romantic pastoral and depopulated 'wilderness', for the past decade or more it has been pushing beyond narrowly conceived, Western understandings of the environment and humanity's place therein.[11]

Transcultural ecocriticism emerges from this milieu. We hope that the following collection of essays is a sign not only of the increasing diversity of knowledge systems that inform ecocritical scholarship, but also of the exciting contributions being made by scholars from around the Pacific Rim, that great site of transcultural permeation, and beyond. Being mindful of the problematic heritage of ecocriticism in romantic thought, however, our response here is not to 'cancel' romanticism or bury it until its absence feeds some form of neurosis, but rather to acknowledge the power of contemporary romantic scholarship and to examine ways in which it might still contribute to transcultural criticism. After all, Kate Rigby reminds us that part of the enduring value of romantic literature lies in its 'capacity to go beyond science in exploring the spiritual, psychological, and ethical implications of existing . . . within a dynamic, unfolding, and signifying universe'.[12] And, while it is true, as Rigby notes, that Martin Heidegger called upon 'the redemptive strand' of romanticism to articulate an ethnocentric, proto-ecological fascism, it is equally true that Theodor Adorno and Max Horkheimer relied upon 'its avant-garde element in developing a proto-ecosocialist critique of industrial modernity'[13] (and inspired the new poetries of which people like Rothenberg were a part). As we show in this book, romanticism is much larger and more interesting than its early ecocritical ambassadors made out.[14]

With this in mind, we seek to interrogate the phenomenological immediacy of the unitary, European subject's experience of unspoiled nature by drawing on the proliferating diversity of subaltern perspectives from around the globe. This tension is reflected in the environmental movement more broadly, which has been spliced, as Ursula Heise has argued, 'between the embrace of and the resistance to global connectedness, and between the commitment to a planetary vision and the utopian reinvestment in the local'.[15] Indeed, since its publication over a decade ago, Heise's seminal *Sense of Place and Sense of Planet* has compelled ecocriticism to engage not only with 'local places' but with 'territories and systems that are understood to encompass the planet'. Rethinking an orthodoxy of early ecological thought, Heise demonstrates with characteristic precision how excessive focus on local belonging can be detrimental to global environmental movements.[16] While a sense of place 'might function as one useful tool among others for environmentally oriented arguments', she cautions that it can become 'a visionary dead end if it is understood as a founding ideological principle'. Environmentalism, she argues, 'needs to foster an understanding of how a wide variety of both natural and cultural places and processes are connected and shape each other around the world, and how human impact affects and changes this connectedness'.[17]

At the same time, what is equally important is that this sense of 'connectedness' does not come at the expense of attention to local ecologies and, in particular, localized Indigenous ecological knowledges and custodial rights. Otherwise, a 'global' sense of the environment risks replicating older and more familiar kinds of colonization. In Heise's terms, this amounts to a challenge to 'imagine local environments less as foundations for an unalienated existence than as habitats that are ceaselessly being reshaped by the encroachment of the global as well as their own inherent dynamism'. With such an open-ended notion of 'place', the focus for environmentalism would not be 'to preserve pristine, authentic ecosystems', but instead to nurture their capacity 'to change and evolve'. Nevertheless, such a resolution 'raises the difficult question of how an endorsement of constant transformation and change would allow one to discriminate between the inherently dynamic evolution of ecosystems and the kinds of disruptive change that might ultimately lead to serious ecosystemic problems and failures'.[18] Across vast regions of the world, with their millennia of attentiveness to more-than-human systems, Indigenous knowledges can, along with the environmental sciences, best determine what constitutes 'disruptive change'.

We present these chapters as a collective response to some of the most pressing concerns in contemporary ecocritical discourse. First of these concerns is that, as a critical methodology that attempts to recover the agencies of all living things and life-worlds, ecocriticism needs to acknowledge the full complexity of earthly histories, including, as Joy Harjo writes, 'the plants, trees, animal life who all have their tribes, their families, their histories, too'.

               Talk to them,
listen to them. They are alive poems.[19]

In citing Harjo, a Muscogee Creek Native American poet, we are also signalling that proper acknowledgement involves the decolonization of Western institutions, knowledges and political systems, not to mention careful consideration of the many inextricable connections between Western thought and Eastern, Indigenous and other knowledge systems since at least the 1500s. Relative to such a project, this collection of essays is, to use a term of Evelyn Araluen's, 'too little'.[20] We urge readers to consider a burgeoning diversity of First Nations scholarship as a central component of any ecocritical method,[21] and in order to avoid the 'fetishised landscape[s]' of an imperial ecological aesthetics.[22] Second of these concerns is that, as it continues to explore and celebrate the local and the immediate, ecological writing needs to be better equipped to deal with the unavoidably powerful shift towards a 'global' imagination and cultural and social diversity. Celebratory, embodied, personal experiences of places are abundant in environmental writing, yet they invariably neglect the complex ways in which access to such places, and the places themselves, rely on much larger networks of climate and capital. At the very same time, however, part of the value of a poetics of place is that it resists the formation of a globally unified constellation of freely flowing, freely accessed capital.

Between 'a poetics of place' and 'an imagination of the global', we locate the 'transcultural' – literally, webs, routes and islands of places which might not lead anywhere, or which might unfold outwards to the scale of a planet, a solar system, a galaxy. For Peter Minter, a pioneer of transcultural ecocriticism, locales and regions are expressions of broader, planetary formations, which themselves are always undergoing modification by what he calls localized or molecular 'archipelagos of sense'.²³ In turn, an ontology embedded in such a lively world requires that the human 'I' must negotiate its particularity with pervasive, dynamic processes. To paraphrase Vicky Kirby, the limits of the transcultural subject are 'chiasmatically given'; thus, '"my" situation is more than local'.²⁴ In a climatic system rapidly approaching crisis, such an ontology is embedded in precariousness, the more-than-local is in danger, and phenomenological immediacy is the intimacy of a threatened sociality. Importantly, as Minter outlines in his chapter, the transcultural is not analogous to the trans*national*. Rather, the transcultural incorporates more-than-human plenitudes within multiple contact zones. Together, these zones produce meanings that are 'opaque or resistant to a bordered and/ or borderless "transnational", which in contrast reifies late-western sociopolitical, economic and aesthetic modernity and globalisation'. As examples of transcultural systems that might assume molecular concretions in particular locales, and which can never be abstracted from these locales, we point here to the various Indigenous Australian and South American knowledge systems. While to some extent such systems can be comprehended by generalized terms such as 'The Dreaming' or 'Pachamama' ('World Mother'), they are thoroughly localized conceptions of much more extensive, transcontinental forces – different parts of which are illuminated in different ways, depending on where and when they are experienced.²⁵

When we first wrote this introduction, we conceived transcultural ecocriticism as a response to the current environmental crisis, which aimed to bring together local and global, and human and non-human perspectives in recognition of the complexity of ecological issues, practices and meanings. As we sat down to revise it, however, the world was in the grip of another crisis, the global coronavirus pandemic. From Wuhan to Rome, New York to La Paz, cities around the world have sought to contain the spread of COVID-19 by entering a state of lockdown, which, along with cancelled flights, temporarily reduced carbon emissions and improved air quality in many urban conurbations. Such outbreaks of zoonotic, pandemic disease are likely to become more common in the future, as a range of factors, including habitat loss, population growth and changes in land use, generate new human and animal interactions. Moreover, the coronavirus pandemic has offered something of a preview of the anticipated effects of climate change. Economic collapse, social polarization, psychological stress, and the inflammation of geopolitical tensions have all provided an insight into what the 'new normal' might be like in an interconnected world defined by major ecological disruption. While COVID-19 probably derived from bats, it has arguably made us more aware of ourselves as a species, though our shared vulnerability to environmental circumstances is shot through with social disparities, economic inequalities and cultural differences. Like climate change, the COVID-19 pandemic is a global crisis with significant local and regional variations. It is clearly harming some communities much more than others, and, in addition to heightening our sense of how our own local places and experiences are shaped by broader global networks, it is foregrounding the precariousness of life in the Anthropocene.

If the Anthropocene has made the issue of scale central to ecocriticism, the chapters in this book recognize that the enmeshing of local and global forces, together with the movement between geological and human horizons, has raised different questions not only in different times and places but in different genres of writing. Part I, 'Planetary Localities', explores ecological concerns in a diverse assortment of imagined globalized places, both urban and rural, ranging from the United States to China and Mozambique, through readings of science fiction, the animal fable and magical realism. Ursula Heise notes that, in climate fiction, the city often functions as a proxy for climate change, as novels, films and other texts examine the significance of urbanization in relation to environmental crisis, along with the way it reshapes planetary ecosystems. This preoccupation with urbanization, a key feature of the Anthropocene, is something novelists and film-makers share with activists, journalists, geographers and urban planners, among others. According to Heise, a common trope in both fictional and nonfictional attempts to reimagine urban futures is the flooded city as a proxy for climate change. In climate fiction, the drowning metropolis often figures as a microcosm of a world thoroughly transformed by extreme global weather, a space in which the same event can be visualized on more than one scale, as individual lives are shown to be tied to the fate of regions, nations and even the planet. So common is the trope of the submarine city that it has become a narrative cliché, as likely to delight in sublime spectacles of urban disaster as to probe the urban dimensions of climate change. As Heise demonstrates, however, the narrative templates of climate fiction are revealingly reworked in Nguyễn-Võ Nghiêm-Minh's film *Nước 2030* (*Water 2030*, 2014), which depicts Saigon, and Kim Stanley Robinson's *New York 2140* (2017), which depicts its titular metropolis. Both of these texts raise subtle questions to do with the effects of climate change on property, value, inequality and institutional structures, while Robinson's novel also intriguingly represents the flooding of New York as a catalyst for ecological restoration.

While climate fiction is concerned with the effects of scale, conceived as shifts in space and time, science fiction more generally, as Heise has argued, has a long history of imagining the issue of scale in terms of the relation between human and non-human agents, whether robots or aliens.[26] Following a similar logic, Chris Danta argues that an attention to the perspectives of *animals*, both non-human and human, is crucial to understanding the Anthropocene. For Danta, there is a major problem in perhaps the most influential account of the Anthropocene, as formulated by Dipesh Chakrabarty. This account puts human history in the context of deep time, privileging the species over the individual, while conceiving human actions as geological forces. One consequence of such movement from the small to the large scale is to regard individual human actions, on mass and over time, in terms of their effects on global ecosystems. But the problem is that this 'scaling up of the imagination of the human', as Danta puts it, risks reproducing the very anthropocentrism it seeks to challenge. For while the geological timescale reorients our consideration away from the human, it nevertheless attributes to us a kind of colossal planetary power. An important solution to this dilemma, Danta contends, is to provide perspectives on the Anthropocene from non-human, as well as human, animals. To this end, Danta reads Ted Chiang's 'The Great Silence' (2014), a short story about a member of a species of parrot, close to extinction, whose intelligence goes unnoticed by their human neighbours, more concerned to look for extraterrestrial life in space than to communicate with non-human life in the here and now. In relation to human agents, this constitutes a significant scaling down from the level of the species to that of individual, interpersonal experience, a shift in viewpoint, which promises to facilitate interaction and communication among different life forms.

Recently, a distinctively African Anthropocene has been proposed as a model for enabling deep time and human history to be brought together in a single frame, or interscalar vision, in which localized spaces such as mines reveal simultaneous geological and political forces.[27] Meg Samuelson explores this African Anthropocene through a reading of Mia Couto's fiction about Mozambique, focusing on his commitment to re-enchantment as a response to colonialism, capitalism and ongoing environmental crisis. Mozambique is on the frontline of climate change, experiencing in the present forms of ecological disruption which await the global North in the future. This is partly because environmental degradation has been accelerated by decades of colonialism and war, causing a displacement of populations and high levels of poverty. To represent this conjunction of global inequality and environmental crisis, as it materializes in Mozambique, Couto develops a 'planetary aesthetic', which acknowledges the interdependency of geopolitical and ecological events. This aesthetic is used by Couto, an ecologist by training, to re-enchant the world through a revival of situated, non-Western knowledges. As animist elements are combined to remake the land into a sacred web, or transcultural mesh, agency is restored to both non-human and human life forms, including the poor of Mozambique.

An engagement with the social and political dimensions of environmental degradation, imagined simultaneously at global and local levels, both in the present and future, is also a prominent feature of contemporary Chinese science fiction. This growing body of fiction, however, explores different ecological problems in very different ways. Mengtian Sun focusses on two contrasting examples of the genre, Chen Qiufan's *Huang Chao* (*The Waste Tide*, 2013), and a couple of related novels by Han Song, namely *Ditie* (*The Subway*, 2011) and *Hongse Haiyong* (*The Red Sea*, 2004). Qiufan gives his science fiction a realistic or didactic quality in order to examine the issue of e-waste, as it is exported from the global North and processed in Guiyu, a town in southern China, which is also the e-waste recycling capital of the world. But, as Sun argues, if e-waste is a global industry, raising questions of environmental justice, such questions are also generated on another scale by northern Chinese migrant workers, whose labour involves not just low wages, but appalling conditions, including illness-inducing stench and poisonous gases. By contrast, Han Song's science fiction eschews realism for a kind of magical, apocalyptic fable. In a reworking of one of the narrative templates of climate fiction, as identified by Heise, Song depicts a dystopian world in the wake of some sort of extreme ecological disaster, where humans have descended into the sea and undergone de-evolution, transforming into aquatic creatures, with fins and gills. According to Sun, this transformation is an unmitigated degeneration, taking place in an increasingly putrid marine environment and encompassing the abandonment of civility for violence. Such examples of Chinese science fiction, then, imagine a future in which humans have become alien, ghostly presences in a blighted, unfamiliar environment.

As is well known, globalization has long been associated with ecological disruption and exchange, first brought about by European empires around 1500 in a process which decimated Indigenous populations and generated new inequalities between human societies across the world. This process reached a new intensity in the romantic period, when an enthusiasm for unpeopled, uncultivated 'nature' developed among European poets, readers and travellers.

During the late eighteenth and early nineteenth centuries, the expansion of British imperial power in India, Australia and the Pacific was aided by natural history and accompanied by the relocation of plants and animals to distant places via botanic gardens, agricultural societies and other scientific institutions, which stretched from Calcutta to Sydney, Cape Town to St Vincent. In his recent book, *Natures in Translation*, Alan Bewell put romantic ecocriticism on an entirely new footing by demonstrating that the notion of 'nature' as localized, stable and non-commercialized was intimately bound up with this other globalized, mobile and commodified 'nature'. As Bewell writes, 'the British came to see nature as something that stood apart from the modern world ... at the same time as they were actively engaged in translating it into the very forms that would allow it to be accessed from a distance, marketed, exchanged, and improved.'[28]

Part II, 'Beyond the Romantic Frontier', engages with this contradiction. Analysing various genres of environmental writing, our contributors consider the ways in which the meanings of trees, flowers, animals and picturesque scenes changed as they moved, whether imaginatively or physically, across different Indigenous, colonial, national and global contexts. Building on insights formulated in his book, Bewell shows that colonial natural history is a fundamentally translational and transcultural activity. As naturalists renamed and described plants, animals and landforms, which had already been given names by Indigenous people, they erased not just these pre-existing names but the relationships such names expressed between people, places and the non-human world. Both settlers and Indigenous people could thus end up being lost in translation, as familiar things seemed strange, and vice versa. In this sense, colonial natural history was a bit like mapping, since it operated as a medium for appropriating flora, fauna and territory, while also authorizing a particular scientific view of such ecological elements and controlling the dissemination of information about them. As Bewell argues, however, it is essential to recover the perspectives that have been lost in the environments that remain if we are to restore polyvocality to the natural world.

Because colonial plants, animals and environments were so often encountered in distant metropolitan locations, perhaps even in silent rooms, through dead botanical and zoological specimens, or images and descriptions in books, there emerged a tendency to privilege their visual appearance over their sounds.[29] This is an issue taken up by Peter Denney in his analysis of the sensory meanings of the natural world in British India, as recorded in travel writing. With an enthusiasm for exotic, uncultivated nature shaped by theories of picturesque taste, most travellers construed Indian landscape in primarily visual terms, at least when they were evaluating its aesthetic qualities. Through this elevation of vision over the other senses, control and distance could be established over foreign territory, and observers could demonstrate their taste, gentility and sensibility. However, as Denney reveals, in British India, non-visual sensory experiences from itchy rashes to noisy frogs could prevent viewers from exercising the undivided attention regarded as necessary for seeing land as landscape. In addition, the environmental determinism, which influenced Enlightenment theories of climate, also made travellers anxious that, while tropical weather might be responsible for the beauty of Indian landscape, it could also generate harmful or irritating bodily effects inimical to the contemplation of natural scenery.

In Britain in the late eighteenth century, both picturesque taste and the romantic ethos attributed enormous value to trees, though this coincided, especially in colonial locations, with a vigorous commitment to deforestation in the name of improvement. Ve-Yin Tee puts this romantic dendrophilia, or love of trees, under scrutiny through an analysis of several poems and other texts by writers from diverse social backgrounds. In doing so, he discloses a 'dark side' of dendrophilia, the legacy of which had a profound impact on forest cover and access to land in post-Company India, and still informs British attitudes today. As Tee argues in an illuminating reading of some poems by William Blake, an elite love of trees led to more large trees being planted in London, but this often occurred on urban common land, which was swiftly enclosed and privatized so as to exclude the labouring classes. Other poets regarded the forest as a realm of liberty, completely ignoring the game laws, which restricted hunting to the property-owning classes, while curtailing freedom of movement among the populace. These inequalities regarding access to trees were imported to India during the period of direct British rule, when they began to inform practices of forest conservation, initiated for commercial rather than ecological ends. For these reasons, concludes Tee, it is not surprising that romantic dendrophilia has found a happy home in political conservatism in Britain. And rather than just profess a love of trees, we need to be vigilant in attending to the unequal power relationships, which accompany certain uses and perceptions of these arboreal life forms.

During the romantic period, close links were forged between admiring, collecting, classifying, studying and writing about plants, as botanical science catalysed the imagination and strong feeling.[30] This was especially the case in relation to colonial botany due to the strangeness and exoticism of plants from distant places. Women, too, participated in the production of natural history, seeing botanical science as a means of claiming cultural authority.[31] Jessica White examines the life and correspondence of one such woman, Georgiana Molloy, who pursued her interest in botany in colonial Western Australia, having migrated to Augusta, originally from Carlisle, in 1830. Molloy was enlisted to collect native seeds by James Mangles, a retired naval officer and fellow of the Royal Society, who, though based in London, had a network of people from across the British world sending him botanical specimens, which he studied, sold, donated to botanical gardens and transplanted to other environments. When Molloy sent Mangles plants previously known only to Indigenous people, she described them in great detail, mixing romantic sentiment with close observation. But, as White acknowledges, she deferred to his authority, and it was Mangles who classified and named the plants. In this way, both scientists contributed, through renaming, to the erasure of existing Indigenous ecological relationships, as discussed by Bewell, and to the translation of their plants into global commodities, objects of scientific knowledge and aesthetic pleasure.

A primary purpose of this collection is to interrogate place-based, localized narratives in light of their connections to global texts, concerns, networks, movements and practices, and similarly to re-evaluate colonial romantic works by juxtaposing their absences and appropriations with decolonial ecological perspectives, which elaborate Indigenous knowledge systems and their encounters, positive and negative, with other modes of understanding the natural world. Part III, 'Decolonial Poetics', explores the transcultural ecological dimensions of a range of Indigenous and non-Indigenous art and literature, including Mapuche poetry, Maya writing and a collaboration between an Aboriginal poet and a non-Indigenous painter. Peter Minter focusses on this cross-cultural collaboration, *meenamatta lena narla puellakanny: Meenamatta Water Country Discussion*, a collection of thirteen poems by puralia meenamatta (Jim Everett) in dialogue with twelve paintings by Jonathan Kimberley. First exhibited in Hobart in 2006, the collaboration constitutes a profound evocation of meenamatta country in northeast Tasmania. The result, according to Minter, is a 'transcultural poetic event'. Specifically, the event encompasses a series of exchanges between puralia's situated eco-philosophy of meenamatta country and Kimberley's attempt to decolonize the Western tradition of landscape art. As Minter demonstrates, this leads to an 'unlandscaping' expression of decoloniality, which opens up a third space, where transcultural interactions and kinship networks between humans, animals, plants and landforms communicate the concept of 'all-life', symbolized by water, the nourisher and connector of all things.

The concept of literary communication, whether oral or written, as relying on networks of usage rather than individual human inspiration is a powerful means of acknowledging the multispecies configuration which makes thought and writing possible. As Stephen Muecke argues, humans often enlist the help not only of devices like telescopes and smartphones but also of plants and animals to enhance their sensory, affective and intellectual engagements with the world. Such an approach has the potential to decolonize aesthetic objects by illustrating their dependence on immediate, networked environments comprising complex chains of life forms and material entities. For Muecke, this kind of ecological framework is valuable because, among other things, it provides an alternative to the old dualism between nature and culture. In turn, the resultant *multinaturalism* debunks the notion of there being one 'real world', while aligning with a kinship system in which animals and plants are linked to humans, as in the sense of territory as 'country'. Conceived in this way, Muecke contends that literature becomes an instantiation of ecological knowledge, and its importance lies not only in its situatedness but in its function as a transcultural work in which local and global forces and movements intersect.

If networked environments offer a productive way of thinking about both Indigenous and non-Indigenous literature, it is important to note that such environments can be associated with different, competing gender identities. For Maia Gunn Watkinson, this is a prominent concern in the work of Maya women writers. Analysing recent narratives by Ana Patricia Martínez Huchim, a Maya ethnographer from Yucatán in southern Mexico, Watkinson shows how the forest, in particular, has been an important site for elaborating Maya identities. To some extent, the chicle industry, which involved the collection of sap from the *sapodilla* tree for use in the production of chewing gum, led to the forest being associated with demanding masculine labour. But as Watkinson reveals, Martínez Huchim reinscribes the forest as a feminine space, drawing a parallel between the exploitation of the forest and the female body. Within her work, this feminist vision is linked to a distinctive ecological framework in which the red-coloured sap from the *sapodilla* tree evokes blood, generating an acknowledgement of networks of kinship between human and non-human communities. Accordingly, the forest is redefined as a site of resistance to the essentialization and marginalization of women in Maya culture, a space of multiple, changing ways of knowing and belonging.

Throughout this book, our contributors aim to emphasize the ways in which environmental problems must be understood in their local and global contexts, in their relation to concerns about social justice, and through transcultural forms of writing capable of elucidating the movement of ecological knowledge across geographical regions. Stuart Cooke addresses all these issues in his account of a wetland, the Humedal Antiñir, in southern Chile, alongside the poetry and activism of its leading advocate, Juan Paulo Huirimilla Oyarzo. Despite its biodiversity and value to the local Huilliche-Mapuche community as a source of medicinal plants, the Humedal is an ecosystem under threat due to the encroachment of industrial and housing developments. For Huirimilla, however, it is a vital ancestral territory for the Mapuche people and an important locus for his own theory of poetics. More specifically, he conceives it as a 'geoterritory', a multidimensional place in which multiple modes of existence coexist and interact, including deep time and human history. Through collaboration with Huirimilla, alongside a study of his poetry, Cooke describes how this notion of heterogeneous place intersects with parallel forms of non-Mapuche ecological knowledge, which themselves intersect with the ecopoetics discussed by Minter with reference to meenamatta country, and the networked, decolonizing environments theorized by Muecke. Thus, as Cooke and Huirimilla collaborate on a series of poetic compositions, their poetry articulates a transcultural interpretation of the ecological significance of the Humedal, taking into account its intertwining of local and global, temporal and spatial, human and non-human, orientations.

Notes

1 Timothy Morton, *Ecology without Nature: Rethinking Environmental Aesthetics*, 2009 edn (Cambridge, MA and London: Harvard University Press, 2007), 178.
2 'Pre-Face (2017)', in Jerome Rothenberg, ed., *Technicians of the Sacred: A Range of Poetries from Africa, America, Asia, Europe, and Oceania*, 50th Anniversary edn (Oakland: University of California Press, 2017), xvii.
3 Rothenberg, *Technicians of the Sacred*, xviii.
4 Rothenberg, *Technicians of the Sacred*, xxi.
5 For more details, see Stuart Cooke, 'Towards an Ethological Poetics: The Transgression of Genre and the Poetry of the Albert's Lyrebird', *Environmental Humanities* 11, no. 2 (2019): 302–23.
6 Marcella Durand, 'The Ecology of Poetry', in *)((ECO(LANG)(UAGE(READER))*, ed. Brenda Iijima (New York: Portable Press, 2010), 118.

7 Ursula K. Heise, *Sense of Place and Sense of Planet: The Environmental Imagination of the Global* (New York: Oxford University Press, 2008), 42.
8 Lynn Keller, *Recomposing Ecopoetics: North American Poetry of the Self-conscious Anthropocene* (Charlottesville: University of Virginia Press, 2017), 13.
9 Keller, *Recomposing Ecopoetics*, 10.
10 Keller, *Recomposing Ecopoetics*, 11.
11 Keller, *Recomposing Ecopoetics*, 14–15.
12 Kate Rigby, *Topographies of the Sacred: The Poetics of Place in European Romanticism* (Charlottesville: University of Virginia Press, 2004), 5.
13 Rigby, *Topographies of the Sacred*, 9.
14 Published only after this manuscript was in production, Rigby's most recent title 'reclaims' these complex, valuable strains of romanticism for a contemporary, decolonial ecopoetics. See Kate Rigby, *Reclaiming Romanticism: Towards an Ecopoetics of Decolonization* (London: Bloomsbury, 2020).
15 Heise, *Sense of Place and Sense of Planet*, 21.
16 Heise, *Sense of Place and Sense of Planet*, 13.
17 Heise, *Sense of Place and Sense of Planet*, 14.
18 Heise, *Sense of Place and Sense of Planet*, 114.
19 'Remember', Joy Harjo, *How We Became Human: New and Selected Poems, 1975-2001*, 2004 edn (New York: WW Norton & Company, 2002), 42.
20 Evelyn Araluen, 'Too Little, Too Much', in A. Whittaker (ed.), *Fire Front: First Nations Poetry and Power Today* (St Lucia: University of Queensland Press, 2020), 39.
21 For a useful compendium that addresses the intersections between ecocriticism and Indigenous studies, see S. Monani and J. Adamson (eds), *Ecocriticism and Indigenous Studies: Conversations from Earth to Cosmos* (Oxford: Routledge, 2016).
22 Araluen, 'Too Little, Too Much', 40.
23 Peter Minter, 'Archipelagos of Sense: Thinking about a Decolonised Australian Poetics', *Southerly* 73, no. 1 (2013): 155–69.
24 Vicky Kirby, *Quantum Anthropologies: Life at Large* (Durham and London: Duke University Press, 2011), 136.
25 See Stuart Cooke, 'Indigenous Poetics and Transcultural Ecologies', *Interdisciplinary Literary Studies* 20, no. 1 (2018): 1–32.
26 Ursula K. Heise, 'Science Fiction and the Time Scales of the Anthropocene', *ELH* 86, no. 2 (2019): 281.
27 Gabrielle Hecht, 'Interscalar Vehicles for an African Anthropocene: On Waste, Temporality, and Violence', *Cultural Anthropology* 33, no. 1 (2018): 109–41.
28 Alan Bewell, *Natures in Translation: Romanticism and Colonial Natural History* (Baltimore: Johns Hopkins, 2017), 6.
29 See, for example, Peter Denney, 'Picturesque Farming: The Sound of "Happy Britannia" in Colonial Australia', *Cultural Studies Review* 18, no. 3 (2012): 85–108.

30 Theresa M. Kelly, *Clandestine Marriage: Botany and Romantic Culture* (Baltimore: Johns Hopkins University Press, 2012), 7–8.
31 Melissa Bailes, *Questioning Nature: British Women's Scientific Writing and Literary Originality* (Charlottesville: University of Virginia Press, 2017), 203.

Bibliography

Araluen, Evelyn. 'Too Little, Too Much'. In *Fire Front: First Nations Poetry and Power Today*, edited by A. Whittaker, 39–45. St Lucia: University of Queensland Press, 2020.

Bailes, Melissa. *Questioning Nature: British Women's Scientific Writing and Literary Originality*. Charlottesville: University of Virginia Press, 2017.

Bewell, Alan. *Natures in Translation: Romanticism and Colonial Natural History*. Baltimore: Johns Hopkins, 2017.

Cooke, Stuart. 'Indigenous Poetics and Transcultural Ecologies'. *Interdisciplinary Literary Studies* 20, no. 1 (2018): 1–32.

Cooke, Stuart. 'Toward an Ethological Poetics: The Transgression of Genre and the Poetry of the Albert's Lyrebird'. *Environmental Humanities* 11, no. 2 (2019): 302–23.

Denney, Peter. 'Picturesque Farming: The Sound of "Happy Britannia" in Colonial Australia'. *Cultural Studies Review* 18, no. 3 (2012): 85–108.

Durand, Marcella. 'The Ecology of Poetry'. In *)((ECO(LANG)(UAGE(READER))*, edited by Brenda Iijima, 114–24. New York: Portable Press, 2010.

Harjo, Joy. *How We Became Human: New and Selected Poems, 1975–2001*. 2004 edn. New York: WW Norton & Company, 2002.

Hecht, Gabrielle. 'Interscalar Vehicles for an African Anthropocene: On Waste, Temporarlity, and Violence'. *Cultural Anthropology* 33, no. 1 (2018): 109–41.

Heise, Ursula K. 'Science Fiction and the Time Scales of the Anthropocene'. *ELH* 86, no. 2 (2019): 275–304.

Heise, Ursula K. *Sense of Place and Sense of Planet: The Environmental Imagination of the Global*. New York: Oxford University Press, 2008.

Keller, Lynn. *Recomposing Ecopoetics: North American Poetry of the Self-Conscious Anthropocene*. Charlottesville and London: University of Virginia Press, 2017.

Kelly, Theresa M. *Clandestine Marriage: Botany and Romantic Culture*. Baltimore: Johns Hopkins University Press, 2012.

Kirby, Vicky. *Quantum Anthropologies: Life at Large*. Durham and London: Duke University Press, 2011.

Minter, Peter. 'Archipelagos of Sense: Thinking about a Decolonised Australian Poetics'. *Southerly* 73, no. 1 (2013): 155–69.

Monani, S. and J. Adamson, eds. *Ecocriticism and Indigenous Studies: Conversations from Earth to Cosmos*. Oxford: Routledge, 2016.

Morton, Timothy. *Ecology without Nature: Rethinking Environmental Aesthetics*. 2009 edn. Cambridge, MA and London: Harvard University Press, 2007.

Rigby, Kate. *Reclaiming Romanticism: Towards an Ecopoetics of Decolonization*. London: Bloomsbury, 2020.

Rigby, Kate. *Topographies of the Sacred: The Poetics of Place in European Romanticism*. Charlottesville and London: University of Virginia Press, 2004.

Rothenberg, Jerome, ed. *Technicians of the Sacred: A Range of Poetries from Africa, America, Asia, Europe, and Oceania*. 50th Anniversary edn. Oakland: University of California Press, 2017.

Part I

Planetary localities

2

Urban narrative and climate change

Ursula K. Heise

Urbanization and Anthropocene

Urbanization is one of the main characteristics of the Anthropocene. The ecologist Eugene Stoermer and the atmospheric chemist Paul Crutzen mentioned a tenfold increase in urbanization over the course of the twentieth century, among many other benchmarks, when they proposed the Anthropocene or 'Age of Humans' in 2000 as a designation for the new geological era in which we are currently living. A few years later, various divisions of the United Nations published data showing that for the first time in the history of the species, more than 50 per cent of humans lived in cities, a percentage that is expected to grow to 70 per cent by mid-century.[1] While some debate has surrounded the definition of the city and the statistical methods that inform these assessments,[2] there is no disagreement with the basic diagnosis: as the global human population continues to grow throughout the twenty-first century, most people will be born in cities in the first place or end up living there, whereas rural populations will continue to shrink.

Urban populations are forecast to increase particularly rapidly in Africa and Asia, in nations that are poor, in municipalities that have limited infrastructure, and under administrations that lack the will or the means to enforce what laws and building codes exist. Cities will grow, in other words, under what are often called conditions of 'informal urbanization' in which citizens typically have no legal title to their homes, no formal employment contracts and no access to urban grids of electricity, water or sanitation. The geographer Mike Davis has more bluntly portrayed these conditions in many of the world's regions as leading to a 'planet of slums'. Rural populations, he argues, are drawn from no longer sustainable agricultural livelihoods to cities, as rural residents in Europe were during the age of industrialization in the nineteenth century.

But as opposed to European cities two centuries ago, metropolises in the global South today offer many fewer possibilities of employment, leading to the growth of an urban underclass with few practical chances of ascending to a working- or middle-class way of life on the European or North American model.

For environmentalism, urbanization poses a new challenge. As environmental studies scholars Kai N. Lee, William R. Freudenburg and Richard B. Howarth have argued, the older challenge of total population growth that has been one focus of environmental concern, from Paul Ehrlich's classic *The Population Bomb* (1968) to Alan Weisman's *Countdown* (2013), has found a clear, if slow, solution in the demographic transition that began in Europe 200 years ago and is now taking place in most regions of the globe, from high birth and death rates to high birth and low death rates and finally both low birth and death rates. By contrast, the new challenge of growth in urban populations – sometimes even under conditions of overall population decline – has no such clear solution. During the lifetime of today's college students, they highlight,

> humans will create, somewhere in the world, urban settlements containing as many people as in all cities that now exist. This is, potentially, a great opportunity: to build a sustainable urban habitat that works economically, environmentally, and socially for its residents. And it is a daunting challenge because this habitat is already being built, willy-nilly, and much of it is locking in a dependence on automobiles and other technologies that will be difficult to implement in an environmentally sustainable fashion.[3]

Urbanization is not just a challenge for the environmental movement because it contributes to socio-economic inequality and creates unsustainable habitats, important as these dimensions are. The growth of cities also forms part of the pervasive reshaping of planetary ecosystems that the concept of the Anthropocene points to. 'Growing cities replace one landscape, largely natural in its functions, with one in which human control dominates. The creation of a human habitat in cities is expensive and permanent in the way it transforms ecosystems. The urban environment may be the greatest unrecognized environmental challenge of the twenty-first century.'[4]

This challenge is increasingly being addressed, however, by research in urban ecology and urban planning that recognizes cities as a novel type of ecosystem with its own climatic characteristics such as the urban heat island effect, its own soils, fauna and flora. Biologists such as Menno Schilthuizen have even pointed to evolutionary processes that are tied to urban environments.⁵ Over the last thirty years, an ever-increasing number of studies and organizations has also addressed urban political ecology – research on the causes and structures that coproduce uneven natural spaces and unequal social conditions – and urban environmental justice, research and advocacy on behalf of those who suffer the consequences of these inequalities, from lack of access to green spaces to pollution exposure and disproportionate vulnerability to other risks such as flooding, water scarcity and fires.

Climate change has loomed large in these reimaginations of urban nature and urban futures. From Matthew E. Kahn's *Climatopolis* (2010) and Peter Calthorpe's *Urbanism in an Age of Climate Change* (2011) to Ashley Dawson's *Extreme Cities* (2017) and Jeff Goodell's *The Water Will Come* (2017), to name just a few, urban planners, geographers, journalists and environmental activists have foregrounded the risks that face coastal cities inhabited by hundreds of millions of humans worldwide. Whether they seek the answer to the urban risks of climate change in the functioning of markets, as Kahn does, or in the wholesale overthrow of capitalist market mechanisms, as Dawson suggests, the city is at the centre of their attention: in particular, the city flooded or drowned because of rising sea levels and increased storms, rather than the city dried up because of heat, drought and aquifer depletion. If the recent water crises in Chennai, Capetown and São Paulo suggest that dry cities may be as likely as flooded ones in the age of climate change, it is nevertheless the drowning or drowned city that has served as the focus of narratives about the future of cities. Indeed, drowning cities tend to loom large even in those studies that are primarily focused not on urbanism but on climate change broadly understood, such as David Wallace-Wells's *The Uninhabitable Earth* (2019). The flooded city, in other words, has become one of the principal proxy images for climate change in public discourse.

In this chapter, I will focus on fictional rather than nonfictional narratives of climate futures to show that in this genre, too, drowning cities have played a crucial role in portraying climate change. In the second section, I will outline some of the typical story templates that recur in many novels, films and short stories whose climate-change scenarios revolve around a flooded city. In the third and fourth sections, I will take a more in-depth look at two works that adopt more unusual and original idioms and plot lines to portray drowning cities: Saigon in Nguyễn-Võ Nghiêm-Minh's film *Nước 2030* (*Water 2030*, 2014) and New York in Kim Stanley Robinson's *New York 2140* (2017).

Drowning cities: An aquatic anatomy

Literary scholars as well as journalists and experts in environmental communication have intensively explored the question of how our most common literary forms might deal with the challenges of portraying an ecologically altered world. The journalist Dan Bloom coined the term 'cli-fi', or climate fiction, in 2007, obviously on the assumption that a new genre had emerged to address if not the Anthropocene in all its dimensions, then at least climate change, its most publicly discussed manifestation. How climate fiction might be defined by anything other than a broadly shared theme, however, is not as yet clear. Literary critics such as Adam Trexler and Timothy Clark and writers such as Amitav Ghosh have foregrounded the difficulty of representing events at the temporal and spatial scales that appear necessary to engage with global warming and other aspects of the Anthropocene, as well as, to a lesser extent, the question of how non-human agency might be portrayed in such contexts.[6] Yet in spite of the doubts and reservations about the ability of current forms of poetry and narrative to portray climate change adequately, several hundred poems, short stories, novels and films about climate change have already been published, and more continue to appear in a variety of languages each year. Many though by no means all of them adopt central themes and narrative strategies of science fiction, which is itself becoming an increasingly common genre even in regions and literatures that do not have a deep tradition in this form of narrative.

How, then, do climate fictions create an image of the world? By what narrative and metaphoric strategies do they represent a global environment caught up in processes of rapid change? In looking for such an anatomy of the climate change story, a few major plot patterns and narrative strategies emerge that repeat themselves across many works with variations. I will briefly highlight three of these story templates here: the climate disaster story, climate dystopia and the climate proxy story.

The most salient of these story templates is no doubt the climate disaster story, equally prevalent in novels and film. It focuses on a major hurricane, flood, fire or other climate catastrophe that is predicted by scientists but ignored by authorities and public, and that ends up causing large-scale and spectacular damage to people and built environments. Environmental film scholar Alexa Weik von Mossner has called this genre the 'Nature Attacks' film, which 'combines spectacular scenes of weather-related disaster with a melodramatic storyline, all the while lecturing viewers about the great risks associated with abrupt climate change. Such disaster scenes need not be scientifically accurate, nor does the natural spectacle itself have to be authentic... the very condition of a dangerously active nature precludes filming the actual thing'.[7] The plot usually revolves around a nuclear family that is threatened by disaster but ultimately saved, usually through the heroic action of the father figure. It is only after the damage is done to society at large that rethinking or reform takes place. In spite of major losses, the ending is, if not happy, usually at least mildly optimistic.[8] Roland Emmerich's feature film *The Day After Tomorrow* (2004), the first film to take on climate change, illustrates all of these narrative ingredients in its focus on the family of a scientist, initially ignored by authorities, who sets out to rescue his son from drowned and frozen Manhattan.[9]

More recent works offer variations on this pattern. In Liz Jensen's *The Rapture* (2009), the protagonist, Gabrielle Fox, is a psychotherapist who has remained paralyzed after a car accident. She is assigned as a patient a disturbed teenager, Bethany Krall, who has murdered her mother. Bethany suffers from what initially seem like paranoid delusions about impending disasters, but her predictive visions become, time after time, ecological realities. Fox's superiors ignore her warnings and belittle her for taking what they think of as her patient's hallucinations seriously. In the meantime, the disasters follow each other, and at the end, London is destroyed in a cataclysmic flood, just as Bethany had predicted. As she looks ahead to the bleak future of 'Bethanyland', Fox discovers she is pregnant – a reassertion of the family motif even after Bethany's own suicide. In Nathaniel Rich's *Odds against Tomorrow* (2013), completed in late 2012 as Hurricane Sandy hit New York, the protagonist is a risk analyst who accurately predicts the dangers that his corporate clients may face in the event of a major storm or flood. He is ignored by most, until an apocalyptic hurricane that devastates New York and the Eastern Seaboard turns him into a cult prophet of sorts. But Rich turns the basic story template into a more original narrative when the protagonist rejects his own cult status, refuses to cash in on his predictive powers and in the end decides to remain in a marginal zone of Brooklyn, outside the urban society of Manhattan, which is eagerly rebuilding. His failure to reintegrate casts doubt on whether anything has really changed for society at large. While the spectacular descriptions of Manhattan underwater perfectly illustrate the conventions of the disaster story template, the protagonist's persistent loneliness and his final isolation mark a departure from the disaster novel's typical family focus.

Climate dystopias also focus on the catastrophic consequences of global warming, but they do so while emphasizing a broader spectrum of changes: rising sea levels and heat waves or storms combine with other social and ecological problems such as population growth, inequality, discrimination, resource scarcity, violence and corruption. Catastrophes unfold more gradually in climate dystopias than in climate disaster stories and typically involve a larger cast of characters so as to create a scenario of structural crisis well beyond one-time disaster. Solutions are more difficult to come by, and the final outlook remains more often pessimistic than in climate disaster stories. In Brazilian novelist Ignacio de Loyola Brandão's *Não Verás País Nenhum (Memorial Descritivo)* (1981; translated as *And Still the Earth*), for example, increasing heat, total deforestation of the Amazon and food and water shortages have led to a military presence and fascist dictatorship that are equal parts futuristic projection and reflections on Brazil's military dictatorship at the time. George Turner's *The Sea and Summer* (1987), set in Melbourne, shows a city beset by climate change and sea level rise that exacerbate gross inequalities between the 'Sweet' and the 'Swill' – shorthands for the wealthy and poor, jobholders and jobless. Paolo Bacigalupi's *The Windup Girl* (2009) juxtaposes the perspectives of four major and a range of minor characters in a future Bangkok devastated by famine, genetic engineering, successive outbreaks of disease and rising waters. In all of these novels, climate change becomes part of a much broader social and political scenario that is criticized with great attention to detail as well as sweeping vistas of entire societies.

A third common story template, the climate proxy story, uses a different narrative strategy. Rather than featuring a wide and diverse array of characters and their differing perspectives, these climate stories focus on an individual character and either a central experience of loss or a series of disappointments that come to stand as a synecdoche for the global losses that are occurring in the background. Finnish novelist Antti Tuomainen's *Parantaja* (*The Healer*, 2010), for example, portrays a poet who searches for his missing journalist wife in a Helsinki that is perpetually rainy, flooded and overrun by climate refugees from much hotter, now uninhabitable regions of the planet. Tapani Lehtinen, the protagonist, as well as other characters explicitly draw parallels between the small-scale tragedies of their lives and the larger ones afflicting the planet. In Megan Hunter's *The End We Start From* (2017), the protagonist's water breaks and she gives birth to a child just as the sea inundates London, in an all-too-obvious parallel that turns parenthood into a proxy for the individual and collective challenges of dealing with climate change. More originally, the geologist in Bulgarian-German novelist Ilija Trojanow's *Eistau* (2011; translated as *The Lamentations of Zeno*) mourns the loss not of a person but of his favourite glacier; here too, melancholy turns into the point of departure and proxy for a broader portrayal, in this case a climate travel narrative.

The climate disaster story, climate dystopia and the climate proxy story are three narrative templates that repeat themselves frequently in climate film and fictions, albeit often with original variations. In these as well as other climate story templates, the scale transition between the experiences of individuals and the fate of regions or even the planet at large is often mediated by the portrayal of a metropolis. This strategy makes sense not only in view of the importance of urbanization as the dominant human habitat in the present and future that I discussed earlier, but also in view of literary-historical traditions. In the history of the novel in the nineteenth and twentieth centuries, cities such as London, Paris, St. Petersburg, New York, Rio de Janeiro, Mexico City, Mumbai, Shanghai and Tokyo have often functioned as narrative microcosms that bring together characters, cultures, technologies and world views from around the globe in uneven, conflictive and sometimes violent encounters. In climate fiction, this figuration of the metropolis as global microcosm takes a new turn as global weather propels characters' migrations and encounters. But as I will show in the third and fourth sections, some earlier strategies of urban narrative resurface in recent works of fiction and film that portray different characters in their struggle with new conditions of existence.

Urban climate narrative draws on the modern tradition of the metropolis as microcosm of the world, but at the same time it often taps into the even older tradition of drowning cities as synecdoches for the passing of civilizations. From the mythic city of Atlantis that Plato claimed was submerged by the gods as a punishment for its antagonism to Athens in *Timaeus* and *Critias* (360 BCE) to the anticipated drowning of Tokyo in Abe Kōbō's 第四間氷期 (*Dai-Yon Kampyōki*; translated as *Inter Ice Age 4*, 1959) and of London in J. G. Ballard's *The Drowned World* (1962), the sunken city has functioned as a major symbol for the end of historical eras, the transience of beliefs and cultures and the eventual downfall of even the most powerful empires. Climate scientists' predictions of increased floods and sea level rise lend a new realism to this age-old trope, which makes it unsurprising that film-makers and novelists have given the drowning or drowned city pride of place in climate fictions and films. From Melbourne under water in Turner's *Sea and Summer* and Denver at the bottom of the ocean in Kevin Reynolds's film *Waterworld* (1995) to New York hit by a tsunami in Emmerich's *Day after Tomorrow*, multiple world cities levelled by floods in Frank Schätzing's novel *Der Schwarm* (*The Swarm*, 2004) and Stephen Baxter's *Flood* (2008), Bangkok drowned in Bacigalupi's *Windup Girl*, London flooded in Jensen's *Rapture* and Hunter's *The End We Start From* and New York navigable only by canoe in Rich's *Odds against Tomorrow*, the spectacular sinking of well-known metropolises has commanded a central significance in climate fiction. The misery and horror of climate catastrophe, especially for those not affluent enough to protect themselves against the floods, are sometimes foregrounded but often enough overshadowed by the long-established pleasures of urban disaster spectacles. Indeed, in spite of the very real dangers of sea level rise for low-lying cities such as Dhaka, Jakarta or Miami, the sinking or sunken city has become so much of a narrative cliché that it has lost a good deal of its power to convey the real-life threats of climate change to urban life.

But innovative writers and film-makers have revived the flooded city as a vehicle of climate narrative, approaching it from different conceptual angles and with the help of narrative and cinematic strategies that twist the story templates I have mentioned earlier into new shapes. Claire Miye Stanford's lyrical short story 'Neither Above nor Below' (2019), for example, portrays Jakarta in the year 2099 in an ecotopian vein as a city of canals to which humans as well as animals have successfully adapted. The American science fiction novelist Kim Stanley Robinson, in his novel *2312* (2012), describes Manhattan in the early twenty-fourth century as a 'SuperVenice' where canals and aerial walkways have replaced streets in an urban landscape that one of the off-world characters perceives as one of the most natural places she has ever experienced, compared to the artificial habitats humans have built on other planets. Robinson has recently returned to this vision of Manhattan underwater in *New York 2140* (2017), a novel I will discuss in the fourth section. But film-makers are also contributing to the reimagination of the sunken city, as the Vietnamese film *Nước 2030* demonstrates in a surrealist-inspired vision culminating in a submarine Saigon that is both memory and future for the characters.

Submarine surrealism: *Nước 2030*

Nguyễn-Võ Nghiêm-Minh's *Nước 2030* (2014) is set largely in the titular year in the Mekong Delta, approximately 100 kilometres south of Ho Chi Minh City (Saigon). A vast area of wetlands and rivers at sea level, the Mekong Delta with its towns, agriculture and dense population is projected to be at extreme risk from king tides, floods and rising seas. A brief paragraph at the beginning of Nguyễn-Võ's futuristic film indicates that by 2030, 80 per cent of the population has been evacuated from the area because of climate change. The ensuing plot is presented to spectators through a frame narrative and three acts. In the frame narrative, which appears at the beginning of the film and the opening of the third act, a young fisher woman, Sáo (Quỳnh Hoa), retrieves the body of her husband, Thi (Thạch Kim Long), from the floating hydroponic farm where he was killed during work. She goes on to seek and find employment at the same farm – perhaps to make a living, but also to find out why and how her husband died. This frame narrative, therefore, cues spectators to expect a somewhat futuristic murder mystery – or a version of the climate proxy story that I outlined in the second section, which uses an individual loss as a synecdoche for collective decline.

But Nguyễn-Võ twists this story template in unusual ways. In the film's first act, Sáo and Thi are shown in the weeks leading up to Thi's death in 2030, leading what looks like the fairly normal life of a poor young couple in the global South: they fish, grow greens, try to conceive a baby and live in a house on stilts in the flooded bay where Thi's land once was. In this part of the film, Nguyễn-Võ cinematically stages an argument that Indigenous and postcolonial scholars have made in more theoretical terms: what is perceived as climate-change apocalypse or dystopia in the global North is often already a lived reality for communities in the global South. Poverty, displacement, precarious food supplies and uncertain futures are nothing new for communities that have experienced colonialism in its various forms. From this perspective, climate change and its consequences are not as new in terms of lived experience as they are in terms of their scientific causes. By the same token, adapting to climate change involves structures of inequality and struggles for justice that have driven progressive political movements for centuries.

The second act adds complications to this basic plot line of a poor young couple coping with difficult circumstances, and of a woman left widowed by her husband's mysterious death. The plot here flashes back to the year 2020, when a university student named Giang (Quý Bình) from Saigon visits the Mekong Delta to do research on plants to be engineered for future climate-resilient farming. Giang and Sáo fall in love after meeting at a bookstore café where she works as a waitress, and Sáo shows him a particular kind of local seaweed that is able to thrive in both fresh and saltwater. This seaweed becomes the core of Giang's research as he genetically modifies it so as to turn it into a crop plant capable of absorbing saltwater – an important asset in the flooded landscapes of southern Vietnam and the world. But at the end of his research, Giang leaves Sáo, returns to Saigon and marries into the wealthy family that funded his research and owns the hydroponic farm where Thi works later on.

In the third act, the film returns to 2030 and the moment where recently widowed Sáo embarks on a quest that combines knowledge, revenge and bare survival. Two versions of Thi's death emerge from her inquiries. Thi's brother, Thanh (Hoàng Phi), tells Sáo that he heard Giang on the floating farm ordering his men to kill Thi, punishing him for allegedly stealing genetically modified seeds for resale on the black market. But Giang himself later tells Sáo a different version of events: he claims that he hired Thi to smuggle seeds out from his family's farm so that they could be made available to the poor, but that Thi was caught and killed in the ensuing tussle. Just how reliable a narrator Giang might be is not easy to tell – and neither is it clear whether Giang and Sáo's continuing (or renewed) attraction might have played a role in bringing about Thi's demise in either Thanh's or Giang's version of the story. But Sáo at least pretends she believes Giang's account. During a typhoon that approaches the floating farm, the two board a submersible and float downward – perhaps to be safe from the storm, and perhaps to take knowledge of the genetically modified plants away from the corporation's possession. They travel through a mysterious underwater city, and then end up lying next to each other on an infinite stretch of sand.

Nước 2030's pace and tone are slow, quiet and lyrical – in stark opposition to the disaster mode of many North American films about climate change. Gradually but inexorably, the film transitions the viewer from the familiar hardships of life for the poor in the global South to a far stranger and more unsettling world. Uncertain concepts of property play a much more central role in this transition out of the ordinary world of everyday life than disaster scenarios. In an early scene, for example, Thi runs his boat into a group of men fishing near a floating sign that reads 'Private property'. He demands they get off his land; they express scepticism that the sea can be owned. In response, he leaps into their boat and starts throwing fists. Not long after, he finds holes in his fishing net and his fish eaten – the revenge of the fishermen he has chased away. At that point, he decides that holding on to his flooded land is not worth the trouble, and paints over the property sign with a 'For Sale' message and a phone number.

It is when his land is up for sale that Thi receives the call that leads to his working for Giang's hydroponic farm. As I already mentioned, property and theft are at the heart of the two conflicting versions Thanh and Giang tell about his death – the question of who owns or should own the genetically modified plant that is cultivated on the farm and that might save poor people like Sáo and Thi from famine. This question concerns material and intellectual as well as public and private property questions. In the second act, which takes viewers back to the years around 2020, one scene shows Giang presenting the findings of his research to the executives of the company he works for. Once he has revealed that he made the breakthrough they were hoping for, a moment of tension arises in the boardroom. Whereas Giang wants to use this technique to seed the ocean itself with produce, the board members suggest partnership with a leading research university and further development of the floating farms, which would turn the plant into a commodity for sale.

At the end of the film, this question re-emerges in Giang's claim that he hired Thi because he wanted the genetically modified produce to become publicly available, whereas the company that employs him – and to whose owners he is related by marriage – wanted it to remain proprietary. But even apart from the company, is the GMO plant Giang's to give away? After all, it was Sáo with her intimate knowledge of the ocean who led him to the original plant in the first place; Giang, the graduate student from Saigon, would not have found it on his own. So one might argue that Giang's academic research originally appropriated Sáo's vernacular knowledge without any compensation. The proxy story of personal loss that the film started out with here combines in increasingly intricate ways with an exploration of possession and ownership. Again and again, the film raises these questions of property in the context of climate change: what belongs to whom, and how ownership functions become uncertain issues in a world that is more ocean than land.

These subtly accumulating questions of ownership against the background of adaptation to life in and with the sea gradually convey a sense of a different world in which old concepts, laws, practices and institutions have only intermittent traction. The strangeness of this new world emerges especially in Nguyễn-Võ's extraordinary underwater scenes: Sáo and Thanh, for example, dive down to lay flowers on Thi's blue coffin at the bottom of the bay – a beautiful gesture of mourning and memory, strangely displaced from a cemetery to the ocean. But it is especially the image of a city underwater at the end of the film that drives home to what extent climate change unsettles ordinary conceptions of reality.

As a typhoon approaches and all the workers have already left the floating hydroponic farm, Giang and Sáo embark in a submersible that floats gently down and then glides across an underwater cityscape. The city is unmistakably Saigon, with one of its architectural landmarks, the Bitexco Tower, clearly visible. This scene does not make logical sense in the storyworld of *Nước 2030*, which is set well south of Saigon: in several earlier scenes, the city skyline was shown on the horizon, well above water. And the underwater city is lit up as if the electricity could still be on. Sáo and Giang then float by the bookstore café where she worked as a waitress and they first met in 2020. The café, the hammocks and even the books are all still implausibly intact, and the scene makes it seem as if it is now the fish reading the books – including one called *2020* in a metafictional allusion to the film itself. Climate-change realism here morphs into the imagery typical of French surrealism with its surprising juxtapositions and self-contradictory metaphors. This mesmerizing combination of beauty and incongruity in the underwater scenes sends the film's clearest signal to viewers that its futuristic storyworld no longer corresponds to the old world before climate change: not because of disasters, destruction and death – the typhoon, for example, is not portrayed as a major threat – but because the omnipresence of the ocean unmoors both collective institutions and individual practices.

In the same slightly disorienting fashion, *Nước 2030* turns its portrait of southern Vietnam into a synecdoche for global change. At three different moments in the film, the camera pulls slowly back from the unfolding scene to show the landscape or seascape through a fish-eye lens that highlights the curvature of the planet. These are not vistas that any of the characters perceive, but ones that the film audience is supposed to see – the planetary story behind the Vietnam plot. Instead of drawing on the familiar story templates and film images of hurricanes, flood waves, displaced crowds and destroyed cities, Nguyễn-Võ draws on the estrangement techniques developed by the high-modernist European avant-garde in the early twentieth century to create an aesthetically appealing but also deeply unsettling vision of land, wealth and culture going underwater.

Urban amphibiguity: *New York 2140*

Experimental narrative forms drawn from the modernisms of the early twentieth century also inform one of Robinson's more recent science fiction novels, set in a climate-change metropolis. Yet rather than the poetic experiments of surrealism, Robinson takes as his model the narrative innovations of John Dos Passos in *Manhattan Transfer* (1925) and the *USA* trilogy (1930–6). These novels, one focused on the city of New York and the others on the United States as a nation, share with other modernist experiments in narrative, such as James Joyce's *Ulysses* (1922), Virginia Woolf's *Mrs. Dalloway* (1925) and Alfred Döblin's *Berlin Alexanderplatz* (1929), the break-up of plot into the perspectives of multiple characters who inhabit the same urban space, but perceive and remember it in divergent ways. Like other modernist novelists, Dos Passos mixed these different character perspectives with bits and pieces of public or collective discourse that populate urban spaces and airways: overheard conversations, radio announcements, newspaper headlines, cinema newsreels, billboards, fragments of legal texts, bits of popular music and many other types of discourse that emanate from human crowds, municipal institutions or communications technologies. Unlike Joyce or Woolf, however, Dos Passos did not foreground the psychological interiority of his characters as a counterpoint to public discourse. Following the legacy of naturalism, his novels tend to emphasize the political, social and economic structures that his characters are forced to confront and that often leave them very limited room for choice. As a consequence, his narratives come closer than those of other modernist writers to not really featuring any clear protagonist; rather, the voices of many different characters have approximately the same weight and presence in the narrative.

Robinson, too, as a writer who has deeply engaged with Marxist and socialist thought, emphasizes institutional contexts and political forces in his portrayal of New York underwater in the middle of the twenty-second century. One of the most obvious manifestations of this emphasis in *New York 2140* is the voice of someone simply called 'the citizen' or 'that citizen', which in some later passages in the novel morphs into 'the city' – a voice that provides a good deal of urban history and much commentary on the contemporary sphere, but is not attached to a clearly defined character. A dozen or so other characters, much more minutely personalized, complement this voice of the municipality itself: Franklin Garr, a stockbroker; Charlotte Armstrong, a refugee advocate who is elected Representative of Congress towards the end of the novel; Gen Octaviasdottir, an African American police woman whose Nordic name alludes to the science fiction novelist Octavia Butler; Vlade Marovich, a building superintendent who originally came from Eastern Europe; two computer hackers, nicknamed Mutt and Jeff, who seek to overturn the capitalist market; Amelia Black, an internet celebrity who travels around the globe in an airship to broadcast live reports on the state of biodiversity and endangered species; two illiterate and orphaned boys, Stefan and Roberto, who spend much of their time with a retired historian whose maps, they hope, will lead them to treasures underwater. All of these characters come from different personal histories and social backgrounds, and inhabit the urban space in different ways even as they also represent larger forces of the market, the political establishment and the media, among others. All of the characters coincide at the MetLife building, where they either live permanently as part of a cooperative of the kind that is common in Manhattan in 2140, or squat temporarily in one of its spaces.

Climate change and rising sea levels are one of the major external forces that all the characters have to contend with. Robinson portrays Manhattan after two major pulses of ice thaw and sea level rise that have raised ocean water by sixty feet – by current scientific standards, an extreme but not impossible future. Under these circumstances, upper Manhattan, which lies 150 feet above sea level, has continued its vertical growth and sports new 'superscrapers' of unprecedented height. Midtown Manhattan has turned into an 'intertidal' zone where waters come and go, and the survival or collapse of buildings has become a prime object of real estate speculation. Lower Manhattan has completely flooded. But this scenario, usually the point of departure for large-scale urban disaster narratives, is far more ambivalent in Robinson's portrayal. The novel leaves no doubt that sea level rise and increased hurricanes have inflicted heavy damage on New York and the many other coastal cities in the age of climate change for which it stands as a proxy. But with its proverbial resilience, New York has not only survived but benefited from the flood. The characters variously call it an 'aquatropolis'[10] or a 'SuperVenice, fashionably hip, artistic, sexy, a new urban legend'.[11] In fact, to some extent, climate change has catalysed social change and utopian experimentation: 'Hegemony had drowned, so in the years after the flooding there was a proliferation of cooperatives, neighborhood associations, communes, squats, barter, alternative currencies, gift economies . . . also free open universities, free trade schools, and free art schools.'[12]

But of course, hegemony has not quite drowned. Just as the flooding of Thi's ancestral land leads to 'amphibiguity' of property values in Nguyễn-Võ's *Nước 2030*, the loss of homes to the rising waters features centrally in *New York 2140*. Climate refugees flood steadily into the city, where Charlotte Armstrong's Householders Union seeks to help them find their way through immigration and housing application procedures. Mutt and Jeff, the two computer programmers, squat on the grounds of the MetLife building's vertical farm because they have no permanent home. Stefan and Roberto, the two orphans whose origins are never clearly determined, do not seem to have any fixed abode either, and end up staying for an extended time at the MetLife building. Their mentor, the retired historian Gordon Hexter, sees the building he inhabits in midtown Manhattan start to shake and 'melt' due to the impact of the tides one day. He is only saved thanks to Stefan and Roberto's intervention at the last minute and then relocates to the MetLife.[13]

Rising waters, in other words, drive some of the characters from their homes, while others find new homes by squatting in buildings that can no longer be officially rented. Yet others seem unable to find a home because housing may be unaffordable to them in the first place. The intertidal areas of New York and other coastal cities have turned into privileged zones for real estate speculation, showing how capitalism itself has adapted to a radically changed world. Franklin Garr, a stockbroker whose first-person narrative and bildungsroman-style development over the course of the plot function as the novel's narrative backbone, not only participates in this speculation on the death and life of great American buildings. He has also created a new stock index, the intertidal property pricing index (IPPI), which is designed to help investors profit from this speculation, 'because if the intertidal has any value at all, even if it's only a million or two, then someone wants to own that. And other people want to leverage that value right out to the usual fifty times whatever it might be.'[14] This kind of speculation can make even risky buildings like Gordon Hexter's too expensive to live in for the young and the poor.

Questions of ownership are at the forefront of this narrative engagement with climate change, even though in Robinson's metropolis these issues are foregrounded more bluntly in their systemic implications than in the personal stories of Nguyễn-Võ's lyrical meditation. Indeed, the plot of *New York 2140* is bookended by two attempts to overturn the capitalist order that keeps real estate speculation alive even and especially when the real estate is going underwater. Mutt and Jeff, in the novel's very first scene, hack the international legal code that underwrites banking and stock market transactions. They cause a disruption of a mere few seconds before their intervention is discovered and reversed – although they are subsequently kidnapped and held captive for several weeks by shadowy corporate agents to prevent any further intrusion into the workings of international markets. The technological elite, however progressively minded, will not be able to bring about any lasting change, in Robinson's view. But at the end of the novel, an unusual alliance between masses of consumers and the governments of most nations does lead to an incisive change. Instigated by activists such as Charlotte and Amelia, millions of customers start to withhold payment on their loans, credits, and mortgages, precipitating international markets into a financial crash on the model of the one that occurred in 2008. In 2140, governments step in and offer to bail out collapsing banks and corporations, as they did in 2008 and 2009 – but this time on condition that the enterprises cede at least 51 per cent of their stock to the government. Effectively, then, the householders' payment strike in combination with government policy leads to the socialization of major enterprises – for Robinson, a step in the right direction, away from the ubiquitous power of capital.

The future city as Robinson portrays it, then, is not just (partly) underwater because of rising sea levels and climate change. It is also 'underwater' in more metaphorical, financial senses. The novel plays extensively on the metaphorical superimposition of money and water in both its plot and its language. 'Combining a housing index with sea level was one way to view the drowned coastlines, and that was at the heart of what I did,' Franklin Garr says about his financial approach.[15] Stefan and Roberto, the penniless orphans who are often referred as 'drowned rats' by the adults and repeatedly come close to actually drowning on their diving expeditions, do end up locating a sunken galleon with the help of Hexter's historical maps and gold bullion worth four billion dollars – although, in an ironic twist, the historic treasure has to be kept confidential and melted down to translate into wealth for them in the capitalist market. The novel's first chapter is entitled 'The Tyranny of Sunk Costs', which according to the citizen is what makes New York New York: 'People can't give up on it . . . once you've put so much time and money into a project, it gets hard to just eat your losses and walk. You are forced by the structure of the situation to throw good money after bad. . . . You persevere unto death, a monomaniacal New Yorker to the end.'[16]

Another chapter is entitled 'Liquidity Trap', in another pun on money and water. And one whole page of the novel is simply an enumeration of real and made-up, present and future idioms and synonyms related to sinking, drinking, drowning and going under water:

> six fathoms under, wet, all wet, moldy, mildewed, tidal, marshy . . . scubaed, plunged, high diving, sloshed, drunk, dowsed, watered, waterfalled, snorkeled, running the rapids, backstroking, waterboarded . . . jawing with Jonah, in the belly of the whale, pilot fishing, leviathanating, getting finny, shnockered, dipped, clammed, clamming, salting, brined, belly-flopping, trawling, bottom-feeding, breathing water, eating water, down the toilet, washing-machined, submarining, going down . . . liquidated, liquefied, . . . inundated, laved, deluged, fluvialized, fluviated, flooded, Noahed, Noah's-neighbored, U-boating, universally solventized, ad aqua infinitum.[17]

The omnipresence of water in Robinson's drowned Manhattan, through these plot twists and linguistic games, takes on multiple meanings that include but are not limited to literal rising sea levels. They also point to social structures, market transactions and historical memories, all of which shape how the different individuals that populate the novel understand and live with the futuristic city they inhabit. Dealing with climate change, in this context, is not only a matter of better technologies (such as waterproof diamond-sheeted buildings), of new construction in devastated urban districts, of biological conservation and restoration, of innovative social experiments or of civic activism – though all of these play important roles in the plot. It is mainly an issue of reimagining value itself, the processes through which value is attached and removed from places, practices, objects and people themselves.

Such a reimagination is possible, in Robinson's perspective, and nowhere is this clearer than in the way in which the flooding of Manhattan has in and of itself turned into a process of ecological restoration. Amelia Black, in the aerial view she describes to her internet viewers, often highlights the way in which greater New York was always a landscape of bays, estuaries and coastlines – an essentially marine landscape. And the citizen celebrates the rebirth of waterborne biodiversity in and around New York that the city's inundation has catalyzed:

> On the floors of the canals, the old sewer holes spew life from below. Up and down life floats, in and out with the tides. Salamanders and frogs and turtles proliferate among the fishes and eels, burrow in the mulm. Above them birds flock and nest in the concrete cliffs of the city. . . . Right whales swim into the upper bay to birth their babies. Minke whales, finbacks, humpbacks. Wolves and foxes skulk in the forests of the outer boroughs. . . . River otters, mink, fishers, weasels, raccoons: all these citizens inhabit the world the beavers made from their version of lumber. Around them swim harbor seals, harbor porpoises. A sperm whale sails through the Narrows like an ocean liner. Squirrels and bats. The American black bear. They have all come back like the tide, like poetry.[18]

Like the stock market transactions, ecological change is here conveyed through the metaphor of the tide – metaphorical nature represents the literal return of nature to the city.

Through his persistent play on water, floods, liquidity and drowning in *New York 2140*, Robinson seeks to realize the narrative quest for what he often refers to as 'optopia'. The neologism seeks to eschew the connotations of static social structures and political authoritarianism that are often attached to older visions of utopia, as well as the idea that only a perfect society is worth striving for. Optopia, in Robinson's approach, is the best society you can achieve, given the circumstances: less than perfect, but better than current conditions. In *New York 2140*, his signal narrative achievement is to base his vision of a future urban and ultimately national and international optopia on precisely the thematic foundation that usually leads authors of speculative fiction to dystopia. Nguyễn-Võ's surrealist submarine Saigon in Giang and Sáo's dream-like voyage offers a more meditative and less optimistic vision of the future, but like Robinson's Venetian Manhattan, it foregrounds the lives of ordinary people seeking for ways to adapt to strange, climate-changed urban landscapes. The city drowned by climate change, in both works, becomes a way of imagining other worlds and sometimes better futures by turning it into a complex meditation on ownership, property, markets and values that sink or swim, come and go with floods and tides.

Notes

1. See UNFPA (United Nations Population Fund), *State of World Population 2007*; United Nations Department of Economic and Social Affairs/Population Division, *World Urbanization Prospects: The 2007 Revision*; and UN-HABITAT (United Nations Human Settlement Programme), *The State of the World's Cities Report 2006/2007*.
2. Neil Brenner and Christian Schmid, 'The "Urban Age" in Question', *International Journal of Urban and Regional Research* 38, no. 3 (2014): 731–55; Thomas Buettner, 'Urban Estimates and Projections at the United Nations: The Strengths, Weaknesses, and Underpinnings of the World Urbanization Prospects', *Spatial Demography* 2, no. 2 (2014), http://citeseerx.ist.psu.edu/viewdoc/download?doi=10.1.1.679.297&rep=rep1&type=pdf.
3. Kai N. Lee, William R. Freudenburg and Richard B. Howarth, *Humans in the Landscape: An Introduction to Environmental Studies* (New York: Norton, 2012), 208.
4. Lee et al, *Humans in the Landscape*, 223.
5. Menno Schilthuizen, *Darwin Comes to Town: How the Urban Jungle Drives Evolution* (New York: Picador, 2018).
6. For a detailed discussion of the insights and shortfalls of these analyses, see Ursula K. Heise, 'Science Fiction and the Time Scales of the Anthropocene', *English Literary History* 86, no. 2 (2019): 275–304.
7. Alexa Weik von Mossner, *Affective Ecologies: Empathy, Emotion, and Environmental Narrative* (Columbus: Ohio State University Press, 2017), 68.
8. Many ingredients of the climate disaster story were already described in the context of nuclear disaster stories by Susan Sontag in her 1965 essay, 'The Imagination of Disaster', in *Against Interpretation and Other Essays* (New York: Picador, 1990), 209–25.
9. For ecocritical analyses of Emmerich's film, see Robin L. Murray and Joseph K. Heumann, *Ecology and Popular Film: Cinema on the Edge* (Buffalo: SUNY Press, 2009), 3–10; Weik von Mossner, *Affective Ecologies*, 137–8, 153–61.
10. Kim Stanley Robinson, *New York 2140* (New York: Orbit, 2017), 285.
11. Robinson, *New York 2140*, 279–80.
12. Robinson, *New York 2140*, 209.
13. Robinson, *New York 2140*, 117.
14. Robinson, *New York 2140*, 120.

15   Robinson, *New York 2140*, 19.
16   Robinson, *New York 2140*, 33.
17   Robinson, *New York 2140*, 138.
18   Robinson, *New York 2140*, 319–20.

Bibliography

Brandão, Ignacio de Loyola. *Não Verás País Nenhum (Memorial Descritivo)*. Rio de Janeiro: Codecri, 1981.

Brenner, Neil and Christian Schmid. 'The "Urban Age" in Question'. *International Journal of Urban and Regional Research* 38, no. 3 (2014): 731–55.

Buettner, Thomas. 'Urban Estimates and Projections at the United Nations: The Strengths, Weaknesses, and Underpinnings of the World Urbanization Prospects'. *Spatial Demography* 2, no. 2 (2014). http://citeseerx.ist.psu.edu/viewdoc/download?doi=10.1.1.679.297&rep=rep1&type=pdf.

Calthorpe, Peter. *Urbanism in an Age of Climate Change*. Washington, DC: Island Press, 2011.

Davis, Mike. *Planet of Slums*. London: Verso, 2006.

Dawson, Ashley. *Extreme Cities: The Peril and Promise of Urban Life in the Age of Climate Change*. London: Verso, 2017.

Ehrlich, Paul. 1968. *The Population Bomb*. Cutchogue: Buccaneer, 1971.

Goodell, Jeff. *The Water Will Come: Rising Seas, Sinking Cities, and the Remaking of Civilizations*. New York: Little, Brown, 2017.

Heise, Ursula K. 'Science Fiction and the Time Scales of the Anthropocene'. *English Literary History* 86, no. 2 (2019): 275–304.

Hunter, Megan. *The End We Start From*. London: Picador, 2017.

Jensen, Liz. *The Rapture*. London: Bloomsbury, 2009.

Kahn, Matthew E. *Climatopolis: How Our Cities Will Thrive in the Hotter Future*. New York: Basic Books, 2010.

Lee, Kai N., William R. Freudenburg and Richard B. Howarth. *Humans in the Landscape: An Introduction to Environmental Studies*. New York: Norton, 2012.

Murray, Robin L. and Joseph K. Heumann. *Ecology and Popular Film: Cinema on the Edge*. Buffalo: SUNY Press, 2009.

Robinson, Kim Stanley. *New York 2140*. New York: Orbit, 2017.

Schilthuizen, Menno. *Darwin Comes to Town: How the Urban Jungle Drives Evolution*. New York: Picador, 2018.

Sontag, Susan. 1965. 'The Imagination of Disaster'. In *Against Interpretation and Other Essays*, 209–25. New York: Picador, 1990.

Stanford, Claire Miye. 'Neither Above Nor Below'. In *A Flash of Silver Green: Stories of the Nature of Cities*, edited by David Maddox, Curtis Walker and Marjorie Lovejoy, 15–21. Guelph: Publication Studio Guelph, 2019.

Trojanow, Ilija. *EisTau*. Munich: Carl Hanser, 2011.

Tuomainen, Antti. 2010. *The Healer*. Translated by Lola Rogers. New York: Henry Holt, 2013.

UN-HABITAT (United Nations Human Settlement Programme). *The State of the World's Cities Report 2006/2007: 30 Years of Shaping the Habitat Agenda*. London: Earthscan for UN-Habitat, 2007. Web. Accessed 7 February 2015. https://sustainabledevelopment.un.org/content/documents/11292101_alt.pdf.

UNFPA (United Nations Population Fund). *State of World Population 2007: Unleashing the Potential of Urban Growth*. New York: United Nations Population Fund, 2007. Web. Accessed 7 February 2015. http://www.unfpa.org/publications/state-world-population-2007.

United Nations Department of Economic and Social Affairs/Population Division. *World Urbanization Prospects: The 2007 Revision*. New York: United Nations, 2008. Web. Accessed 8 February 2015. Accessed 7 February 2015. http://www.unfpa.org/publications/state-world-population-2007.

Wallace-Wells, David. *The Uninhabitable Earth: Life after Warming*. New York: Penguin Random House, 2019.

Weik von Mossner, Alexa. *Affective Ecologies: Empathy, Emotion, and Environmental Narrative*. Columbus: Ohio State University Press, 2017.

Weisman, Alan. *Countdown: Our Last, Best Hope for a Future on Earth?* New York: Little, Brown, 2013.

3

Scaling down our imagination of the human
Ted Chiang and the fable of extinction
Chris Danta

Scale effects

The Anthropocene is an idea currently reshaping our thinking about what it means to be human. In a 2000 article for the *Global Change Newsletter*, Nobel-Prize-winning atmospheric chemist Paul J. Crutzen and biologist Eugene F. Stoermer proposed using the term 'Anthropocene' to designate the current geological epoch. According to Crutzen and Stoermer, the impacts of human activities on the earth and atmosphere have escalated to such a degree over the past three centuries that humankind has become a major geological and environmental force.[1] Anthropocene, from the Greek roots *anthropo* (human) and *cene* (new), is a term intended to take account of what Crutzen calls in a 2002 article in *Nature* 'the geology of mankind'. 'It seems appropriate to assign the term "Anthropocene" to the present, in many ways human-dominated, geological epoch', Crutzen writes in that article, 'supplementing the Holocene – the warm period of the past 10-12 millennia'.[2]

The Anthropocene has yet to gain official sanction as a new geological epoch in Earth history. But the term has captured the imagination of scholars working not just in the environmental sciences but also in the humanities. One reason for this, I suggest, is the growing fascination in various fields with how the problem of scale affects our understanding of the human. The Anthropocene narrative achieves its forcefulness through a grotesque magnification of the scale of human agency. As the historian Dipesh Chakrabarty notes in his influential 2009 article 'The Climate of History: Four Theses':

> To call human beings geological agents is to scale up our imagination of the human. Humans are biological agents, both collectively and as individuals. They

have always been so. There was no point in human history when humans were not biological agents. But we can become geological agents only historically and collectively, that is, when we have reached numbers and invented technologies that are on a scale large enough to have an impact on the planet itself.³

Thinking about the human – and the humanities – in the age of the Anthropocene involves thinking about the problem of scale.⁴ As Chakrabarty notes in a 2012 essay on climate change and postcolonial studies, 'the current conjuncture of globalisation and global warming leaves us with the challenge of having to think of human agency over multiple and incommensurable scales at once.' The issue of anthropogenic environmental change, he argues, enjoins us to conceive of the human in two apparently contradictory registers: on the one hand, as a political agent that is the bearer of rights and, on the other, as a geological agent that is indifferent to 'questions of intrahuman justice'.⁵ Novelist Amitav Ghosh echoes and extends Chakrabarty's point when he notes in *The Great Derangement*: 'Climate change is often described as a "wicked problem". One of its wickedest aspects is that it may require us to abandon some of our most treasured ideas about political virtue: for example, "be the change you want to see".' For Ghosh, to understand the Anthropocene, we must think the human beyond the scale of individual experience: 'What we need . . . is to find a way out of the individualising imaginary in which we are trapped.'⁶

Literary ecocritic Timothy Clark has famously argued that a derangement of the human scale characterizes the Anthropocene. 'We understand distance, height and breadth in terms of the given dimensionality of our embodied existence', Clark writes in *Ecocriticism on the Edge*:

> A particular human scale is inherent to the intelligibility of the Earth around us. . . . The Anthropocene entails the realization of how deeply this scale may be misleading, underlining how (worryingly) our 'normal' scales of space and time must be understood as contingent projections of a biology that may be relatively inexorable. This is now manifest in the disjunctions between the scale of planetary environmental realities and of those things that seem immediately to matter to human engagement from one day to another.⁷

According to the *OED*, a scale effect is 'an effect occurring when the scale of something is changed, as a result of contributory factors not all varying in proportion'.⁸ For Chakrabarty, Ghosh and Clark, the Anthropocene illustrates unsettling disjunctions between the effects of human action on the individual and planetary scales. Clark writes: 'The Anthropocene is itself an emergent "scale effect". That is, at a certain, indeterminate threshold, numerous human actions, insignificant in themselves (heating a house, clearing trees, flying between continents, forest management) come together to form a new, imponderable physical event, altering the basic ecological cycles of the planet.'[9]

Scaling up our imagination of the human to account for anthropogenic climate change is both mentally and emotionally taxing. The idea of the Anthropocene infects us with a strange kind of proportion sickness, as we find ourselves unable to reconcile the traditional view of the human as biological, social and political agent with the emergent view of the human as impersonal geological force. Chakrabarty relates his own sense of disorientation in the face of the climate-change crisis in 'The Climate of History', which in some sense takes the form of a conversion narrative. 'As the crisis gathered momentum in the last few years', he writes, 'I realized that all my readings in theories of globalization, Marxist analysis of capital, subaltern studies, and postcolonial criticism over the last twenty-five years, while enormously useful in studying globalization, had not really prepared me for making sense of this planetary conjuncture within which humanity finds itself today'. The climate-change crisis has taught him that the boundary usually thought to separate natural or deep history from human history no longer exists: 'The geologic now of the Anthropocene has become entangled with the now of human history.'[10] Bruno Latour coins the phrase 'our common *geostory*' to account for the collapse of the distinction between natural and human history. 'The problem for all of us in philosophy, science, or literature', Latour writes, 'becomes: how do we tell such a story?'[11]

A great challenge in writing about the Anthropocene is how to tell 'our common *geostory*' without at the same time succumbing to pessimism. Literary critic Mark McGurl detects in arguments like Chakrabarty's, which he labels 'the new cultural geology', 'a certain pessimism about the ability of human beings to do anything about the crisis their actions have precipitated'. 'Having dramatically increased the spatial and temporal scale at which human history will be viewed', McGurl continues,

> human agency itself becomes visible as something nested in forces beyond its control. Thus the terror we see in the not-quite empty sky is the terrifying nature of our ethically unconscious selves. We are the terror, but only insofar as 'we' are discovered to be 'non-human' in precisely the way a stone is – in being careless of the fate of the other.[12]

The Anthropocene narrative, as both Chakrabarty and Clark tell it, asks us to scale up our imagination of the human to account for the detrimental effect of our species on the planet's atmosphere. It nonetheless asserts, perplexingly, that we cannot understand this larger scale of experience in the terms given to us by the smaller scale of experience. As Chakrabarty argues:

> When [biologist] E. O. Wilson . . . recommends in the interest of our collective future that we achieve self-understanding as a species, the statement does not correspond to any historical way of understanding and connecting pasts with futures through the assumption of there being an element of continuity to human experience. . . . Who is the we? We humans never experience ourselves as a species. We can only intellectually comprehend or infer the existence of the human species but never experience it as such. There could be no phenomenology of us as a species.[13]

Even though Chakrabarty argues that the Anthropocene enjoins us to think human agency across multiple scales at once, in his account big history trumps little history: that is, the larger scale of natural history renders inoperative – and invalidates – concepts that work at the smaller scale of human history. Consider when Chakrabarty writes: 'A geophysical force – for that is what in part we are in our collective existence – is neither subject nor an object. A force is the capacity to move things. It is pure, nonontological identity.' The claim here is that the distinction between subject and object that operates at the smaller scale of human history ceases to operate at the larger scale of the Anthropocene. 'In becoming a geophysical force on the planet', Chakrabarty writes, 'we have developed a form of collective existence that has no ontological dimension. Our thinking about ourselves now stretches our capacity for interpretive understanding.'[14]

But must we accept Chakrabarty's pessimistic conclusion that there could be 'no phenomenology of us as a species'? Ursula K. Heise, for one, rejects this conclusion in her book *Imagining Extinction*. Heise writes in direct response to Chakrabarty:

> Granted, humans may not normally be able to experience themselves as a species – any more than they are able to experience themselves as a nation: unless, that is, communities produce institutions, laws, symbols, and forms of rhetoric that establish such abstract categories as perceptible and liveable frameworks of experience. . . . Surely what being a 'species' means, from a biological and ecological as well as a social perspective, is to be situated in a network of lived, existential relations with other species and with the inanimate environment (soil, water, atmosphere, weather patterns).[15]

Heise here helps us to see the central problem with Chakrabarty's anthropology of the Anthropocene: it is too abstract, too petrified and, ultimately, too nihilistic. By imagining *Homo sapiens* to have become a geophysical force that somehow transcends the distinction between subject and object, Chakrabarty removes humans from 'the network of lived, existential relations with other species and with the inanimate environment'.

This becomes particularly apparent when we consider the subject of Heise's book: extinction. The notion of extinction requires us to think at the level both of the individual creature and of the species. As Deborah Bird Rose, Thom van Dooren and Matthew Chrulew point out in the introduction to their recent edited collection *Extinction Studies*: 'Extinction . . . is, by definition, a collective death, the end of a living kind. But this larger ending is pieced together out of the deaths of countless individual organisms. In a range of different ways, at various scales, death is central to extinction processes.' In framing their approach to extinction studies, Rose, van Dooren and Chrulew refuse to let big history trump little history:

> By *staying with* the lives and deaths of particular, precious beings; by refusing to allow the perspectives afforded by evolutionary deep time or genetic codification – invaluably unsettling as they are – to invalidate the fragile temporalities by which singular living communities make their worlds and make their ways in ours; by *holding together* the agencies of different animal species and those of human actors . . . we hope to open up a place and a moment for a reflective gathering of energies *against* extinction but also *creative* of new modes of survival and fragile flourishing.

For Rose, van Dooren and Chrulew, telling extinction stories – addressing the problem of death at the level of the species – also requires us to pay close and careful attention to the small scale of human history. It means reflecting on the 'many ways in which human communities are affected by and suffer through extinction . . . [and] the specific political, economic, and cultural forms of organization most responsible for any given extinction'.[16]

Understanding the phenomenon of extinction requires us to move between the large scale of species experience and the small scale of individual experience. Our nomenclature is impoverished in regard to this second enterprise of delineating the particular experiences of near-extinct things. As Robert M. Webster and Bruce Erickson point out in the correspondence section of the 4 April 1996 issue of *Nature*, we lack a word in English to designate the final survivor of a lineage: 'There is a need for a word in taxonomy, and in medical genealogical, scientific, biological and other literature, that does not occur in English or any other language. We need a word to designate the last person, animal or other species in his/her/its lineage.'[17] Webster and Erickson propose the Tolkienesque neologism *endling* to designate the last of its kind.

A famous twentieth-century endling is Martha, the last known Passenger Pigeon, who died at 1.00 pm on 1 September 1914 in the Cincinnati Zoo, Ohio. In her lyrical afterword to *Extinction Studies*, Vinciane Despret wonders what it must have been like for Martha before she died as the last of her lineage. Despret notes that what disappears when a species goes extinct is that species' unique point of view on the world:

> What the world has lost . . . is the unique, sensual, living, warm, musical, and colourful point of view that the Passenger Pigeons created upon it and with it. . . . The happiness of being an immense wing traversing infinite spaces; the feeling of being a cloud above Earth and of creating changing shapes on it, flowing and shadowy: the sensation of the fields and the woods that, far below, fly like the images of an accelerating film.[18]

Despret helps us to see here that the act of scaling up our imagination of the human to take account of the Anthropocene comes at a hermeneutic cost: it prevents us from adopting the perspective of an endling such as Martha. Ghosh argues that we must escape the individualizing imaginary in which we are trapped. But, as I try to show in the final section of this chapter when I turn to the American science fiction writer Ted Chiang's short story about an endangered species of parrot, 'The Great Silence', representing the individual perspective of an endangered non-human animal can be a powerful way of critiquing human behaviour in the time of anthropogenic extinction.

Discourse on the Anthropocene in the humanities tends to fetishize both the idea of scalar disjunction and the sense of cognitive failure that result from contemplating massive scales. Chakrabarty's discussion of the difficulty a social scientist such as himself experiences in trying to place the human in the larger context of deep time recalls Charles Darwin's observation in the *Origin of Species* that a non-specialist reader will experience a sense of incomprehension when contemplating the lapse of geological time. Darwin writes:

> It is hardly possible for me to recall to the reader, who may not be a practical geologist, the facts leading the mind feebly to comprehend the lapse of [geological] time. He who can read Sir Charles Lyell's grand work on the Principles of Geology, which the future historian will recognise as having produced a revolution in natural science, yet does not admit how incomprehensibly vast have been the past periods of time, may at once close this volume.[19]

In his work on the Anthropocene, Chakrabarty positions himself as a kind of future historian of the principles of the geology of humankind. He assumes that the move from the smaller scale of human history to the larger scale of deep time is a move from a human and anthropocentric point of view to a non-human and non-anthropocentric point of view. He writes in a recent article on 'The Future of the Human Sciences in the Age of Humans':

> an awareness of 'deep time' is what will inform the social sciences of the future. Man will have to be placed in the larger context of the deeper history of life on this planet. This does not mean that our usual disputations about intra-human in/justice, inequalities, oppressive relationships will not continue; they will. But the climate crisis leaves us more aware of the obsessively human-centric nature of the social sciences. Such anthropocentrism may be necessary but will increasingly seem inadequate if one looks at the impact of the human ecological footprint on other forms of life and on the planet itself. So our inevitable anthropocentrism will need to be supplemented (not replaced) by 'deep time' perspectives that necessarily escape the human point of view.[20]

But do deep time perspectives necessarily escape the human point of view? Is the act of scaling up our imagination of the human to take account of anthropogenic climate change sufficient to circumvent the problem of anthropocentrism?

I suggest in this chapter that it is not, that escaping anthropocentrism requires more than just scaling up our imagination of the human. What I find problematic about the Anthropocene narrative is that it puts the human on the side of the massive. It is one thing to scale up our imagination of the passage of time, as Darwin does in the *Origin*, from human history to geological time. This type of scaling up has the effect of diminishing the importance of the human species by placing it within a larger, evolutionary timeframe. Here, attention to the movement of the earth's geological forces works to make the human seem small and insignificant. As John Durham Peters puts it, 'Geological time shames our anthropocentric tenderness.'[21] But it is quite another thing to scale up our imagination of the human, as Chakrabarty and others do, so that the human becomes equivalent to a geological force of nature. This second type of scaling up risks the charge of anthropocentrism by putting the human on the side of the massive. While the fossil record and the geologic time scale are blows to theological anthropocentrism, the proposal that we recognize ourselves as a geological agent has the opposite effect of transforming the human into something powerful and titanic – a 'giant Atlas', as Latour puts it in *Facing Gaia*.[22]

The Anthropocene narrative overdetermines the role of human agency in the production of the earth's present geological state so that the only solution to the problem of a damaged planet becomes further intervention by humans. In *Extinction Studies*, Rose, van Dooren and Chrulew observe that actions and stories in the era of the Anthropocene 'all too often revert to comfortable, all-too-human scripts, whether heroic epics of conservation and, increasingly, resurrection and de-extinction, enamored of the salvific power of scientific control . . . or nihilistic fables of fated human escape or disappearance, erasing all unique forms of nonhuman value in narratives of accelerated progress or inevitable decline'.[23] According to the Anthropocene narrative, we can act heroically and solve the problem we have created, or else it is too late and no action on our part will change things. The problem with both of these scenarios – the heroic and the nihilistic – is that they emphasize human agency to the exclusion of non-human agency. In so doing, they separate humans from other biological and non-biological forms of life on Earth. This is perhaps why the American biologist Edward O. Wilson prefers to call the Anthropocene the Eremocene – or the Age of Loneliness.[24]

The non-human perspective

So how might we tell 'our common *geostory*'[25] without at the same time overdetermining the role of human agency or failing to take account of our evolutionary entanglement with other species of life on the planet? We might present the Anthropocene from the point of view not just of humans but also of non-humans. Chakrabarty ends 'The Climate of History' by calling for a universal history of the human species: 'Climate change is an unintended consequence of human actions and shows, only through scientific analysis, the effects of our actions as a species. Species may indeed be the name of a placeholder for an emergent, new universal history of humans that flashes up in the moment of the danger that is climate change'.[26] While proposing the idea of a universal history of the human species, Chakrabarty remains largely silent on the topics of non-human agency and the history of other species of animal. Jeremy Davies criticizes Chakrabarty for underplaying the agency of non-human geophysical actors in the Anthropocene:

> The Anthropocene does not . . . require a turn away from the critique of sociopolitical power relations (globalization, capitalism, imperialism, and so on) toward a universal history of the human species. Instead, to understand the Anthropocene means widening the focus of sociopolitical critique and working toward *an analysis of the power relations between geo-physical actors, both human and nonhuman.*[27]

Literature offers unique conceptual resources with which to carry out 'an analysis of the power relations between geo-physical actors, both human and nonhuman', because literary writers imaginatively present the perspectives of non-human actors in their fiction. Much recent literary criticism addresses the 'question of storytelling in the Anthropocene', of how anthropogenic climate change has been and should be represented in literature.[28] For Ghosh, climate change requires us to think in more animistic ways. He explains the strangeness of the Anthropocene in *The Great Derangement* through the example of something apparently inanimate suddenly coming to life. One of the uncanniest effects of the Anthropocene, he remarks, is a 'renewed awareness of the elements of agency and consciousness that humans share with many other beings, and even perhaps the planet itself'. He points out that many people in the world have never lost this awareness in the first place: 'In the Sundarbans . . . the people who live in and around the mangrove forest have never doubted that tigers and many other animals possess intelligence and agency. For the first peoples of the Yukon, even glaciers are endowed with moods and feelings, likes and dislikes.' Searching for more animistic ways of thinking and of telling stories, Ghosh turns away from the modern novel, with its focus on the individualizing human imaginary, towards other literary genres such as epic, science fiction and fantasy. In his potted history of the novel, he associates the emergence of anthropogenic climate change in the eighteenth century with a rise in anthropocentrism in the literary imagination: 'It was in exactly the period in which human activity was changing the earth's atmosphere that the literary imagination became radically centred on the human. Inasmuch as the nonhuman was written about at all, it was not within the mansion of serious fiction but rather in the outhouses to which science fiction and fantasy had been banished.'[29]

Making literary genres such as science fiction and fantasy useful in thinking about the Anthropocene is the fact that they readily allow for the fictional presentation of non-human perspectives on the human. As Heise notes in relation to science fiction: 'For at least one hundred and fifty years, science fiction has often featured nonhuman agents, from robots to aliens and artificial intelligences. It has routinely focused on extraordinary events such as the discovery of new planets, encounters with aliens, and revolutionary technological change.'[30] To Ghosh's list of literary genres that allow for the presentation of non-human perspectives on the human (epic, science fiction and fantasy), I would add the genre of the fable. Like these other genres, the fable presupposes that humans share elements of agency and consciousness with many other beings.

According to anthropologist John Hartigan: '[Fables] stage other species as capable of speaking to us. This is, of course, not unfettered or human speech; the fables can rightfully all be charged with ventriloquizing nonhumans in shamelessly moralistic manners. But they do present both the possibility and problem of how we might listen to and then learn from other species.'[31] Fables help to mitigate anthropocentrism by imaginatively implicating the human in its environmental and evolutionary milieu. They gift animals the power of human speech and reason to show us not only that we have something to learn from other animals, but also that we are animals. The form of the fable allows writers to critique human hubris by developing animal perspectives on the human. Distinguishing the fable from other literary genres such as science fiction, fantasy and epic is that it scales down our imagination of the human. Fables often serve to puncture the unfounded species pride of their central characters. They express a practical, earthy form of wisdom that inevitably undercuts the possibility of idealism. Especially after Darwin, they challenge our belief in the exceptionality of our species by showing the human to be, as H. G. Wells puts it in his 1898 novel *The War of the Worlds*, 'an animal among the animals'.[32]

According to McGurl, 'Aggrieved partisans of genre fiction are forever lobbying for its recognition as serious literature, which is fine, but it is just as important to draw the philosophical lesson embedded in its apparent lowliness, which points altogether beyond the pale of aesthetic redemption.'[33] A philosophical lesson embedded in the apparent lowliness of genres such as science fiction, fantasy and fable is that these genres allow writers to critique the human from below, so to speak, from the so-called lowly perspective of the non-human agent. Animal fables present individual animal characters that are at the same time representatives of their species. These characters are anti-novelistic in the sense that they bear the name of their species rather than the name of an individual member of the species. But this generalizing, abstract, anti-novelistic feature of the fable is precisely what allows the genre to embark on a unique form of species thinking and even species critique.

Ted Chiang's 'The Great Silence'

Let me conclude this chapter by showing how the fable offers itself to the contemporary writer as an ideal mode with which to comment on the relation between humans and non-humans in the time of anthropogenic extinction. My example text is science fiction writer Ted Chiang's 2014 short story 'The Great Silence', a heartrending Anthropocene fable that uses a non-human point of view to criticize the tendency of humans to scale up their imagination of themselves. As we will see, in 'The Great Silence', Chiang adopts the fictionalized consciousness of a member of a dying species of parrot, a sort of endling, to capture the essential dilemmas of scale and perspective that we face in the Anthropocene.

Chiang's story originally formed the subtitle text of a 2014 video installation by artists Jennifer Allora and Guillermo Calzadilla called *The Great Silence*. 'There are actually two pieces titled, "The Great Silence"', Chiang tells us in the story notes to his 2019 collection *Exhalation*, 'only one of which can fit in this collection'. He then explains how he came to write the story as an anthropomorphic fable told from the perspective of an endangered Puerto Rican parrot:

> In 2014 Jennifer got in touch with me about the possibility of collaborating with her and her partner, Guillermo. They wanted to create a multiscreen video installation about anthropomorphism, technology, and the connections between the human and nonhuman worlds. Their plan was to juxtapose footage of the radio telescope in Arecibo [in Puerto Rico] with footage of the endangered Puerto Rican parrots that live in a nearby forest, and they asked if I would write subtitle text that would appear on a third screen, a fable told from the point of view of one of the parrots, 'a form of interspecies translation'. I was hesitant, not only because I had no experience with video art, but also because fables aren't what I usually write. But after they showed me a little preliminary footage I decided to give it a try, and in the following weeks we exchanged thoughts on topics like glossolalia and the extinction of languages.[34]

Chiang's stories often take language as their theme. In a 2012 interview with *The New Yorker*, Chiang identifies the search for a perfect language as one of his enduring concerns. 'There's a book by Umberto Eco called "The Search for the Perfect Language"', he tells Joshua Rothman. 'It's a history of the idea that there could be a language which is perfectly unambiguous and can perfectly describe everything. At one point, it was believed that this was the language spoken by angels in Heaven, or the language spoken by Adam in Eden. Later on, there were attempts by philosophers to create a perfect language.' This idea of a perfect language appeals to him in an abstract way, Chiang continues, despite its impossibility.[35]

Chiang is fascinated not just by the search for a perfect language but also by the possibility of interspecies communication. His best-known work, 'Story of Your Life' (1998), on which Denis Villeneuve's 2016 Hollywood film *Arrival* is based, tells of a human linguist who starts to see into her future after she learns to think in an alien language called Heptapod B.[36] 'The Great Silence' concerns the more realistic and mundane possibility of humans communicating with non-human animals here on Earth. Like a number of traditional animal fables,

Chiang's anthropomorphic fiction has a basis in ethological observation. Chiang has noted that he researched the story by reading American psychologist Irene M. Pepperberg's 2008 animal memoir *Alex & Me*.[37] Pepperberg's book would have appealed to Chiang as a source for 'The Great Silence' not just because she wrote it in the immediate wake of the death of her beloved African Grey parrot Alex in 2007, but also because she originally conceived the name Alex as an acronym for Avian Language Experiment (before revising it to Avian Learning Experiment).[38]

At one point in its dramatic monologue, Chiang's parrot-narrator refers to Pepperberg's research into parrot communication:

> There was an African gray parrot named Alex. He was famous for his cognitive abilities. Famous among humans, that is.
>
> A human researcher named Irene Pepperberg spent thirty years studying Alex. She found that not only did Alex know the words for shapes and colors, he actually understood the concepts of shape and color.
>
> Many scientists were sceptical that a bird could grasp abstract concepts. Humans like to think that they're unique. But eventually Pepperberg convinced them that Alex wasn't just repeating words, that he understood what he was saying.
>
> Out of all my cousins, Alex was the one who came closest to being taken seriously as a communication partner by humans. (232)

Here, Chiang cleaves closely to Pepperberg's presentation of the cognitive capacity of parrots in *Alex & Me*. As Pepperberg writes there:

> Scientifically speaking, the single greatest lesson Alex taught me, taught all of us, is that animal minds are a great deal more like human minds than the vast majority of behavioral scientists believed. . . . A vast world of animal cognition exists out there, not just in African Grey parrots but in other creatures, too. It is a world largely untapped by science. Clearly, animals know more than we think, and think a great deal more than we know. . . . [Alex] taught us that our vanity had blinded us to the true nature of minds, animal and human; that so much more is to be learned about animal minds than received doctrine allowed.[39]

Chiang follows Pepperberg in attributing our ignorance about the nature of other animal minds to our unfounded belief in human exceptionality.

Chiang uses the literary form of the fable in 'The Great Silence' to imagine both the intelligence and the sociality of non-human animals. His choice of speaking creature is essential to his story's meaning. As Despret explains:

'parrots have a pragmatic rather than a referential conception of language. They cannot speak if they don't feel they are speaking to someone'.[40] What makes Chiang's choice of a parrot for narrator so apt is the fact that his fable concerns the very problem of humans refusing to communicate with intelligent non-human earthlings in favour of searching outer space for signs of extraterrestrial intelligence. Chiang's parrot-narrator begins the story by noting the irony of humans using giant radio telescopes like the one at the Arecibo Observatory in Puerto Rico to detect extraterrestrial life, when they are surrounded by intelligent non-human life:

> The humans use Arecibo to look for extraterrestrial intelligence. Their desire to make a connection is so strong that they've created an ear capable of hearing across the universe.
>
> But I and my fellow parrots are right here. Why aren't they interested in listening to our voices?
>
> We're a nonhuman species capable of communicating with them. Aren't we exactly what humans are looking for? (231)

'The Great Silence' generates a sense of pathos by playing its animal narrator's pragmatic conception of language off against humans' more referential conception of language. While it presents parrots as pragmatic communicators who seek immediate, intimate interlocutors, it presents humans as idealistic stargazers who dream of one day encountering intelligent aliens from outer space (preferably like the peaceful heptapods in 'Story of Your Life' rather than the belligerent Martians in *The War of the Worlds*).

Chiang thus frames the problem of the relation between human and non-human animals as a problem of scale. While non-human animals operate on the smaller scale of the earth, humans operate on the larger scale of the universe. The moral of this Anthropocene fable is that the scientific act of humans scaling up their imagination, in this case by directing the Arecibo telescope towards the great silence of the universe in the hope of discovering extraterrestrial intelligence, has the detrimental effect of exacerbating species extinction here on Earth. Sherryl Vint puts it well in her review of Chiang's *Exhalation*: '"The Great Silence" . . . is written in the voice of a parrot and asks us to contemplate whether interspecies forgiveness is possible in this era of anthropogenic extinction.'[41]

According to Heise: 'One way in which science fiction rethinks and relativizes human exceptionality is through the confrontation with aliens, species with whom humans have not coevolved. Such "species fictions", as we might call them, plunge their readers head-on into questions of multispecies assemblies and multispecies justice.'[42] While 'Story of Your Life' conforms to this narrative pattern in science fiction, 'The Great Silence' diverges from it. 'The Great Silence' 'rethinks and relativizes human exceptionality' through the confrontation with a near-extinct species of bird with which humans have co-evolved. The story invokes aliens, but only to compare their fates to the fates of non-human animals on Earth. As the parrot-narrator tells us:

> The Fermi Paradox is sometimes known as the Great Silence. The universe ought to be a cacophony of voices, but instead it is disconcertingly quiet.
>
> Some humans theorize that intelligent species go extinct before they can expand into outer space. If they're correct, then the hush of the night is the silence of the graveyard.
>
> Hundreds of years ago, my kind was so plentiful that the Rio Abajo Forest resounded with our voices. Now we're almost gone. Soon this rain forest may be as silent as the rest of the universe. (232)

Notice how the narrator shifts our focus in this passage from the larger scale of the universe (the predominant venue of the human imagination) to the smaller scale of the Rio Abajo Forest (the predominant venue of the parrot imagination). Scaling down our imagination of the human is one of its chief rhetorical strategies in the story. By redirecting the human gaze and ear away from the stars and the possibility of communication with distant aliens and towards the earth and the possibility of communication with neighbouring non-humans, Chiang's parrot-narrator tries to force its human audience to take responsibility for damaging the planet that it shares with so many other species of animal.

'The Great Silence' resembles Franz Kafka's 1917 short story 'A Report to an Academy' in the sense that it is a dramatic monologue delivered by an animal narrator who has been harmed by human activity. Kafka's animal narrator Red Peter tells the members of the academy of how a hunting expedition from the Hagenbeck company in Hamburg shot and captured him one day while he was coming to drink with his troop of apes at a watering hole in the Gold Coast – in what he calls 'a criminal assault'.[43] Chiang's narrator and its fellow parrots find themselves the victims of anthropogenic environmental damage. The greatest silence in both these modern fables is the silence of their human audiences. Each story intensifies the sense of separation between human and non-human animals by foreclosing the possibility of dialogue. Each at times makes its animal protagonist seem more human than humans. Like Kafka's ape-narrator, Chiang's parrot-narrator tries to usurp the realm of emotion from humans in order to shame humans into acknowledging its intelligence and existentially precarious situation. We can see this strategy at play when it narrates the sudden death of its cousin, the African Grey parrot Alex (on 7 September 2007, at the age of thirty-one):

> Alex died suddenly, when he was still relatively young. The evening before he died, Alex said to Pepperberg, 'You be good. I love you.'
>
> If humans are looking for a connection with a nonhuman intelligence, what more can they ask for than that? (232)

For rhetorical reasons, Chiang's narrator here downplays the properly dialogical nature of Pepperberg's final exchange with Alex on 6 September 2007. As Pepperberg recounts in *Alex & Me*, when she put him back in his cage that evening, Alex said to her: "'You be good. I love you.' She replied, "I love you, too." He then asked her, as he usually did when they parted, "You'll be in tomorrow?" She replied, "Yes, I'll be in tomorrow."[44]

For Chiang, Pepperberg's open, empathetic and dialogical engagement with the non-human animal remains the exception rather than the rule. In his fable, he thus emphasizes the indifference of the majority of humans to the plight of non-human animals in the time of anthropogenic extinction. He shows emotional communication originating from the parrot but receiving no reply from the human (just as the message broadcast by humans from the Arecibo Observatory in 1974 has yet to receive a reply from intelligent non-humans in outer space). By excluding humans from the realm of interpersonal communication in this way, Chiang critiques the human tendency to privilege the larger over the smaller scale. As we saw earlier, Chakrabarty and Clark call for us to scale up our imagination of ourselves to take account of the Anthropocene. For Chiang's parrot, by contrast, the act of humans scaling up their imagination of themselves by developing technology such as the Arecibo Observatory is precisely what has rendered them indifferent to the fate of other species of animal on Earth in the first place. The solution to the problems of interspecies communication and anthropogenic extinction, as far as our animal narrator is concerned, is for humans to scale down their imagination of themselves so that they might recognize once more their kinship with other non-human earthlings.

The form of the fable perfectly suits Chiang's task of showing how human scientific hubris is imperilling other species of animal on Earth for fables undercut human idealism by privileging physical over intellectual reality and the body over the mind. In 'The Great Silence', the narrator's last effort to draw humans closer to parrots is to appeal to the two species' shared sense of embodiment:

> It's no coincidence that 'aspiration' means both hope and the act of breathing.
> When we speak, we use the breath in our lungs to give our thoughts physical form. The sounds we make are simultaneously our intentions and our life force.
> I speak, therefore I am. Vocal learners, like parrots and humans, are perhaps the only ones who fully comprehend the truth of this. (234)

'As its Latin name indicates', Jacques Derrida writes, 'a fable is always and before all else speech – *for, fari*, is to speak, to say, to celebrate, to sing, to predict, and *fabula* is first of all something said, a familiar piece of speech, a conversation.'[45] Fables are performative speech acts that assert the primacy of the oral. The wolf speaks to the lamb in Aesop's well-known fable 'The Wolf and the Lamb', but only in order to eat it.[46] Little Red Riding Hood says to the wolf who has eaten and impersonated her grandmother, 'Grandma, you have such big teeth!' before he replies, 'That's to eat you up.'[47] Chiang's fable asserts the primacy of the oral much more gently than this, by shifting our focus from conversational speech to something more physically primal than speech: sound. In an astonishing sequence of animistic thoughts, our parrot-narrator locates the source of life and spirituality in the act of syllabic vocalization. 'There's a pleasure that comes with shaping sounds with your mouth', it says. 'It's so primal and visceral that, throughout their history, humans have considered the activity a pathway to the divine. . . . Only a species of vocal learners would ascribe such importance to sound in their mythologies. We parrots can appreciate that' (234).

Once again, we see how the parrot seeks to understand the larger scale of the universe in terms of the smaller scale of body. From its point of view, the single mouth shaping sound forms an image of the creative force in the universe:

> According to Hindu mythology, the universe was created with a sound: 'om'. It's a syllable that contains within it everything that ever was and everything that will be.
> When the Arecibo telescope is pointed at the space between stars, it hears a faint hum.
> Astronomers call that the cosmic microwave background. It's the residual radiation of the Big Bang, the explosion that created the universe fourteen billion years ago.

> But you can also think of it as a barely audible reverberation of that original 'om.' That syllable was so resonant that the night sky will keep vibrating for as long as the universe exists.
> When Arecibo is not listening to anything else, it hears the voice of creation. (235)

Chiang's central protagonists tend to remain hopeful even in the face of the direst predicament. In 'The Great Silence', the parrot-narrator never stops hoping that humans will hear and respond to its plea for them to recognize the extent of non-human intelligence on Earth. It also refuses to blame humans for bringing its species to the edge of extinction. 'They didn't do it maliciously', it says. 'They just weren't paying attention' (235). Despite the impending death of its kind, the narrator draws consolation from the fact that the act of embodied vocalization connects it to the very source of life and meaning in the universe – 'the voice of creation'.

Chiang's parrot-narrator ends its Anthropocene fable by linking the large scale of species extinction to the small scale of individual animal vocalization:

> My species probably won't be here for much longer; it's likely that we'll die before our time and join the Great Silence. But before we go, we are sending a message to humanity. We just hope the telescope at Arecibo will enable them to hear it.
> The message is this:
> You be good. I love you. (236)

Here, the narrator re-vocalizes Alex the African Grey parrot's final words to human scientist Irene Pepperberg – and so links Alex's premature death to the premature extinction of its species. Once more, we see the parrot's rhetorical strategy of responding to human indifference by scaling down from the level of the species to the level of the individual and the interpersonal. Its final act of vocalization has two effects, one negative and the other positive. First, it reinforces the parrot rather than the human as the primary source of emotion in the story. Fables such as 'The Great Silence' and 'A Report to an Academy' convey the tragic message that, in modern times, it is left up to the animal to remind humans of how to feel for another creature. Second, and more positively, the parrot's repetition of Alex's final words to Pepperberg asserts that the small scale on which the speaker of the fable operates – that of interpersonal, embodied vocalization – is nonetheless adequate to account for the mystery of the world. Here is where Chiang's story comes to express a paradoxical sense of hope. Even in times of anthropogenic extinction, species redemption might still be sought and found in the smallest acts of interspecies kindness and communication.

Notes

1. Paul J. Crutzen and Eugene F. Stoermer, 'The "Anthropocene"', *Global Change Newsletter* 41 (2000): 17–18.
2. Paul J. Crutzen, 'Geology of Mankind', *Nature* 415, no. 23 (2002): 23.
3. Dipesh Chakrabarty, 'The Climate of History: Four Theses', *Critical Inquiry* 35, no. 2 (2009): 205–6.
4. In 2019, two literary journals have dedicated special issues to the topic of scale. See 'Essays from The English Institute 2017: Scale', *ELH* 86, no. 2 (2019) and 'What Is the Scale of the Literary Object?', *Modernism/Modernity Print Plus* 3, Cycle 4 (1 February 2019).
5. Dipesh Chakrabarty, 'Postcolonial Studies and the Challenge of Climate Change', *New Literary History* 43, no. 1 (2012): 1, 14.
6. Amitav Ghosh, *The Great Derangement: Climate Change and the Unthinkable* (Chicago: University of Chicago Press, 2016), 135.
7. Timothy Clark, *Ecocriticism on the Edge: The Anthropocene as a Threshold Concept* (London: Bloomsbury, 2015), 30.
8. 'Scale, n.3'. *OED Online*, June 2019. Oxford University Press, https://www.oed.com/view/Entry/171737?rskey=4qAHU4&result=3&isAdvanced=false (accessed 13 December 2019).
9. Clark, *Ecocriticism on the Edge*, 72.
10. Chakrabarty, 'The Climate of History', 199, 212.
11. Bruno Latour, 'Agency at the Time of the Anthropocene', *New Literary History* 45, no. 1 (2014): 3.
12. Mark McGurl, 'The New Cultural Geology', *Twentieth-Century Literature* 57, nos. 3–4 (2011): 388.
13. Chakrabarty, 'The Climate of History', 220.
14. Chakrabarty, 'Postcolonial Studies and the Challenge of Climate Change', 13.
15. Ursula K. Heise, *Imagining Extinction: The Cultural Meanings of Endangered Species* (Chicago: University of Chicago Press, 2016), 224–5.
16. Deborah Bird Rose, Thom van Dooren and Matthew Chrulew, 'Telling Extinction Stories', in *Extinction Studies: Stories of Time, Death, and Generations*, ed. Rose, van Dooren and Chrulew (New York: Columbia University Press, 2017), 6–9; emphasis in original.
17. Robert M. Webster and Bruce Erickson, 'The Last Word', *Nature* 380 (1996): 386.
18. Vinciane Despret, 'It Is an Entire World That Has Disappeared', trans. Matthew Chrulew, in *Extinction Studies*, ed. Rose, van Dooren and Chrulew, 220–1.
19. Charles Darwin, *On the Origin of Species by Means of Natural Selection, or the Preservation of Favoured Races in the Struggle for Life* (London: John Murray, 1859), 208.

20 Dipesh Chakrabarty, 'The Future of the Human Sciences in the Age of Humans', *European Journal of Social Theory* 20, no. 1 (2017): 42.
21 John Durham Peters, '3³ + 1 Vignettes on the History of Scalar Inversion', *ELH* 86, no. 2 (2019): 320.
22 Bruno Latour, *Facing Gaia: Eight Lectures on the New Climatic Regime*, trans. Catherine Porter (Cambridge: Polity, 2017), 39.
23 Rose, van Dooren and Chrulew, 'Telling Extinction Stories', 8.
24 Edward O. Wilson, *Half-Earth: Our Planet's Fight for Life* (New York: Liveright, 2016), 20.
25 Latour, 'Agency at the Time of the Anthropocene', 3.
26 Chakrabarty, 'The Climate of History', 221.
27 Jeremy Davies, *The Birth of the Anthropocene* (Oakland: University of California Press, 2016), 62; emphasis in original.
28 Ursula K. Heise, 'Science Fiction and the Time Scales of the Anthropocene', *ELH* 86, no. 2 (2019): 279. See, for example, Mark McGurl, 'The Posthuman Comedy', *Critical Inquiry* 38, no. 3 (2012): 533–53, Adam Trexler, *Anthropocene Fictions: The Novel in a Time of Climate Change* (Charlottesville: University of Virginia Press, 2015) and the essays in Tobias Menely and Jesse Oak Taylor, eds., *Anthropocene Reading: Literary History in Geologic Times* (University Park: Pennsylvania State University Press, 2017).
29 Ghosh, *The Great Derangement*, 63–6.
30 Heise, 'Science Fiction and the Time Scales of the Anthropocene', 281.
31 John Hartigan Jr., *Aesop's Anthropology: A Multispecies Approach* (Minneapolis: University of Minnesota Press, 2014), 53.
32 H. G. Wells, *The War of the Worlds*, ed. Martin A. Danahay (Peterborough: Broadview, 2003), 160. For more on how fables critique human species pride, see Chris Danta, *Animal Fables after Darwin: Literature, Speciesism, and Metaphor* (Cambridge: Cambridge University Press, 2018).
33 McGurl, 'The Posthuman Comedy', 539.
34 Ted Chiang, *Exhalation* (London: Picador, 2019), 347. Hereafter cited in the text. A single-screen version of Chiang's collaboration with Allora and Calzadilla can be viewed at https://vimeo.com/195588827.
35 Joshua Rothman, 'Ted Chiang's Soulful Science Fiction', *The New Yorker*, 5 January 2012, https://www.newyorker.com/culture/persons-of-interest/ted-chiangs-soulful-science-fiction (accessed 13 December 2019).
36 Ted Chiang, 'Story of Your Life', in *Arrival* (London: Picador, 2016), 111–72.
37 See Karen Burnham and Karen Lord, 'Episode 23: In Conversation with Ted Chiang: "The Great Silence"', *SF Crossing the Gulf*, podcast, 11 February 2019, https://locusmag.com/2019/02/sf-crossing-the-gulf-in-conversation-with-ted-chiang/ (accessed 13 December 2019).

38 Irene M. Pepperberg, *Alex & Me: How a Scientist and a Parrot Discovered a Hidden World of Animal Intelligence – and Formed a Deep Bond in the Process* (New York: Collins, 2008), 83–4. Pepperberg explains in *Alex & Me* that she changed what the acronym Alex stood for because she felt Avian Learning Experiment was 'less provocative' than Avian Language Experiment. 'In scholarly settings', she writes, 'I was ever more careful to describe Alex's vocal productions as "labels", not "words"' (84–5). Christopher Peterson discusses Pepperberg's hesitations about ascribing language to non-human animals in *Monkey Trouble: The Scandal of Posthumanism* (New York: Fordham University Press, 2018), 35–40.
39 Pepperberg, *Alex & Me*, 214–19.
40 Vinciane Despret, 'The Becomings of Subjectivity in Animal Worlds', *Subjectivity* 23 (2008): 125.
41 Sherryl Vint, 'The Technologies that Remake Us: On Ted Chiang's "Exhalation: Stories"', *The Los Angeles Review of Books*, 25 May 2019, https://lareviewofbooks.org/article/the-technologies-that-remake-us-on-ted-chiangs-exhalation-stories/ (accessed 13 December 2019).
42 Heise, *Imagining Extinction*, 227.
43 Franz Kafka, 'A Report to an Academy', in *Metamorphosis and Other Stories*, trans. Michael Hofmann (London: Penguin, 2008), 227.
44 Pepperberg, *Alex & Me*, 207.
45 Jacques Derrida, *The Beast & the Sovereign*, vol. 1, trans. Geoffrey Bennington (Chicago: University of Chicago Press, 2009), 34.
46 Aesop, 'The Wolf and the Lamb', in *Aesop's Fables*, trans. Laura Gibbs (Oxford: Oxford University Press, 2002), 130.
47 Charles Perrault, 'Little Red Riding Hood', trans. Christine A. Jones, in *Marvelous Transformations: An Anthology of Fairy Tales and Contemporary Critical Perspectives*, ed. Christine A. Jones and Jennifer Schacker (Peterborough: Broadview, 2013), 176.

Bibliography

Aesop. *Aesop's Fables*. Translated by Laura Gibbs. Oxford: Oxford University Press, 2002.

Burnham, Karen and Karen Lord. 'Episode 23: In Conversation with Ted Chiang: "The Great Silence"'. *SF Crossing the Gulf*. Podcast. 11 February 2019. https://locusmag.com/2019/02/sf-crossing-the-gulf-in-conversation-with-ted-chiang/

Chakrabarty, Dipesh. 'The Climate of History: Four Theses'. *Critical Inquiry* 35, no. 2 (2009): 197–222.

Chakrabarty, Dipesh. 'The Future of the Human Sciences in the Age of Humans'. *European Journal of Social Theory* 20, no. 1 (2017): 39–43.

Chakrabarty, Dipesh. 'Postcolonial Studies and the Challenge of Climate Change'. *New Literary History* 43, no. 1 (2012): 1–18.

Chiang, Ted. *Arrival*. London: Picador, 2016.

Chiang, Ted. *Exhalation*. London: Picador, 2019.

Clark, Timothy. *Ecocriticism on the Edge: The Anthropocene as a Threshold Concept*. London: Bloomsbury, 2015.

Crutzen, Paul J. 'Geology of Mankind'. *Nature* 415, no. 23 (2002): 23.

Crutzen Paul J. and Eugene F. Stoermer. 'The "Anthropocene"'. *Global Change Newsletter* 41 (2000): 17–18.

Danta, Chris. *Animal Fables after Darwin: Literature, Speciesism, and Metaphor*. Cambridge: Cambridge University Press, 2018.

Darwin, Charles. *On the Origin of Species by Means of Natural Selection, or the Preservation of Favoured Races in the Struggle for Life*. London: John Murray, 1859.

Davies, Jeremy. *The Birth of the Anthropocene*. Oakland: University of California Press, 2016.

Derrida, Jacques. *The Beast & the Sovereign*. Translated by Geoffrey Bennington. 2 vols. Chicago: University of Chicago Press, 2009.

Despret, Vinciane. 'The Becomings of Subjectivity in Animal Worlds'. *Subjectivity* 23 (2008): 123–39.

Despret, Vinciane. 'It Is an Entire World That Has Disappeared'. Translated by Matthew Chrulew. *Extinction Studies: Stories of Time, Death, and Generations*. Edited by Deborah Bird Rose, Thom van Dooren and Matthew Chrulew, 217–22. New York: Columbia University Press, 2017.

Ghosh, Amitav. *The Great Derangement: Climate Change and the Unthinkable*. Chicago: University of Chicago Press, 2016.

Hartigan, John Jr. *Aesop's Anthropology: A Multispecies Approach*. Minneapolis: University of Minnesota Press, 2014.

Heise, Ursula K. *Imagining Extinction: The Cultural Meanings of Endangered Species*. Chicago: University of Chicago Press, 2016.

Heise, Ursula K. 'Science Fiction and the Time Scales of the Anthropocene'. *ELH* 86, no. 2 (2019): 275–304.

Jones, Christine A. and Jennifer Schacker, eds. *Marvelous Transformations: An Anthology of Fairy Tales and Contemporary Critical Perspectives*. Peterborough: Broadview, 2013.

Kafka, Franz. *Metamorphosis and Other Stories*. Translated by Michael Hofmann. London: Penguin, 2008.

Latour, Bruno. 'Agency at the Time of the Anthropocene'. *New Literary History* 45, no. 1 (2014): 1–18.

Latour, Bruno. *Facing Gaia: Eight Lectures on the New Climatic Regime*. Translated by Catherine Porter. Cambridge: Polity, 2017.

McGurl, Mark. 'The New Cultural Geology'. *Twentieth-Century Literature* 57, nos. 3–4 (2011): 380–90.

McGurl, Mark. 'The Posthuman Comedy'. *Critical Inquiry* 38, no. 3 (2012): 533–53.
Menely, Tobias and Jesse Oak Taylor, eds. *Anthropocene Reading: Literary History in Geologic Times*. University Park: Pennsylvania State University Press, 2017.
Pepperberg, Irene M. *Alex & Me: How a Scientist and a Parrot Discovered a Hidden World of Animal Intelligence – and Formed a Deep Bond in the Process*. New York: Collins, 2008.
Peters, John Durham. '3^3 + 1 Vignettes on the History of Scalar Inversion'. *ELH* 86, no. 2 (2019): 305–31.
Peterson, Christopher. *Monkey Trouble: The Scandal of Posthumanism*. New York: Fordham University Press, 2018.
Rose, Deborah Bird, Thom van Dooren and Matthew Chrulew, eds. *Extinction Studies: Stories of Time, Death, and Generations*. New York: Columbia University Press, 2017.
Rothman, Joshua. 'Ted Chiang's Soulful Science Fiction'. *The New Yorker*, 5 January 2012. https://www.newyorker.com/culture/persons-of-interest/ted-chiangs-soulful-science-fiction
Trexler, Adam. *Anthropocene Fictions: The Novel in a Time of Climate Change*. Charlottesville: University of Virginia Press, 2015.
Vint, Sherryl. 'The Technologies that Remake Us: On Ted Chiang's "Exhalation: Stories"'. *The Los Angeles Review of Books*, 25 May 2019. https://lareviewofbooks.org/article/the-technologies-that-remake-us-on-ted-chiangs-exhalation-stories/
Webster, Robert M. and Bruce Erickson. 'The Last Word'. *Nature* 380 (1996): 386.
Wells, H. G. *The War of the Worlds*. Edited by Martin A. Danahay. Peterborough: Broadview, 2003.
Wilson, Edward O. *Half-Earth: Our Planet's Fight for Life*. New York: Liveright, 2016.

4

'Re-enchanting the world' from Mozambique

The African Anthropocene and Mia Couto's poetics of the planet

Meg Samuelson[1]

Cyclone Idai tore through southeastern Africa in March 2019, temporarily transforming central Mozambique into an inland sea and leaving a long wake of destruction in one of the more precarious regions of the planet. It was to date the most catastrophic weather event to hit the coast of Africa and among the more extreme to register in the southern hemisphere. While erasing villages and farms deep into the interior, the storm surge destroyed or damaged an initially estimated 90 per cent of the port city of Beira.[2] The fate suffered by Mozambique's second largest city bears out Amitav Ghosh's observation that the 'Anthropocene has reversed the temporal order of modernity: those at the margins are now the first to experience the future that awaits all of us'.[3] Concurrently, this immiserated and submerged African shore throws into relief the critical question of who constitutes the 'we' of the Anthropocene. Mia Couto, a Beira-born writer and ecologist,[4] takes up and redirects such questions in a oeuvre that – though not isolating or even foregrounding environmental catastrophe – offers compelling if confounding meditations on the planetary condition as it takes shape in the global margins and which responds to it by 're-enchanting the world'.[5]

In a resonant proposal, Morris Berman presents 're-enchantment' as 'the only hope' for a world in which the 'disenchantment' forecast by Max Weber has 'very nearly wrecked the planet'.[6] Couto adds to this diagnosis a more located sense of ruination as well as of the possibilities for regeneration. In the midst of the deluge, he issued 'A Call for Solidarity with Mozambique' and followed it with an essay on 'life after a cyclone in Mozambique'.[7] The latter observes that Beira 'has always been prone to such calamities'. In an earlier reflection on the city, which he describes lyrically and yet tragically as the 'Waters of My Beginning', he notes how its origins as a colonial port imposed the structural vulnerability that Idai has now exposed: its precarity is a legacy of its construction as a vessel of imperial extraction.[8] His address to the world registers its implication in the disaster – as much as its magnitude – when it locates it as a 'calamity on a global scale'. In turn, he appeals to the 'solidarity of all', evoking not the 'we' of an assumed sameness but rather commonality-in-relation. The terms of this appeal from the frontline of an 'African Anthropocene' inform both his literary and ecological practice, which derive a poetics of the planet from the particularities of place.[9]

Mozambique is among the poorest and most-aid-dependent countries in the world today.[10] Before its battering by Cyclone Idai – and Cyclone Kenneth, which followed almost immediately – the country's natural resources – including human labour – had been plundered over centuries by chartered companies and colonial powers. It has suffered also from post-independence experiments in scientific socialism and subsequent neoliberal economic policies imposed by the IMF and other donors, as well as from venal administrators.[11] Finally, it was devastated by a prolonged civil war that broke out soon after independence and which consumed the country for more than a decade. As noted in a report that Couto co-compiled in his capacity as environmental consultant, the war displaced an estimated 50 per cent of the peasantry, who comprised over 75 per cent of the national population.[12] This massive social upheaval was in large part driven by the extensive planting of landmines across the countryside and resulted also in significant biodiversity loss in the regions into which refugees fled as well as those to which they later returned. Deforestation and the 'decimation' of wildlife populations are identified by Couto and his co-authors as ranking among the enduring legacies of the war.[13]

With nearly half of its human population displaced from lands that had been rendered uninhabitable, and non-human populations collapsing due to over-exploitation, Mozambique might be seen to emerge from the war as an anticipatory figure of the climate crisis. Yet, while allegorizing this planetary condition, it also brings into focus the uneven distribution of vulnerability within it. It thus underlines what Rob Nixon identifies as the imperative 'to approach the question of vulnerability from the perspective of two of the greatest crises of our time: the environmental crisis and the inequality crisis' in order to find ways of narrating 'the age of the human' at a time in which 'the idea of the human is breaking apart'.[14]

Grounded in Mozambique's geohistory and what his essays present as its rural 'cosmovisions' (or world views),[15] along with his own training as a biologist,

Couto's practice of writing as 're-enchantment' presents modes of narration capable of drawing together questions of ecology and economic inequality, the geological and the geopolitical and literature and science. Through biology, he searches for 'a familiarity with other living creatures that have a different logic and language from ours'; on the other hand, the poetry with which he infuses his narratives denies the 'arrogance of understanding'.[16] While refusing this anthropocentric assumption, he registers also the imperial pretensions of rationality, identifying as a 'last bastion of racism [...] the arrogance of assuming that there is only one system of knowledge, and of being unable to accept philosophies that originate in impoverished nations'.[17] The local philosophies on which he draws anticipate and advance recent calls to 're-enchant the world' in the face of planetary devastation.[18]

In contrast to conceptions of 'the environment' as externality, the cosmovisions that Couto encounters in rural Mozambique recognize that 'things don't revolve around us, but we, along with them, form one world; people and things dwell within one indivisible body'.[19] 'Mozambicans', he elaborates, 'have a different notion of the borders between what is human and not human – what is alive and not alive' – and deny the 'frontier dividing that which is "cultural" from that which is "natural"' in favour of recognizing the 'interconnected world'.[20] Translating these insights into fiction, Couto composes narratives that are invariably situated on the tremulous and permeable border between human and non-human, or the living and the dead, and which traverse the 'visible and invisible worlds' that comprise African realities.[21] He emphasizes, however, that the 'magic' infusing his fiction is not drawn from an essentialist 'tradition' and nor does it function as 'folkloric exoticism'; instead, it 'originates in our ability to exchange culture [... and] our capacity to be ourselves while being others'.[22]

As a medium through which to 're-enchant the world', literature can enable this ability, says Couto, in that it offers 'a chance to migrate from ourselves, a chance to become others inside ourselves'.[23] He ascribes this capacity also to Mozambique's geohistory: referencing the extent of its coastline, which comprises a third of the continent's eastern seaboard, he presents the country as 'a balcony over the ocean' and celebrates its long history of 'commerce with the universe'.[24] Much of Mozambique falls within the monsoon belt – the weather system that connected the Indian Ocean region for over a millennium and which brought Arab, Indian, Chinese and, ultimately, European traders to its shores. Couto claims that the 'dense web of exchanges' that was spun on the loom of this ocean has produced 'a capacity for cultural hybridity' that is the wellspring of the marvellous realities conveyed in his fiction.[25] Far from evoking a discrete and exceptional African ontology, or affirming difference, enchantment is thus presented as the modality of a transcultural poetic that is planetary in reach and implication while recomposing a world rent and depleted by war and extraction.[26]

Recomposing 'the sacred web' amid a 'harvest of death'

Mozambique has been 'contaminated' by war in various guises.[27] These include most prominently the post-independence conflict that delivered a 'harvest of death',[28] along with imperial offensives and the anti-colonial struggle, as well as the assault on the earth and on creaturely life by extractive economies such as mining and trophy hunting, and the earlier trade in ivory, slaves and contract labour. War has also spilled across the 1992 Peace Accord in the form of the arms trade and sporadic landmine explosions that continue to afflict Mozambique, as well as in the persistent predations and deprivations suffered by women, the poor and other creaturely life,[29] and in what one of Couto's characters identifies as a 'coup against the past', which denies the land 'that weave of interdependent existences we call tenderness' and authorizes its 'pillaging'.[30] Taking as its task the work of recomposing the 'sacred web' that has unravelled through Mozambique's cataclysmic history,[31] Couto's writing exemplifies the insight presented as aphorism in *Woman of the Ashes*: 'Life is made like string. We need to braid it until we can no longer distinguish its thread from our fingers.'[32] He crafts narrative modes akin to those that Donna Haraway gathers under the rubric 'SF'; encompassing string figures, science fact, speculative fabulation and speculative feminisms, these are practices of 'response-ability' that dissolve distinctions between the thread of life and the braiding finger, and which thus realize enchantment's etymological implication of being *in* the song.[33]

Couto's first two books of fiction – the collection of stories *Voices Made Night* and the novel *Sleepwalking Land* – were written during the civil war and while he was training as an ecologist. Imprinted with pervasive desperation, delusion and death, they are at the same time enlivened by the desire 'to enter into kinship with the world' and 'to gain the companionship of the living and non-living creatures' with which we share it.[34] For Couto, this means reactivating dreaming in a population inured to the deadening conditions of poverty and war; in short, it depends on 're-enchanting the world'.[35]

After presenting a nightmarish landscape strewn with charred corpses and in which all living creatures have entered the 'resigned apprenticeship of death',[36]

Sleepwalking Land introduces the first of a series of interleaved notebooks that ultimately dissolve into the frame narrative and which import wonder into the desolate opening scene, summoning the moon to bathe it in silver light. It also offers two material figures for thinking through the war. In the first, the sea dries up and palm trees sprout golden gourds when the notebook writer's father dies. The deceased cautions against harvesting these 'sacred fruit', warning that 'the destiny of our world was held together by delicate threads' and that severing them would unleash 'disorder and a whole succession of disasters to ensue'. But the machete-bearing men are unmoved and assault the trees for being 'inhuman'. As forecast, the plain floods, 'swallowing up everything and everyone'.[37] The second figure is similarly revelatory of how the desperation imposed on the people of Mozambique has frayed the 'sacred web':

> The whale was expiring, exhausted in its death throes. The people rushed over to cut bits of its flesh, strip after strip weighing kilos. It hasn't yet died and its bones were already gleaming in the sunlight. Now, I saw my country like one of those whales that come to breathe their last on the shore. Death hadn't even occurred and knives were already stealing chunks of it, each one trying to get a bigger piece for himself. As if it were the very last animal, the last chance to gain a share.[38]

While granted substantial narrative presence in its own right, the flensed whale also provides a concrete image with which to apprehend the rapacious assault on the country. At the same time, the whale's magical materiality as the being 'whose sigh causes the ocean to fill and ebb' ensures that the allegory scales up from Mozambique to the planet.[39]

Published on the eve of the Peace Accord, *Sleepwalking Land* concludes with the hopeful dream of a song welling up 'like a memory of before we became people', and which sounds out a 'new beginning'.[40] Instead of entering this anticipated state of enchantment, however, Mozambique embarked on a process of 'disenchantment' through an aggressive modernization programme that condemned so-called traditional practices as 'superstition' or 'backwardness that had to be overcome'.[41] While the 'scientific socialism' initially espoused by the ruling party soon gave way to free market ideologies, the condescension displayed towards the peasantry has remained consistent and Mozambique's recent incorporation into global capitalism has further hastened the 'erasure' of local cultural practices.[42] Couto's subsequent novels, *Under the Frangipani* and *The Last Flight of the Flamingo*, adapt detective genres but conclude with perplexing revelations as they contend with this 'coup against the past' and what he elsewhere describes as the consequent 'erosion' of culture and thus of creativity.[43] The suggestive image of a nation stripped of top soil adds fecund layers of meaning to the verb 'recomposing' that this chapter takes up with a nod to Bruno Latour, who notes that the term 'composition' also carries the 'pungent but ecologically correct smell of "compost"',[44] and Haraway's SF 'Children of Compost', which, though grounded in distinct geohistories and cosmovisions, shares Couto's concern with 'repairing damaged places and making flourishing multispecies futures'.[45] Like a true compositionist and composter, he proceeds through proliferating agencies rather than via 'the revelation of the world of beyond'.[46]

The setting of *Under the Frangipani* is an old colonial fort built to export slaves and ivory, and to defend Portugal's mercantile shipping routes. Having been repurposed as a prison for revolutions during the anti-colonial struggle, it becomes a 'makeshift refuge' for the aged after independence. In the narrative present, it is also being used as an arsenal: unbeknown to his charges, the refuge director is involved in the arms trade. When they discover his deadly horde, the aged residents align with planetary forces to rid the earth of what they recognize to be the 'seeds of another war' and 'the burning coals of a hell which had already burnt everyone's feet'.[47] The director is consequently murdered by his corrupt cohorts when they return to find that the arsenal has vanished: this is the mystery ostensibly unveiled in the chapter titled 'The Revelation'. The novel insists, however, that the 'real crime being committed here is that they are killing the world of the past'.[48] The investigative mode is thus appropriated to recompose the cosmovisions of its 'guardians', which have been ridiculed and proscribed under the diktat of both coloniality and the modern state.[49] At the same time, the narrative does not endorse a character's desire to 'shut off the road to the future';[50] that this desire is seen to reproduce the injurious logic of war becomes evident when it takes the form of replanting landmines around the refuge.

Rejecting the repudiation of old ways without in turn seeking to arrest time, Couto's re-enchanting fiction seeks to convey past potentialities into the present and future, thereby recomposing a regenerative temporality.[51] War is said to have introduced a temporality that is simultaneously circular and linear: establishing an entrapping 'cycle of blood', it has torn through the time of 'seasons' and 'harvests' and drawn a line that divides life into 'before the war, after the war'.[52] The novel's emblematic frangipani tree, in contrast, manifests organic time (that it is a non-Indigenous species introduced from South America into southern Africa by the Portuguese maritime empire is apposite to the transcultural nature of Couto's poetics). During a climatic confrontation in which the aged fend off what the policeman perceives as a helicopter bearing arms traffickers and what they receive as the *wamulambo* or cyclonic storm snake, the tree is burnt in what initially appears to be the relentless reiteration of the temporal rupture effected by war. But in the marvellous conclusion, the deceased narrator – who had journeyed back to the world of the living – restores the tree 'into the fullness of life' and then himself 'enter[s] plant life, preparing for [his] own arborescence'.[53] Closing with the narrator 'losing the language of men to take up the earth's dialect', the story opens to life beyond, rather than simply 'after', war.

Regenerative time is restored in this novel through the mutual re-composition of both the poetic and planet: 'tak[ing] up the earth's dialect', the narrator in turn composts into it the stories we have ostensibly been reading, for he carries with him the notebook in which he had 'record[ed] the words of the elders': 'The little notebook will rot away along with my remains. The creatures of the soil will feed upon these ancient voices.'[54] Decaying into microbic multiplicity while retaining singularity, this is a literature that embraces the 'chance to become others inside ourselves' and which seeks to 'disappear and to allow the presence of those who seem to be absent', to quote from Couto's manifesto for 're-enchanting the world'.[55] Such writing becomes a means of 'transgressing [the] human condition', as suggested in his later novel, *Tuner of Silences*.[56] The mystery driving this plot is 'resolved' when a deceased character is finally understood to be speaking through the writing hand of his living son: 'Your hand, your writing, have given me a voice. You alone composed these manuscripts. I wasn't the only one responsible for dictating them. It was the voice of the earth, the river's turn of phrase.'[57]

The landmines through which Couto figures the iterative rupture imposed by war in *Under the Frangipani* feature also in the denouement of *The Last Flight of the Flamingo* where the deadly circularity of 'the war of business and the business of war' is again in play.[58] The mystery here is that UN Peacekeepers are inexplicably exploding in a Mozambican town, leaving behind just their tell-tale blue helmets and severed penises. The plot behind these 'improbable' events is eventually revealed: 'local leaders' have been replanting explosives in order 'to prolong the mine clearance programme' and thus continue 'siphon[ing]' illicit income off a lucrative stream of international revenue.[59] The informant observes that the occasional mortality conveniently lent credibility to the scheme without inviting unwanted attention ('they were nameless people, in the interior of an African country that could hardly sustain its name in the world').[60] However, '[w]hen foreigners began to get blown up, the scam fell apart.'[61]

Embroidered between the plots of *Under the Frangipani* and *The Last Flight of the Flamingo* is an argument in favour of interdependency. It repudiates the autonomy promised in returning the refuge to the isolation imposed on it by war as well as the penetration of the country by global capitalism and the dependence on foreign aid that has shackled a hard-won independence and corrupted its leadership. At the same time, it registers the uneven distribution of vulnerability and grievability across the globe.[62] The affirmation of interdependency in Couto's oeuvre is moreover simultaneously geopolitical and eco- or biological. He observes that the 'human species [...] is made from mixtures' and has 'been able to survive because of this diversity',[63] and his fiction makes insistent reference to 'mulatto-ness' and multiplicity, such as in the syntactical confusion from which one of his early stories launches:

> I are sad. No, I'm not mistaken. What I'm saying is correct. Or perhaps: we am sad? Because inside me, I'm not alone. I'm many. And they call fight over my one and only life. [...] That's why, when I tell my story, I mix myself up, a mulatto not of races, but of existences.[64]

Bill Ashcroft observes of Couto's fiction that 'the subtext of the vision of multiple worlds is the violence of the drawn-out war in Mozambique, a conflict between very polarized worlds'.[65] The same may be said for the enthralling entanglements spun in and by his fiction in the wake of a destructive history of external predation and internal discord. Revaluing the entwined nature of Mozambican culture, it seeks to return the country to a condition of enlivening exchange while insisting on reciprocal relations and, thus, on mutual responsibilities.

Though it may run the risk of appropriation on an uneven globe, hybridity, as Couto conceives it, is an expression of cultural vitality that recognizes Mozambican agency and Mozambique's contribution to the world, and which refuses Africa's casting as benighted continent: 'if we enter into hybrid relationships', he maintains, 'it means that someone else, on the other side, has received something that was ours'.[66] The implicit distinction between what is received and what is extracted or purloined is critical, so too is the redistribution of agency in Couto's formulation: as Chirevo Kwenda has noted through his 'ecological' proposal to recompose 'civil society' in an environment of patronage, colonial powers – while seeking to grasp the planet – maintained the pretence of *giving without receiving*.[67] Elsewhere, Couto writes of the need to 'create a bridge' between rural Mozambique and the world at large that 'both takes and brings in equal measure' in contrast to 'those bridges built to take everything out without giving anything back'.[68] The context for this last remark is an essay about establishing mutually meaningful ecological discourses with the human inhabitants of an 'underdeveloped' and 'isolated' biodiversity hotspot: 'The inhabitants of Matatuine don't know the word. But they know perfectly well what biodiversity is. It's not a conceptual issue. They live on the back of biodiversity.' Mutual intelligibility initially flounders when advisers from the capital fly in to protect animals that are understood to be threatening villagers' lives and livelihoods, but Couto finds a bridge in the language of the 'sacred', noting how it has successfully regulated fishing in the lagoon. Moreover, while ecological concerns are often cast as a luxury in the deprived communities with which Couto engages as both writer and environmentalist, he implicitly echoes Édouard Glissant's recognition that

> [t]he politics of ecology has implications for populations that are decimated or threatened with disappearance as a people. For, far from consenting to sacred intolerance, it is a driving force for the relational interdependence of all lands, of the whole Earth.[69]

The enchanting nature of the 'sacred web' recomposed in Couto's fiction insists on such planetary 'response-abilities' and summons the 'solidarity of all' in an African Anthropocene determined by extraction and immiseration.

The eviscerated earth and re-animated planet

The poetics of the planet that Couto reactivates in an African Anthropocene is, as Glissant anticipates, as much one of 'disruption and intrusion' as it is one of 'connection.' 'An aesthetics of the earth? In the half-starved dust of Africa? [...] In epidemics, masked forms of exploitation, flies buzz-bombing the skeleton skins of children? [...] In mud huts crowning goldmines?', asks Glissant: 'Yes. But an aesthetics of disruption and intrusion.'[70] In Couto's fiction, the global margins are again shown to be anticipatory of the 'catastrophic times' that Isabelle Stengers has characterized as 'the intrusion of Gaia' – 'this "nature" that has left behind its traditional role and now has the power to question us all' – and which impresses upon 'us' the 'obligation "to dream other dreams"'.[71] Couto's oeuvre responds to this question while informing it with that with which this chapter opened: who constitutes the 'we' of the Anthropocene? In delineating an 'African Anthropocene', Gabrielle Hecht has shown how an unqualified use of the term obscures both African geohistories and their planetary effects. For instance, she notes that '[m]inerals from Africa played a big role in motivating colonialism and powering industrialization.'[72] Their extraction fuelled the Anthropocene.'[72] Those on which she focuses – gold and uranium – are both mined in neighbouring South Africa, where migrant workers from across the region, and particularly from Mozambique, have 'tunneled deeper underground than anywhere else on the planet' under particularly dangerous and exploitative conditions.[73]

The apocalyptic events that comprise the crisis of many of Couto's narratives ultimately disclose an animated planet provoked by extraction and/or the pollution of war – and of which the mining of minerals and the planting of landmines are respectively the most eviscerating and explosive manifestations. In *Under the Frangipani*, the earth voids weapons into an abyss in order to rid the world inhabited by the living and the dead of their contaminating presence; in *The Last Flight of the Flamingo*, the earth's rejoinder to nations that fail to 'love' the land and 'respect' their fellows is to swallow worlds in their entirety – 'people, animals, plants, rivers and mountains'.[74] The obverse occurs in the novel *A River Called Time* when the earth responds to violations of the 'sacred web' by 'refusing to open its belly to human design'.[75] Enabling interscalar thinking, the novel shows local transgressions to have planetary effects: the crisis that Couto embeds on a small riverine island escalates into one that is 'catastrophic and global in proportion' as the ground on 'every continent' grows 'impenetrable', disrupting the infrastructure of development and extraction by halting '[c]onstruction projects, mines, [and the] dredging of ports'.[76]

Opening with an epigraph from the imperial chronicler João de Barros that anticipates 'rivers of gold' flowing out of Africa, Couto's most recent novel to be translated into English, *Woman of the Ashes*, revisits a late nineteenth-century colonial conflict in order to bring mining into sharper focus and connect it to other extractive industries as well as to the arms trade.[77] There is again an 'intrusion of Gaia' when a trader who deals in human and non-human life accepts a commission to run guns for the imperial cause. When one of his exploited porters raises a load of 'ivory and animal pelts', something extraordinary happens:

> along with the bundle, he lifted all the ground around it. As if it were a towel, the surrounding earth was raised, and a cloud of dust hung suspended in the air. All around the porter, a bottomless abyss opened up. With apparent ease, the man hoisted the surrounding terrain above him. Then he deposited the world on his head.[78]

Combined with the novel's attention to the conflagrating conflicts of imperial expansion and labour migration to Mozambique's sub-imperial neighbour, this uncanny occurrence entwines the consumption of the earth and its creatures with the burden borne by those it has impoverished in the concrete figure of the porter 'deposit[ing] the world on his head'. Explicitly relating the extinction of creaturely life to the predation on a people, the narrator of Woman of the Ashes observes that the Portuguese invaders have killed all the elephants in the locality before concluding:

> That's how it will be when you've eviscerated the earth to steal all its minerals. You'll order the blacks to pile themselves up, one on top of another, until they reach the moon. And then Chopi miners will begin to dig for lunar silver.[79]

Drawing human immiseration and environmental degradation into conjunction, the abysses pitting Couto's narrative worlds reference the mines – both extractive and explosive – that are consuming African life and the planet itself. They manifest the unevenness of the globe as well as the coherence of the earth's response.

The coherence of this intrusion is detailed in the choreographed climax of Under the Frangipani when the *halakavuma*, or scaly anteater, 'assemble[s] the forces of this and the other world' to repulse the returning arms traders (the *halakavuma* is identified as one of the last remaining 'messengers' between the living and the dead and is thus a medium of enchantment in a disenchanted world).[80] It is evident also in the disposal of the arsenal. The elders apprehend the risk that the arsenal presents to creaturely life and appreciate that '*[t]he earth isn't the place to bury arms*', but their 'meagre strength' and the fear of detection prevent them from throwing the hoard into the sea.[81] Instead, an old woman who has been vilified as a witch casts a spell that induces the earth to open a 'bottomless hole' and together the aged 'emptied the weapons into the abyss'.[82] Theirs is an enchanted enactment of what Nixon calls 'the environmentalism of the poor'. This seldom-recognized environmentalism is often triggered when 'official landscapes' (such as the arsenal established by an administrator and men 'in uniform' in Couto's narrative) are 'imposed on a vernacular one', 'severing webs of accumulated cultural meaning and treating the landscape as if it were uninhabited by the living, the unborn, and the animate deceased'.[83] To the 'guardians' of the world that coloniality and the postcolonial state alike have sought to disenchant, the land is composed of such a 'sacred web': 'trees and animals, animals and men, men and stone' are understood to be 'all related, created out of the same matter'.[84]

Mozambique's post-independence leadership maintained that peasants were enthralled by 'the false hope that magic equaled power'.[85] The animist understanding of the world that informs the actions of Couto's characters has, however, 'often provided avenues of agency for the dispossessed in colonial and postcolonial Africa', as Harry Garuba notes with reference to examples from Nigeria.[86] The '*continual re-enchantment of the world*' that animism performs thus not only exposes the vitality of the earth but also contends with the manner in which agency is being stripped from marginalized subjects at the very time in which 'the human' is said to be coalescing into a 'geological force'.[87] As Jane Bennett divines from her enquiry into 'vibrant matter':

> the figure of enchantment points in two directions: the first toward the humans who *feel* enchanted and whose agentic capacities may be thereby strengthened, and the second toward the agency of the things that *produce* (helpful, harmful) effects in human and other bodies.[88]

A recent revaluation of enchantment notes that, '[i]n an enchanted world [...] any object [...] can turn out to be a subject. This is the great insight of animism.'[89]

Deriving a poetics of the planet from insights such as these that flourish in the most impoverished part of the world, Couto's oeuvre also redistributes agency among humans, thereby composing an 'all' who might 'dream other dreams' without assuming that 'we' are similarly located in the planetary condition. Maintaining wonder even as it demystifies the local and global machinations driving human immiseration and environmental degradation, Couto draws readers into the 'sacred web' while denying them the 'arrogance' of grasping its meanings. The planetary poetics of re-enchanting the world thus ultimately invoke an enlivening ecocritical method: denying modes of reading-as-extraction and inviting instead reading-as-relation.[90]

Notes

1 This chapter is dedicated to the memory of Harry Garuba (1958–2020).
2 See, inter alia: Abdur Rahman Alfa Shaban, '90% of Mozambican City of Beira Destroyed by Cyclone Idai–Red Cross', *AfricaNews* (18 March 2019).
3 Amitav Ghosh, *The Great Derangement: Climate Change and the Unthinkable* (Chicago: University of Chicago Press, 2016), 62.
4 Having previously abandoned his medical studies to join the national liberation struggle and thereafter working as a journalist, Couto returned to study biology during the civil war and completed his degree between publishing his first two books of fiction; he now runs an environmental consultancy in Maputo and is Mozambique's most prominent writer both locally and abroad. He has received the major accolades of the African and Lusophone literary spheres and was awarded the

2014 Neustadt International Prize for his body of work in English translation (for which he was also shortlisted for the Man Booker International Prize in 2015). This chapter focuses on the substantial portion of his oeuvre that has been translated into English by David Brookshaw; the risks of reading in translation are matched by the rewards of extending the participatory entanglements that this chapter associates with re-enchantment.

5   Mia Couto, 'Re-enchanting the World: The 2014 Neustadt Prize Lecture', trans. Paul Fauvet, *World Literature Today* (January/February 2015).
6   Morris Berman, *The Reenchantment of the World* (Ithaca: Cornell University Press, 1981), n.p.
7   Mia Couto, 'Call for Solidarity from Mozambique: A Message from 2014 Neustadt Prize Laureate Mia Couto', *World Literature Today* (21 March 2019); Couto, 'A Second Soul: Mia Couto on life after a cyclone in Mozambique', trans. Miranda France, *Times Literary Supplement* (10 May 2019).
8   Mia Couto, 'Waters of My Beginning', in *Pensativities: Essays and Provocations*, trans. David Brookshaw (Winsor: Biblioasis, 2015); Ghosh notes that this is a feature of many of the cities that now face the threat of deluge.
9   See Gabrielle Hecht, 'The African Anthropocene', *Aeon* (6 February 2018), on the need to qualify the proposed epoch and disaggregate the 'we' on which its naming depends; and on a resonant call for an 'eco-cosmopolitanism' that mediates between place and planet, see Ursula K. Heise, *Sense of Place and Sense of Planet: The Environmental Imagination of the Global* (Oxford: Oxford University Press, 2008).
10 John Hatton, Mia Couto and Judy Oglethorpe, *Biodiversity and War: A Case Study of Mozambique* (Washington, DC: Biodiversity Support Program, 2001), 14, 22; Marlyn Newitt, *A Short History of Mozambique* (New York: Oxford University Press, 2017).
11 For an excellent analysis of Couto's novels vis-à-vis state policy (although I dispute its titular casting of Couto), see Philip Rothwell, *A Postmodern Nationalist: Truth, Orality, and Gender in the Work of Mia Couto* (Lewisburg: Bucknell University Press).
12 Hatton, Couto and Oglethorpe, *Biodiversity and War*, 11.
13 Hatton, Couto and Oglethorpe, *Biodiversity and War*, 15.
14 Rob Nixon, 'The Great Acceleration and the Great Divergence', *Profession* (2014), n.p.
15 Couto, *Pensativities* ('What Africa does the African Writer Write About?' and 'Languages we Don't Know We Know'), n.p.
16 Couto quoted in Gracie Jin, 'Q&A with Mia Couto, The Writer Who Just Won the "American Nobel Prize"', *Mic* (4 November 2013).
17 Couto, *Pensativities* ('Languages We Don't Know We Know').
18 Berman, *Reenchantment*; see also Patrick Curry, *Enchantment: Wonder in Modern Life* (Floris Books, 2019), and the promotion of 'material ecocriticism' as 'a story-

laden mode of reenchantment' in Jeffrey Jerome Cohen, 'Foreword: Storied Matter', *Material Ecocriticism*, ed. Serenella Iovino and Serpil Oppermann (Bloomington: Indiana University Press, 2014), x.
19 Couto, *Pensativities* ('Languages We Don't Know We Know'), n.p.
20 Couto quoted in Jin, 'Q&A'; Couto, *Pensativities* ('Animal Conservation').
21 Bill Ashcroft, 'The Multiple Worlds of Mia Couto', in *A Companion to Mia Couto*, ed. Grant Hamilton and David Huddart (London: James Currey, 2016), n.p.
22 Couto, *Pensativities* ('The Frontier of Culture').
23 Couto, 'Re-enchanting the World', 50.
24 Mia Couto, *Under the Frangipani*, trans. David Brookshaw (London: Serpent's Tail, 2001; first published in Portuguese in 1996), 44; Gaurav Desai, *Commerce with the Universe: Africa, India, and the Afrasian Imagination* (New York: Columbia University Press, 2013).
25 Couto, 'A Sea of Exchanges, an Ocean of Myths', *Pensativities*.
26 For further discussion of how Couto's narratives are shaped by the littoral circumstances of Mozambique, see Meg Samuelson, 'Coastal Form: Amphibian Positions, Wider Worlds and Planetary Horizons on the African Indian Ocean Littoral', *Comparative Literature* 69, no. 1 (2017): 16–24.
27 Mia Couto, *Sleepwalking Land*, trans. David Brookshaw (London: Serpent's Tail, 2006; first published in Portuguese in 1992), 1.
28 Couto, *Frangipani*, 3.
29 One of his later novels includes the chapter epigraph: 'The difference between war and peace is as follows: in war, the poor are the first to be killed; in peace, the poor are the first to die. For us women, there's another difference too: in war, we get raped by those we do not know' (Mia Couto, *Woman of the Ashes*, trans. David Brookshaw (New York: Farrar, Straus and Giroux, 2018; first published in Portuguese in 2015), 71).
30 Couto, *Frangipani*, 99; Mia Couto, *The Last Flight of the Flamingo*, trans. David Brookshaw (London: Serpent's Tail, 2001; first published in Portuguese in 1996), 87.
31 Couto in Jin, 'Q&A'.
32 Couto, *Woman of the Ashes*, 3.
33 Donna J. Haraway, *Staying with the Trouble: Making Kin in the Chthulucene* (Durham: Duke University Press, 2016), 18.
34 Couto, *Pensativities* ('A Word of Advice and Some Advice without Words').
35 The author's foreword to his first collection claims that '[t]he most harrowing thing about poverty' is that its sufferers 'abstain from dreams, depriving themselves of the desire to be others' (Mia Couto, *Voices Made Night*, trans. David Brookshaw (Portsmouth: Heinemann, 1990; first published in Portuguese in 1986), n.p.).
36 Couto, *Sleepwalking*, 1.
37 Couto, *Sleepwalking*, 13.
38 Couto, *Sleepwalking*, 16.

39 Couto, *Sleepwalking*, 15.
40 Couto, *Sleepwalking*, 211.
41 Newitt, *Short History*; James Ciment, *Angola and Mozambique: Postcolonial Wars in Southern Africa* (New York: Facts on File, 1997).
42 Newitt, *Short History*; Rothwell, *Postmodern Nationalist*, 79.
43 Couto, *Frangipani*, 99; Couto, *Pensativities* ('Seven Dirty Shoes').
44 Bruno Latour, 'An Attempt at a "Compositionist Manifesto"', *New Literary History*, 41 (2010): 474.
45 Haraway, *Staying with the Trouble*.
46 Latour, '"Compositionist Manifesto"', 478.
47 Couto, *Frangipani*, 140.
48 Couto, *Frangipani*, 53.
49 Couto, *Frangipani*, 53.
50 Couto, *Frangipani*, 110.
51 He emphasizes elsewhere that the 'cosmovisions' recomposed in his fiction are by no means 'resistant to time and the dynamics of exchange' (Couto, 'Languages We Don't Know', *Pensativities*).
52 Couto, *Frangipani*, 123.
53 Couto, *Frangipani*, 150, 149.
54 Couto, *Frangipani*, 18. This recurrent motif is inaugurated in the conclusion to *Sleepwalking Land* when the notebooks comprising half the narrative are scattered 'by wind born not from the air but from the ground itself' until 'one by one, the letters turn into grains and sand, and little by little, all my writings are transformed into the pages of the earth' (213).
55 Couto, 'Re-enchanting the World', 50.
56 Mia Couto, *The Tuner of Silences*, trans. David Brookshaw (Biblioasis, 2012; first published in Portuguese in 2009), 228.
57 Couto, *Tuner of Silences*, 212.
58 Couto, *Last Flight*, 154.
59 Couto, *Last Flight*, 154.
60 Couto, *Last Flight*, 154.
61 Couto, *Last Flight*, 155.
62 See Judith Butler, *Precarious Life: The Powers of Mourning and Violence* (London: Verso, 2004).
63 Couto, *Pensativities* ('Citizenship in Search of Its City').
64 Couto, *Voices Made Night*, 41 ('So You Haven't Flown Yet, Carlota Gentina?').
65 Ashcroft, 'Multiple Worlds'.
66 Couto, *Pensativities* ('What Africa Does the African Writer Write About').
67 Chirevo V. Kwenda, 'Beyond Patronage: Giving and Receiving in the Construction of Civil Society', *Journal of Theology for Southern Africa* 101 (1998): 1–10.
68 Couto, *Pensativities* ('The Waters of Biodiversity').

69 Édouard Glissant, *Poetics of Relation*, trans. Betsy Wing (University of Michigan Press, 1997; first published in French in 1990), 146; the poetics of the planet that Couto elaborates from Mozambique's geohistory and its rural cosmovisions is in many respects comparable to the 'poetics of relation' that Glissant elaborates from an archipelagic Antillanité.

70 Glissant, *Poetics*, 151.

71 Isabelle Stengers, *In Catastrophic Times: Resisting the Coming Barbarism*, trans. Andrew Goffey (Open Humanities Press, 2015; first published in French in 2009), 13; Deborah Danowski and Eduardo Vivieros da Castro, *The Ends of the World*, trans. Rodrigo de Castro (Cambridge: Polity, 2017; first published in Portuguese in 2014), n.p.

72 Hecht, 'African Anthropocene'.

73 Hecht, 'African Anthropocene'; on the supply of migrant labour from Mozambique to South Africa's mines, see Newitt, *Short History*.

74 Couto, *Last Flight*, 174–5.

75 Mia Couto, *A River Called Time*, trans. David Brookshaw (London: Serpents Tail, 2008; first published in Portuguese in 2002), 166.

76 Couto, *River Called Time*, 166.

77 Couto, *Woman of the Ashes*; this is the first volume of a projected trilogy titled 'Sands of the Emperor'; the second volume was published in Portuguese in 2016.

78 Couto, *Woman of the Ashes*, 176.

79 Couto, *Woman of the Ashes*, 227–8.

80 Couto, *Frangipani*, 146, 138.

81 Couto, *Frangipani*, 140–1; emphasis in original.

82 Couto, *Frangipani*, 142.

83 Rob Nixon, *Slow Violence and the Environmentalism of the Poor* (Cambridge, MA: Harvard University Press, 2011), 17; Couto, *Frangipani*.

84 Couto, *Frangipani*, 63–4.

85 Ciment, *Angola and Mozambique*, 66.

86 Harry Garuba, 'Explorations in Animist Materialism: Notes on Reading/Writing African Literature, Culture, and Society', *Public Culture* 15, no. 2 (2003): 285. For more detailed analyses of *Under the Frangipani* vis-à-vis Garuba's categories of 'animist materialism' and 'animist realism', see Meg Samuelson, 'Melancholy States, Statist Mourning and the Poetics of Memory in Post-Conflict Fiction from Southern Africa', *Journal of Social Studies* 115 (2007): 45–68, and Hubbert, '"Ask Life": Animism & the Metaphysical Detective', *A Companion to Mia Couto*, ed. Hamilton and Huddart.

87 See Dipesh Chakrabarty, 'The Climate of History: Four Theses', *Critical Inquiry* 35, no. 2 (2009): 197–222.

88 Jane Bennett, *Vibrant Matter: A Political Ecology of Things* (Durham: Duke University Press, 2010), xii.

89 Curry, *Enchantment,* n.p.
90 On reading for enchantment, see Rita Felski, *Uses of Literature* (Malden: Blackwell, 2008).

Bibliography

Ashcroft, Bill. 'The Multiple Worlds of Mia Couto'. In *A Companion to Mia Couto*, edited by Grant Hamilton and David Huddart, n.p. London: James Currey, 2016. Kindle.

Bennett, Jane. *Vibrant Matter: A Political Ecology of Things*. Durham: Duke University Press, 2010.

Berman, Morris. *The Reenchantment of the World*. Ithaca: Cornell University Press, 1981.

Butler, Judith. *Precarious Life: The Powers of Mourning and Violence*. London: Verso, 2004.

Chakrabarty, Dipesh. 'The Climate of History: Four Theses'. *Critical Inquiry* 35, no. 2 (2009): 197–222.

Ciment, James. *Angola and Mozambique: Postcolonial Wars in Southern Africa*. New York: Facts on File, 1997.

Cohen, Jeffrey Jerome. 'Foreword: Storied Matter'. In *Material Ecocriticism*, edited by Serenella Iovino and Serpil Oppermann, ix–xii. Bloomington: Indiana University Press, 2014.

Couto, Mia. 'Call for Solidarity from Mozambique: A Message from 2014 Neustadt Prize Laureate Mia Couto'. *World Literature Today Blog*, 21 March 2019. https://www.worldliteraturetoday.org/blog/news-and/events/call-solidarity-mozambique-message-2014-neustadt-prize-laureate-mia-couto.

Couto, Mia. *The Last Flight of the Flamingo*. Translated by David Brookshaw. London: Serpent's Tail, 2004.

Couto, Mia. *Pensativities: Essays and Provocations*. Translated by David Brookshaw. Winsor: Biblioasis, 2015.

Couto, Mia. 'Re-enchanting the World: The 2014 Neustadt Prize Lecture'. Translated by Paul Fauvet. *World Literature Today* (January/February 2015): 50–3.

Couto, Mia. *A River Called Time*. Translated by David Brookshaw. London: Serpent's Tail, 2008.

Couto, Mia. 'A Second Soul: Mia Couto on Life after a Cyclone in Mozambique'. Translated by Miranda France. *Times Literary Supplement*, 10 May 2019. https://www.the-tls.co.uk/articles/second-soul-mozambique-cyclone/

Couto, Mia. *Sleepwalking Land*. Translated by David Brookshaw. London: Serpent's Tail, 2006.

Couto, Mia. *The Tuner of Silences*. Translated by David Brookshaw. Emeryville: Biblioasis, 2012.

Couto, Mia. *Under the Frangipani*. Translated by David Brookshaw. London: Serpent's Tail, 2001.
Couto, Mia. *Voices Made Night*. Translated by David Brookshaw. Oxford: Heinemann, 1990.
Couto, Mia. *Woman of the Ashes*. Translated by David Brookshaw. New York: Farrar, Straus and Giroux, 2018. Kindle.
Curry, Patrick. *Enchantment: Wonder in Modern Life*. Edinburgh: Floris Books, 2019. Kindle.
Danowski, Deborah and Eduardo Vivieros da Castro. *The Ends of the World*. Translated by Rodrigo de Castro. Cambridge: Polity, 2017. Kindle.
Desai, Gaurav. *Commerce with the Universe: Africa, India, and the Afrasian Imagination*. New York: Columbia University Press, 2013. Kindle.
Felski, Rita. *Uses of Literature*. Malden: Blackwell, 2008. Kindle.
Garuba, Harry. 'Explorations in Animist Materialism: Notes on Reading/Writing African Literature, Culture, and Society'. *Public Culture* 15, no. 2 (2003): 261–85.
Ghosh, Amitav. *The Great Derangement: Climate Change and the Unthinkable*. Chicago: University of Chicago Press, 2016. Kindle.
Glissant, Édouard. *Poetics of Relation*. Translated by Betsy Wing. Ann Arbor: University of Michigan Press, 1997.
Haraway, Donna J. *Staying with the Trouble: Making Kin in the Chthulucene*. Durham: Duke University Press, 2016. Kindle.
Hatton, John, Mia Couto and Judy Oglethorpe. *Biodiversity and War: A Case Study of Mozambique*. Washington, DC: Biodiversity Support Program, 2001.
Hecht, Gabrielle. 'The African Anthropocene'. *Aeon*, 6 February 2018. https://aeon.co/essays/if-we-talk-about-hurting-our-planet-who-exactly-is-the-we
Huddart, David. '"Ask Life": Animism & the Metaphysical Detective'. In *A Companion to Mia Couto*, edited by Grant Hamilton and David Huddart, n.p. London: James Currey, 2016. Kindle.
Jin, Gracie. 'Q&A with Mia Couto, The Writer Who Just Won the "American Nobel Prize"'. *Mic*, 4 November 2013. Available at: https://www.mic.com/articles/71373/q-a-with-mia-couto-the-writer-who-just-won-the-american-nobel-prize#.TxVx1SK8W
Kwenda, Chirevo V. 'Beyond Patronage: Giving and Receiving in the Construction of Civil Society'. *Journal of Theology for Southern Africa* 101 (1998): 1–10.
Latour, Bruno. 'An Attempt at a "Compositionist Manifesto"'. *New Literary History* 41 (2010): 471–90.
Newitt, Marlyn. *A Short History of Mozambique*. New York: Oxford University Press, 2017. Kindle.
Nixon, Rob. 'The Great Acceleration and the Great Divergence: Vulnerability in the Anthropocene'. *Profession*, 2014. https://profession.mla.org/the-great-acceleration-and-the-great-divergence-vulnerability-in-the-anthropocene/

Nixon, Rob. *Slow Violence and the Environmentalism of the Poor*. Cambridge, MA: Harvard University Press, 2011.

Rothwell, Philip. *A Postmodern Nationalist: Truth, Orality, and Gender in the Work of Mia Couto*. Lewisburg: Bucknell University Press, 2004.

Samuelson, Meg. 'Coastal Form: Amphibian Positions, Wider Worlds and Planetary Horizons on the African Indian Ocean Littoral'. *Comparative Literature* 69, no. 1 (2017): 16–24.

Samuelson, Meg. 'Melancholic States, Statist Mourning and the Poetics of Memory in Post-Conflict Fiction from Southern Africa'. *Journal of Social Studies* 115 (2007): 42–68.

Shaban, Abdur Rahman Alfa. '90% of Mozambican City of Beira Destroyed by Cyclone Idai–Red Cross'. *AfricaNews*, 18 March 2019. https://www.africanews.com/2019/03/18/90-percent-of-mozambican-city-of-beira-destroyed-by-cyclone-idai-red-cross//

Stengers, Isabelle. *In Catastrophic Times: Resisting the Coming Barbarism*. Translated by Andrew Goffey. London: Open Humanities Press, 2015.

5

Ecological imaginations in contemporary Chinese science fiction

Mengtian Sun

I see that the dream of ruling the sea has appeared again. I see that I have become a pile of dancing white bones.

– Han Song, *Hongse Haiyang* (*The Red Sea*)

On 5 June 2019, World Environment Day was hosted by China with the theme of air pollution. For anyone who is even the slightest familiar with China, it's well known that air pollution has been a major environmental issue in the last two decades. Beijing, China's capital, has especially received global attention in a variety of major newspapers and websites: 'On Scale of 0 to 500, Beijing's Air Quality Tops "Crazy Bad" at 755' according to *The New York Times*;[1] 'China pollution: First ever red alert in effect in Beijing' according to *BBC News*;[2] 'Beijing chokes on off-the-charts air pollution as thick smog settles over northern China' according to *The Washington Post*;[3] 'Beijing hit by new air pollution crisis as huge sandstorm blows in', according to *The Guardian*.[4] The list goes on. However, accompanying these kinds of news reports showing how serious the air pollution is in China, there are also another set of news reports that noticed a different aspect of the story: 'Beijing announces emergency measures amid fog of pollution';[5] 'Beijing confiscates barbecues in drive to cut air pollution';[6] 'Beijing Takes Steps to Fight Pollution as Problem Worsens';[7] 'Beijing factories ordered to shut or cut output after pollution red alert';[8] 'Smog Police: New Beijing Force Created To Tackle Air Pollution'.[9]

The fact that China is the host of the 2019 World Environment Day with the theme of air pollution epitomizes China's environmental problems as is shown in the short curation of news headlines mentioned earlier: the seriousness of air pollution in China and the tremendous endeavours to deal with it. It is also an acknowledgement of the early successes of the battle against air pollution in China. Dechen Tsering, director of the UN Environment's Asia Pacific Regional Office, says China was chosen as the host because Beijing is 'a good example of how a large city in a developing country can balance environmental protection and economic growth'.[10] Even though some measures that the Chinese government have taken are only temporary (e.g. shutting down factories during some major national and international events, such as APEC and the National People's Congress) or just a matter of relocating of pollution (e.g. relocating chemical plants from Beijing to other areas), the comprehensive measures taken did bring about some improvement in the air pollution problem.

However, air pollution is just one of the many environmental and ecological problems that China is facing and tackling. Like most other third world countries who went through industrialization and modernization in a short period of time, China's economic success is accompanied by an array of ecological problems such as water pollution, deforestation and industrial and electronic waste, among others. They have become a large portion of the daily reality that Chinese people are living with nowadays. And it comes without surprise that ecological concerns have become one of the main themes in contemporary Chinese literature. Whereas ecological imaginations in mainstream literature have received wide academic attention in both China and the West,[11] in Chinese science fiction, they have received comparatively little attention. This chapter examines how contemporary Chinese writers use science fiction to contemplate on China's ecological issues. It will especially focus on the works by Han Song and Chen Qiufan, who have written some of the works that most actively engage with and criticize the ecological problems in contemporary China. By looking at these two representative writers' works, this chapter attempts to map out some of the major ecological concerns and ways of thinking about them in contemporary Chinese science fiction.

Chen Qiufan and the global cycle of waste

Chen Qiufan's *Huang Chao* (荒潮 *The Waste Tide* 2013) is one of the most environmentally conscious and outspoken science fiction novels in contemporary China. As can be seen from the title of the book, the main problem addressed is waste, e-waste to be more specific. This novel was written and published during a period when the issue of waste, especially the exportation of e-waste from developed (global North) to less developed countries (global

South), was receiving increasing global attention, beginning around the turn of the twenty-first century. This issue especially gained global attention with the publication of an investigation report by BAN (The Basel Action Network) and SVTC (Silicon Valley Toxic Coalition), entitled 'Exporting Harm: The High-Tech Trashing of Asia', published in 2002, along with a corresponding short video documentary by the same name. In the documentary, Guiyu, a southern Chinese town, is taken as an example of e-waste exporting destinations in Asia. The documentary explains how e-waste was processed in Guiyu and describes the various ecological and human health hazards that the process brings to the local community.

Almost a decade after the publication of 'Exporting Harm', Chen wrote *The Waste Tide*. Similar to the documentary, the novel is set in Guiyu and reveals how e-waste is processed there, focusing on the damages that it brings to the environment and people's health (especially in the first three chapters). This is no coincidence, considering how famous Guiyu is in the discussion of global e-waste circulation. For a long time, Guiyu has been 'the largest E-waste recycling site in the world'.[12] Chen also has a personal tie to the place. As is shown in the afterword of the book, Chen set this novel in his hometown as a dedication to it. Guiyu is a small town in Shantou municipal city, where Chen was born. The novel is a tribute to his hometown, which is no longer what it was, because of the fast development of modernization in China.

Although thematically similar to the report, the novel gives a much more vivid description and in-depth discussion of e-waste recycling in Guiyu. Since the novel is narrated by five narrators who have different backgrounds, readers are offered different perspectives on the e-waste industry in this particular town. Chen gives the most detailed and comprehensive description of e-waste recycling through the narrator Scott Brandle, an American businessman who comes to visit Guiyu for the first time. Clearly, Brandle provides the point of view of the foreigner, who sees the effect of e-waste recycling at Guiyu for the first time. He is shocked to discover that:

> Metal chassis, broken displays, circuit boards, plastic components and wires, some dismantled and some awaiting processing, were scattered everywhere like piles of manure, with laborers, all of them migrants from elsewhere in China, flitting between the piles like flies. The workers sifted through the piles and picked out valuable pieces to be placed into the ovens or acid baths for additional decomposition to extract copper and tin, as well as gold, platinum, and other precious metals. What was left over was either incinerated or scattered on the ground, creating even more trash. No one wore any protective gear.[13]

He continues to describe the damages of e-waste recycling in Guiyu in detail, noticing how 'everything was shrouded in a leaden miasma, an amalgamation of the white mist generated by the boiling aqua regia in the acid baths and the black smoke from the unceasing burning of PVC, insulation, and circuit boards in the fields and on the shore of the river'.[14] He also observes how laundry was done 'in black water with bare hands', and how children played on the black shores 'where fiber glass and the charred remains of circuit boards twinkled'.[15]

The ecological damage of e-waste at Guiyu is also depicted through the eyes of Chen Kaizong, another narrator in the novel, who was born in Guiyu but went to the United States with his parents when he was young. He is returning to Guiyu for the first time since he has grown up. In Chen's eyes, Guiyu has transformed from a pastoral paradise to a dumping ground of e-waste, which is ironically called modernity. Guiyu, as remembered by him, used to be 'poor but lively and hopeful', 'the water in the pond was clear and the air smelled of the salty sea', and '[o]n the beach one could pick shells and crabs'.[16] What they have now is dioxins and furans, acid fog, 'water whose lead content exceeded the safe threshold by 2400 times', 'soil whose chromium concentration exceeded the EPA limit by 1338 times', and 'men and women who had to drink this water and sleep on this soil'.[17]

The novel provides an even closer look at e-waste recycling at Guiyu, especially the social problems related to it, through the character of Xiao Mi. She came to Guiyu from a northern town when she was very young. She represents the tens of millions of people who migrated from northern to southern China during the 1990s, where opportunities were supposed to lie and where modernization in China was most pronounced (because of the prioritization of industrialization and urbanization in southern cities by the Chinese government). This wave of domestic labour force migration was famously called 'nan xia' (南下, Going Down to the South). As an embodiment of the 'nan xia' social phenomenon, Xiao Mi's story in the novel reveals the dark side of China's fast industrialization and urbanization 'miracle'. Like tens of millions of other rural migrant workers, Xiao Mi came to the south with hopes for a better future, only to realize that the future that they helped to build never belonged to them. Because of discrimination against rural migrant workers and China's hukou system which makes it hard to become an 'official' local with all the social benefits (such as education, medical care and so on), they have always occupied the lowest class and been treated as outsiders and disposable tools. When Xiao Mi migrated to Guiyu, she saw this strange and futuristic city, and the novel depicts her lamenting: 'nothing in this city belonged to them . . . but this is what the poor lives on' – the false hope that they are part of the future too.[18]

Although the fast industrialization and urbanization of cities in China would not have been possible without these marginalized migrants, they are excluded from any benefits of this future. Through Xiao Mi, the novel reveals how, with almost no work rights and extremely poor working condition, rural migrant workers are dehumanized and considered as disposable tools. Every morning at 7.00 am, she and another seven workers living in the same room would get up and work.[19] Their work involves sorting through a large pile of plastic garbage – like a stray dog sniffing in pile of discarded bones, and sorting out the different types of plastic garbage by burning the edge and smelling them, as the poisonous gas makes them vomit more than they eat every day.[20] There is a kind of electronic device that can detect the smell too, but

> the price of a single electronic nose was enough to hire a hundred young women like her, and the machine was unlikely to be as efficient. Moreover, the instrument might break down and require repairs, while the girls could simply be sent home with a few yuan if they fell sick, not even requiring medical insurance.[21]

The novel not only looks at e-waste from the point of view of migrant workers, but also from an international perspective. It puts e-waste in the context of globalization and points out how the local and the global are interconnected in a closed circle. Specifically, China's e-waste problem is represented as a global problem:

> It was said that the crushed plastic would then be melted down, cooled, formed into pellets to be sold to coastal factories, where they would be turned into cheap plastic products the bulk of which were exported to countries around the world so that everyone around the globe could benefit from the affordable 'Made in China' merchandise; when those wares broke down or became stale, they turned into trash to be shipped back to China, and the cycle would begin again.
>
> The world ran on such cycles, which Mimi found fascinating and marvelous: the cycles kept the machines roaring and the workers busy.[22]

As can be seen, the novel situates Guiyu's e-waste in a global capitalist system, where, as Zygmunt Bauman famously observes, lands and population are arranged into different functions and 'a hierarchy of castes'.[23] The developing countries, or the global South, can only participate in the global capitalist marketplace by assuming the subordinate role that is assigned to them – both the world's factory and its garbage bin. It is the only way through which they might eventually become 'developed', or join the global North, after the devastation of the ecosystem and the creation of severe class division. And even in the case of China, who is on a promising path of moving from the global South to the global North, the transition is accompanied by the creation of a local, more polarized global North and global South in itself. Not to mention that development and modernization is not guaranteed due to the devastation of its ecosystem and the destruction of its social fabric. Consequently, the peripheral and subordinate role of the global South is largely perpetuated in the global capitalist system, as is represented by the cycle of waste in the novel.

By looking at e-waste at Guiyu from a global perspective, the novel also criticizes how the neoliberal nature of global capitalism brings about global environmental injustice. Chen places this theme at the forefront of the novel, prefacing it with an epigraph that imitates a Wikipedia explanation of the Basel Convention:

> The Basel Convention on the Control of Transboundary Movements of Hazardous Wastes and Their Disposal, usually known as the Basel Convention, is an international treaty that was designed to reduce the movements of hazardous waste between nations, and specifically to prevent transfer of hazardous waste from developed to less developed countries (LDCs).
>
> The Convention was opened for signature on 22 March 1989, and entered into force on 5 May 1992. As of May 2013, 179 states and the European Union are parties to the Convention.
>
> The United States, the leading producer of electronic waste, has never ratified the Convention.
>
> –Wikipedia entry on 'Basel Convention'[24]

The Basel Convention is an international effort to help promote environmental justice in the face of neoliberal globalization. It tries to prevent industrialized countries from profiting by 'exploiting the precarious economic positions of developing nations',[25] which are forced to prioritize economic development over environmental concerns. The principle of environmental justice 'asserts that no people, based on their race or economic status should be forced to bear a disproportionate burden of environmental risks'.[26] However, without regulation, global capitalism, whose only concern is economic profit, dictates that hazardous waste will always end up taking the economic path of least resistance. As is stated in the 'Exporting Harm' report, '[a] free trade in hazardous waste leaves the poorer people of the world with an untenable choice between poverty and poison.'[27] From a global perspective, the transboundary flow of e-waste does not simply move pollution from one place to another, but creates much more severe environmental damage than it would on the place where it originates due to the superior treatment regimes of developed countries. By contrast, in developing countries, recycling is done 'using primitive techniques and little regard for worker safety or environmental protection'.[28]

The neoliberal tendency of the global capitalist system dictates that the less developed countries are always forced to accept the position of the garbage dumping ground, before they become economically strong enough to say no to such refuse. In the case of China, only after it had developed its economy significantly was it able to say no to the global influx of toxic waste. In January 2018, five years after the publication of the novel, the 'National Sword' policy was enacted which banned the import of various types of waste. China might be one of the few cases where a global South country is on the road to becoming part of the global North, though considering its severely damaged environment and the class division, whether it can be considered as belonging to the global North in the near future is still doubtful. However, this transition of China, successful or not, does not change at all that the global South is perpetuated in certain functions and caste relations in the global capitalist system. China's ban on hazardous waste only means the diversion of such waste to other global South areas, such as Southeast Asia.

Alongside the epigraph, the novel mainly criticizes the neoliberal tendencies of global capitalism through the character Scott. He is a business representative of a large multinational corporation. According to Scott, just as e-waste management and eco-pollution is moved to the global South, so too are high risk drug trials: '[s]ince the FDA strictly regulated clinical trials conducted in the United States, many high-risk drug trials had been moved to developing countries'; in these 'corruption-ridden, mismanaged regions of the world, hundreds, even thousands, volunteered to be trial subjects for pennies'.[29] This is a win-win situation except for the poor in the global South: the pharmaceutical companies obtain data; hospitals and doctors who carry out the trials get money; but the poor trial subjects are left with 'a few wrinkled dollar bills, a free breakfast, unknown side effects, the risk of a lengthy incubation period, and a high probability of dying from complications'.[30] The novel criticizes how globalization, without regulation, will always end up exploiting the poor and contribute to the widening division between the global North and the global South. Just as Bauman points out, whereas the global elite have become mobile, international and free from spatial determination, the poor are fixed in their locality.[31] It is always the locally bound who are left doing 'wound-licking, damage-repair and waste-disposal',[32] while the free-to-move (usually MNCs) pack up and leave with loads of money.

As can be seen, *The Waste Tide* not only gives readers a detailed description of the e-waste recycling at Guiyu, but also makes readers actively think about it in relation to China's modernization process and the larger global context. It reveals that in the era of globalization, the local and the global cannot be separated. Local problems need both local and global visions and solutions. As Bruno Latour observes, there is no longer such place as outside or away, 'where we could discharge the refuse of our activity'.[33] What circles the planet is 'not only Magellan's ship, but also our refuse, our toxic wastes and toxic loans'.[34]

Han Song and *The Red Sea*

Set in Guiyu and with a writing style that is defined by Chen himself as 'science fiction realism', *The Waste Tide* represents a type of Chinese ecological imagination that is closely grounded in reality and looks at China's ecological problems from a global perspective. The ecological imagination of another major contemporary Chinese science fiction writer, Han Song, however, represents the opposite – a form of hyper metaphorical and fantastical science fiction. Often acclaimed as one of the 'big three' of contemporary Chinese science fiction writers,[35] Han's works are described by many critics, such as Li Guangyi,[36] Jia Liyuan[37] and Wang Yao,[38] as obscure and 'guiyi', a Chinese word which means uncanny and weird. This is also the main reason why, compared to Liu Cixin, another of the 'big three', Han's works have received far less attention from Western scholars. His works are hard to understand even for native Chinese readers, not to mention Westerners. But this is a shame, because his stories, characterized by Carlos Rojas as 'apocalyptic fables',[39] often focus on fundamental issues that are common to all humankind.

In a recent interview, Chiara Cigarini, a Chinese Studies scholar, asked Han why his writing style is so 'cryptic and obscure'. Han explains that he 'thought there must be some change, but I cannot work out a plan, so the story becomes obscure'.[40] He also points out that form is content; taking his novel *Ditie* (*The Subway*) as an example, he says that he 'used a lot of very sharp and colourful words, sometimes controversial'[41] to represent the subway. In the same interview, he explains how he felt 'the whole [Chinese] society is behaving just like in the subway: people are squeezed together, and they struggle for money, food, basically everything'.[42] As can be seen, the subway is a metaphor for the social condition in modern China. With uncanny and obscure language and images,

Han is trying to present the very experience of modern China, which he regards as uncanny and obscure.

Han's ecological imagination needs to be looked at in this context too. I will especially focus on two of his most representative novels, including *Ditie* (*The Subway*, 2011) and *Hongse Haiyang* (*The Red Sea*, 2004). Both of these novels are 'notoriously' hard to understand, not only because of the uncanny and weird language and images and the non-realist setting, but also because both novels contain several previously independently published short stories, which are only loosely related to each other. There is no easily discernible plot line that runs through every story from the beginning to the end. However, when looked at together, the two novels mutually inform each other and together they form a complete story (or rather fable) of human civilization. Although *Hongse Haiyang* possesses a more ecological orientation, *Ditie* is key to understanding the background and the overall theme of the two novels.

The main motif of *Ditie* (and also most of his other works) can be seen in the preface where Han explains why he is writing a story about the subway. He writes that the fast development of the railway system in China epitomizes its modernization dream and struggle;[43] the subway is a concentrated repository of contemporary Chinese people's emotions, desires, values and fates.[44] Everyone wants to catch this train of modernization at any cost.[45] However, the novel shows how instead of marching towards the bright future on this 'subway', people enter and become trapped in a yi shijie (an alien world). A passenger on the train breaks out of the window and attempts to reach the driver's carriage to see what has gone wrong. On his way there, he observes how people on board have become 'kongxin chengke' (hollow-souled passengers),[46] and the various ways they have devolved: in one carriage, he notices that everyone is fast asleep, like they are hibernating or are dead;[47] in another carriage, he sees that people are pacing up and down the corridor on all fours like wolves trapped in a cage;[48] and in yet another carriage, people are killed for eating food,[49] and then all they do is have sex with each other. On the train, people become old very fast, children are born one after another, and space becomes more and more limited.[50] In the end, people, 'all naked', have 'lost their human form', and 'devolved into all kinds of weird and strange creatures'.[51]

This is where the second chapter ends. Until this point, the novel has shown how on this train, which is travelling at a break-neck speed supposedly into the future, humans are descending into pristine forms and undergoing de-evolution, developing and going backwards. However, humans are not the only thing that has become 'alien' in this world. So, too, has the environment. In chapter three, we are shown the world above ground, which is no less uncanny than in the subway. Above the ground is the city, where the 'visible light is black, the basic colour of the city';[52] the rain, acidic and dark red, the colour of industrial pigments, pours day and night;[53] the streets are filled with spit, waste, sperms and all kinds of weird-shaped plants and flowers, genetically mutated;[54] many genetically modified mice walk upright on the pavements along the streets;[55] and 'rich people' have 'implanted artificial gills that look like measles to filter the dirty, poisonous air'.[56]

As can be seen, everything – nature, human and other life forms – has mutated and become alien, from the black light to the red rain, the weird-shaped plants, the standing mice and the fish-like humans. This dystopian imagination is accompanied by an atmosphere of looming disaster throughout the novel. In order to hide and flee from the pending apocalypse, some people bought tickets on spaceships to fly to other planets; some, who can not afford spaceship tickets, went underground and de-evolved into diku ren (underground cave men); and some went to hide under the sea. Intriguingly, *Hongse Haiyang (The Red Sea)* is a novel about this last group of people who went to the sea to escape the catastrophe above ground.

Hongse Haiyang contains some of the weirdest images of nature, especially the sea, and people's relation with it in contemporary Chinese science fiction. The novel starts with first-person narration, as the story is told of 'I', who is an aquatic human. It starts from 'my' birth and follows 'my' growth into a man. Finally, this protagonist 'I' becomes the leader of a group of aquatic humans. Readers gradually learn that this is the present of human history, where people have evolved (or de-evolved) into aquatic mammals with fins and gills, after the apocalypse hinted at in *Ditie* has happened and the land and its species have been destroyed. However, the sea that they live in is no longer the blue sea that we are familiar with:

> This sea is red everywhere. Water in the depth or at the surface are all bright like fire. Countless germs, benthons,[57] plankton,[58] nekton,[59] acquired the ability to be luminous all at once; hundreds of millions of red metal fragments, which no one knows where they came from, keep flying and glittering in the water like spore, making the endless sea boil with a high temperature that is unseen in history.[60]

This red, boiling sea is another uncanny image in Han's works that symbolizes an 'alien' nature, resulting from human destruction. Just like in *Ditie*, not only has the nature become 'alien' and uncanny, but humans themselves have become 'alien' and de-evolved into pristine creatures. Like other sea animals, aquatic humans grow fast but have a much shorter life span. They also have short memories. The only two things that concern them are food and sex. This degeneration of humans is especially epitomized in the novel through the treatment of women. In the red sea, women are reduced to sex tools, and the responsibility of rearing the offspring falls solely on them. Whenever the food source in one area of the sea becomes scarce, men will migrate to another area, leaving women and children behind, because there are many ferocious animals in the sea and bringing women and children with them would pose a threat to their own lives. So every time a tribe of men passes by, women in the caves offer sex in exchange for food.

The mistreatment of women in the novel not only epitomizes the degeneration of humans, but also symbolizes their destruction of nature, represented by the sea. On several occasions, the sea is compared to women (and vice versa). At the very beginning, when 'I' was born, 'the first thing that I saw was mom's young and beautiful naked body, which left me a weird impression that the gender of the sea is actually female'.[61] However, the comparison between women and the sea also changes as the story develops. Whereas at the beginning it is related to the image of a mother and the birth of lives, later, the sea is often compared to women who either are dead or are about to die, especially after 'I' encounters the tribe of men called 'Predators'. These 'Predators' represent a new stage of degeneration – cannibalism – for humankind under the sea. As it turns out, the environment in the red sea continues to worsen. The salinity, acidity and temperature of the water continue to rise; the amount of oxygen continues to drop; and microbes, plankton and fishes continue to die. The red sea has become 'a sea of floating corpses'.[62] Since the food source has become extremely scarce, some aquatic men now have engaged in cannibalism.

When 'I' and the other members of the 'Predators' have killed all the men in another tribe and are eating them, 'I' see the women wriggling their bodies in excitement as a sign of welcome. This is the result of human nature's metamorphosis under the sea: 'these women instinctively thought, these viscous men who came from elsewhere must be the victor in this survival struggle.'[63] According to the narrator, if they can replace their useless fathers and brothers with these men to protect them, they will have a much better chance of survival against the sea rats (the enemy of aquatic humans).[64] As 'I' watched the women, 'I' remembered 'mom' (who was already dead at that moment), and 'I remembered Shuicao, Baihe, and all my dead sisters, and the sea itself'.[65] Both Shuicao and Baihe are 'my' childhood female friends who are now dead. By listing them together, the sea again is compared to women; but instead of relating to the birth of life, the image of dead women is invoked to symbolize the dying of the sea. These women of the other tribe did turn out dead in the end – slaughtered and eaten by the very men who they thought could be their new protectors against the sea rats. Not only used as sex tools by men, women have also become food eaten by men. As a symbol of the sea, women in the novel represent how nature has been used and destroyed by mankind.

The degeneration of both humankind and nature is a theme that is not only reflected in the content of the novel, but also the form. The novel is composed of four sections, each of which is named, respectively, 'Our Present', 'Our Past', 'Our Past's Past' and 'Our Future'. Each section has a different writing style. The first section is written in first-person narration, depicting life under the sea long after humans have become aquatic creatures. The middle two sections go back in time and tell, in third-person narration, the story of what happened both after and before humans went under the sea. It turns out that at the beginning, when humans first went under sea, human civilization still hadn't degenerated much in terms of physiology, morality and technology. Back then, humans built massive underwater domes, strong enough to withstand the boiling sea water, seaquakes and the attack of sea rats.[66] There were lots of fish, and humans had the technology to gather and raise them in sea ponds.[67] They also had underwater cars with which they travelled around the world (underwater of course). However, in the present timescale, humans live in caves, and have to fight for scarce food sources with sea rats, and even eat themselves. As can be seen, the retrospective narrative in the novel foregrounds how both humans and nature have degenerated from the 'past' (in the novel) to the future.

The last section, which is composed of several short stories, gives the novel an even more estranging effect. Although entitled 'Our Future', the stories are set in the past, featuring real people in history, such as Li Daoyuan, a famous Chinese geologist (470–527), and Zheng He, the celebrated Chinese voyager, who lived during the Ming period. In this last section, the aquatic humans' future and past encounter each other and become one, forming a closed time loop of past-present-future. The story 'Tianxia Zhi Shui' ('All the Water in the World') is the most representative one in this section. It is set in the 500s, and the style of language also resembles that of ancient Chinese. The story is about Li Daoyuan, the famous Chinese geologist who wrote *Shuijing Zhu* (*Commentary on the Water Classics*). As an expansion of the Chinese classic *The Rivers*, *Shuijing Zhu* describes more than a thousand rivers in China and the geology, weather, folk customs, historical events and myths in the region of each of the rivers.

In the short story, one day, Li had a dream about red water. In order to find it, he went to Mengmen along the Yellow River. In a forest nearby, he stumbles across a small lake whose colour is exactly red. The way the red lake is described reminds readers of the red sea – both are compared to women. When Li reaches out to the water in the lake, he is surprised to feel 'a warmth that resembles the skin of a young woman'.[68] An old hermit living in a hut beside the lake tells Li that the lake is actually a living being. The lake has told the hermit that it has forgotten whether it came from the past or the future, but it does remember that in ancient times, it lived on the land like humans do. Later, there was a world war, which destroyed the ecosystem on land completely. They modified themselves into aquatic creatures to live under the sea. At the very beginning, they still resembled humans, but after hundreds of millions of years undergoing evolution, they merged and became one with the sea. But one day, a new disaster came and they had to migrate again. Something went wrong, however, and they ended up coming here. Li wonders whether the red lake is his past or his future.

As can be seen, the red lake is the future of aquatic humans described in the former few sections of the novel. In this story, the future of humans encounters the past of humans. Together with *Ditie*, *Hongse Haiyang* paints a picture of human history from the present (in *Ditie*), to the future (the present in *Hongse Haiyang*), and to the past-future (in 'Tianxia Zhi Shui'). From *Ditie* to *Hongse Haiyang*, Han Song shows the degeneration of humans in modern society and their destruction of the environment, which led to humans suffering further degeneration (into pristine, cannibalistic aquatic humans). Although unlike Chen's *The Waste Tide*, which is set in a realistic setting and criticizes specific contemporary environmental and social problems, Han's *Ditie* and *Hongse Haiyang*, with their linked, highly symbolic settings and stories, are equally powerful critiques of humans' destruction of the environment. By presenting a circular conception of history/time and the final merging of humankind and the sea, Han's ecological imagination reminds people of their connection to, and dependence on, nature, and that we can not afford to be naïve and think of history as linear progress, where everything will become better as human society develops.

An alien self in an alien world

From the waste land to the dehumanizing subway and the red sea, contemporary Chinese science fiction writers imagine a future in which humans and the environment have become alien. For Chinese people who have experienced the dramatic changes modernization has brought in a short span of thirty years – urbanization, industrialization, grey skies, hazardous air and waste-filled land, among others – it comes as no surprise that estrangement is a notable experience. Science fiction, famously defined by Darko Suvin as 'cognitive estrangement', has become a powerful means of expression for Chinese writers to convey that experience and also criticize its future (often dystopian) tendencies. As Han cautions in the interview with Chiara Cigarini, 'Chinese people are themselves becoming monsters. We're eating everything: the environment, our culture, our people'.[69] Han's comments can safely be extended to humankind more generally. As representations of the experience of modernity and criticism of the social and ecological problems brought about by it, Han's and Chen's novels deal not with China-specific problems, but global problems that haunt everyone on Earth. Their stories will sound familiar to all of us, who have become aliens in an alien world. And hopefully, they will also inspire actions to prevent their variously imagined dystopian futures from becoming reality.

Notes

1 Edward Wong, 'On Scale of 0 to 500, Beijing's Air Quality Tops "Crazy Bad" at 755', *The New York Times,* 13 January 2013, https://www.nytimes.com/2013/01/13/science/earth/beijing-air-pollution-off-the-charts.html.
2 'China Pollution: First Ever Red Alert in Effect in Beijing', *BBC News*, 8 December 2015, https://www.bbc.com/news/world-asia-china-35026363.
3 Angela Fritz, 'Beijing Chokes on Off-the-Charts Air Pollution as Thick Smog Settles over Northern China', *The Washington Post*, 30 November 2015, https://www.washingtonpost.com/news/capital-weather-gang/wp/2015/11/30/beijing-chokes-on-off-the-charts-air-pollution-as-thick-smog-settles-over-northern-china/.
4 Tom Phillips, 'Beijing Hit by New Air Pollution Crisis as Huge Sandstorm Blows in', *The Guardian*, 4 May 2017, https://www.theguardian.com/world/2017/may/04/beijing-new-air-pollution-crisis-sandstorm.
5 Paul Armstrong and Feng Ke, 'Beijing Announces Emergency Measures Amid Fog of Pollution', *CNN*, 23 October 2013, https://edition.cnn.com/2013/10/23/world/asia/china-beijing-smog-emergency-measures/index.html.
6 'Beijing Confiscates Barbecues in Drive to Cut Air Pollution', *The Guardian*, 27 November 2013, https://www.theguardian.com/world/2013/nov/27/china-barbecues-air-pollution.
7 Edward Wong, 'Beijing Takes Steps to Fight Pollution as Problem Worsens', *The New York Times*, 30 January 2013, https://www.nytimes.com/2013/01/31/world/asia/beijing-takes-emergency-steps-to-fight-smog.html.

8 'Beijing Factories Ordered to Shut or Cut Output after Pollution Red Alert', *ABC News*, 18 December 2016, https://www.abc.net.au/news/2016-12-17/china-orders-beijing-factories-to-shut-or-cut-output/8129752.
9 Merrit Kennedy, 'Smog Police: New Beijing Force Created to Tackle Air Pollution', *NPR*, 9 January 2017, https://www.npr.org/sections/thetwo-way/2017/01/09/508965737/smog-police-new-beijing-force-created-to-tackle-air-pollution.
10 'China to Host World Environment Day 2019 on Air Pollution', *China Daily*, 16 March 2019, http://www.chinadaily.com.cn/a/201903/16/WS5c8c1e9fa3106c65c34eeeb5.html.
11 For example, see Yang Jincai's 'Ecological Awareness in Contemporary Chinese Literature', *Neohelicon* 39 (2012): 107–18, and Wang Ning's 'Global in the Local: Ecocriticism in China', *Interdisciplinary Studies in Literature and Environment* 21, no. 4 (2014): 739–48.
12 Brett H. Robinson, 'E-waste: An Assessment of Global Production and Environmental Impacts', *Science of the Total Environment* 408 (2009): 187.
13 Chen Qiufan, *Huang Chao* (Wuhan: Changjiang Literature and Art, 2013), 32.
14 Chen, *Huang Chao*, 32.
15 Chen, *Huang Chao*, 32.
16 Chen, *Huang Chao*, 39.
17 Chen, *Huang Chao*, 25.
18 Chen, *Huang Chao*, 50.
19 Chen, *Huang Chao*, 50.
20 Chen, *Huang Chao*, 51.
21 Chen, *Huang Chao*, 51.
22 Chen, *Huang Chao*, 51–2.
23 Zygmunt Bauman, *Wasted Lives: Modernity and Its Outcasts* (Oxford: Polity, 2004), 59.
24 Chen, *Huang Chao*, 22.
25 Sejal Choksi, 'The Basel Convention on the Control of Transboundary Movements of Hazardous Wastes and Their Disposal: 1999 Protocol on Liability and Compensation', *Ecology Law Quarterly* 28, no. 2 (2001): 512.
26 Jim Puckett and Ted Smith, 'Exporting Harm: The High-Tech Trashing of Asia', 2002, 3.
27 Puckett and Smith, 'Exporting Harm', 2.
28 Robinson, 'E-Waste', 184.
29 Chen, *Huang Chao*, 181.
30 Chen, *Huang Chao*, 181.
31 Bauman, *Wasted Lives*, 2.
32 Bauman, *Wasted Lives*, 8.
33 Bruno Latour, 'Spheres and Networks: Two Ways to Reinterpret Globalization', *Harvard Design Magazine* 30 (2009): 144.

34 Latour, 'Spheres and Networks', 144.
35 Song Mingwei, 'Variations on Utopia in Contemporary Chinese Science Fiction', *Science Fiction Studies* 40, no. 1 (2013): 87.
36 Li Guangyi, 'Uncanny and Uncertainty–Han Song's Science Fiction' (Guiyi yu Buqueding Xing), *Contemporary Writers Review* (*Dangdai Zuojia Pinglun*) 1 (2007): 102–6.
37 Jia Liyuan, 'Han Song and "Ghostly China"' (Han Song yu Guimei Zhongguo), *Contemporary Writers Review* (*Dangdai Zuojia Pinglun*) 1 (2011): 83–90.
38 Wang Yao, 'Maze, Mirror and Round Dance' (Migong, Jingxiang yu Huanwu), *Masterpieces Review* (*Mingzuo Xinshang*) 8 (2014): 49–51.
39 Carlos Rojas, 'Han Song and the Dream of Reason', *Chinese Literature Today* 7, no. 1 (2018): 35.
40 Chiara Cigarini, 'Science Fiction and the Avant-Garde Spirit: An Interview with Han Song', *Chinese Literature Today* 7, no. 1 (2018): 22.
41 Cigarini, 'Science Fiction and the Avant-Garde Spirit', 21.
42 Cigarini, 'Science Fiction and the Avant-Garde Spirit', 21.
43 Han Song, *Ditie* (Shanghai People's Publishing House, 2010), 9.
44 Han, *Ditie*, 11.
45 Han, *Ditie*, 11.
46 Han, *Ditie*, 17.
47 Han, *Ditie*, 73.
48 Han, *Ditie*, 73.
49 Han, *Ditie*, 74.
50 Han, *Ditie*, 81.
51 Han, *Ditie*, 88.
52 Han, *Ditie*, 93.
53 Han, *Ditie*, 93.
54 Han, *Ditie*, 93.
55 Han, *Ditie*, 95.
56 Han, *Ditie*, 94.
57 Organisms dwelling in the benthos.
58 Animals and plants that can only float passively in the water.
59 Living organisms that are able to swim and move independently of currents.
60 Han Song, *Hongse Haiyang* (Shanghai Science Popularization Publishing House, 2004), 15.
61 Han, *Hongse Haiyang*, 15.
62 Han, *Hongse Haiyang*, 35.
63 Han, *Hongse Haiyang*, 42.
64 Han, *Hongse Haiyang*, 42.
65 Han, *Hongse Haiyang*, 42.
66 Han, *Hongse Haiyang*, 30.

67 Han, *Hongse Haiyang*, 30.
68 Han, *Hongse Haiyang*, 224.
69 Cigarini, 'Science Fiction and the Avant-Garde Spirit', 22.

Bibliography

ABC News. 'Beijing Factories Ordered to Shut or Cut Output after Pollution Red Alert'. *ABC News*, 17 December 2016. https://www.abc.net.au/news/2016-12-17/china-orders-beijing-factories-to-shut-or-cut-output/8129752

Armstrong, Paul and Feng Ke. 'Beijing Announces Emergency Measures amid Fog of Pollution'. *CNN*, 23 October 2013. https://edition.cnn.com/2013/10/23/world/asia/china-beijing-smog-emergency-measures/index.html

Bauman, Zygmunt. *Wasted Lives: Modernity and Its Outcasts*. Oxford: Polity, 2004.

BBC News. 'China Pollution: First ever Red Alert in Effect in Beijing'. *BBC News*, 8 December 2015. https://www.bbc.com/news/world-asia-china-35026363

Berman, Douglas Scott. 'Chinese Ecocriticism: A Survey of the Landscape'. *Literature Compass* 12, no. 8 (2015): 396–403.

Chen, Qiufan. *Huang Chao (The Waste Tide)*. Wuhan: Changjiang Literature and Art, 2013.

Choksi, Sejal. 'The Basel Convention on the Control of Transboundary Movements of Hazardous Wastes and Their Disposal: 1999 Protocol on Liability and Compensation'. *Ecology Law Quarterly* 28, no. 2 (2001): 509–39.

Cigarini, Chiara. 'Science Fiction and the Avant-Garde Spirit: An Interview with Han Song'. *Chinese Literature Today* 7, no. 1 (2018): 20–2.

Duggan, Jennifer. 'Beijing's Mayor Announces "All-Out Effort" to Tackle Air Pollution'. *The Guardian*, 17 January 2014. https://www.theguardian.com/environment/chinas-choice/2014/jan/16/china-beijing-air-pollution-hazardous

Fritz, Angela. 'Beijing Chokes on Off-the-Charts Air Pollution as Thick Smog Settles over Northern China'. *The Washington Post*, 1 December 2015. https://www.washingtonpost.com/news/capital-weather-gang/wp/2015/11/30/beijing-chokes-on-off-the-charts-air-pollution-as-thick-smog-settles-over-northern-china/

Han, Song. *Ditie (The Subway)*. Shanghai: Shanghai People's Publishing House, 2010.

Han, Song. *Hongse Haiyang (The Red Sea)*. Shanghai: Shanghai Science Popularization Publishing House, 2004.

He, Weihua. 'The Last "Hero" and Jia Pingwa's Ecological Concerns in Remembering Wolves'. *Comparative Literature Studies* 55, no. 4 (2018): 761–72.

Jia, Liyuan. 'Han Song and "Ghostly China"' (Han Song yu Guimei Zhongguo). *Contemporary Writers Review* (*Dangdai Zuojia Pinglun*) 1 (2011): 83–90.

Kennedy, Merrit. 'Smog Police: New Beijing Force Created to Tackle Air Pollution'. *NPR*, 9 January 2017. https://www.npr.org/sections/thetwo-way/2017/01/09/508965737/smog-police-new-beijing-force-created-to-tackle-air-pollution

Latour, Bruno. 'Spheres and Networks: Two Ways to Reinterpret Globalization'. *Harvard Design Magazine* 30 (2009): 138–44.

Li, Guangyi. 'Uncanny and Uncertainty – Han Song's Science Fiction' (Guiyi yu Buqueding Xing). *Contemporary Writers Review (Dangdai Zuojia Pinglun)* 1 (2007): 102–6.

Phillips, Tom. 'Beijing Hit by New Air Pollution Crisis as Huge Sandstorm Blows in'. *The Guardian*, 4 May 2017. https://www.theguardian.com/world/2017/may/04/beijing-new-air-pollution-crisis-sandstorm

Puckett, Jim and Ted Smith. 'Exporting Harm: The High-Tech Trashing of Asia'. 2002. http://svtc.org/wp-content/uploads/technotrash.pdf

Robinson, Brett H. 'E-waste: An Assessment of Global Production and Environmental Impacts'. *Science of the Total Environment* 408 (2009): 183–91.

Rojas, Carlos. 'Han Song and the Dream of Reason'. *Chinese Literature Today* 7, no. 1 (2018): 33–41.

Shang, Biwu. 'Delving into a World of Non-Human Experience: Unnatural Narrative and Ecological Critique of Chen Yingsong's The Last Dance of a Leopard'. *Comparative Literature Studies* 55, no. 4 (2018): 749–60.

Song, Mingwei. 'Variations on Utopia in Contemporary Chinese Science Fiction'. *Science Fiction Studies* 40, no. 1 (2013): 86–102.

The Guardian. 'Beijing Confiscates Barbecues in Drive to Cut Air Pollution'. *The Guardian*, 27 November 2013. https://www.theguardian.com/world/2013/nov/27/china-barbecues-air-pollution

Wang, Ning. 'Global in the Local: Ecocriticism in China'. *Interdisciplinary Studies in Literature and Environment* 21, no. 4 (2014): 739–48.

Wang, Yao. 'Maze, Mirror and Round Dance' (Migong, Jingxiang yu Huanwu). *Masterpieces Review (Mingzuo Xinshang)* 8 (2014): 49–51.

Wei, Qingqi. 'Chinese Ecocriticism in the Last Ten Years'. In *The Oxford handbook of ecocriticism*, edited by Greg Garrard, 537–46. New York: Oxford University Press, 2014.

Wong, Edward. 'Beijing Takes Steps to Fight Pollution as Problem Worsens'. *The New York Times*, 30 January 2013. https://www.nytimes.com/2013/01/31/world/asia/beijing-takes-emergency-steps-to-fight-smog.html

Wong, Edward. 'On Scale of 0 to 500, Beijing's Air Quality Tops "Crazy Bad" at 755'. *The New York Times*, 12 January 2013. https://www.nytimes.com/2013/01/13/science/earth/beijing-air-pollution-off-the-charts.html

Yang, Jincai. 'Ecological Awareness in Contemporary Chinese Literature'. *Neohelicon* 39 (2012): 107–18.

Part II

Beyond the romantic frontier

6

The colonial translation of natures

Alan Bewell

Coming upon the title page of the first volume of Thomas Pennant's *Arctic Zoology*, published in 1784, one might seriously question his qualifications as a naturalist and wonder whether he qualifies, perhaps, for having made the biggest blunder in the history of natural history (Figure 6.1). The competition for this dubious honour has been fierce. The English parson naturalist Gilbert White, for instance, apparently driven by the inability to accept that his favourite birds – the house swallows – could possibly desert the village of Selbourne every winter, insisted, despite all signs to the contrary, that instead of migrating to Africa, they hid underwater or in underground caves near the parish. Samuel Taylor Coleridge also famously compared the air-born melodies of the Eolian harp to the songs of the Indonesian Greater Bird of Paradise, which, he claimed, 'Footless and wild . . . Nor pause, nor perch, hovering on untamed wing!'[1] The poet can probably be pardoned for thinking that these birds had no feet and were thus forced to be in constant flight, because he could not have known that the species had been given its scientific name, *Paradisaea apoda*, that is, the 'footless bird-of-paradise', because the feet (as well as the wings) of the first specimens to arrive in Europe had been removed when the skins were prepared for shipping. When George Shaw, the zoologist and natural history curator at the British Museum, first saw a specimen of an Australian platypus, he was not going to fall prey to a crude hoax perpetrated by people living in a distant convict colony. 'Of all the Mammalia yet known', he writes, the animal 'seems the most extraordinary in its conformation, exhibiting the perfect resemblance of the beak of a Duck engrafted on the head of a quadruped'. He initially believed that the specimen was the result of a 'deceptive preparation', but when, after 'the most minute and rigid examination', he could not find any sutures attaching its beak to its head, he was forced to conclude that the blunder was in nature itself and named it *Platypus anatinus*, a 'duck-like flat-foot'.[2] Albrecht Dürer, who

Figure 6.1 Title page from Thomas Pennant's *Arctic Zoology* (1784), courtesy of the Thomas Fisher Rare Book Library, University of Toronto.

had never seen a living Indian rhinoceros, famously portrayed the animal as being clothed in riveted armour and as having, along with the formidable nose horn from whence it derives its name, another delicate little horn mounted like a car-hood ornament between its shoulders. Even so, Dürer still knew that he was drawing a rhinoceros and *not* a hippopotamus. That is why the idea that Pennant, one of the most distinguished of eighteenth-century British naturalists, writing a book on Arctic zoology, would not know a 'moose' when he saw one is almost inconceivable, yet this appears to have been the case, for the caption to the illustration reads: 'the head of the Elk . . . before it was arrived at full age'.[3]

Later in the volume, Pennant seems to compound his error by reproducing George Stubbs's famous painting *The Duke of Richmond's First Bull Moose*, drawn in 1770, from a living specimen sent as a gift by the governor general of Canada Guy Carlton to the Duke of Richmond[4] (see Figure 6.2).

The caption to the engraving reads: 'A full-grown male Elk or Moose, with the velvet, or young horns; and a full-grown pair on the ground. From a painting by Mr. Stubbs, communicated to me by the late Dr. Hunter.'[5] Although one might easily conclude that Pennant was simply hedging his bet by deliberately avoiding identifying the animal as either an 'Elk or Moose', his written entry on the animal

Figure 6.2 Engraving of George Stubb's *The Duke of Richmond's First Bull Moose* in Thomas Pennant's *Arctic Zoology* (1784), courtesy of the Thomas Fisher Rare Book Library, University of Toronto.

makes it clear that he actually believed that 'the Elk and the Moose are the same species'.[6] Here it might seem that we are dealing with an extraordinary failure of identification, as the name of one of the most iconic animals of North America seems to have somehow gotten mixed up with another when it was introduced into the pages of a British natural history text. However, such a conclusion would be wrong, for although Pennant's judgement is not likely to win many converts these days, if there is an error here, it is not his, but ours, because the 'elk' and the 'moose' are, indeed, the same animal. Long before Europeans had ever heard of a 'moose', the same animal, called an 'elk' by Europeans, had long inhabited the northern temperate regions of Eurasia from Scandinavia to Siberia and China. The European elk (i.e. the 'moose') disappeared from Britain around 1500 BC, but a small population of the animal continued to inhabit Scandinavia during the eighteenth century. The Anglo-Saxon word 'Elk' comes from the Middle High German 'Elch', and the Latin scientific name of the 'moose' is *Alces alces* (i.e. 'Elk elk'), so I guess we should admit that Pennant really did know an 'elk' when he saw one. Still, this is not to say that during the 1780s he was not himself acting a bit like a moose, stubbornly and aggressively holding his ground as a loner by insisting that this species should be called an 'elk' when almost everyone else, for reasons that I will go into in greater depth, had adopted an anglicized version of its Indigenous Algonquian name.

Given the scarcity of 'elk' still in existence in Europe, few of the early New England settlers would have known what an 'elk' actually looked like, beyond its referring to a large deer. Even fewer would have been able to consult Edward Topsell's *History of Four-Footed Beasts* (1607), so they did what European settlers often did when they encountered an animal that was unfamiliar to them: they coined the Algonquian and Cree name for the animal, '*mos*' or '*mooswa*', meaning 'twig eater' (see Figure 6.3). The name stuck, not only because during the eighteenth century there were substantially more 'moose' in North America than 'elk' in Europe, but also because no other animal captured so powerfully the symbolic dimensions of the vast North American wilderness and the difference between this nature and the natures found in Europe. One effect of European settlers' tendency to borrow Indigenous names for animals that were strikingly different from those that they knew in Europe is that the continuing traces of North American Indigenous languages were registered and preserved not in the animals and plants that settlers recognized, but in those that they did not. Thus,

Figure 6.3 From Edward Topsell's *History of Four-Footed Beasts* (1607), courtesy of the Thomas Fisher Rare Book Library, University of Toronto.

the name 'caribou' was taken from the French pronunciation of the Mi'kmaq word *qaripu* (itself an earlier form of *qalipu*), which captured the fact that the animal uses its antlers to clear snow to obtain food. The 'raccoon' derives from the Virginian Algonquian *aroughcun*, meaning 'the animal who scratches with its hands'. The 'opossum' also came from Virginia Algonquian *opassom*, meaning 'white dog'; while the 'skunk', coined from the Western Abenaki *segôgw* and Unami Delaware *šká:kw*, links 'urine' with 'fox', perhaps to say 'stinking fox'. Other animals whose names recall a time before conquest and settlement when all North American animals had Indigenous names are the 'chipmunk', 'muskrat', 'woodchuck', and 'wapiti'.

Animal names reflect human beings' understanding of their relationship to animals. Pennant's unwillingness to accept the idea that a European 'elk' had been renamed as a 'moose', though ostensibly based on scientific principles, was both political and personal. When he completed his work on the four-volume *British Zoology* (1766–7), Pennant had planned to write an even more ambitious 'sketch of the Zoology of *North America*'.[7] European naturalists possessed natures and asserted their authority by renaming them, so the idea of a British naturalist writing the natural history of North America was a grand imperial gesture. These plans were disrupted, however, by the outbreak of the American Revolution in 1775, its first consequence being that Pennant lost the connections that he had assiduously cultivated with field correspondents in America. In 1783, there followed 'that fatal and humiliating hour' when he had to admit that he could no longer consider himself as the 'humble Zoologist' of a nation that could 'boast of ruling over half of the New World'.[8] The project had to be revised, and he recast it as an arctic rather than a North American zoology. Having already lost half of the territory that he had planned originally to survey as an imperial naturalist, Pennant was in no mood to lose an animal, especially one of the size and stature of the European 'elk', to the Americans. In what might be considered a bold shot across the bow, Pennant provided an illustration of a young bull 'elk' on the title page of the first volume of the *Arctic Zoology*. If so, he must have lost his nerve, for he placed the caption for the illustration, identifying it as an 'elk', in the List of Plates. Apparently Pennant did not want his 'elk' to become his albatross.

At the same time as early New England settlers were adopting the Algonquian name for the European elk, they were also encountering another large antlered deer (*Cervus elaphus canadensis*), which, unlike the solitary 'moose', moved in large herds. Indigenous peoples called it by different names: 'wampoose' in Algonquian, 'wawaskeesh' in Athapaskan, 'waskasiw' in Plains Cree and 'waapiti' in Shawnee and Cree. Initially, New Englanders also called this deer a 'moose', distinguishing between these two large deer by their colour. In the 1721 *Philosophical Transactions,* Paul Dudley writes: 'There are two sorts of *moose,* the common light *grey moose* and the large or *black moose*; The former the Indians call *Wampoose;* they are more like the ordinary deer, spring like them and herd sometimes to the number of 30 together'.[9] Summarizing the situation, one could say that among settlers in the American colonies prior to the 1730s, there were two species of 'moose' but no 'elk'.[10] With a better knowledge of the substantial physical and behavioural differences between these two deer, American settlers eventually began to call the 'grey moose' an 'elk'. By a strange historical irony, there was a brief moment when the confusion might have been sorted out, but they gave the name 'elk' to the wrong deer, that is to the 'grey' rather than the 'black' 'moose', so we have been living with the consequences of this translation mistake ever since.

The British naturalist Mark Catesby, who wrote the first published natural history of the flora and fauna of North America, clearly recognized the problem and stressed that these light coloured herding deer were being 'improperly called Elks'. He further noted their similarity with the British 'stag' or 'red deer' (*Cervus elaphus*), writing that the 'Stag of America', most nearly 'resembles the European Red Deer in colour, shape and form of the horns, though it is a much larger animal'.[11] Thomas Jefferson, also a respected naturalist, offered a different solution to this naming problem, suggesting that Americans should treat both the 'moose' and the North American elk as two different kinds of elk, with the 'moose' being called a 'palmated elk' and the North American elk, a 'round horned elk'.[12] If Jefferson had been successful, the United States would have lost its 'moose' and gained two kinds of 'elk'. He would have also erased the linguistic connection between these animals, Indigenous peoples and the pre-conquest wilderness of America. As it turned out, both Catesby's and Jefferson's suggestions fell upon deaf ears. Americans, by this time, were pretty firmly convinced, at least in their own minds, that they knew the difference between an 'elk' and a 'moose', and in a nation that wanted linguistic as much as political independence from colonial authority, they had no intention of losing either their 'elk' to a British 'stag' or 'red deer' or their 'moose' to a European 'elk', no matter what any naturalist, British or otherwise, might say.

The American Revolution separated the United States not only from Britain but also from Canada, which would continue as a British colony continually shifting between a political and cultural allegiance to Britain and a growing desire for independence. Attitudes towards the American 'elk' (*Cervus elaphus canadensis*) were not immune to these shifts. Throughout much of the eighteenth and nineteenth centuries, particularly among fur traders, the animal was known as a 'red deer', though occasionally also as a 'stag', while Indigenous people referred to it as a 'waskasiw' or a 'wawaskeesh'.[13] In Britain, the word 'stag' was traditionally used to refer to a male deer, and it was seen as the pre-eminent British game animal, integrally associated with the aristocracy and with hunting culture. Although by the middle of the eighteenth century, few 'red deer' remained in the wild in either England or Scotland, they continued to be raised on crown lands and parks. Perhaps not surprisingly, this is the name that Pennant opted for in *Arctic Zoology*. By using the name 'red deer' in referring to the American elk, fur traders affirmed the connection between Canada and Britain, while distancing themselves from its aristocratic values.

Many of the Indigenous names for settlements, meeting places, rivers and lakes in Canada derive from the animals that were once found there. The translation or renaming of Indigenous animals thus led to a substantial renaming of many places in Canada that originally had Indigenous names. These places often continue to exist in a translated form, for instance, as Sturgeon River, Moose Lake, Pine River or Gull Lake, and as such, they provide a kind of geographical mapping of the original distribution of plants and animals across Indigenous territories. These translated toponyms connect the present to the past, even if, in many cases, they are all that remain of the natures that they refer to. Near Fort Macleod, Alberta, is the World Heritage Site called Head-Smashed-In, which translates the Blackfoot *Estipah-skikikini-kots*. It marks the place where for centuries the Blackfoot people hunted bison by herding and driving them over a cliff to their deaths. The city of Red Deer, Alberta, which was first incorporated as a town in 1901, is a testimony to the ways in which national politics found expression in how colonial natures were translated. Situated on the banks of the Red Deer River, where for centuries the Plains Cree, Blackfoot and Stony peoples used to meet, the city can be said to have been named after an animal translation that failed to be adopted. Since Canadians nowadays all have come to accept the American naming of the 'elk' – the establishment in 1958 of the famous 'Elk Island National Park' only 200 kilometres away from Red Deer being a good indication of that change – it is doubtful that many of the 100,000 people who now live in Red Deer would guess that the city is named after the 'elk' that still inhabit the surrounding foothills. Few too would guess that Waskasoo Creek, which flows into the Red Deer River in the city, also refers in Cree to the same animal, and that this creek is all that remains of the great river that the Cree once called *Waskasoo Seepee*, that is, the Red Deer River. What should be stressed is that colonial translation both reveals and conceals competing histories of how different peoples and cultures have understood and related to the natures around them, and these names and translations are a part of that history.

Given the confusion that arose from having two different animals with the same name – 'elk' – nineteenth-century naturalists attempted to resolve matters by adopting the American naturalist Benjamin Smith Barton's suggestion in 1806 that the Shawnee and Cree nation name 'wapiti', meaning 'white rump', be used to refer to the North American elk.[14] As John Richardson notes in his 1829 entry on the 'Wapiti', the 'trivial name of "wapiti" has been only recently adopted in scientific works, but is preferable to the appellations either of elk, grey-moose, or red-deer, which have already been the means of confounding it with other species'.[15] One effect of the scientific turn to 'wapiti' is that, at least in scientific circles, the connection between these two animals and North American Indigenous cultures is now explicit.

Any consideration of the role that translation played in colonial natural history needs to focus on not just the transformations in our relationship to animals produced by linguistic translation, but also the changes resulting from the managed transportation, intentionally and otherwise, of plants and animals from one part of the globe to another: translation in the older sense of a movement between places. One of the distinctive features of colonial natures was that they moved across the globe on a scale never seen before. Plants, animals and other kinds of biota were as active in global migration and resettlement as people, with the result that colonialism was shaped by new encounters between people, plants and animals, and the actual biological distribution of species across the globe was transformed. This was a translation not only in the languages by which global natures were grasped, but also in the nature of environments themselves, as settler cultures extended the privilege of travel and settlement to plants and animals as much as to people. In the late nineteenth century, North American elk and moose became part of this global migration. It started in the 1860s, with the resurgence of game hunting among aristocrats and the wealthy in Britain, America, Canada and South Africa. British stags, which had largely been exterminated in Scotland during the eighteenth century, were reintroduced at this time, and tenant farmers and blackface sheep were cleared from the land in order to make this possible. In an effort to promote trophy deer hunting in New Zealand, British stags were then exported to the Fiordlands, where they would later be joined by American elk and moose at the beginning of the twentieth century. New Zealand thus became the only place on Earth where both red deer and American elk live together in the wild. Without any natural enemies, populations of red deer and elk rapidly increased, so the New Zealand government decided in the 1930s to begin culling them, leaving a small number to support big game hunting. In the 1970s, these animals would form the basis of a new commercial deer farming industry in New Zealand. Although the elk were larger in size and had faster growth rates, they proved difficult to raise domestically, so farmers cross-bred female red deer or 'hinds' with male elk to produce a new hybridized breed of deer suitable for commercial farming. To improve this new breed additional wild elk were imported from Banff National Park, Canada. Lacking a name for this new hybrid stock, yet nevertheless wanting to avoid confusing the cross-bred deer with their wild counterparts – the 'elk' and the 'red deer' – New Zealand farmers decided to call this new breed of deer 'wapiti'. Whether their goal was to use a North American Indigenous name to make clear that these animals were not 'native' to New Zealand or whether they were resurrecting nineteenth-century colonial stereotypes concerning the hybridity of Indigenous peoples, whatever their goal it has resulted in the word 'wapiti' now referring to two different animals in the United States and New Zealand and expressing very different attitudes towards them.

I have devoted time to discussing the complex translational history that underpins the naming of the 'moose' and 'elk' in order to suggest the degree to which colonial natural history can be understood as a translational activity. If at times this discussion has seemed like a sequel to the movie *Lost in Translation*, it is because these natures were undergoing changes wrought by translation: settlers and indigenes alike encountered worlds in which strange things seemed somehow familiar and familiar things took on an uncanny strangeness because the relationship between things and their names had become uncertain, because both words and things were no longer tied to places, but were instead moving. The colonial experience of nature was not simply a feeling of being *between places*: of settlers who left their homelands to live in places that were foreign and strange, or of Indigenous peoples who stayed in place and witnessed the appearance of new natures that supplanted their traditional environments. It was also an experience of inhabiting *in-between places*, that is, of moving through places where plants and animals and the names that had once been used to talk about them were being mixed together in new and uncanny ways. Europeans discovered that they were not the only beings that could move: the natures around them were also doing so, as were the names that were being attached to these natures, often by metropolitan scientists who had never set foot upon the lands or experienced the living natures that they claimed the sovereign and scientific authority to name.

European colonial societies were at their core translational cultures because they recognized that tremendous power and profit came from the capacity to control the movement not only of plants and animals across the globe, but of the names associated with them. That is why natural history emerged as the première science of the period through its commitment both to naming and renaming plants and animals everywhere and to developing new technologies and practices aimed at redistributing them across the globe. If translation is understood as a process that transforms something in order to transfer it across the distance separating languages, cultures or peoples, colonial translation not only worked with different species of plants and animals on a global scale, but also crucially focused on the naming and renaming of global species, the principles and restrictions governing their naming, and the authority underpinning and authorizing the global renaming of species. Remaking the diversity of global environments so that they reflected European colonial values and needs was never a neutral process. Colonial naturalists often portrayed their descriptions, classifications, and scientific names as elucidating an already-established order of nature that had been brought into confusion by the diversity or Babel of human languages and by the ignorance of Indigenous peoples. That is why naturalists only recognized a species as being a species if it had been properly described and named by an appropriate authority in a recognized publication; prior to that moment it was a 'non-descript'. Oral knowledge and oral languages were thus excluded, even if scientists depended upon them in their written descriptions.

In its emphasis upon the importance of inscription, colonial natural history can be likened to the mapping or marking of territory, possessing natures through the process of naming or describing them – possession *in* and *through* translation. Colonial naming took place within contexts of power, negotiation and conflict because it operated in a world in which plants and animals had already been named. To give a plant or an animal a new name was thus to rename it and, by so doing, to replace it in some way. It was also to understand that nature in a new way. Although the 'mooswa', the anglicized 'moose', and the European elk can be treated as being the same animal within the globalizing taxonomies of natural history, they were also different insofar as each belonged to a different language, place and culture, and their names expressed different symbolic and emotional connections with these animals. Scientific naming was thus inherently a cross-cultural activity that redefined pre-existing relationships between human beings and the non-human world, establishing the preconditions of a global understanding of nature by replacing local natures embedded within a diversity of cultures with a single nature that was independent of time, place and history. As centuries of ecological destruction and the devastation of Indigenous cultures have sadly made clear, however, 'one law for the lion and the ox is oppression'.[16]

*　*　*

Susan Bassnett observes that 'translation . . . is a primary method of imposing meaning while concealing the power relations that lie behind the production of that meaning'. Using censorship as an example, she notes that 'it is easy to see how translation can impose censorship while simultaneously purporting to be a free and open rendering of the source text. By comparing the translated version with the original, the evidence of such censorship is easy to see where written texts are concerned.'[17] Developing in close connection with governmental colonial administrations and the navy, British natural history was an ideal medium for controlling who had the authority to speak for nature, how the natural world would be represented and how information about global natures would be disseminated. Under the banner of Enlightenment, naturalists promoted the idea that there was only one nature, that this nature was subject to universally recognized laws, and that its scientific understanding was first and foremost a textual activity, aimed at producing published materials that were accessible to educated individuals and which could be scrutinized, verified and amended. Its revolutionary power and its global reach were derived from its being a science whose observations appeared in books, with scientific names all being in Latin. These procedures explicitly promoted European polite culture and interests, while making Indigenous natural knowledge, which was primarily local and oral, trivial and insignificant, a kind of noise that had to be removed from natural history texts. An enormous silence thus informs these books, for they actively posit the view that Indigenous peoples do not have the right to speak about the natures around them and what they have to say is of little importance to this polite science. If Indigenous lands were a *terra nullias*, the Indigenous understanding of them was little better. Colonial naturalists saw themselves as being engaged in translating oral knowledges and histories into a new form of knowledge that was understood as being distinctly European, something that was modern, scientific, highly technical, addressed to an educated elite and disseminated in books. Evidence of the role that Indigenous people played in the production of these texts was progressively removed. Unlike most translations, however, where one can compare texts to see what has been lost, forgotten or erased in translation, the knowledge that these texts drew upon was difficult to access without consulting Indigenous peoples. In his well-known 1968 Boyer lectures *After the Dreaming*, W. E. H. Stanner first suggested that the history of Australia had been shaped by a powerful mode of forgetting, 'something like a cult of forgetfulness practised on a national scale', in its apparent incapacity to talk about the place of Aboriginal people within the history of the country. He argued that 'the other side of a story' needed to be told, 'over which the great Australian silence reigns; the story of the things we were unconsciously resolved not to discuss with them or treat with them about; the story, in short, of the unacknowledged relations between two racial groups within a single field of life'.[18] Colonial natural history books played a major role in promoting this 'great silence'. To properly write, that is, to rewrite the history of colonial natural history, these books need to be set in relation to the other story of colonial natural history that has yet to be properly told.

As I indicated earlier, colonists and professional naturalists rarely drew upon Indigenous names for a species of plant or animal except in those cases where it seemed to be endemic and exhibited little in common with a European species with which they were familiar. When Sir Joseph Banks, who joined Captain Cook on the First Voyage, came upon what looked like a gigantic jumping mouse sporting a thick long tail and a pouch for its young, he acknowledged that he could not fit the animal into any previously known scientific category, so he recorded the name that the Guugu Yimithirr people of Queensland had given it (*Gangurru*) as 'Kangooroo'. The Darug people of the Sydney region were the source of the name 'koala' which comes from the dharug word 'koolah', meaning 'no water or no drink'. They also provided the convict settlement with additional Indigenous names that were taken up by settlers and naturalists, such as 'dingo', 'wallaby' and 'wombat'. In the case of the koala, the settlers apparently were unsatisfied with just borrowing the Indigenous name for the animal, seeking to make this marsupial a little more familiar by calling it a 'koala bear' or a 'Native' or 'Australian bear'.

Robert Southey, in his *Botany Bay Eclogue* 'Elinor', imagines that in Australia, instead of listening to the pastoral sounds of 'lowing herds' and 'the music of the bleating flocks', all that can be heard is 'the Kangaroo's sad note – Deep'ning in distance'.[19] Unaware that the animal communicates by thumping its hind legs, the poet was wrong to assume, in this case, that its name is onomatopoeic and that kangaroos are 'rueful' (even if the early experience of the colonists was), but he was not wrong to believe, as would a poet, that the sound of Australian Indigenous animal names might do more than simply represent the appearance of an animal and that they might also somehow communicate the sounds and feelings of a place. Frequently, Australian Indigenous names, especially bird names, such as the 'budgerigar', 'currawong' and 'kookaburra', do seek to capture how a creature sounds rather than how it looks. Indigenous naming captures a distinctive aspect of the soundscape of Indigenous Australia, and it also often gives one access to how Indigenous peoples heard these songs. Transforming a 'budgerigar' into a 'budgie' may convey domestic affection, but it also truncates the almost ceaseless banter, the gregarious noisiness, of these very social birds when they are together. One of the most distinctive sounds of the Australian bush is the call of the Eastern Whipbird or Whipcoach bird (*Psophodes olivaceus*). Where the common English name seeks to describe the whip crack sound of the bird's call, the name given to it by the Wonnarua people – '*Djou*' – focuses on capturing its sound. Given how striking the bird's call is, it is worth noting that its scientific name is silent about this distinctive aspect of the bird, instead focusing on its 'olive' colour. This oversight is easily explained. The English ornithologist John Latham, who in 1801 gave the bird its name, had never been to Australia and had never heard its call. Working in silence, in another part of the world, he based his scientific descriptions and the names that he gave to Australian birds on dead birds that he had seen in collections or on illustrations taken of them. For Latham, the 'Djou' was unremarkably a 'White-Cheeked crow' (*Corvus olivaceus*).[20] In contrast, the Indigenous naming of plants and animals reflected the Indigenous understanding both of what made these birds distinctive and emerged in situ, in landscapes that were not simply seen, but also filled with sounds. In seeking to create a nature that could be appreciated anywhere, colonial natural history reduced nature to what still could be seen when plants and animals were removed from their unique social and physical environments.

Recent work on eighteenth-century ideas about the relationship between sounds and civility suggests that one reason for the censorship of Indigenous sounds in colonial natural history texts has to do with anxieties about the manner in which Indigenous voices and natures conflicted with European notions of polite civility.[21] Also this turning away from an obvious immediate source for the names of Indigenous species in favour of translating or renaming them in English was a way of possessing or colonizing a foreign nature inhabited by foreign peoples by making it seem less silent and forbidding and more familiar. The wholesale importation of domestic animals and food crops certainly played an important role in making Australia look more English, and later in the century Australian settlers would expand on these efforts by introducing into Australia familiar wild British animals, such as rabbits, but particularly birds, like starlings, house sparrows, skylarks, European blackbirds, goldfinches and Eurasian tree sparrows.[22] When the animals could not actually be moved to make Australia physically more like England, naming a species after a well-known English one could make it sound that way, providing a symbolic means of achieving the same goal. In England and France, for instance, the 'redbreast' (*Erithacus rubecula*) is such a beloved bird that both countries added the diminutive of 'Robert' to 'redbreast' and then eventually often referred to the 'robin redbreast' only by its pet name. Wordsworth calls it 'the bird whom Man loves best, / The pious bird with the scarlet breast, / Our little English Robin'.[23] Although there is only *one* 'robin' in England, there are at least *two* in the Americas. In North America, there is the well-known American robin. In Jamaica a much-loved little, bright green-headed bird with a ruby throat, the Jamaican tody, is frequently also called a 'robin redbreast' when it is not being referred to as the 'rasta bird'. Apparently, sometime after the 1930s, the national love for 'robin' was replaced with a new love for Ras Tafar. If the American robin, as a thrush, has little in common with its English counterpart beyond sharing with it a red breast, this little bird has even less in common. The settlers of Australia and New Zealand apparently also loved the 'robin redbreast', for the region now boasts forty-four species of 'Australian robins' or *Petroicidae*. Some of these birds have brightly coloured breasts – rose, pink, orange and yellow – but most do not, and they too are only distantly related to the European robin. The fact that the *name* of a single bird that lives in England and Europe has succeeded in being replicated across the globe suggests the ways in which renaming colonial natures was a way of claiming affective connections with them.

If this process made colonial natures a little more English, thus strengthening affective ties linking colonists with a British homeland, its effect upon Indigenous people was the opposite, because it separated them from the Indigenous names by which their natures had been previously known and dreamed. Scientific and English common plant and animal names alienated Aboriginal people from their land, their history and their nature, which no longer spoke to them as it once did. Replacing the Indigenous name *gadi* with the scientific name *Xanthorrhoea australis* may not seem to change much in how one might relate to the grasstree or grass gum tree. If one knows, however, that the Gadigal clan of the Sydney region derive their name from the *gadi*, the erasure of the name erases the knowledge of their historical connection to this plant.

I hope that what I have said about colonial natures stands in sharp contrast to the nostalgia that dominates most accounts of the relationship between nature and place during the eighteenth and nineteenth centuries. There can be little question that, beginning with the romantics, nature was increasingly seen as providing an alternative to modern society. To experience nature was supposed to allow one to recover feelings of wholeness, connectedness and continuity, rather than the many dislocating emotions occasioned by the speed and disruptions of modern life. If, to a degree, the experience of nature in England functioned this way, this was not how most colonists or Indigenous people experienced colonial natures. Instead of being places that spoke of the unchanging endurance of nature, in which all species were understood as having been designed to occupy the places in which they were found, colonial natures were undergoing often rapid transformations. As a result, these natures mirrored the inequities, divisions and conflicts of the societies in which they were found, with native species engaged in their own life-and-death struggles with powerful biotic newcomers coming from elsewhere. Long before the historical dimensions of their own natures were recognized by Europeans, they were being dramatically displayed in the changing landscapes of the colonial world.

My goal here is not to engage in a simplistic critique of the colonial translation of natures. Instead, I would argue that when we are dealing with colonial environments, we are not so much dealing with natures, but natures in translation. As such, it is incumbent upon us to recognize that where one nature now stands, another nature once stood. Since the history of colonialism is the story of the translation and erasure of precolonial natures, however, we are talking about translations whose originals were fractured by this very process. If we are to recover these natures, and to make our current environments a home for everyone, we need to enter into a much deeper dialogue with Indigenous peoples. We also need to see what has been lost in what remains, seeing the history of these landscapes and natures and seeking to find the voices and relationships that were written into them and almost translated out of existence. If we are to recover the history of the struggles that are imbedded in these texts and landscapes, and if we are to recover a more polyvocal understanding of the richness and diversity of the natural world, seeking more collaborative ways of understanding place, we must recognize that present-day natures continue to speak to us as the textualized products of colonial history. They censor how we see, think about, relate to and care for the natures around us. In recognizing that colonial natures, as physical environments and as discursive constructs, are translations that have replaced their originals, we need to find more ways to read them against the grain, seeking to discover what has been lost in translation. A better knowledge of Indigenous languages and more Indigenous scholars of colonial history would be an important start.

In addressing the environmental and cultural legacies of colonialism, therefore, postcolonial and Indigenous criticisms should not seek to do away with the idea of historical natures, but instead should respond to them as complex and diverse forms of translation. In 'Learning Bundjalung on Tharawal', Evelyn Araluen captures the challenge and uncertainty that faces an Indigenous poet as she seeks to find her voice 'in this new and ancient place'. 'Trying to sing like hill and saltwater' requires that she unlearn the language of empire and recover

> old words from an old country that I have never walked on:
> *bundjalung jagum ngai, nganduwal nyuyaya,*
and god, I don't even know
> if I'm saying it right.[24]

If we are to understand these natures in all their historical complexity; if we are to better understand the places that Indigenous people now share with settler cultures; if we are to understand how Indigenous peoples have felt and continue to feel about these places; and if we are to better grasp the complex interrelations of plants, animals and different peoples, we need to think much more creatively and critically about the relationship between translation and the natural world.

* * *

One of the most powerful articulations of contemporary Canadian Indigenous experience is Bill Reid's *The Spirit of Haida Gwaii, the Black Canoe*, which is located in the pool in the courtyard of the Canadian Embassy in Washington, D.C. A second casting of the sculpture in green patina, the Jade Canoe, is located in the Vancouver Airport International Terminal, while the original plaster prototype of the sculpture is on display in the Grand Hall of the Canadian Museum of Civilization in Ottawa. More than nineteen feet long, eleven feet wide and twelve feet high, the sculpture presents an extraordinary image of a people travelling through time and history, going somewhere, yet also staying in place. Reid's decision to represent the Haida nation as a collectivity situated in a canoe points to their traditional status as a coastal nation, but it also asks us to think about indigeneity, colonialism and modernity in a different way, recognizing that it was not just settler nations that set out in boats to rebuild their cultures in new parts of the globe. Indigenous nations were also set adrift and required to set a new course and to remake themselves in the face of the changes wrought by colonial settlement. Mobility and change were not the sole privilege of the newcomers but affected everyone in the contact zones. In Richard Wagamese's novel *Indian Horse*, we learn that the family of the protagonist Saul Indian Horse was given a new name when his great grandfather, the shaman Shabogeesick (Slanting Sky), after listening to the land, went on a long journey and returned home with a horse, a creature that the Anishinaabe had never seen before. Seeing into the future, Shabogeesick recognized that the traditional ways of his people would no longer be sufficient and that his people would need to 'learn to ride each of these horses of change'.[25] Reid's Black Canoe also conveys an image of a people on the move, even as they remain deeply linked to place. What makes the sculpture so emblematic of North American Indigenous cultures and the concerns that have shaped this chapter is that Reid refused to understand the Haida Spirit as being solely composed of human beings. Instead, he recognized that in order to move forward, the Haida also needed the *sghaana* or myth creatures that – in words, images and stories – had shaped and guided the Haida from the beginning. 'We are all in the same boat', remarked Reid in his published meditation on the sculpture.[26] The search for another home could not be accomplished without the spirit animals whose stories gave meaning and coherence to their culture. They do the paddling.

Thirteen travellers, some human, some half-human and some animal, but all mythically translated in some way, are crowded onto the boat, looking 'superficially more or less what they always were, symbols of another time when the Haidas, all ten thousand of them, knew they were the greatest of all nations'.[27] At the front sits Bear, *Xuuaji*, his back to the future, his 'eyes firmly and forever fixed on the past', trying to believe that 'things are still as they were'. Bear Mother, who is human, stares out upon an indefinite future as she cares for her twin bear cubs. The legendary trickster and shape-shifter, the Raven or *Xuuya*, is located at the back of the boat, holding the steering oar, while his mother, Mouse Woman or *Kugaan Jaad*, who brings prosperity to those who see her, hides beneath his tail. Other spirit creatures join in paddling towards their future, among these the half-human Dogfish Woman, Qaaxhadajaat; the beaver, *Tsing*; the frog, *Hlkyan qquustan*; the wolf, *Guuji*; and the Eagle, *Guudaay*. Reid stressed that even though a culture is remembered for its 'warriors, artists, heroes and heroines', it needs survivors if it is to continue, so he included in the boat a figure drawn from Carl Sandburg's poem 'Old Timers' that was also a self-portrait: the 'Ancient Reluctant Conscript' who embodies the disenfranchised and displaced peoples in history. His primary task is to survive, to be there to start the process of rebuilding when the culture collapses through the excesses of its rulers. At the centre of the canoe stands the tall figure of the shaman, holding a speaker's staff. He is a leader, but where he is directing the boat to go is not clear. As Reid commented, he 'may or may not be the Spirit of Haida Gwaii leading us . . . to a sheltered beach beyond the rim of the world, as he seems to be, or is he lost in his own dreamings? The boat goes on, forever anchored in the same place.'[28]

Reid's sculpture is essentially a mythic narrative that insists that the spirit of a people cannot survive and cannot go anywhere if it does not preserve its deep, imaginative relationships with non-human beings, whether they live in nature or in dreams. The sculpture looks both to the past and to the future, and in so doing it asks its viewers to think not only of the past, but of the continuing need for imaginative relationships with the natural world (and with other cultures) if human beings are to have a future worth living. The direction that this boat is taking and where it will end up, however, is uncertain, because that future is still in the process of being dreamed.

Notes

1. Samuel Taylor Coleridge, 'The Eolian Harp', in *The Collected Works of Samuel Taylor Coleridge, Volume 16: Poetical Works I, Poems (Reading Text)*, ed. J. C. C. Mays (Princeton: Princeton University Press, 2001), 16, pt 1:1, lines 24–5.
2. George Shaw, *The Naturalist's Miscellany; or Coloured Figures of Natural Objects Drawn and Described Immediately from Nature* (London: Nodder, 1789–1813), 10:228.
3. Thomas Pennant, *Arctic Zoology*, 2 vols (London: Henry Hughs, 1784–5), 1:6. The description of the plate is provided in the List of Plates.
4. For a valuable discussion of the painting and its historical context, see Lisa Vargo, 'The Romantic Prospects of the Duke of Richmond's Moose', *European Romantic Review* 24, no. 3 (2013): 297–305.
5. Pennant, *Arctic Zoology*, 1:7.
6. Pennant, *Arctic Zoology*, 1:18.
7. Pennant, *Arctic Zoology*, 1:3.
8. Pennant, *Arctic Zoology*, 1:3–4.
9. Paul Dudley, 'A Description of the Moose-Deer in America', *Philosophical Transactions* 31 (1721–2): 165.
10. The naming of the American elk as a 'grey moose' can still be seen in Oliver Goldsmith's *An History of the Earth, and Animated Nature* (1774), one of the most popular natural history books of the late eighteenth century.

11   Mark Catesby, *The Natural History of Carolina, Florida, and the Bahama Islands: Containing the Figures of Birds, Beasts, Fishes, Serpents, Insects, and Plants*, 2 vols (London: Benjamin White, 1771), 1: xxviii. Currently there is debate over whether the American elk (*Cervus elaphus canadensis*) is a separate species or only a subspecies of the red deer or stag (*Cervus elaphus*).
12   Thomas Jefferson, *Notes on the State of Virginia* (London: Stockdale, 1787), 82, 86.
13   In the 1772 manuscript that the Hudson's Bay chief factor Andrew Graham and Thomas Hutchins included with the specimens that they sent to the Royal Society, they translated the 'Was, ka, seu' as 'Red Deer or Stag' and noted that 'it is not so large as the Elk, or moose'. 'Thomas Hutchins' Manuscript Accompanying Bird and Mammal Specimens Submitted to England from York Factory, 28 August, 1772', ed. C. Stuart Houston. Supplementary Document #2 to: Stuart Houston, Tim Ball and Mary Houston (eds), *Eighteenth-Century Naturalists of Hudson Bay* (Montreal: McGill-Queen's University Press, 2003), http://www.mqup.mcgill.ca/books/eighteenth-century/hutchins.
14   Benjamin Barton, 'An Account of the Cervus Wapiti or Southern Elk of North America', *Philadelphia Medical and Physiology Journal* 3, no. 1 (March 1806), 36–55.
15   John Richardson, *Fauna Boreali-Americana; or the Zoology of the Northern Parts of British America*, 4 vols (London: John Murray, 1829-37), 1:252.
16   William Blake, 'The Marriage of Heaven and Hell', in *The Complete Poetry and Prose of William Blake*, ed. David V. Erdman (New York: Random House, 1988), plate 24.
17   Susan Bassnett, 'The Translation Turn in Cultural Studies', in *Constructing Culture: Essays on Literary Translation* (Clevedon: Multilingual Matters, 1998), 136.
18   W. E. H. Stanner, *The 1968 Boyer Lectures: After the Dreaming* (Sydney: Australian Broadcasting Commission, 1974), 24–5.
19   Robert Southey, 'Elinor', *Southey's Poetical Works* (London: Longman, Brown, Green and Longmans, 1845), 103.
20   John Latham, *Supplementum indicis ornithologici sive systematis ornithologia* (London: Leigh & Sotheby, 1801), xxvi.
21   See Peter Denney, Bruce Buchan, David Ellison and Karen Crawley (eds), *Sound, Space and Civility in the British World, 1700-1850* (London: Routledge, 2019).
22   See Thomas R. Dunlap, *Nature and the English Diaspora* (Cambridge: Cambridge University Press, 1999).
23   William Wordsworth, 'The Redbreast Chasing the Butterfly', in *The Poetical Works of William Wordsworth*, ed. Ernest de Selincourt, 5 vols (Oxford: Clarendon, 1952), 2:149–50.
24   Evelyn Araluen, 'Learning Bundjalung on Tharawal', *Overland*, 223 (Winter 2016), https://overland.org.au/previous-issues/issue-223/nakata-brophy-prize-evelyn-araluen/
25   Richard Wagamese, *Indian Horse* (Madeira Park: Douglas and McIntyre, 2012), 7.

26 Bill Reid, 'The Spirit of Haida Gwaii', in *Solitary Raven: The Selected Writings of Bill Reid*, ed. Robert Bringhurst (Vancouver: Douglas & McIntyre, 2000), 230.
27 Reid, 'Spirit of Haida Gwaii', 228.
28 Reid, 'Spirit of Haida Gwaii'.

Bibliography

Araluen, Evelyn. 'Learning Bundjalung on Tharawal'. *Overland* 223 (2016). https://overland.org.au/previous-issues/issue-223/nakata-brophy-prize-evelyn-araluen/

Barton, Benjamin. 'An Account of the Cervus Wapiti or Southern Elk of North America'. *Philadelphia Medical and Physiology Journal* 3, no. 1 (1806): 36–55.

Bassnett, Susan. 'The Translation Turn in Cultural Studies'. In *Constructing Culture: Essays on Literary Translation*, edited by Susan Bassnett and André Lefevere, 123–40. Clevedon: Multilingual Matters, 1998.

Blake, William. *The Complete Poetry and Prose of William Blake*. Edited by David V. Erdman. New York: Random House, 1988.

Catesby, Mark. *The Natural History of Carolina, Florida, and the Bahama Islands: Containing the Figures of Birds, Beasts, Fishes, Serpents, Insects, and Plants*. 2 vols. London: Benjamin White, 1771.

Coleridge, Samuel Taylor. *Collected Works of Samuel Taylor Coleridge, Volume 16: Poetical Works I, Poems (Reading Text)*. Edited by J. C. C. Mays. Princeton: Princeton University Press, 2001.

Denney, Peter, Bruce Buchan, David Ellison and Karen Crawley, eds. *Sound, Space and Civility in the British World, 1700–1850*. London: Routledge, 2019.

Dudley, Paul. 'A Description of the Moose-Deer in America'. *Philosophical Transactions* 31 (1721–22): 165–8.

Dunlap, Thomas R. *Nature and the English Diaspora*. Cambridge: Cambridge University Press, 1999.

Houston, Stuart, Tim Ball and Mary Houston, eds. *Eighteenth-Century Naturalists of Hudson Bay*. Montreal: McGill-Queen's University Press, 2003.

Jefferson, Thomas. *Notes on the State of Virginia*. London: Stockdale, 1787.

Latham, John. *Supplementum Indicis Ornithologici Sive Systematis Ornithologia*. London: Leigh & Sotheby, 1801.

Pennant, Thomas. *Arctic Zoology*. 2 vols. London: Henry Hughs, 1784–85.

Reid, Bill. 'The Spirit of Haida Gwaii'. In *Solitary Raven: The Selected Writings of Bill Reid*, edited by Robert Bringhurst, 228–30. Vancouver: Douglas & McIntyre, 2000.

Richardson, John. *Fauna Boreali-Americana; or the Zoology of the Northern Parts of British America*. 4 vols. London: John Murray, 1829–37.

Shaw, George. *The Naturalist's Miscellany; or Coloured Figures of Natural Objects Drawn and Described Immediately from Nature*. 24 vols. London: Nodder, 1789–1813.

Southey, Robert. *Southey's Poetical Works*. London: Longman, Brown, Green and Longmans, 1845.

Stanner, W. E. H. *The 1968 Boyer Lectures: After the Dreaming*. Sydney: Australian Broadcasting Commission, 1974.

Vargo, Lisa. 'The Romantic Prospects of the Duke of Richmond's Moose'. *European Romantic Review* 24, no. 3 (2013): 297–305.

Wagamese, Richard. *Indian Horse*. Madeira Park: Douglas and McIntyre, 2012.

Wordsworth, William. *The Poetical Works of William Wordsworth*. Edited by Ernest de Selincourt. 5 vols. Oxford: Clarendon, 1952.

7

Sensing empire

Travel writing, picturesque taste and British perceptions of the Indian sensory environment

Peter Denney

At a meeting of the Royal Society in London, in 1789, Joseph Banks read a report by the naturalist Robert Saunders, who was then working in Bengal for the East India Company. By this time, Banks had emerged as Britain's preeminent scientific organizer. Committed to the improvement of nature at home and across the world, he sought to ensure that botany would be of commercial benefit to empire.[1] Through his oversight of an imperial network of botanists, Banks facilitated the global exchange of plants, crops and natural knowledge with the aim of maximizing the productivity of colonial territories.[2] Saunders was a minor participant in this network. Several years earlier, he had joined a diplomatic mission from Bengal to Tibet via Bhutan, spending much of the trip gathering new ecological information. It was his account of the plants, soil and mineral resources he observed during this journey, which Banks communicated to fellow members of the Royal Society.

In his report, however, Saunders expressed a keen interest not only in the properties of plants, animals and rocks but also in the aesthetic qualities of places. Observing one curious geological structure, he emphasized its 'beautiful and picturesque appearance' before noting its potential value as a source of slate.[3] But the most extraordinary feature, according to Saunders, was the way in which the landscape changed dramatically when he crossed the border from Bhutan to Tibet. From an eminence looking south, the mountains of Bhutan could be seen covered in foliage and greenery. By contrast, looking north, the 'eye took in an extensive range of hills and plains', but there was 'not a tree, shrub, or scarce a tuft of grass' anywhere in sight. 'Thus, in the course of a mile', Saunders summarized, 'we bid adieu to a most fertile soil, covered with perpetual verdure, and enter a country where the soil and climate seem inimical to the production of every vegetable.'[4] Writing about a decade later, this observation greatly interested William Gilpin, the chief exponent of picturesque landscape taste. In his account of his tour of western England, Gilpin remarked that, from a ridge between Guildford and Farnham, two very different views were presented to the tourist. On one side was an uninterrupted, remote landscape, while on the other side was a broken, cluttered scene, with an array of hills preventing any clear line of vision to the distance. Such 'violent contrasts', thought Gilpin, were 'rather uncommon in nature', and even though there were a few examples in England, its topography was too small in scale for them to 'strike the imagination with so much grandeur'.[5] For the best instance of this rarity, where a divided landscape appeared picturesque in one direction and unsightly in another, it was necessary to visit the border between Bhutan and Tibet, as described by Saunders. From the eminence marking this boundary, a look to the south showed mountains and trees 'beautifully' organized into a kind of picture, its various shades of green imparting pleasure to the viewer, while expressing the fertility of the region. But by turning north, the 'eye was received by a vast dreary waste', with no trace of vegetation, a source of disgust rather than delight.[6] Through his use of this illustration, Gilpin seemed to indicate that picturesque landscape taste was perhaps best exemplified by the scenery of South Asia.

Most British travel writers, who visited India during the late eighteenth and early nineteenth centuries, represented themselves as refined observers, dedicated to providing a chiefly visual account of the plants, animals, people and scenery of the subcontinent. This emphasis on observation took many different forms. For writers of natural history, concerned to record information about flora, fauna and geology, observation was a scientific practice implying empirical accuracy. Other observers, however, focused on the visual appearance of the Indian environment, evaluating its aesthetic qualities according to a standard of picturesque taste. Much travel writing, therefore, tended to privilege vision over the other senses.[7] And yet travelling was a fundamentally bodily activity, involving discomfort as well as pleasure, with both scientific and aesthetic pursuits frequently being accompanied or disrupted by all manner of acoustic, olfactory, culinary and tactile events. In tropical colonial locations, especially, the climate was regularly criticized for its deleterious effects on the skin and the nervous system. Although the genres of picturesque landscape description and natural history marginalized myriad non-visual experiences, British travel writers in India observed ecological and human phenomena in a multisensory environment.

This essay examines the meanings of the senses in British travel writing about India in the early romantic period, focusing on the connections between picturesque vision and the interpretation of acoustic, olfactory, gustatory and haptic phenomena. Through an analysis of texts by William Hodges, George Forster and several other writers, it argues that the treatment of sensory experiences tended to reinforce the authority of the visual language of the picturesque, as the primary means of finding aesthetic value in the natural world. In doing so, this way of seeing affirmed the civilized identity of the viewer and depicted Britain as an enlightened global power. It also translated Indian land into imperial landscape, a portable commodity to be consumed in books by educated metropolitan readers rather than recognized as a complex web of cultural, social and ecological relationships. At the same time, however, the unavoidable acknowledgement of non-visual senses threatened to disrupt the distanced view of the environment, which was both a hallmark of picturesque beauty and a vehicle of colonial exploitation.

If the objectifying, distancing and appropriative character of picturesque vision facilitated territorial control, it was British territorial expansion in India during the second half of the eighteenth century which made travel possible in the first instance. After Robert Clive defeated Siraj ud-Daulah at the Battle of Plassey in 1757, British control over Bengal began to increase exponentially. A watershed was reached in 1765, when, as part of the Treaty of Allahabad, the Mughal emperor granted the English East India Company the *diwani*, the right to collect tax revenues in Bengal and its affiliated provinces.[8] In the years that followed, the Company was transformed from a commercial to a political power.[9] Under Company rule, officials amassed immense fortunes.[10] And there were ecological consequences, too. When Warren Hastings was governor general, between 1771 and 1784, large numbers of trees were denuded in order to create a new road linking Calcutta to Benares.[11] As part of this process, the Bengal Army violently displaced many forest dwellers, exploiting their environment for timber resources. Another milestone was the Permanent Settlement of 1793. Aiming to encourage agricultural improvement, the Permanent Settlement of Bengal fixed tax revenues, which were to be paid by *zamindars* in return for private property rights, the goal being to create a class of Indian landowners likely to invest in the land and increase its productivity.[12] This proved profitable for the Company, while inducing *zamindars* to adopt a British model of farming. Further expansion continued apace, and in 1799 the defeat of Tipu Sultan was accompanied by the annexation of the state of Mysore. All this not only increased the territorial power of the Company, but kindled British interest in the subcontinent and opened up additional parts of the region for travel. In related fashion, there emerged a growing demand for more information about the Indian environment, including its geography, climate, flora, fauna and scenery. As the painter William Hodges asserted in 1793, it was a 'matter of surprize' that, of a 'country so nearly allied to us, so little should be known' of its 'face', or visual appearance, along with its 'arts, and natural productions'.[13]

It was inevitable that, of all the travel writers in the late eighteenth century, Hodges would most explicitly suggest that British territorial expansion in India necessitated a detailed examination of its visual appearance. As a painter schooled in contemporary theories of landscape taste, he was not only deeply interested in Indian topography. But he was also concerned with what such topography revealed about the past and present state of Indian society, drawing on Enlightenment ideas regarding the connections between geography, climate, morality, civilization, empire and political governance.[14] From 1772 to 1775, Hodges had been the official artist on Captain Cook's second voyage to the Pacific. On this voyage, he gained experience in applying or adapting stadial theories of social development to the portrayal of non-European places and their Indigenous inhabitants.[15] A similar tendency characterized both his written and visual representations of India, which he visited between 1780 and 1783. According to Hodges, his extensive experience of global travel guaranteed the validity of his statements, for unlike philosophers, his claims had an empirical foundation, based on what he had '*seen*' in 'various climates and parts of the world'.[16] This emphasis on direct observation attributed enormous authority to vision as a medium for the production of knowledge. It also implied a notion of travel as, primarily, a visual activity. Moreover, Hodges claimed that, as a traveller, his way of seeing was superior to that of Company officials and other British colonialists who had lived in India for any substantial period of time.[17] Whereas the 'stranger' was alive to the 'first impression' and responsive to the appreciation of 'novelty', he asserted, residents were likely to downplay 'observation' in favour of abstract 'reasoning'.[18] This appreciation of novelty was not only typical of imperial, or global, travel. As theorized by William Gilpin, it was also a key feature of picturesque vision, an association, which made both visual and written images of the Indian environment appealing to enthusiasts of landscape, including metropolitan readers of travel literature.[19]

Hodges published *Travels in India* in 1793, about a decade after he left India, having stayed there for almost four years under the patronage of the Governor General Warren Hastings. Initially employed to provide a visual record of Hastings's tour through Bengal and Bihar, his journeys were facilitated by the East

India Company, which afforded military protection in what were often recently conquered and still highly contested territories. Upon his return to London, between 1785 and 1788, Hodges published a series of aquatints, based on his sketches, and he also exhibited, throughout the late 1780s and early 1790s, a large number of oil paintings in which India was represented as a land of romantic wonder and picturesque beauty. His book *Travels in India* included several engravings alongside written descriptions of the scenery, climate, agriculture, architecture and some of the social and religious customs he observed during his journeys. As well as offering British readers a novel account of the 'face of the country' in northern India, it also defended Hastings at a crucial time in his impeachment for corruption. During Hastings's tenure, in those areas under Company rule, Hodges intimated, Indian inhabitants flourished in a pastoral paradise, whereas in Mughal-controlled districts, the land was sterile and empty, though not necessarily lacking in picturesque appeal.[20]

The importance of vision to understanding India was emphasized in several reviews of Hodges's travel account. One reviewer praised his 'observations', noting that he 'faithfully' exhibited to the 'eye' the 'appearances' as well as the 'ideas' of 'places and manners'.[21] Similarly, another reviewer remarked that Hodges presented British readers with the first 'faithful' record of the 'interior parts of a beautiful and picturesque region'.[22] In such reviews, vision was aligned with taste as well as knowledge, enabling a refined and accurate account of Indian nature.

If vision was associated with knowledge and taste, it was also regarded as a faculty, which had been most developed in contemporary Europe, where Enlightenment philosophers credited the eye of the educated observer with an unprecedented ability to discern both the physical properties and aesthetic qualities of the natural world. In his preface, as we have seen, Hodges celebrated the observational acuity of the traveller. And following this line of thought, he commenced his narrative by remarking that, when one first arrived in India, the 'clear, blue, cloudless sky', the 'bright sandy beach' and the 'dark green sea' presented a 'combination totally new to the eye of an Englishman', a source of visual gratification and meteorological information.[23]

By contrast, Hodges's first impression of Indian people suggested an allegedly opposing Asian tendency to privilege non-visual sensory experiences, especially sound and touch. This became evident as 'crowds' began boarding his ship, even before it had anchored in the port of Madras, his first destination in India. As he wrote:

> This is the moment in which an European feels the great distinction between Asia and his own country. The rustling of the linen, and the general hum of

unusual conversation, presents to his mind for a moment the idea of an assembly of females.... The first salutation he receives from these strangers is by bending their bodies very low, touching the deck with the back of the hand, and the forehead three times.[24]

For Hodges, as for many travel writers, the difference between Europe and Asia was registered in sensory terms. Indian people were identified with unintelligible, feminized conversation and with touch, one of the lowest-ranking senses, through their performance of strange bodily rituals. Conversely, a privileged visual orientation was associated with a European way of perceiving the world.

The authority assigned to vision by travel writers in India was, to a large extent, a consequence of the influence of picturesque landscape taste, which reached its height in Britain in the late eighteenth century. A flexible term, 'picturesque' had a wide range of meanings and applications. It could refer to a type of terrain, or a way of viewing the natural world, or even a kind of tourism.[25] Picturesque scenery encompassed irregular, uncultivated and often isolated geographical features, such as mountains, forests, ravines and rock formations. For these features to be viewed in a picturesque light, however, they had to be seen as if they were elements within a 'landscape', a combination of Earth, water, plants and perhaps animals, which resembled a picture and conformed to aesthetic principles regarding beauty. As William Gilpin noted in 1782 in his first published work on picturesque tourism, this form of travel involved 'not barely examining the face of a country; but of examining it by the rules of picturesque beauty: that of not merely describing; but of adapting the description of natural scenery to the principles of artificial landscape'.[26] Arguably the most important of these principles was variety. According to Gilpin, the 'ingredients' of picturesque landscape – 'trees – rocks – brokengrounds – woods – rivers – lakes – plains – valleys – mountains – and distances' – could themselves produce '*infinite variety*', but they were also 'varied' by '*combination*' and by '*different lights and shades, and other aerial effects*'.[27] Needless to say, as a pictorial view of the natural world, picturesque vision was also, in theory at least, an entirely visual one. As the aesthetic theorist Richard Payne Knight put it, 'the picturesque is merely that kind of beauty which belongs exclusively to the sense of vision; or to the imagination guided by that sense.'[28] So it followed that for places to conform to this standard of picturesque taste, they had to be divested of their sounds, smells, tastes and textures.

While British travel writers in India did not deploy the picturesque in the pure form espoused by Gilpin, they all demonstrated a tendency to conceive nature in overwhelmingly visual, often pictorial, terms. A number of observers, Hodges among them, referred to landforms in relation to their position in a 'fore ground' or 'distance', clearly searching for a view of terrain, which would approximate a painting.[29] One common example of this way of seeing was the prospect view, an extensive vision of a region from an elevated vantage point. While the prospect view became a prevalent aspect of the picturesque interpretation of India, it had been a component of landscape aesthetics in Britain since early in the eighteenth century. About two miles from Mongheir, Jemima Kindersley, who lived in Bengal in the late 1760s, rhapsodized on the 'romantic and delightful prospect', which could be observed from the 'top of a very high hill' commanding 'a vast extent of country'. From this high viewpoint, according to Kindersley, the Ganges combined with hills, valleys, woods, villages, cornfields, gardens, mosques, elephants, buffalos, camels, cattle and people to produce a 'landscape of great variety, in miniature'.[30]

The advantage of the prospect view was that it maximized the variety of a particular scene, while establishing a sense of visual control over nature. In turn, such control separated the spectator from the region being surveyed. And this separation symbolized the distance between humankind and nature, which Enlightenment philosophers regarded as a precondition of civilized identity. Journeying through the lowland Jungle Terry district, Hodges expressed some excitement at coming across a chain of hills, where, from the 'summits', the spectator could see 'beautiful and extensive prospects', 'diversified by the meandering of the Ganges' and the 'varied face of the country'.[31] Another traveller, Viscount Valentia, also seemed to feel more comfortable on open, elevated ground than in dark, occluded and thickly vegetated places, especially the jungle, that abode of tigers and other wild animals. Undertaking a kind of grand tour of India in the early 1800s, shortly after the British subjugation of Mysore, the aristocratic Valentia was more interested in botany than natural scenery, often preferring to collect plants than compose prospects.[32] And yet he evidently used a sliding scale of picturesque beauty to evaluate the Indian countryside. During a trip up the Ganges, at a location not far from Allahabad, Valentia remarked that the banks of the river were 'more picturesque' than usual due to the 'mixture of jungle with the mango and tamarind trees'.[33] At Ngombo, in Ceylon, however, the countryside was 'less picturesque' than it should be, given its combination of landforms, plants and so on.[34]

While the representation of India as an embodiment of picturesque beauty took a wide range of forms, these all coalesced to increase the authority of vision as a means of understanding and judging the natural world. Intriguingly, Hodges even valued Indian birds for their visual appearance rather than their songs, even though such songs were one of the few non-visual sensory experiences, which regularly featured in picturesque landscape description. In pastoral mode, George Forster remarked that a 'variegated view of populous villages', in Kashmir, was 'enlivened by the notes of a thousand birds', filling the 'mind with harmony and delight'.[35] For Hodges, by contrast, the birds, which filled the woods of Bihar, namely parrots, were remarkable for their 'beautiful colours', while peacocks, of course, dazzled the 'eyes of the traveller' through their display of exquisite plumage.[36] Revealingly, the only sounds that birds made in Hodges's account were the 'screams' of cormorants, a discordant noise, which complemented the sterility, disarray and decline of a landscape, supposedly in need of British rule.

Alongside picturesque vision, there were a number of other visual practices, which also functioned to commodify, transform or appropriate Indian nature in order to facilitate British governance and expansion. Surveying, map-making and geographical examination all involved imposing a new visual order on India so that it could be more effectively controlled, familiarized and optimized for productivity.[37] Natural history, too, encompassed collecting, observing and classifying plants and other resources. This meant redefining plants as objects of knowledge or sources of profit, thereby neglecting or erasing their social, ecological and multisensory contexts. Clearly, the utilitarian character of these scientific visual practices distinguished them from picturesque modes of seeing. Nevertheless, there were also affinities between, say, the empirical observation of plants, the survey of terrain and the appreciation of natural scenery. Not only were such pursuits united by a scopic orientation, they also frequently interpenetrated as naturalists, cartographers and Company officials identified as men of taste, able to admire the picturesque beauty of this land of novelty. A case in point was the enthusiasm for natural scenery shown by James Rennell, the surveyor-general of Bengal from 1767 to 1777. For Rennell, Kashmir valley was a pastoral paradise in which the 'scenery is beautifully picturesque; and a part of the romantic circle of mountains, makes up a portion of every landscape'.[38]

Because the picturesque representation of India entailed a predominantly visual interpretation of the natural world, other sensory experiences were often downplayed or excluded, when travel writers were concerned with aesthetic matters. More than this, the appreciation of picturesque beauty was frequently linked to a conception of nature as silent, or quiet, devoid of sound, movement and often people. Such silence was believed to enhance the aesthetic pleasure derived from the contemplation of landscape, not least because solitude was deemed to aid visual attention. In addition, as Hodges revealed in his sweeping, elevated view of the land around Agra, a silent landscape could also stimulate moral reflection and a gratifying feeling of melancholy, experiences which allegedly testified to the ethical concern, refined taste and deep sensibility of the traveller:

> From the summit of the minarets in the front a spectator's eye may range over a prodigious circuit of country, not less than thirty miles in a direct line, the whole of which is flat and filled with ruins of ancient grandeur: the river Jumna is seen at some distance, and the glittering towers of Agra. This fine country exhibits, in its present state, a melancholy proof of the consequences of a bad government, of wild ambition, and the horrors attending civil dissentions; for when the governors of this country were in plenitude of power, and exercised their rights with wisdom, from the excellence of its climate, with some degree of industry, it must have been a perfect garden; but now all is desolation and silence.[39]

For Hodges, the silence of the countryside around Agra, together with its ancient architectural ruins, evoked picturesque beauty despite being a source of moral condemnation. As several scholars have noted, Hodges saw this silent, ruined, uncultivated landscape as evidence of the luxury, despotism and violence of contemporary Mughal rule.[40] From this perspective, the Mughal empire, during its heyday under Akbar, was considered to have created a grand and prosperous civilization, but a long period of decline now required British intervention if the land was to be transformed, once again, into a kind of garden. Hodges illustrated the point by depicting the British-controlled region of Bhagalpur as a 'perfect paradise' in which he saw the 'manufacturer at his loom, in the cool shade, attended by his friend softening his labour by the tender strains of music.'[41] But despite this idealized image of India under Company rule as a land animated by the songs that accompany happy artisanal labour, Hodges virtually nowhere else attributed any positive value to the sound of human activity. On the contrary, his clear aesthetic preference was for a silent landscape, viewed from a distant, elevated situation, which rendered the countryside inaudible, whether populated or not.

It was not surprising that Hodges, a painter, had a tendency to perceive the Indian countryside in pictorial terms as a silent object of contemplation, occasioning melancholy reflection. But a similar valuation of silence, or quietness, characterized many British travel writers in India, especially when they were commenting on the aesthetic qualities of places. The Company employee George Forster, who travelled through much of South Asia during the 1780s, noted of his visit to Punjab that the frequent 'prospect of a deserted village' or 'desolate country' destroyed every 'chearful or pleasing idea.'[42] And yet, in Mazandaran, a region in Iran along the southern coast of the Caspian Sea, his arrival in cultivated country after journeying through 'extensive forest' was marked by immense delight at the sight of a silent, varied but inhabited landscape. As Forster remarked, 'the vallies now opened and exhibited a pleasing picture of plenty and rural quiet', a 'scene' of hills, dales, villages and 'streams of delicious water', which 'gave the mind ineffable delight'.[43]

According to Hodges, another key cause of the silence of the Indian environment was the catastrophic Bengal famine of 1770, when as many as ten million people died of starvation or some hunger-related disease. This famine witnessed a turning point in British perceptions of Bengal, as an old image of the province as a bountiful garden came to be contested by a rival emphasis on its poverty, misery and return to a state of savage, unrestrained nature.[44] Such apparent regression was symbolized by prowling tigers, roaming elephants and the loud, incessant noise of frogs and insects. The famine had been exacerbated by the punitive extraction of tax revenues by the East India Company, weakening the capacity of Indian people to cope with any subsistence crisis, but many observers, like Hodges, depicted it as a purely ecological catastrophe. There was widespread agreement, however, that both the social misery and ecological disturbance created by the famine led to sensory disorder. As villages were depicted resounding with the agonizing cries of starving people, dogs, jackals, pigs, vultures and other scavengers were recorded emerging to feed on human carcasses.[45] During a period when Enlightenment philosophers defined mastery over nature as a precondition of full humanity, one corollary of this new image was the representation of Indian people as subordinated to a hostile environment. For Hodges, travelling more than a decade after the famine, Bengal had once been 'highly cultivated, and filled with industrious husbandmen', but now 'depopulation' had ushered in a reign of 'silence', punctuated only by the anti-pastoral noise of discordant birds.

In the rigid version of picturesque taste explicated by William Gilpin, this way of seeing nature was anti-utilitarian, ascribing aesthetic value to views of semi-wild, or uncultivated, places, while eschewing signs of agriculture, industry and labour. As we have seen, India was frequently regarded as a 'favoured' land abounding in 'picturesque beauties'.[46] And on occasion, British travel writers praised uncultivated areas, whether mountains or exotic, thickly vegetated sites, for providing pleasing views of supposedly untouched nature. Travelling through the recently subjugated Mysore district, northeast of Bangalore, Viscount Valentia commented approvingly on the 'savageness of the scene' before him, with its 'foreground' of small hills and, in the distance, mountains 'shaded' by jungle.[47] From an elevated situation on top of one of these mountains, he even claimed that the prospect was superior to anything that could be seen in that hotspot of British picturesque tourism: 'Herefordshire, with the distant view of the Welsh mountains'.[48] Similarly, Francis Buchanan could be equally enthusiastic about the picturesque qualities of what he interpreted as primeval nature in parts of Mysore and adjacent territories. Admiring the countryside around the Eastern Ghats, where the Palar River threads through the mountains, Buchanan remarked in 1800 that 'from the rising ground, those who delight in rude scenes of nature may enjoy a most beautiful prospect', one striking feature of which was a 'very rough' valley, with 'few people and little cultivation'.[49] As long as they were observed from a distance, such semi-wild, picturesque places could be assigned a positive aesthetic value, even though their unimproved state was also regarded as a moral deficiency, a failure of land management and political governance.

While the picturesque representation of India as a once majestic civilization now lying in ruins generated aesthetic pleasure or romantic wonder, it also elicited moral condemnation from most British travellers. From this moral perspective, the Indian environment was seen not so much as agreeably wild, but as either sterile or overrun by luxuriant vegetation due to some combination of famine, war or despotism. Of Rajmahal, in Bengal, on the west bank of the Ganges, James Rennell claimed that the settlement was in a 'ruinous state', possessing a 'situation' which was 'romantic, but not pleasant'.[50] Hindoostan, Rennell inferred from this example, 'presented . . . nothing beyond a wild scene', since it lacked the 'soft and beautiful' elements of 'European landscapes'.[51] In 1779, William Mackintosh observed that one-third of Bengal had 'grown up into woods, and become the residence of wild beasts', forcing many Indian people to leave their villages.[52] According to Mackintosh, this reforestation and related depopulation was the result of 'European rapacity'. Specifically, it stemmed from the involvement of Warren Hastings in the Rohilla War in which, as Edmund Burke likewise argued,[53] the governor general revealed himself to be an arbitrary ruler in pursuit of pecuniary gain. Rendered despotic by the corrupting influence of empire, Hastings's unethical conduct entailed assisting the Nawab of Oudh to annex the country of Rohilla Afghans. Despite such ambivalence to empire constituting a minor theme in British writing about India in the late eighteenth century, most travellers associated the 'ruined' state of its countryside with the regular, bitter conflicts between its local rulers or the idle habits of its inhabitants. As Mackintosh himself pronounced, whereas in 'European nations' there was 'a love of novelty, and an ardour of improvement', Indian people preferred conservation to invention.[54] Expressing a similar prejudice, Forster pontificated that the 'natives of India' were 'not much addicted to curious investigation', since their hot climate and abundant vegetation permitted the pursuit of 'indolent and languid' pleasures.[55]

If there was enthusiasm, then, for the picturesque scenery of India, this tended to be qualified by a contradictory concern for the 'improvement' of its environment. Such improvement was held to involve, among other things, the drainage of wetlands, the culling of wild animals, and the adoption of more efficient forms of agriculture. For this reason, views of cultivated nature were often considered to be as pleasing as wild scenes, and British travel writers developed a hybrid aesthetic, which sometimes combined picturesque and georgic modes of representation and, at other times, alternated between them.[56] After ascending a 'steep incline' in order to take a prospect of the landscape around the Netravati River, a few miles from Mangalore, Valentia recognized that the 'country was not picturesque, from the hills being divided into terraces for the purposes of cultivation; but the appearance of general prosperity fully compensated for the diminution of beauty'.[57] This was typical of the way in which, in British writing about India, picturesque taste coexisted with a more utilitarian strain of seeing the land in terms of its actual or potential productivity.

The importance of agricultural improvement was recognized throughout the British empire, influencing policies and practices in settler and plantation colonies as well as in India.[58] Uniting scientific rationality with principles of private property, labour discipline and technological innovation, improvement was a key aspect of elite Enlightenment culture. In Bengal, the famine of 1770 prompted much criticism of existing farming systems by Company officials and other British commentators. Moreover, the belief that private property was a requirement of agricultural improvement resulted in the governor general, Lord Cornwallis, introducing the Permanent Settlement in 1793.[59] This new legal arrangement aimed to bring about the improvement of Bengal by securing the private property rights of a group of Indian landowners known as *zamindars*. In addition, by providing these *zamindars* with an incentive to invest in methods for maximizing the productivity of their land, it was assumed that the Permanent Settlement would induce them to support Company rule.

Whether in Bengal or elsewhere, British travel writers habitually evaluated the Indian environment according to its state of improvement, prizing views of cultivated, ordered and highly populated countryside. In a survey of the condition of agriculture in Bengal, published in Calcutta in 1795, Henry Thomas Colebrooke contrasted the 'neatness' of the huts of affluent farmers with the 'miserable hovels' of 'peasants'.[60] He also lamented the 'neglect' of 'enclosures' in the region, and his 'eye' was offended when he observed some 'weeders' sitting down while they worked, as if such idle habits added to the slovenly appearance of the land no less than its inefficient use.[61] Similarly, en route from Madras to the recently conquered Mysore district, in 1800, Francis Buchanan commented on the 'slovenly cultivation' of the countryside around Venkatagiri, where rice fields were the principal sites of agricultural production, but accounted for only one-twentieth of the arable land. The 'dry fields' here looked 'very ill', being 'bare' and 'devoid of vegetation'. And yet, according to Buchanan, the land was 'perfectly fitted for the English manner of cultivation', so that both its appearance and fertility would be improved if the ground was 'enclosed with hedges', perhaps using *Euphorbia tirucalli*, which made 'beautiful fences'.[62] A botanist and surgeon, who worked for the East India Company, Buchanan was sent to Madras in 1800 by the Governor General, Lord Wellesley, to undertake a survey of the Mysore territory, which had been captured from Tipu Sultan in the previous year. This survey included an inventory of its natural resources, along with an assessment of its agriculture and productive potential as well as myriad descriptions of its topography and scenery. It was the dry season when Buchanan travelled into the Indian interior, but he ignored this climatic variable as he cast his eye over what he perceived as a broken, barren landscape, ruined by war and despotism.[63] On the whole, such unimproved land was seen as both disagreeable and unproductive, lacking the visual order of the green, enclosed fields of rural England. According to Buchanan, however, since the defeat of Tipu, British rule had functioned as a stimulus to improvement, prompting the inhabitants of Mysore to swap idleness for industry. As he wrote of Seringapatam, where 'desolation' was 'to be seen' everywhere, 'now' the countryside began to 'wear an aspect of beginning restoration'. 'The villages are rebuilding', Buchanan observed, 'the canals are clearing; and in place of antelopes and forest guards, we have the peaceful bullock returning to his useful labour'.[64]

Despite their differences, both picturesque and georgic descriptions of India tended to conceive nature in predominantly visual terms. In fact, views of cultivated land were frequently framed by a pictorial aesthetic, seen in prospect from an elevated vantage point. Travelling through the Concan district, for example, James Forbes was struck by how a 'cultivated plain, encircled by verdant hills' formed a 'pastoral landscape', which was enlivened by 'villages, and a busy peasantry'.[65] Similarly, as Valentia looked over a 'cheering prospect' of paddy fields, with 'lofty hills' in the background, not far from Bombay, he pronounced that 'high cultivation and picturesque scenery have no where in India been so perfectly united'.[66] In this way, picturesque and georgic modes of evaluation could be reconciled through a shared visual orientation to nature, one which marginalized the other senses.[67]

By conceiving Indian nature, in aesthetic fashion, as a picture, British travellers assumed that, like a painting, the environment should be characterized by stillness, solitude and silence. According to Forbes in 1772, the abundance of pepper vines in southern Malabar gave the region the same 'picturesque style' as the Campagna Felix, though his 'chief' pleasure here was to travel through the forest near Anjengo, where he could engage in some 'solitary musings' amid the 'solemn stillness of uncultivated nature'.[68] This way of seeing meant that a wide range of social and ecological sound came to be classified as undesirable noise, a disturbance which detracted from the proper appreciation of landscape. In the vicinity of Bombay, Mackintosh complained that the 'loud croaking noise' of giant frogs in the reservoirs and fields took the place of the 'melody of European birds'.[69] Such noise created a discordant soundscape in which the cries, calls and songs of Indian creatures were too strange to be heard as background music, facilitating the enjoyment of otherwise quiet scenery. Edward Ives also remarked that he 'heard no singing birds' on his journey through South Asia, and this absence made him even more irritated by the 'buzzing noise' of mosquitoes and other insects.[70] Paradoxically, it was as if the aesthetic pleasure associated with silent, uncultivated nature amplified the noise of unfamiliar creatures, causing both psychological and physical discomfort.

For many British travellers, a propensity to make noise was associated with a lack of civility, and this connection was often used to suggest that the various inhabitants of South Asia were as untamed as the places in which they lived. Forster, for instance, claimed that the Hybers, an apparently 'lawless' group of Afghans, spoke a 'harshly guttural' language, shaped by the chain of rocky mountains comprising their environment.[71] While some commentators found Indian people 'quiet' and 'inoffensive',[72] Forster depicted both 'Hindoos and Mahometans' as exhibiting a 'love of shew and noise'.[73] This fondness of loud or disorderly sound was incompatible with what he elsewhere represented as the civilized activity of contemplating silent, picturesque scenery.

The contemplation of landscape was held to be superior to other sensory engagements with the natural world, in part because vision was associated with refinement and intellectual activity. At the same time, however, if British travellers regarded the aesthetic evaluation of the Indian environment as a primarily visual pursuit, travel itself was an inescapably bodily affair. On more than one occasion, Forster referred to his own journeying as 'very painful', which was not surprising given that he often travelled alone and incognito through uncharted, difficult, unconquered terrain.[74] In Afghanistan, after travelling through the night on a camel, crammed into a small compartment alongside a young mother and crying baby, he described his 'joy' at reaching his destination, where he was 'relieved from a complication of discordant sounds, and a cramp which had benumbed all my body'.[75] Physical discomfort was not only something, which travellers suffered as they moved between places, but it could also accompany the appreciation of scenery, when one was in a particular location. Climate was identified as the principal source of this irritation, though there was also a sense that an unsightly landscape could generate a combination of aesthetic, psychological and physical displeasure. At Nurpur, in northern India, not far from Kashmir, Forster observed, from the 'top of a hill', the 'beauty' of an 'open' country with a 'winding stream'. When he looked in the opposite direction, however, 'mountains' contracted the 'view', causing his 'eyes' to 'ache'. Nevertheless, these mountains had their 'uses', Forster declared, because they contributed to the mild climate of the region, at least during the early summer months.[76] By contrast, as we shall see, places with a more extreme, tropical climate were perceived as injurious to health, carriers of disease, which made the contemplation of landscape a potentially hazardous pursuit.

The notion of India as exemplifying picturesque beauty existed in an uneasy relationship with an alternative mode of perceiving it as a land of hypersensory stimulation. Whether preoccupied with natural history or aesthetic pleasure, British travel writers registered their experiences of sound, smell, touch and taste even though their main focus was on the visual aspects of the environment.[77] The scent of flowers and the taste of exotic fruits were often mentioned, alongside the olfactory qualities of the air and the effects of the climate on both internal and external parts of the body. There was an emphasis, too, on the heightened character of such sensory experiences. From this perspective, the Indian countryside became allied with sensuality, as did its inhabitants. But this was a profoundly ambivalent image, as the sensual dimensions of land, plants, animals and people were attributed both negative and positive meanings. Writing in 1779 in a generalized way about the plains on the Deccan Plateau, Mackintosh remarked:

> I have often walked abroad in the morning in a *Batta* field, after the grain was cut down, in order to enjoy the fragrance of the newly-shorn herbs. The serenity of the sky, the genial warmth of the climate, the spicy odours that were diffused around me, afforded a pleasure unknown in the climates of Europe, and strongly disposed to a species of enjoyment still more voluptuous.[78]

Resonating with the orientalist revision of pastoral imagery inaugurated by William Jones,[79] this idealized portrayal made the alluring, gratifying aroma of plants typical of Indian nature. For Mackintosh, indeed, the 'luxury of fumes and perfumes' were 'no where [sic] cultivated but in Asia'.[80] During this period, some commentators argued that smell had important and potentially beneficial effects on the body and mind, and doctors studied the scent of plants for medicinal properties, while new norms regarding private and public hygiene made people hypersensitive to different odours.[81] Nevertheless, there remained, among Enlightenment philosophers, a belief that smell, as a proximate bodily sense, became less prominent as society became more civilized, when the distancing faculty of vision took over as the pre-eminent sense for discerning truth no less than beauty. A desire for 'fumes and perfumes' was also regarded with moral suspicion as an expression of enervating luxury. For this reason, other British travellers were less likely than Mackintosh to revel in the voluptuous olfactory qualities of the environment, especially when they were demonstrating their civility through an appreciation of its picturesque elements.

While the picturesque vision of India tended to comprise deodorized views of a quiet countryside, such views were sometimes punctuated or disrupted by overpowering odours, inimical to the refined contemplation of landscape. British travellers associated the strong smells of the Indian environment not just with the pleasurable fragrance of exotic plants, but with what they perceived as the undesirable stench of other ecological and social phenomena. Mackintosh described Calcutta as 'an undistinguished mass of filth and corruption, equally offensive to human sense and health'.[82] This pejorative interpretation did not involve any simple contrast between the foetid city and the fragrant countryside. On the contrary, Mackintosh depicted Calcutta as overrun by nature in a process of decline, which resulted in a disorderly sensory ecosystem, where jackals and vultures fed on waste, as smoke pervaded the atmosphere. Forster similarly criticized Benares for its 'intolerable stench' during the dry season, equating this with the 'many pieces of stagnated water' in the town.[83] According to Forster, another cause of the 'ill smells', which were so 'offensive to the European inhabitants of this city', were the allegedly unhygienic habits of its Hindu residents, notably a tendency to throw 'filth . . . indiscriminately . . . into the streets'.[84] In this way, the depiction of Benares as a malodorous space was part of a broader disparagement of Hindu people as still dominated by, or immersed in, nature, in stark contrast to European observers, whose separation from the Indian environment was everywhere exemplified by their distanced views of landscape. Ironically, though, such stench reduced Forster's enjoyment of the expansive 'prospect' of the surrounding countryside, since, by entering his body, it provoked a level of irritation, which distracted his visual attention.

The ambivalent attitude to non-visual sensory experiences in British travel writing about India was partly a consequence of the complex interaction between picturesque landscape taste and the emergent field of medical geography. Constituting a novel version of environmental determinism, medical geography referred to the study of the influence of topography and climate on disease, and the distribution of disease across global space.[85] Its development in the late eighteenth century coincided with British territorial expansion in India, and travellers increasingly applied its ideas to their interpretation of the region. The founding principle of medical geography was the notion that bodies were porous and, through the senses, open to external environmental factors, which affected health. Pre-eminent among such factors was air, though atmospheric conditions were themselves shaped by topographical features as well as global geographical locations. In addition to evaluating the Indian environment in aesthetic terms, then, British travellers were equally concerned with identifying the pathogenic or healthy qualities of different places. And while their appraisals of the effects of geographical phenomena on health privileged observation,[86] they could hardly avoid registering, also, the wide range of other sensory experiences, which either signalled the presence of disease, or facilitated its transmission.

Intriguingly, a number of travel writers suggested that the bodily effects of an unhealthy environment were incompatible with the appreciation of picturesque beauty. In 1771, for instance, the artist James Forbes took a commanding prospect from the top of Dazagon Hill, where, seated beneath a mango tree, he began sketching a 'beautiful landscape . . . bounded by verdant hills and lofty mountains'. But, he noted, 'short are all rural pleasures between the tropics', for after only an hour, his enjoyment of the scenery was cut short by 'what are emphatically called the *hot-winds*', forcing him to pack away his sketchbook and brushes.[87] For Forster, by contrast, an exposure to such winds did not just cause temporary annoyance, but risked permanent debilitation. After his long residence in India, his body, he complained, had become 'open to every touch of those rude blasts', weakening his physical vigour.[88] Like Forbes, the surgeon and leading early writer on tropical medicine James Johnson was sometimes prevented from demonstrating his taste in picturesque landscape by the injurious physical effects of the Indian environment. In 1803, Johnson recorded how, about a month after arriving in India, he was afflicted with that 'pest of hot climates, the *prickly heat*', a rash which generated 'indescribably tormenting' 'sensations'.[89]

At times, some travel writers suggested that the picturesque beauty of Indian landscape, especially its dense, abundant vegetation, actually produced disease.

Johnson, for instance, described the eastern coast of Ceylon as 'romantic', but unhealthy. He clearly took aesthetic delight in its 'almost impenetrable forests of lofty trees, underwood, and jungle', together with the valleys and ravines which were 'choked up' with 'all the wild exuberance of tropical vegetation'.[90] And yet, such luxuriant, tangled vegetation was, during the monsoon season from May to July, a major cause of cholera morbus due to the high humidity of the region. Conversely, Valentia argued that the climate of Benares was 'very healthy', but its visible appearance was lacking in picturesque qualities, being characterized by 'nakedness' due to the 'want of trees'. The removal of trees was 'necessary' in India, however, for otherwise British colonialists would be 'devoured by mosquitoes'.[91] Patently, this emphasis on deforestation as a means of improvement, transforming a pathogenic environment into a healthy one, provided another justification of Company rule.

While picturesque taste was sometimes in direct conflict with medical geography in the evaluation of Indian nature, more commonly there was an alignment between the two contrasting modes of environmental representation. Specifically, almost all travel writers noted that an elevated situation not only enabled the land to be seen, from a distance, as an expansive, silent landscape, but that such a situation was also more likely to impede the contraction of disease, despite the inimical effects of an extreme, tropical climate. As one observer recorded in 1799, travellers should, where possible, choose to position themselves on a 'dry elevated situation', for it was 'a general maxim that every low situation is unhealthy, especially in the neighbourhood of swamps and marshes'.[92] Similarly, Johnson contended that, compared to the 'atmospherical vicissitudes' of Bombay, the 'marsh effluvia' of Bengal, and the 'scorching heat of Madras', Penang Island possessed a 'very salubrious' climate. And to illustrate the point, he ascended a mountain from where the 'most romantic, extensive, and picturesque views' were presented to his 'delighted eye, contributing greatly to mental amusement and corporeal renovation'.[93] This was a particularly revealing example, since Johnson was claiming that the contemplation of landscape, when seen from a high viewpoint, had a therapeutic function. As the body was revived by such a pleasing prospect, it was also quarantined from undesirable sensory experiences in a process, which enabled visual control to be re-imposed on the land. Accordingly, from this seemingly disembodied perspective, travellers represented India as a wild, pathogenic land inimical to civility, while also asserting the need for British improvement, not least via an elevation of vision over the other senses in the picturesque construction of colonial space.

Notes

1. John Gascoigne, *Science in the Service of Empire: Joseph Banks, the British State and the Uses of Science in the Age of Revolution* (Cambridge: Cambridge University Press, 1998), 111–46.
2. David Mackay, 'Agents of Empire: The Banksian Collectors and Evaluation of New Lands', in *Visions of Empire: Voyages, Botany, and Representations of Nature*, ed. David Philip Miller and Peter Hanns Reill (Cambridge: Cambridge University Press, 1996), 38–57.
3. Robert Saunders, 'Some Account of the Vegetable and Mineral Productions of Boutan and Thibet', *Philosophical Transactions of the Royal Society* 79 (1789): 89.
4. Saunders, 'Some Account', 91.
5. William Gilpin, *Observations on the Western Parts of England, Relative Chiefly to Picturesque Beauty* (London, 1798), 36–7.
6. Gilpin, *Western Tour*, 37–8.
7. David Arnold, *The Tropics and the Traveling Gaze: India, Landscape, and Science, 1800-1856* (Seattle: University of Washington Press, 2006), 22–4.
8. P. J. Marshall, 'The British in Asia: From Trade to Dominion', in *The Oxford History of the British Empire: The Eighteenth Century*, ed. P. J. Marshall (Oxford: Oxford University Press, 1998), 492.
9. Philip Lawson, *The East India Company: A History* (London: Routledge, 1993), 86–102.
10. C. A. Bayly, *Indian Society and the Making of the British Empire* (Cambridge: Cambridge University Press, 1998), 51–3.
11. Michael H. Fisher, *An Environmental History of India: From Earliest Times to the Twenty-First Century* (Cambridge: Cambridge University Press, 2018), 122.
12. Fisher, *Environmental History of India*, 124.
13. William Hodges, *Travels in India* (London, 1793), iv.
14. See Geoff Quilley, 'William Hodges: Artist of Empire', in *William Hodges, 1744-1797: The Art of Exploration*, ed. Geoff Quilley and John Bonehill (New Haven: Yale University Press, 2004), 2–5.
15. See Harriet Guest, *Empire, Barbarism, and Civilisation: Captain Cook, William Hodges, and the Return to the Pacific* (Cambridge: Cambridge University Press, 2007), 10–20.
16. Hodges, *Travels in India*, 66.
17. For this privileging of travel over residency, see Nigel Leask, *Curiosity and the Aesthetics of Travel Writing, 1770-1840: 'From an Antique Land'* (Oxford: Oxford University Press, 2002), 158–61.
18. Hodges, *Travels in India*, iv.
19. On novelty in picturesque perceptions of India, see Hermione de Almeida and George H. Gilpin, *Indian Renaissance: British Romantic Art and the Prospect of India* (Aldershot: Ashgate, 2005), 193–4.

20 See Beth Fowkes Tobin, *Colonizing Nature: The Tropics in British Arts and Letters, 1760-1830* (Philadelphia: University of Pennsylvania Press, 2005), 122-6.
21 *Monthly Review* 11 (1793): 133.
22 *British Critic* 1 (1793): 14.
23 Hodges, *Travels in India*, 2.
24 Hodges, *Travels in India*, 2-3.
25 For the best study of the picturesque, see Malcolm Andrews, *The Search for the Picturesque: Landscape Aesthetics and Tourism in Britain, 1760-1800* (Aldershot: Scolar Press, 1989), 24-66.
26 William Gilpin, *Observations on the River Wye, and Several Parts of South Wales, Relative Chiefly to Picturesque Beauty* (London, 1782), 1-2.
27 William Gilpin, *Three Essays: On Picturesque Beauty; On Picturesque Travel; and On Sketching Landscape* (London, 1792), 42; emphasis in original.
28 Richard Payne Knight, *The Landscape*, 2nd edn (London, 1795), 19.
29 See, for example, Hodges, *Travels in India*, 14, 123.
30 Jemima Kindersley, *Letters from the Island of Teneriffe, Brazil, the Cape of Good Hope, and the East Indies* (London, 1777), 91.
31 Hodges, *Travels in India*, 90-1.
32 Leask, *Curiosity and the Aesthetics of Travel Writing*, 180-1.
33 Viscount Valentia, *Voyages and Travels to India, Ceylon, the Red Sea, Abyssinia, and Egypt*, 3 vols (London, 1809), 1:208.
34 Valentia, *Voyages and Travels to India*, 1:324.
35 George Forster, *A Journey from Bengal to England through the Northern part of India, Kashmire, Afghanistan, and Persia, and into Russia, by the Caspian Sea*, 2 vols (London, 1798), 2:8.
36 Hodges, *Travels in India*, 24-5.
37 See Matthew Edney, *Mapping an Empire: The Geographical Construction of British India, 1765-1843* (Chicago: University of Chicago Press, 1997), 39-76.
38 James Rennell, *Memoir of a Map of Hindoostan* (London, 1788), 105.
39 Hodges, *Travels in India*, 123.
40 See Tobin, *Colonizing Nature*, 126-9; Kate Teltscher, *India Inscribed: European and British Writing on India, 1600-1800* (Delhi: Oxford University Press, 1995), 127-8.
41 Hodges, *Travels in India*, 27.
42 Forster, *Journeys from Bengal to England*, 1:235.
43 Forster, *Journeys from Bengal to England*, 2:196.
44 David Arnold, 'Hunger in the Garden of Plenty: The Bengal Famine of 1770', in *Dreadful Visitations: Confronting Natural Catastrophe in the Age of Enlightenment*, ed. Alessa Johns (New York: Routledge, 1993), 90-3.
45 Arnold, 'Hunger in the Garden of Plenty', 82-8; for a contemporary account, see *The Gentleman's Magazine* 41 (1771): 402-4.

46 Thomas Daniell and William Daniell, *A Picturesque Voyage to India; by the Way of China* (London, 1810), ii.
47 Valentia, *Voyages and Travels to India*, 1:449.
48 Valentia, *Voyages and Travels to India*, 1:450.
49 Francis Buchanan, *Journeys from Madras through the Counties of Mysore, Canara, and Malabar*, 3 vols (London, 1807), 2:186.
50 Rennell, *Memoir of a Map of Hindoostan*, 60.
51 Rennell, *Memoir of a Map of Hindoostan*, 61.
52 William Mackintosh, *Travels in Europe, Asia, and Africa*, 2 vols (London, 1782), 2:234.
53 See Richard Bourke, *Empire and Revolution: The Political Life of Edmund Burke* (Princeton: Princeton University Press, 2015), 639–46.
54 Mackintosh, *Travels in Europe, Asia, and Africa*, 1:300–1.
55 Forster, *Journey from Bengal to England*, 1:13.
56 See Arnold, *Tropics and the Traveling Gaze*, 74–109; Pramod Nayar, *English Writing and India, 1600-1920: Colonizing Aesthetics* (London: Routledge, 2008), 66–81.
57 Valentia, *Voyages and Travels to India*, 1:452–3.
58 C. A. Bayly, *Imperial Meridian: The British Empire and the World, 1780-1830* (Harlow: Longman, 1989), 121–2.
59 Fisher, *Environmental History of India*, 124; Ranajit Guha, *A Rule of Property for Bengal: An Essay on the Idea of Permanent Settlement* (Durham: Duke University Press, 1996), 16–18.
60 Henry Thomas Colebrooke, *Remarks on the Present State of the Husbandry and Commerce of Bengal* (Calcutta, 1795), 64.
61 Colebrooke, *Remarks*, 23, 26, 61.
62 Buchanan, *Journeys from Madras*, 1:30.
63 Arnold, *Tropics and the Traveling Gaze*, 83–4.
64 Buchanan, *Journeys from Madras*, 1:82–3.
65 James Forbes, *Oriental Memoirs: A Narrative of Seventeen Years Residence in India* (1813), ed. Countess de Montalembert, 2 vols (London, 1834), 1:120.
66 Valentia, *Voyages and Travels to India*, 2:107–8.
67 See Arnold, *Tropics and the Traveling Gaze*, 86.
68 Forbes, *Oriental Memoirs*, 1:219–20.
69 Mackintosh, *Travels in Europe, Asia, and Africa*, 2:51.
70 Edward Ives, *A Voyage from India to England* (London, 1773), 313.
71 Forster, *Journey from Bengal to England*, 2:58.
72 Ives, *Voyage from India to England*, 48.
73 Forster, *Journey from Bengal to England*, 2:147.
74 Forster, *Journey from Bengal to England*, 2:262.
75 Forster, *Journey from Bengal to England*, 2:94–5.

76 Forster, *Journey from Bengal to England*, 1:232.
77 Arnold, *Tropics and the Traveling Gaze*, 24–5.
78 Mackintosh, *Travels in Europe, Asia, and Africa*, 2:25.
79 See William Jones, *Poems Consisting Chiefly of Translations from the Asiatic Languages* (Oxford, 1772), 173–99.
80 Mackintosh, *Travels in Europe, Asia, and Africa*, 2:25.
81 Carolyn Purnell, *The Sensational Past: How the Enlightenment Changed the Way We Use Our Senses* (New York: W. W. Norton, 2017), 102–22.
82 Mackintosh, *Travels in Europe, Asia, and Africa*, 2:174–5.
83 Forster *Journey from Bengal to England*, 1:32.
84 Forster, *Journey from Bengal to England*, 1:32.
85 Alan Bewell, *Romanticism and Colonial Disease* (Baltimore: Johns Hopkins University Press, 1999), 29–34.
86 See Mark Harrison, *Climates and Constitutions: Health, Race, Environment and British Imperialism in India* (Oxford: Oxford University Press, 1999), 66–7.
87 Forbes, *Oriental Memoirs*, 1:105–6; emphasis in original.
88 Forster, *Journey from Bengal to England*, 2:143–4.
89 James Johnson, *The Oriental Voyager* (London, 1807), 90–1.
90 James Johnson, *The Influence of Tropical Climates on European Constitutions* (London, 1818), 222.
91 Valentia, *Voyages and Travels to India*, 1:440–1.
92 John Taylor, *Travels from England to India*, 2 vols (London, 1799), 2:78.
93 Johnson, *Influence of Tropical Climates*, 227–8.

Bibliography

Andrews, Malcolm. *The Search for the Picturesque: Landscape Aesthetics and Tourism in Britain, 1760–1800.* Aldershot: Scolar Press, 1989.

Arnold, David. 'Hunger in the Garden of Plenty: The Bengal Famine of 1770'. In *Dreadful Visitations: Confronting Natural Catastrophe in the Age of Enlightenment*, edited by Alessa Johns, 81–112. New York: Routledge, 1993.

Arnold, David. *The Tropics and the Traveling Gaze: India, Landscape, and Science, 1800–1856.* Seattle: University of Washington Press, 2006.

Bayly, Christopher Alan. *Imperial Meridian: The British Empire and the World, 1780–1830.* Harlow: Longman, 1989.

Bayly, Christopher Alan. *Indian Society and the Making of the British Empire.* Cambridge: Cambridge University Press, 1998.

Bewell, Alan. *Romanticism and Colonial Disease.* Baltimore: Johns Hopkins University Press, 1999.

Bourke, Richard. *Empire and Revolution: The Political Life of Edmund Burke*. Princeton: Princeton University Press, 2015.

Buchanan, Francis. *Journeys from Madras through the Counties of Mysore, Canara, and Malabar*. 3 vols. London, 1807.

Colebrooke, Henry Thomas. *Remarks on the Present State of the Husbandry and Commerce of Bengal*. Calcutta, 1795.

Daniell, Thomas and William Daniell. *A Picturesque Voyage to India; by the Way of China*. London, 1810.

de Almeida, Hermione and George H. Gilpin. *Indian Renaissance: British Romantic Art and the Prospect of India*. Aldershot: Ashgate, 2005.

Edney, Matthew. *Mapping an Empire: The Geographical Construction of British India, 1765–1843*. Chicago: University of Chicago Press, 1997.

Fisher, Michael H. *An Environmental History of India: From Earliest Times to the Twenty-First Century*. Cambridge: Cambridge University Press, 2018.

Forbes, James. *Oriental Memoirs: A Narrative of Seventeen Years Residence in India* (1813). Edited by Countess de Montalembert. 2 vols. London, 1834.

Forster, George. *A Journey from Bengal to England through the Northern part of India, Kashmire, Afghanistan, and Persia, and into Russia, by the Caspian Sea*. 2 vols. London, 1798.

Gascoigne, John. *Science in the Service of Empire: Joseph Banks, the British State and the Uses of Science in the Age of Revolution*. Cambridge: Cambridge University Press, 1998.

Gilpin, William. *Observations on the River Wye, and Several Parts of South Wales, Relative Chiefly to Picturesque Beauty*. London, 1782.

Gilpin, William. *Observations on the Western Parts of England, Relative Chiefly to Picturesque Beauty*. London, 1798.

Gilpin, William. *Three Essays: On Picturesque Beauty; On Picturesque Travel; and On Sketching Landscape*. London, 1792.

Guest, Harriet. *Empire, Barbarism, and Civilisation: Captain Cook, William Hodges, and the Return to the Pacific*. Cambridge: Cambridge University Press, 2007.

Guha, Ranajit. *A Rule of Property for Bengal: An Essay on the Idea of Permanent Settlement*. Durham: Duke University Press, 1996.

Harrison, Mark. *Climates and Constitutions: Health, Race, Environment and British Imperialism in India*. Oxford: Oxford University Press, 1999.

Hodges, William. *Travels in India*. London, 1793.

Johnson, James. *The Influence of Tropical Climates on European Constitutions*. London, 1818.

Johnson, James. *The Oriental Voyager*. London, 1807.

Jones, William. *Poems Consisting Chiefly of Translations from the Asiatic Languages*. Oxford, 1772.

Kindersley, Jemima. *Letters from the Island of Teneriffe, Brazil, the Cape of Good Hope, and the East Indies*. London, 1777.

Knight, Richard Payne. *The Landscape*. 2nd edn. London, 1795.

Lawson, Philip. *The East India Company: A History*. London: Routledge, 1993.

Leask, Nigel. *Curiosity and the Aesthetics of Travel Writing, 1770-1840: 'From an Antique Land'*. Oxford: Oxford University Press, 2002.

Mackay, David. 'Agents of Empire: The Banksian Collectors and Evaluation of New Lands'. In *Visions of Empire: Voyages, Botany, and Representations of Nature*, edited by David Philip Miller and Peter Hanns Reill, 38-57. Cambridge: Cambridge University Press, 1996.

Mackintosh, William. *Travels in Europe, Asia, and Africa*. 2 vols. London, 1782.

Marshall, P. J. 'The British in Asia: From Trade to Dominion'. In *The Oxford History of the British Empire: The Eighteenth Century*, edited by P. J. Marshall, 487-507. Oxford: Oxford University Press, 1998.

Nayar, Pramod. *English Writing and India, 1600-1920: Colonizing Aesthetics*. London: Routledge, 2008.

Purnell, Carolyn. *The Sensational Past: How the Enlightenment Changed the Way We Use Our Senses*. New York: W. W. Norton, 2017.

Quilley, Geoff. 'William Hodges: Artist of Empire'. In *William Hodges, 1744-1797: The Art of Exploration*, edited by Geoff Quilley and John Bonehill, 1-7. New Haven: Yale University Press, 2004.

Rennell, James. *Memoir of a Map of Hindoostan*. London, 1788.

Saunders, Robert. 'Some Account of the Vegetable and Mineral Productions of Boutan and Thibet'. *Philosophical Transactions of the Royal Society* 79 (1789): 79-111.

Taylor, John. *Travels from England to India*. 2 vols. London, 1799.

Teltscher, Kate. *India Inscribed: European and British Writing on India, 1600-1800*. Delhi: Oxford University Press, 1995.

Tobin, Beth Fowkes. *Colonizing Nature: The Tropics in British Arts and Letters, 1760-1830*. Philadelphia: University of Pennsylvania Press, 2005.

Valentia, Viscount. *Voyages and Travels to India, Ceylon, the Red Sea, Abyssinia, and Egypt*. 3 vols. London, 1809.

8

The dark side of romantic dendrophilia[1]

Ve-Yin Tee

British people love trees. Stereotypically inhibited and irreligious, historically seen as more interested in establishing trade than in building churches, many seem willing enough however to emote very religiously and very publicly for a big old tree. In his column for *The Japan Times*, the Welsh-born environmentalist C. W. Nicol relates his encounter as a young man with the massive Jomon Sugi of Yakushima forest in these terms: 'I imagined that I could see an ancient face in the trunk, and my reaction ... was to feel that this was no mere tree, but a deity.'[2] 'From mighty oaks to humble hazels, our sylvan treasures have never been more highly valued', runs the byline of *The Independent* newspaper's 'Green Giants: Our Love Affair with Trees',[3] which attributes the end of the 'chainsaw massacre' of urban trees to the adoption in 2007 of CAVAT (Capital Asset Value for Amenity Trees), a system for evaluating trees in monetary terms. Indeed, with record numbers of Britons supposedly planting saplings, *The Guardian* predicts the land area under forest will soon return to the 15 per cent level that existed back in 1086.[4]

But why do British people love trees? Though there are many reasons why all of us might love trees, one reason more applicable to them than to the rest of us is because they have so few. Even 15 per cent forest cover would still be far below the European average of 40 per cent.[5] Moreover, there are disturbing signs that the actual situation on the ground might not be quite as rosy as city journalists like to believe. According to the Country Land and Business Association (CLA), whose members own half the rural land in England and Wales, 'thousands of land managers are disengaging from agri-environmental schemes' as a result of the reduction in funding they receive from Europe under the Common Agricultural Policy, which, quite apart from being 'the worst yet', is anticipated to cease altogether with Brexit.[6] Considering the estimates offered by government and international organizations, as well as the predictions of future trends, trees probably occupy somewhere between 10 per cent and 14 per cent of British land.

Incidentally, it was in the eighteenth century, when the area covered by trees first fell to current levels,[7] that they started capturing the public imagination.[8] Given the ecological catastrophe that has been wreaked on the land, as well as on the plants and animals that live on the land, the greening of romantic literary studies is a welcome development. The romantics should not be expected to have all the answers however. Indeed, as one leading ecocritic has conceded, 'aspects of romanticism might turn out to be part of the problem of modernity rather than its hoped-for solution.'[9] Referring to the representations of writers from different social backgrounds in the late eighteenth and early nineteenth century (William Blake and Gilbert White, Francis Noel Clarke Mundy and Sarah Johanna Williams, respectively), I argue that the contemporary love of trees is the legacy of a romantic dendrophilia that reinforces rather than resists ecological degradation. In the context of colonization and globalization, it is a structure of feeling that has impacted, even as it has been modified by, the culture of different places and different times. In order to communicate this, as well as something of the context of unintended consequences that arise when feelings are acted upon, I discuss at some length tree activism in colonial and postcolonial India.

British people love long-lived trees, which were reified in the romantic period as nigh-immortal repositories of ordinary human experience. Katey Castellano argues that the graveyard in memorializing former ways of living becomes for Wordsworth an important site of 'communal intergenerational intimacy'.[10] What she says of Wordsworth and tombstones may also be said of many other British people at the time in relation to large deciduous trees, as William Blake's 'The Ecchoing Green' indicates:

> Old John with white hair
> Does laugh away care,
> Sitting under the oak,
> Among the old folk.
> They laugh at our play,
> And soon they all say,
> Such such were the joys,
> When we all girls & boys,
> In our youth time were seen,
> On the Ecchoing Green.[11]

Spoken from the perspective of a child young enough to think everyone sitting under the oak 'old folk', the tone is melancholic, evoking associations of loss and mortality. 'Old John', the dominant presence in the verse because of his

Figure 8.1 'The Pleystow, vulg: The Plestor', in Gilbert White, *The Natural History and Antiquities of Selborne* (London: Bensley, 1789), facing page 345, from the author's personal collection.

advanced age, is visually supplanted by 'the oak', which, in providing him, his children and grandchildren with shade manifestly facilitates communal intergenerational intimacy. Trees and tombstones were loved for the stability and durability they signified, which were made to stand in sharp contrast to the people they were connected to. The transitoriness of human life is emphasized in 'The Ecchoing Green', for example, through a title drawing attention to something as ephemeral as the echo of children's voices and through a narrative that spans but a single day.

Idealizing human and non-human relationships, 'The Ecchoing Green' is typical of the poems Blake collected for the *Songs of Innocence* (1789). Readers commonly assume that the setting is a village green.[12] Certainly, the illustration of a large tree in the middle of a field matches Gilbert White's contemporaneous representation of Selborne market place (Figure 8.1), which also served as a play area:

> This *Pleystow*, *locus ludorum*, or play-place, is a level area near the church of about forty-four yards by thirty-six, and is known by the name of *Plestor*.
>
> It continues still, as it was in old times, to be the scene of recreation for the youths and children of the neighbourhood; and impresses an idea on the mind that this village, even in *Saxon* times, could not be the most abject of places,

when the inhabitants thought proper to assign so spacious a spot for the sports and amusements of it's [sic] young people.[13]

Blake was a metropolitan poet however, and up until the end of the eighteenth century had spent all his life in London. Rather than a village playground, perhaps it was one of the urban green spaces near where he lived that he had in mind.

Featuring tree-lined walks, a statue to Charles II and a mock Market Cross building, Soho Square in Central London looks like a little park estate today. A city is 'often seen as the antithesis of nature', with 'buildings and pavements' displacing 'forests and fields'. 'Yet', as Henry W. Lawrence has observed, 'in most cities, the artificial human landscape includes elements of living nature selectively woven into its hard fabric'.[14] Originally called King's Square, Soho Square was laid out with gardens of small flowering plants and shrubs. Over Blake's lifetime however, one by one the town squares to which public access had been maintained for centuries by common rights were closed off with railings and gates. It is easily forgotten that land enclosure was an urban as well as a rural phenomenon. Once converted into residential squares, larger tree species were planted to give more privacy to the people who had the keys.[15] The large trees and iron palings of Soho Square are, in other words, survivals of an estate development process that disenfranchised people lower down the social ladder from the land. By 1833, a parliamentary select committee found that the only open spaces available to the 'humble classes' were Hyde Park and Green Park at the far western edge of town.[16] As their report outlined,

> confined as they are during the week-days as Mechanics [...] in heated Factories: [...] on their day of rest [...] it is probable that their only escape from the narrow courts and alleys (in which so many of the humble classes reside) will be [...] drinking-shops, where [...] they waste the means of their families, and [...] destroy their health.[17]

What the poems glorify in *Songs of Innocence*, those in *Songs of Experience* – which Blake put together several years later – criticize. For example, 'Nurses Song' depicts the envy a caretaker feels at the 'children . . . heard on the green',[18] and 'London' the miserable trapped lives many working people led:

> I wander thro' each charter'd street,
> Near where the charter'd Thames does flow
> And mark in every face I meet
> Marks of weakness, marks of woe.

> In every cry of every Man,
> In every Infants cry of fear,
> In every voice: in every ban,
> The mind-forg'd manacles I hear[19]

This current of disaffection would have been reinforced by the decision Blake took to print the *Songs of Innocence* and the *Songs of Experience* as a single work from 1794.

Something has gone amiss with almost every single human being portrayed in the *Songs of Experience*, since they are all alienated in some way from green places. In 'London', where bodies and lives are up for sale, where the commercial interests driving enclosure have managed to capture the River Thames itself, plants and trees are completely absent. As for 'Nurses Song', the jealousy the persona feels becomes more understandable if her young charges are actually playing on an urban residential green, which servants like her and their children no longer have access to. The current status of Soho Square and similar urban green spaces as public parks has not fully reversed the injustice of their removal from the lives of working-class people. For, as common land, unlike the purely recreational function public parks are restricted to, they could be employed for the grazing of farm animals, the drying and bleaching of cloth, mustering soldiers and even shooting practice if they were large enough.[20] Moreover, bearing in mind the fact that the largest trees in the metropolis were the result of projects aimed at housing the wealthy, a conservation programme such as CAVAT in which the value of a tree is determined by its size would only reinforce the status quo: leafy residences for the haves, leafless concrete for the have-nots.

Trees are also loved for the services they render. While the British biogeographer Philip Stott objects to the popular understanding of forests as 'the lungs of the earth' or a 'living carbon sink',[21] an instrumentalist perspective on trees has been an integral part of forest advocacy since the romantic period. Both this idealism and instrumentalism are evident in Francis Noel Clarke Mundy's *Needwood Forest* (1776) and Sarah Johanna Williams's *Sherwood Forest* (1832). In the late eighteenth and early nineteenth centuries, people distinguished (as we do not) between 'forest' and 'woodland', with the former meaning 'land' – not necessarily tree growing – 'subject to forest laws'. These laws were comprehensively defined and strictly enforced under the Normans and their medieval successors, who were widely held to have returned the country to a wilder state. By contrast, the UK Forestry Commission charts an unremitting decline in 'woodland' from 15 per cent in 1086 to less than 6 per cent in 1900.[22]

Until at least as late as the 1970s, scholars tended to suggest an increase from the eleventh to the thirteenth century, when royal forests (i.e. 'forests' in the stricter, romantic sense of the word) alone were presumed to cover from 'a fifth' to 'one-third of England'.[23] Though Needwood and Sherwood were already in noticeable decline in the seventeenth century as forest laws fell into 'total disuse',[24] the period '1770 to 1860' – in which Mundy and Williams published their work – 'was the most destructive in their history'.[25] It marked the peak in the wave of parliamentary enclosure acts, where the surviving parts were removed from the jurisdiction of forest law (in legal speak, disafforested) and sold off. This frequently resulted in tree loss[26] (in other words, plain deforestation) as many of these new landowners 'attempted, in the fashion of the times, to plough and cultivate'.[27]

Under the rhetoric of forest advocacy, trees were promoted as living records of the past. With Mundy, the spotlight is given to the 'SWILCAR Oak', the largest and oldest tree in Needwood, who speaks directly to the reader of human exploits dating back to the days of Henry III.[28] In employing anthropomorphism as a device in the service of non-human beings, Mundy was possibly following the lead of Anna Seward. She too was from the affluent classes and the Midlands, but representing local trees in this way was becoming more common among women poets in general.[29] Moreover, the large oaks of Sherwood about thirty miles away were also being dubbed 'living historians', because they were 'several hundred years old and had witnessed great events'.[30] Sarah Williams took this process a step further in the nineteenth century by adopting the extraordinary approach of conceptualizing Sherwood Forest as a museum:

> 'Tis sweet through time's long vista to look back,
> To commune, as with nations now no more;
> And Nature's fastnesses can never lack
> Some trace of generations gone before,
> Though art, where'er she treads, should shroud the
>   things of yore.[31]

I am reminded here of Raymond Williams's perception 'that the idea of nature contains, though often unnoticed, an extraordinary amount of human history'.[32] Before these lines, Sarah Williams directed attention to the Roman remains buried beneath the trees. Later she developed her conceit of the forest as a storehouse of ancient artefacts to give the impression that Britishness was an identity forged out of a thousand years of victimization by foreign powers, from the Romans down to 'the Saxon', 'Danish', 'and the Norman . . . foe'.[33]

The amenities ascribed to trees and forests during the romantic period do sometimes have distinctively modern equivalents. Of the study of ethnobotany at Harvard in the 1980s, the Canadian anthropologist Wade Davis recalls, 'We all had a mantra that we had to save the rainforest because it was a repository of natural drugs.'[34] In *The Fall of Needwood* (1808), Mundy lamented the destruction of the forest in these terms:

> Fresh, vigorous and countless here,
> You, happy fox-gloves, as you fell,
> In triumph clos'd each purple bell;
> Proud that the bark of fam'd Peru
> Was rival'd, British plant, by you.
> Philosophy and Science rare
> Had pitied Dropsy's sad despair,
> And pour'd your healing treasure forth;
>
> ...
>
> Your honours on Hygiea's shrine,
> Where pleas'd Apollo stoop'd to yield
> To Darwin's hand his lyre and shield.[35]

Even at its most progressive and internationalist however, romantic dendrophilia is at its root profoundly parochial. Malaria had been until the nineteenth century Indigenous to England,[36] and Peruvian bark was a remedy that Erasmus Darwin had touted as a physician. As a fellow poet not only had he written a dedicatory poem praising *Needwood Forest*, but he had also recently passed away. Hence, the appearance of Apollo and in dual capacity as god of poetry and medicine (i.e. with 'lyre and shield').

Mundy and Williams portrayed the forest as the very cradle of freedom. It was the refuge of the beasts of the land and the birds of the air, the hunting of which was upheld as a means to maintain health, strength and martial prowess. Only the Crown and the local gentry had the right to hunt in Sherwood and Needwood however. For the vast majority hunting would have been regarded as poaching, one of the most frequently prosecuted crimes.[37] Both poets passed over without comment the inequitable game laws, which would have undermined the argument that the forest was a public good. It was the source of wood for the navy for example, and thus the foundation of national self-determination. Williams alluded to Sherwood Forest as the haunt of the legendary Robin Hood,[38] who, in the popular ballads and chapbooks of the day, defeated the aristocracy and the clergy, but was in turn bested by artisans and small tradespeople. Mundy referred to Needwood as 'the poor man's friend',[39] because they could enter it 'to collect stool wood (tree roots), blackthorn and windblown branches'.[40] The Act of 1801 'enclosing the Forest or Chase of Needwood'[41] extinguished along with the privileges and prohibitions accorded by forest law common rights such as these.

As a strategy for resisting deforestation, romantic dendrophilia however has proven ineffective. It is generally accepted that the area covered by trees in Britain continued to fall throughout the nineteenth century, reaching perhaps its nadir in 1913 at 'no more than c.5.2 per cent'.[42] The 420-hectare Sherwood Forest National Nature Reserve today is a tiny remnant of its former size during the romantic period, when it covered over 70,000 acres.[43] In 1805, twenty-nine years after Mundy's spirited defence of Needwood Forest, 10,857 trees worth £11,009 3s. 6d. were cut down and used to fence the allotments of the new owners. Between 1802 and 1845, another 38,317 trees valued at £34,100 4s. 9d. were harvested for 'timber merchants at Uttoxeter, Hatton, Barton-under-Needwood and Uxbridge, Middlesex'.[44] Mundy's *Fall of Needwood*, which recounts the deforestation, evokes his return to a veritable wasteland with considerable pathos. There, 'fenced off', on a spot of green, 'where not another tree remains', Swilcar still stands:

> Horrid! – I see thee far – defac'd –
> In fetters on a dreary waste,
> With outstretch'd arms and bosom bare,
> Appealing to the troubled air;
> Yet taxing not the pelting storm;
> But those, more cruel, who deform
> Thy rich retreats, thy turf defile
> With fence, and road, and uses vile;
> Nor of the whole, which Nature gave,
> Leave thee enough to make thy grave,
> When comes, as come it must, thy fall,
> Lear of the Forest, robb'd of all![45]

I am reminded here of the powerful image captured by T. J. Watt of a lone tree activist standing atop the stump of a giant conifer, which was used in the poster for the American documentary film *If a Tree Falls: A Story of the Earth Liberation Front* (2011). Anna Seward herself, in 'Sonnet LXIII. To Colebrooke Dale' (1799), had cast doubt on the pathetic fallacy 'as a cultural strategy for resisting the modern conquest of nature'.[46] The film shows how the members of the earth Liberation Front (ELF) are unable to kill or hurt for trees, and how the fear of losing their loved ones causes them to admit guilt and to betray each other to the FBI. Apart from driving home the point that our love of trees is hopelessly outmatched by our love for each other, this kind of activism is problematically retrospective: Mundy's *Fall of Needwood* and Watt's *Protester* acquire their pathos only after the event of deforestation.

Trees are caught up in networks of human power relations, and the elision of such links by Mundy and Williams has been particularly egregious in the light of the elitist history of forest protection. As Rigby has noted, 'the etymology of the word "forest" recalls that the first conservationists were the medieval monarchs who laid claim to areas . . . as royal hunting reserves: *foris* means "outside", implying that an "afforested" place was one that was off limits to commoners.'[47] Indeed, Sherwood Forest at this time may have covered as much as one-quarter of Nottinghamshire,[48] or twice the expanse that existed at the end of the eighteenth century. If the condition of the royal forests was contingent on their survival as hunting grounds, then Mundy's *Needwood Forest* constituted a last-ditch attempt to engage the country sports faction, which along with the forest itself was in severe decay:[49] 'It was a truth universally acknowledged by English gentlemen that they had the leisure to enjoy what everyone else wished to.'[50] In the case of hunting, as I have mentioned, it was also a pursuit they tried to monopolize by strenuously upholding game laws.[51] While tenants and labourers were included in fox hunting, they participated as foot followers in a sport that one had to be on horseback to fully enjoy.[52] While there is evidence of 'a strong association between shooting, tree planting and woodland management',[53] the green arguments of the supporters of field sports continue to be hampered by the perception of them as atavistic country toffs.[54] Considering the aspersions of elitism the environmental movement routinely accrues in British mainstream society, this has been unhelpful to say the least.

Worse, given the context of colonization, the British version of forest conservation was imposed over a truly vast territory. What chance was there for a more equitable alternative developing overseas if the forest advocates were unwilling to call out the stark inequality of access to land designated as forest at home? Trees probably covered a third of the Indian subcontinent in the romantic period.[55] By the end of British rule, forest cover had fallen to about 16 per cent.[56] Though the scarcity of big teak trees for foreign export seems to have been noticed by the colonial administration as early as 1838,[57] the rapid decline of India's forests did not take place until the second half of the nineteenth century, when more wood was required domestically 'to fuel a growing iron smelting industry, and for railroad ties to build the Indian Railways'.[58] The elitist orientation of forest conservation was nakedly transparent in the series of Forest Acts ushered in at this time, which curtailed the customary practices of forest communities. The shifting cultivation employed by tribespeople for centuries was banned; villagers living near forests who had for generations gathered the fallen branches for fuel, or who used them to graze livestock, found it increasingly difficult to do so. They were supposed to accept these as sacrifices 'for the good of all', meaning – as one historian acidly puts it – 'conserving forests for colonial commercial needs'.[59] The prohibitions were deeply resented and there was widespread civil disobedience. Each time 'the movement was crushed, or collapsed, after some time it would re-emerge'.[60] Disputes over forest rights were a recurring phenomenon, and as Ramachandra Guha observes, '[they] persisted when post-colonial governments in countries such as India and Indonesia reproduced the imperial model of forest management'.[61]

Given the power differential that exists between subsistence users and commercial exploiters of the environment, it was thus with considerable pleasure that I learnt from Guha of the success of the Chipko movement. In 1973, men, women and children from the Himalayan district of Chamoli stopped fourteen ash trees from being cut down simply by hugging them when the lumbermen came. The villagers had applied for official permission to harvest the trees to make agricultural tools, and were stung when they were allocated instead to a sporting goods company hundreds of miles away in Allahabad. Other communities whose needs were sidelined by big business were galvanized into similar acts of nonviolent resistance. In the neighbouring district of Tehri, for example, the iron leaves that had been inserted into chir trees to tap them for resin were removed and trees bandaged to a reciting of the Bhagavad Gita.[62] The turpentine and rosin distilled from the resin had widespread commercial applications, but the tapping meant that the local people could no longer use the wood of the chir for timber and fuel, harvest the twigs for their marriage ceremonies, pick the needle-like leaves for the bedding of their livestock or the cones for decoration and for firecrackers during the festival of Diwali.[63] The disturbances spread across the state of Uttarakhand until the government was eventually persuaded to safeguard traditional rights by limiting the commercial exploitation of the forests. Guha has stressed the historical connections between Chipko and the anti-colonial struggles in India and elsewhere over forest rights; indeed, he goes so far as to align them with popular uprisings all the way back to 'the peasant revolts of medieval Europe'.[64] The work of Guha has encouraged Carl Griffin to reinterpret examples of labouring people maiming or cutting down trees on parks, plantations and orchards in eighteenth- and early nineteenth-century Britain as forms of protest.⁶⁵ To reach for manifestations on a more everyday level, perhaps poaching and wood theft – two common ways by which forest law and property rights were infringed – could be re-evaluated too as acts of resistance to a proletarianization process that was pushing people in ever greater numbers to the towns and cities.

These cultural crossings have their place and are to an extent necessary in the formation of alliances to counter an environmentally destructive capitalism that is as much local and immediate as it is global and long-term. The Chipko story has certainly influenced people in other 'parts of the world who employ it for their own struggles', including environmental activists here in the so-called First World.⁶⁶ But if Foucauldian antihumanists, ecofeminist and postcolonial critics have taught me anything it is to pay close attention to specific contexts and peculiar intersections of power. I cannot help but notice, for example, the distances our tree-sitting activists (including the members of the ELF) traverse in order to defend trees that otherwise have little connection with their daily lives. With respect to Chipko, it is the divergences that are in fact the most interesting, notably how they were able to succeed where so many others had failed. Reading Guha's work, with the benefit of Priyamvada Gopal's insights into subaltern history writing,⁶⁷ what stands out to me is their sheer political acumen.⁶⁸ According to Guha, it was the Gandhian social activist Chandi Prasad Bhatt, who had suggested 'the tree-hugging technique of protest'.⁶⁹ This narrative is allowed to coexist with Sunderlal Bahuguna's idea that Chipko was inspired by the eighteenth-century example of Amrita Devi,⁷⁰ who lost her life along with hundreds of other Bishnoi Hindus when they hugged the Khejri trees that the men of the maharaja of Jodhpur were sent to cut down. I marvel at the forbearance that must have been required to involve these members of the elite. Bhatt and Guha are of the highest Brahmin caste, who have described the Chipko activists as 'unlettered peasants'.⁷¹ Bahuguna, though not a Brahmin, was hardly plebeian either: the son of a forest officer, he had served as the Congress secretary of Uttar Pradesh in his twenties. Through Bhatt, the Chipko protesters had access to the latest activist techne. Bahuguna provided a window into the minds of the people governing the country, and evoking the romance of Devi's sacrifice was instrumental in galvanizing the broad support of Hindu women who formed the backbone of the organization. Finally, without the work of scholars like Guha, it is difficult to imagine Chipko attaining the international stature it currently enjoys.

The forest cover in India has been increasing gradually ever since the 1970s, 'a remarkable achievement given India's human and livestock population'.⁷² Satellite data analysis indicates that the area of the country under trees has surpassed 24 per cent, which was 'ranked 10th in the world' in 2017.[73] The national target is an even more impressive 33 per cent, but it is precisely because 17 per cent of the human and 18 per cent of the livestock population are sustained on only 2.4 per cent of the world's land surface that its appropriateness has come under question.[74] Mayank Aggarwal perceives it as a 'colonial hangover', as the target was first set in 1952, 'Soon after . . . independence from Britain in 1947'.[75] About 33 per cent – one-third of the land area of India – was the 'original cover',[76] or, to put it more bluntly, the extent of the forest before the depredations of British colonial rule. The negative impact of this reforestation is nowhere more keenly felt in India than in the very region from which Chipko originated and in which it has been the most successful.[77] It is one thing for the government of a country like Britain to try and get its people to sacrifice economic development for the sake of the environment, quite another to obligate a people at one-twentieth of the per capita GDP of a First World economy to continue making the same tradeoff. Also, as Chipko and Hindutva have a similar base in terms of geography and religious populism, it is disturbing how easy it has been for the former to be co-opted by the latter as an exemplar of the positive contribution of Hinduism to the environment. Under 'BJP rule, [the] government began to actively fund temples, pilgrimage sites and religious cults for reforestation and maintenance of sacred groves', with the result that 'left-wing religious environmentalism has become in-distinguishable from the "dharmic [sic] ecology" propagated by the champions of Hinduism'.[78]

I would like to conclude with two illustrations: John Smith's engraving of *Swilcar Oak* (1807) and Andriy Ivanchenko's woodblock printing 'Bleeding Heart' (2017). The first (Figure 8.2), which shows Mundy's 'kingly oak'[79] sheltering red deer under its broad canopy, is fairly revealing of the conservative political orientation of romantic dendrophilia. As a conservation ethic, it is problematic in generating visions of Arcady that sentimentalize rather than end the violence of deforestation. Moreover, whether sentimental (as White's was), or political (in the case of Blake, or the eighteenth- and twenty-first-century tree activists), or commercial (as it is with CAVAT), in favouring the large and spectacular, such a conservationist impulse is very much the twin sister of that structure of feeling which motivates the elitist preservation of tigers, rhinos, polar bears, whales and other charismatic megafauna. Due to the attention drawn to big old oak trees by middle- and upper-class poets, writers and artists, they were spared when the land was disafforested. Swilcar Oak remained standing well into the reign of Queen Victoria; there are other famous British oak trees which still stand,

Figure 8.2 *Swilcar Oak (in Needwood Forest) Staffordshire*. Engraving by John Smith of a drawing by H. Moore. London: Vernor Hood and Sharpe, 1807, from the author's personal collection.

like Major Oak, tellingly solitary on a plain of grass. Romantic dendrophilia is also charged with nationalism. The oak is the national tree of England. A figure of 15 per cent is the level of 'woodland cover' currently proffered to the British public as existing in 1086; it is the British equivalent of 'original cover', in the context of Euroscepticism, marking the extent of woodland before European domination. The second illustration (Figure 8.3), inspired by the backstory of the Russian language role-playing game *Domus et Animae*, depicts a fanatic who sacrifices his humanity to imitate the tree-like angels of his religion. Originally entitled 'Guerdian v.2', it offers an interesting critique of First World ecocriticism troubled by decoloniality and anti-humanism. The solution – I think – isn't disengagement, for humans to leave nature alone and fade away. Neither is it de-anthropocentrism, to abandon our ways of feeling and seeing so as to become more tree-like. No, what postcolonialism and posthumanism demand of us is better engagement. The Chipko activists have shown us the level of commitment and the broad-based involvement environmentalists need to foster in order to succeed. We also have to be attentive to local circumstances, sensitive to unequal power relations and ceaselessly reflexive, or we will lose touch with the present and fall prey to the law of unintended consequences as Chipko may have done.

Figure 8.3 'Bleeding Heart' is not only a pejorative label that can be applied to an environmentalist, it is also the name of a tree with red, heart-shaped leaves that is indigenous to Australia. Woodblock print by Andriy Ivanchenko, reproduced with the artist's permission. *Deviantart*, 2017. https://www.deviantart.com/an-kang/art/Guerdi an-v-2-715795196.

Notes

1 This project would not have been possible without the resources I was able to access because of the Grant-in-Aid for Scientific Research (C) for the 2015 academic year. I would also like to acknowledge Simon White's very helpful comments on the first draft of this chapter, and that if there are any omissions and oversights they are all my own.
2 C. W. Nicol, 'Hailing the Benefits of Raising a Stink', *The Japan Times*, 30 April 2016, https://www.japantimes.co.jp/life/2016/04/30/environment/hailing-benefits-raisin g-stink/#.XTLtsS2B1sM.
3 Michael McCarthy, 'Green Giants: Our Love Affair with Trees', *The Independent*, 25 April 2008, https://www.independent.co.uk/environment/nature/green-giant s-our-love-affair-with-trees-815329.html.
4 Bibi Van der Zee, 'England's Forests: A Brief History of Trees', *The Guardian*, 27 July 2013, https://www.theguardian.com/travel/2013/jul/27/history-of-englands-forests.
5 Food and Agriculture Organization of the UN, 'Forest Area (% of Land Area) European Union', https://data.worldbank.org/indicator/AG.LND.FRST.ZS?location s=EU.

6 Country Land and Business Association, 'Future of the Natural Environment after the EU Referendum', Report for the UK Environmental Audit Committee dated 2 September 2016, http://www.cla.org.uk/influence/policy-library/future-natural-environment-after-eu-referendum.

7 The early English statistician Gregory King estimated there were six million acres of woodland, forests, parks and commons (16% of England and Wales) in the 1690s. About two and a half million acres (6% of England and Wales) seems to have been enclosed in the eighteenth century (G. D. H. Cole, *A Short History of the British Working Class Movement* (1925; repr., London: Routledge, 2002), 3:28; N. D. G. James, *A History of English Forestry* (Oxford: Blackwell, 1981), 167), and even assuming this invariably led to deforestation (which it did not) this still leaves tree cover in 1800 at 10 per cent. Modern estimates over the same period are considerably lower. For example, the UK Forestry Commission has 'woodland cover' at about 7 per cent during this time. One explanation for the discrepancy is the stricter terminology, such as 'forest area' by the World Bank, or 'woodland cover' by the Forestry Commission, which typically exclude tree plantations, orchards and tree stands (whether planted or natural) in urban parks and gardens. I am going to suggest however that this difference is ideological.

8 Keith Thomas, *Man and the Natural World* (1983; repr., London: Penguin, 1984), 212.

9 Kate Rigby, *Topographies of the Sacred* (Charlottesville: University of Virginia Press, 2004), 2.

10 Katey Castellano, *The Ecology of British Romantic Conservatism* (New York: Palgrave Macmillan, 2013), 62.

11 William Blake, 'The Ecchoing Green', in *Songs of Innocence and of Experience* (1794; repr., London: Rupert Hart-Davis, 1967), st. 2. Citations refer to the transcript by Geoffrey Keynes rather than to the colour plates.

12 See Stewart Crehan, *Blake in Context* (Dublin: Gill and Macmillan, 1984), 96; Stephen Daniels, 'Political Iconography of Woodland', in *The Iconography of Landscape*, ed. Dennis Cosgrove and Stephen Daniels (Cambridge: Cambridge University Press, 1998), 53; and Nick Rawlinson, *William Blake's Comic Vision* (Hampshire: Palgrave Macmillan), 173.

13 Gilbert White, *The Natural History and Antiquities of Selborne* (London: Bensley, 1789), 345.

14 Henry W. Lawrence, 'The Greening of the Squares of London', *Annals of the Association of American Geographers* 83, no. 1 (1993): 91.

15 Lawrence, 'Squares of London', 101–6.

16 UK Parliament, House of Commons, *Report from the Select Committee on Public Walks* (London: House of Commons, 1833), 5.

17 UK Parliament, 9.

18 Blake, 'Nurses Song', st. 1.
19 Blake, 'London', lines 1–8.
20 Lawrence, 'Squares of London', 94; Aslet, *Villages of Britain* (London: Bloomsbury, 2010), 122.
21 Philip Stott, *Tropical Rainforest* (London: Institute of Economic Affairs, 1999), 50.
22 UK Forestry Commission, *Government Forestry and Woodlands Policy Statement* (London: Defra, 2013), 21.
23 Oliver Rackham, *Trees and Woodland in the British Landscape* (1976; repr., London: J. M. Dent, 1983), 153; Nicholls, 'On the Evolution of a Forest Landscape', *Transactions of the Institute of British Geographers* 56 (1972): 57.
24 William Blackstone, *Commentaries on the Laws of England* (Oxford: Clarendon Press, 1765–9), 3:73.
25 Rackham, *Trees and Woodland*, 157.
26 Not always though. Some of the disafforested land was converted to the large-scale plantation of oak and other hardwoods. Especially from 1757 to 1835, when the Royal Society for the Encouragement of the Arts awarded gold and silver medals to stimulate such projects (see Thomas, *Man and the Natural World*, 210).
27 Thomas Hinde, *Forests of Britain* (London: Victor Gollancz), 227.
28 Francis Noel Clarke Mundy, *Needwood Forest* (Lichfield: Jackson, 1776), 42–4.
29 Sylvia Bowerbank, *Speaking for Nature* (Baltimore: John Hopkins University Press, 2004), 19.
30 Bowerbank, *Speaking for Nature*, 57.
31 Sarah Johanna Williams, *Sherwood Forest, a Poem* (Nottingham: Stretton, 1832), st. 19.
32 Raymond Williams, *Culture and Materialism* (1980; repr., London: Verso, 2005), 67.
33 Williams, *Sherwood Forest*, st. 24.
34 Quoted by John Richard Stepp, *Ethnoecology and the Medicinal Plants of the Highland Maya* (Cham: Springer, 2018), 81.
35 Francis Noel Clarke Mundy, *The Fall of Needwood* (Derby: J. Drewry, 1808), 22.
36 Tom Williamson, *An Environmental History of Wildlife in England 1650–1950* (London: Bloomsbury, 2013), 102.
37 Douglas Hay, 'Legislation, Magistrates, and Judges', in *The British and their Laws in the Eighteenth Century*, ed. David Lemmings (Suffolk: Boydell Press, 2005), 64.
38 Williams, *Sherwood Forest*, st. 30.
39 Mundy, *Needwood Forest*, 21.
40 Nicholls, 'Forest Landscape', 66.
41 UK Parliament, House of Lords, *Journals of the House of Lords* (London: House of Lords, 1801), 43:307.
42 Williamson, *Environmental History*, 152.
43 James, *English Forestry*, 87

44 Nicholls, 'Forest Landscape', 69.
45 Mundy, *Fall of Needwood*, 33–4.
46 Bowerbank, *Speaking for Nature*, 163.
47 Rigby, *Topographies*, 215.
48 James, *English Forestry*, 86.
49 Nicholls, 'Forest Landscape', 63–9.
50 Donna Landry, *The Invention of the Countryside* (Hampshire: Palgrave, 2001), 3.
51 See also Kirby Chester, 'The English Game Law System', American Historical Review 38, no. 2 (1933): 240–3.
52 Landry, *The Invention of the Countryside*, 47–8.
53 Graham Cox, '"Listen to Us!" Country Sports and the Mobilization of a Marginalized Constituency', in *The Contested Countryside*, ed. Jeremy Burchardt and Philip Conford (London: Tauris, 2008), 151.
54 George Monbiot, 'Class War on the Hoof', *The Guardian*, 13 September 2004, https://www.theguardian.com/politics/2004/sep/14/hunting.uk.
55 Indian historians estimate that the country lost 40 to 50 per cent of its forest from the 1860s to the 1990s (see Jagdish Krishnaswamy, 'Forest Management and Water in India', in *Forest Management and the Impact on Water Resources*, ed. Pablo A. Garcia-Chevesich, Daniel G. Neary, David F. Scott, Richard G. Benyon and Teresa Reyna (Paris: UN Educational, Scientific and Cultural Organization, 2017), 87). If the forest cover hovered between 19.27 per cent and 19.45 per cent in the 1990s, as government statistics suggest, that would mean the 'original cover' was at least 32 per cent.
56 Kiran Kumar, R. Patil, G. R. Manjunatha and Chandrakanth Mysore, 'Demand for Forest Products in India', *Indian Journal of Ecology* 43, no. 2 (2016): 486.
57 Atluri Murali, 'Whose Trees? Forest Practices and Local Communities in Andhra, 1600-1922', in *Nature, Culture, Imperialism*, ed. David Arnold and Ramachandra Guha (Delhi: Oxford University Press, 1995), 97–8.
58 Emily K. Brock, 'New Patterns in Old Places', in *The Oxford Handbook of Environmental History*, ed. Andrew C. Isenberg (Oxford: Oxford University Press, 2014), 161.
59 Murali, 'Whose Trees?', 111.
60 Mark Poffenberger, 'The Resurgence of Community Forest Management in the Jungle Mahals of West Bengal', in *Nature, Culture, Imperialism*, ed. Arnold and Guha, 368.
61 Ramachandra Guha, *How Much Should a Person Consume?* (Berkeley: California University Press, 2006), 91.
62 Ramachandra Guha, *The Unquiet Woods* (Berkeley: California University Press, 2001), 161–2.
63 Chandra Prakash Kala, 'Indigenous Uses and Structure of Chir Pine Forest in Uttaranchal Himalaya, India', *International Journal of Sustainable Development and World Ecology* 11, no. 2 (2004): 205–10.

64 Guha, *The Unquiet Woods*, 171.
65 Carl Griffin, 'Protest Practice and (Tree) Cultures of Conflict', *Transactions of the Institute of British Geographers* 33, no. 1 (2007): 98–103.
66 Haripriya Rangan, *Of Myths and Movements* (London: Verso, 2000), 2.
67 Priyamvada Gopal, 'Reading Subaltern History', in *The Cambridge Companion to Postcolonial Literary Studies*, ed. Neil Lazarus (Cambridge: Cambridge University Press, 2004), 139–61.
68 I suspect the central influence here is the hill tribe leader of the women activists Vimla Bahunguna. Her first name is variously spelt as Vimala, Bimla or Bimala, and she is also known under the maiden name Behn, which she had adopted while she was with Gandhi's English disciple Sarah Behn. See Vandana Shiva, *Staying Alive* (1988; repr., London: Zed Books, 2002), 70.
69 Ramachandra Guha and Juan Martinez-Alier, *Varieties of Environmentalism* (London: Earthscan, 1997), 154.
70 Guha, *The Unquiet Woods*, 173.
71 For example Madhav Gadgil and Ramachandra Guha, *Ecology and Equity* (London: Routledge, 1995), 23.
72 Pranab Mukhopadhyay and Priya Shyamsundar, 'Economic Growth and Ecological Sustainability in India', in *The Oxford Handbook of the Indian Economy*, ed. Chetan Ghate (New York: Oxford University Press, 2012), 608.
73 Sahana Ghosh, 'State of the Forest Report says that India's Forest and Tree Cover has Increased by 1 Percent', *Mongabay-India*, 16 February 2018, https://india.mongabay.com/2018/02/state-of-forest-report-says-that-indias-forest-and-tree-cover-has-increased-by-1-percent/.
74 Ghosh, 'Forest Report'.
75 Mayank Aggarwal, 'India's Forest Cover Target Influenced by Colonial Policies rather than Scientific Basis', *Mongabay-India*, 21 January 2019, https://india.mongabay.com/2019/01/indias-forest-cover-target-influenced-by-colonial-policies-rather-than-scientific-basis-says-study/.
76 Krishnaswamy, 'Forest Management', 87.
77 See Rangan, *Myths and Movements*, 6–8.
78 Meera Nanda, 'Dharmic Ecology and the Neo-Pagan International', paper presented at the *18th European Conference on Modern South Asian Studies* (2004), 1–5.
79 Mundy, *Fall of Needwood*, 32.

Bibliography

Aggarwal, Mayank. 'India's Forest Cover Target Influenced by Colonial Policies rather than Scientific Basis'. *Mongabay-India*, 21 January 2019. https://india.mongabay.co

m/2019/01/indias-forest-cover-target-influenced-by-colonial-policies-rather-than-scientific-basis-says-study/

Aslet, Clive. *Villages of Britain: The Five Hundred Villages that Made the Countryside.* London: Bloomsbury, 2010.

Blackstone, William. *Commentaries on the Laws of England.* 4 vols. Oxford: Clarendon Press, 1765–1769.

Blake, William. *Songs of Innocence and of Experience.* 1789, 1794. Reproduction of Copy C, with an introduction by Geoffrey Keynes. London: Rupert Hart-Davis, 1967. (Citations refer to the transcript rather than to the colour plates.)

Bowerbank, Sylvia. *Speaking for Nature.* Baltimore: Johns Hopkins University Press, 2004.

Brock, Emily K. 'New Patterns in Old Places: Forest History for the Global Present'. In *The Oxford Handbook of Environmental History*, edited by Andrew C. Isenberg, 154–77. Oxford: Oxford University Press, 2014.

Castellano, Katey. *The Ecology of British Romantic Conservatism, 1790–1837.* New York: Palgrave Macmillan, 2013.

Chester, Kirby. 'The English Game Law System'. *American Historical Review* 38, no. 2 (1933): 240–62.

Cole, George Douglas Howard. *A Short History of the British Working Class Movement 1789–1848.* 1925. 3 vols. London and New York: Routledge, 2002.

Country Land and Business Association. 'Future of the Natural Environment after the EU Referendum'. Report for the UK Environmental Audit Committee dated 2 September 2016. http://www.cla.org.uk/influence/policy-library/future-natural-environment-after-eu-referendum

Cox, Graham. "Listen to Us!" Country Sports and the Mobilization of a Marginalized Constituency'. In *The Contested Countryside*, edited by Jeremy Burchardt and Philip Conford, 145–66. London: Tauris, 2008.

Crehan, Stewart. *Blake in Context.* Dublin: Gill and Macmillan, 1984.

Daniels, Stephen. 'The Political Iconography of Woodland in later Georgian England'. In *The Iconography of Landscape*, edited by Dennis Cosgrove and Stephen Daniels, 43–82. Cambridge: Cambridge University Press, 1998.

Food and Agriculture Organization of the UN. 'Forest Area (% of Land Area) European Union'. Accessed 20 July 2019. https://data.worldbank.org/indicator/AG.LND.FRST.ZS?locations=EU

Gadgil, Madhav and Guha Ramachandra. *Ecology and Equity.* London: Routledge, 1995.

Ghosh, Sahana. 'State of Forest Report says that India's Forest and Tree Cover has increased by 1 Percent'. *Mongabay-India*, 16 February 2018. https://india.mongabay.com/2018/02/state-of-forest-report-says-that-indias-forest-and-tree-cover-has-increased-by-1-percent/

Gopal, Priyamvada. 'Reading Subaltern History'. In *The Cambridge Companion to Postcolonial Literary Studies*, edited by Neil Lazarus, 139–61. Cambridge: Cambridge University Press, 2004.

Griffin, Carl. 'Protest Practice and (Tree) Cultures of Conflict'. *Transactions of the Institute of British Geographers* 33, no. 1 (2007): 91–108.
Guha, Ramachandra. *How Much Should a Person Consume?* Berkeley: California University Press, 2006.
Guha, Ramachandra. *The Unquiet Woods*. Berkeley: California University Press, 2001.
Guha, Ramachandra and Juan Martinez-Alier. *Varieties of Environmentalism: Essays North and South*. London: Earthscan, 1997.
Hay, Douglas. 'Legislation, Magistrates, and Judges'. In *The British and their Laws in the Eighteenth Century*, edited by David Lemmings, 59–79. Suffolk: Boydell Press, 2005.
Hinde, Thomas. *Forests of Britain*. London: Victor Gollancz, 1985.
James, Noel David Glaves. *A History of English Forestry*. Oxford: Blackwell, 1981.
Kala, Chandra Prakash. 'Indigenous Uses and Structure of Chir Pine Forest in Uttaranchal Himalaya, India'. *International Journal of Sustainable Development and World Ecology* 11, no. 2 (2004): 205–10.
Krishnaswamy, Jagdish. 'Forest Management and Water in India'. In *Forest Management and the Impact on Water Resources*, edited by Pablo A. Garcia-Chevesich, Daniel G. Neary, David F. Scott, Richard G. Benyon and Teresa Reyna, 87–104. Paris: UN Educational, Scientific and Cultural Organization, 2017.
Kumar, Kiran, R. Patil, G. R. Manjunatha and Chandrakanth Mysore. 'Demand for Forest Products in India – Role of Institutions'. *Indian Journal of Ecology* 43, no. 2 (December 2016): 482–90.
Landry, Donna. *The Invention of the Countryside*. Hampshire: Palgrave, 2001.
Lawrence, Henry W. 'The Greening of the Squares of London'. *Annals of the Association of American Geographers* 83, no. 1 (1993): 90–118.
McCarthy, Michael. 'Green Giants'. *The Independent*, 25 April 2008. https://www.independent.co.uk/environment/nature/green-giants-our-love-affair-with-trees-815329.html
Monbiot, George. 'Class War on the Hoof'. *The Guardian*, 13 September 2004. https://www.theguardian.com/politics/2004/sep/14/hunting.uk
Mukhopadhyay, Pranab and Priya Shyamsundar. 'Economic Growth and Ecological Sustainability in India'. In *The Oxford Handbook of the Indian Economy*, edited by Chetan Ghate, 591–618. New York: Oxford University Press, 2012.
Mundy, Francis Noel Clarke. *The Fall of Needwood*. Derby: J. Drewry, 1808.
Mundy, Francis Noel Clarke. *Needwood Forest*. Lichfield: Jackson, 1776.
Murali, Atluri. 'Whose Trees? Forest Practices and Local Communities in Andhra, 1600–1922'. In *Nature, Culture, Imperialism*, edited by David Arnold and Ramachandra Guha, 86–122. Delhi: Oxford University Press, 1995.
Nanda, Meera. 'Dharmic Ecology and the Neo-Pagan International'. Paper presented at the *18th European Conference on Modern South Asian Studies*, Lunds University, Sweden, July 2004. http://www.sacw.net/DC/CommunalismCollection/ArticlesArchive/072004_D_Ecology_MeeraNanda.pdf

Nicholls, Philip H. 'On the Evolution of a Forest Landscape'. *Transactions of the Institute of British Geographers* 56 (1972): 57–76.
Nicol, Clive William. 'Hailing the Benefits of Raising a Stink'. *The Japan Times*, 30 April 2016. https://www.japantimes.co.jp/life/2016/04/30/environment/hailing-benefits-raising-stink/#.XTLtsS2B1sM
Poffenberger, Mark. 'The Resurgence of Community Forest Management in the Jungle Mahals of West Bengal'. In *Nature, Culture, Imperialism*, edited by David Arnold and Ramachandra Guha, 336–69. Delhi: Oxford University Press, 1995.
Rackham, Oliver. *Trees and Woodland in the British Landscape*. 1976. London: J. M. Dent, 1983.
Rangan, Haripriya. *Of Myths and Movements*. London: Verso, 2000.
Rawlinson, Nick. *William Blake's Comic Vision*. Hampshire: Palgrave Macmillan, 2003.
Rigby, Kate. *Topographies of the Sacred*. Charlottesville: University of Virginia Press, 2004.
Shiva, Vandana. *Staying Alive*. London: Zed Books, 2002. First published 1988 by Kali for Women (New Delhi).
Stepp, John Richard. *Ethnoecology and Medicinal Plants of the Highland Maya*. Cham: Springer, 2018.
Stott, Philip. *Tropical Rainforest*. London: Institute of Economic Affairs, 1999.
Thomas, Keith. *Man and the Natural World*. 1983. London and New York: Penguin, 1984.
UK Forestry Commission. Department of Environment, Food & Rural Affairs. *Government Forestry and Woodlands Policy Statement*. London: Defra, 2013. https://assets.publishing.service.gov.uk/government/uploads/system/uploads/attachment_data/file/221023/pb13871-forestry-policy-statement.pdf
UK Parliament. House of Commons. *Report from the Select Committee on Public Walks*. London: House of Commons, 1833.
UK Parliament. House of Lords. Vol. 43 of *Journals of the House of Lords*. London: House of Lords, 1801.
Van der Zee, Bibi. 'England's Forests: A Brief History of Trees'. *The Guardian*, 27 July 2013. https://www.theguardian.com/travel/2013/jul/27/history-of-englands-forests
White, Gilbert. *The Natural History and Antiquities of Selborne*. London: Bensley, 1789.
Williams, Raymond. *Culture and Materialism*. 1980. London: Verso, 2005.
Williams, Sarah Johanna. *Sherwood Forest, a Poem*. Nottingham: Stretton, 1832.
Williamson, Tom. *An Environmental History of Wildlife in England 1650–1950*. London: Bloomsbury, 2013.

9

Shaping selves and spaces

Romanticism, botany and south-west Western Australia

Jessica White

'Lost to the Sight'

In 1828, Georgiana Kennedy, a young woman born in Carlisle in 1805, made a journey through the Scottish lochs near Rosneath to Gourock, Greenock, Rothesay, the Isle of Bute, Tarbert and Inverary. She had quitted a home in which her sister grappled with alcoholism and her mother was unable, or unwilling, to remedy her sister's illness. Looking at Dunbartonshire, across the water from Greenock, she wrote:

> the beautiful shades which a bright July evening cast over those blue and varied mountains can only be imagined by those of a warm and ardent temperament whose mind is just recovering from many painful circumstances. . . . The Clyde was unrippled and of a palish sapphire blue[,] two [or] three skiffs lay moored off the Beach, and the dark smoke emitted by some steam vessels plying from Greenock lighted on the dark green woods of Roseneath and was lost to the sight, the sky all the while, [was] most beautifully blue and mingled with soft white clouds.[1]

The peace conveyed by the 'unrippled' Clyde and the gentleness of its colour, together with the steam and softness of the air, suggests Kennedy had arrived at a more tranquil place than the one she left behind, and that the natural world was a palliative for her. Raised not far from the cradle of romantic writers such as Dorothy and William Wordsworth, and identifying with at least one of its poets, Robert Burns, her writing shows the influences of this period, which include an intense rapport with nature.

A year later, Georgiana Kennedy was married and on her way to Australia. At the age of twenty-four, with her options narrowing, she had met John Molloy, a soldier who fought in the Napoleonic War, and agreed to sail with him to the fledgling colony of Swan River (now Perth) in south-west Western Australia. When the Molloys arrived in 1830, they found that there was no land left to the colonizers in this area, and sailed south to Augusta. In this unique region, now designated a biodiversity hotspot because of the extraordinary diversity of its plant life, Molloy's romantic visions met with the Enlightenment enterprise of collecting and classifying the natural world. At the behest of a botanical connoisseur, Captain James Mangles, who lived in London, Molloy began collecting seeds and specimens. She also wrote Mangles long, detailed letters about her interactions with plants and included them with her boxes of seeds.

Through a comparison of Molloy's early writing – specifically her account of her journey through the lochs leading to Inverary – with her later letters to Mangles, this chapter explores how Molloy's engagement with the culture and literature of the romantic period shaped her initial perception of her Australian environment, and how this was transformed by her botanical project. In doing so, it exemplifies how, as Alan Bewell has outlined in *Natures in Translation*, colonial environments were shaped 'as much by the immigration of plants and animals as by the immigration of people'.[2] However it also provides an important point of depature by illuminating how Molloy's acquisition of botanical knowledge was shaped by her gender. Molloy's transposition to Australia opened up her life in marvellous and unexpected ways. Through her story and its interconnection with Noongar peoples, the longstanding custodians of the south-west's land, waters and other living inhabitants, we might perceive and respond ethically and urgently to Australia's remarkable flora amid the pressures of our environmental crisis.

Romantic visions

Molloy, the granddaughter of a mayor of Carlisle,[3] grew up in Crosby Lodge, a large Georgian building with a walled garden, within which she learned about plants and gardening. Her family circle touched that of a number of romantic writers. Her mother, Elizabeth Kennedy (née Dalton), was a friend of Robert Southey, a poet and friend of the Wordsworths. Wordsworth's friend and benefactor Richard Calvert was married to Mary Calvert, the daughter of John Mitchison, who was Mrs Kennedy's guardian.[4] Mrs Kennedy was also said to have received an offer of marriage from another of Southey's friends, Dr Andrew Bell.[5] Her mother's imbrication in this world of romantic writers, as well as Molloy's proximity to the landscape about which they wrote, suggests that she would have been familiar with their writing and how it represented the natural world.

Molloy was also interested in the poet Robert Burns, taking an 1824 edition of his *Songs Chiefly in the Scottish Dialect* with her to Australia.[6] A few weeks prior to Burns's death in 1796 from endocarditis, his doctor recommended that he taste the spring waters of the Brow Well near Ruthfield in Dumfries, and wade up to his neck in the cold waters of Solway Firth, the body of water which forms part of the border between England and Scotland. The firth is some seventeen miles from Crosby Lodge, and if Molloy did not know of Burns's death as she was growing up, she would have understood the closeness of its location to her home when the poet's work came into her possession.

Although sometimes marginalized in discussions of British romanticism, other approaches have placed Burns at its 'heart'.[7] The poet likely provided solace for Molloy when she was struggling to settle herself after her difficult family situation and her uncertain marriage prospects, given that his poetry was a medium that 'embodied genuine feeling and, crucially, made it live for ever. Again and again, people turned to Burns to find suitable words for expressing their own feelings, confident that his lines were able to stand the test of time.'[8] Molloy's decision to take the volume with her to Australia indicates a strong connection to his writing.

While Burns has often been read in the context of Scottish national identity and dialect, social inequality and ideas of constraint and freedom, he was also deeply embedded in the natural world. As the son of tenant farmer, he was raised in poverty and struggled to make a living when he became a farmer himself. When his first volume of poems sold well, he was relieved of his planned journey to the slave plantations of Jamaica to raise an income. His agricultural background shaped him into a man 'with his feet firmly on the ground'.[9] Instead of 'imitating literary convention, he felt his environment, recreating his responses in poetry'.[10] Ecocritical readings of his work reveal that he made hundreds of references to flowers, trees, rivers, mountains, woods, the seasons and the weather, and that he protested when he saw nature and its inhabitants degraded.[11] Like Burns, Molloy was a passionate person who responded emotionally to the natural world, and these references perhaps resonated with her.

The clearest indication that Molloy's perspectives were influenced by romantic culture is her account of her travels through the lochs. In the influential study,

Romanticism and the Materiality of Nature (2002), Onno Oerlemans observes that romantic writers expressed a profound interest in the natural world:

> Their distinctive passion was marked by the rage for the picturesque tour, a pronounced interest in landscape painting, the celebration and detailed descriptions of natural settings, a seeming rejection of the city and the culture it represented, as well as a notable interest in the physical sciences.[12]

Molloy's account exhibits many of the characteristics which Oerlemans describes. First, her journey through the lochs was an echo of domestic tours taken at the end of the eighteenth century. These excursions had become as popular as the Grand Tour to the Continent, prompted by the dangers of the French Revolution and European-wide war, alongside a resurgence of British patriotism.[13] They were part of the blossoming of the picturesque in Britain, a way of describing the landscape as though it were a painting, which 'takes in caves, quarries and mines, as well as lochs, pikes and gills'.[14] It depended on contrast and ruins for effect, as well as a sense of obscurity created by twilight, moonlight, mist or cloud,[15] elements which appear in Molloy's account. 'At East Loch Tabert', she wrote, there 'is a castle in ruins of great antiquity'.[16] From Greenock she saw the mountains opposite recede 'into a deep purple mist' while, on a bright evening she saw Roseneath, also opposite, forming 'a rich contrast to the grey parts of the mountains receding from it'.[17] Molloy also created 'a sketch of Loch Striven with which I was much pleased',[18] which gestures to the interest in landscape painting, as mentioned by Oerlemans.

Another aspect of romantic ecological sensibility in Oerlemans's account – an attention to the physical sciences – is illuminated by Molloy's interest in botany. On her trip she collected several flowers 'as souvenirs of the different places'[19] she visited, including grass from the graves of men wrecked by the *Comet* in 1825 after its collision with a steamer. Sixty-two of the estimated eighty passengers were killed, including the son-in-law of John Anderson, a friend of the Scottish poet Robert Burns. Molloy's association between collecting and emotional responsiveness – she writes that her thoughts on the wreck were 'tinged with melancholy'[20] – is clear in her actions, and when Molloy moved to Australia, this link between collecting and emotion prompted her to radically reshape her perception of her environment.

Translocation

In 1800, Nicholas Baudin, captain of the corvette *Le Geographé*, set off from Le Havre on the coast of France. He arrived on the west coast of Australia in

1801 and charted the length of this coast and some of the south coast. This voyage, like other French voyages to this region, were primarily undertaken because of France's commitment to science and discovery rather than a compulsion to colonize, although the voyagers were requested to take political and mercantile considerations into account.[21] The journals of successive French commanders to the Pacific Bougainville, La Pérouse and Baudin underscore this priority, being focused more on practical, aesthetic or scientific matters 'while remaining alert to the resources and opportunities for trade presented by the places they visited'.[22] Nonetheless, the British were nervous about the French presence.[23] On 21 January 1827, Major Lockyer took possession of the western third of Australia for the British crown. The Swan River colony, at what is now Perth, was established two years later, under the governance of James Stirling, and colonizers such as the Molloys began to arrive.

Although Molloy had great mental fortitude – evidenced by her decision to leave her difficult family, marry John Molloy and accompany him to the other side of the world – nothing could have prepared her for the privations that were to come when she landed on the shores of Augusta. A few days after her arrival, she gave birth to her daughter in a tent in pouring rain. Over the course of ten days, her baby weakened and died. In an echo of Burns's passionate reactions to the natural world, Molloy's response was elemental: 'I felt inclined to rush out into the open air and charge the winds with what weighed so heavy at my bursting head.'[24] Her lingering despair was so overwhelming that she could not describe it with words. Three years afterwards, she wrote in a letter to her friend Helen Storey, 'language refuses to utter what I experienced when mine died in my arms in this dreary land, with no one but Molloy near me'.[25] Instead, she tried to create meaning through symbolic acts: placing a blue native flower in her baby's grave and, later, planting British clover on top of it. Her tentative embrace of her environment, signalled by her picking of the blue flower, was engulfed by the magnitude of her grief and the impenetrable surrounding bush. She continued in her letter, 'Its grave, though sodded with British clover, looks so singular and solitary in this wilderness, of which I can scarcely give you an idea.'[26]

Molloy's vision, as has been indicated, was shaped in Cumbria and Dunbartonshire, and as such she scrambled for descriptors of the jarrah and karri forests which surrounded her. In a letter to her sister Elizabeth, written two and a half years after she arrived in Australia, she wrote, 'This is certainly a beautiful place – but were it not for domestic charms the eye of the emigrant would soon weary of the unbounded limits of thickly clothed dark green forests where nothing can be described to feast the imagination.'[27] These lines indicate Molloy's inability to distinguish between the surrounding mass of vegetation.

While her earlier description of Dunbartonshire included the 'dark green woods of Roseneath' forming a backdrop to the 'beautifully blue' sky,[28] here the Australian woods fail to ignite her mind. Conditioned by the parameters of the picturesque, which features contrast (between landscape forms and between light and shade), she did not have a visual or literary vocabulary for her new world.

Molloy was not alone in finding herself at a loss for words. Thomas Watling, who was sentenced for fourteen years to the penal colony in New South Wales for forgery, wrote to his aunt in Dumfries in 1792, 'The air, the sky, the land are objects entirely different from all that a Briton has been accustomed to see before.'[29] Watling's reference to vision and Molloy's phrase 'the eye of the emigrant' indicate how they were accustomed to perceiving the world with a particular framework, and how their imagination was disorientated by this new experience of colonial nature.

As indicated by her account of her journey through the lochs, Molloy relied upon this world to ignite her imagination. In the passage which opened this chapter, she refers to her pained emotions, which prompt her imaginative engagement with 'the beautiful shades which a bright July evening cast'.[30] She was part of the movement in which, towards the end of the eighteenth century, 'an insistence on reason as the predominant human faculty had run its course and the imagination began to emerge as another force'.[31] Romantic aesthetics have since come to be commonly associated with the valorization of imagination.[32] Yet in this new country, Molloy's inability to find coordinates with her new world meant that her imagination remained closed, bounded like the forests around her.

Molloy went on to raise a family with her husband, but had little domestic help in what, to her, would have been primitive conditions. She bore another three daughters and a son, and moved with her family north to Busselton. In 1836, when Molloy's son was nineteen months old, he fell into a well and drowned. This prompted what Molloy described as a 'dangerous illness',[33] most likely a nervous breakdown, which nonetheless contained the seeds for her rejuvenation.

Shipping and seeds

Just prior to her son's death, Molloy received a box of seeds and a letter from Captain James Mangles (1786–1867). Mangles's grandfather Robert was a ship chandler and oilman. When he died in 1788, the year Captain Arthur Phillip arrived in Sydney Cove with a fleet of convicts, he bequeathed the business to Mangles's father John and uncle James. Another uncle, Robert, joined the business in 1805.[34] In 1811, the business, F. and C.F. Mangles, launched *Surry* (also known as *Surrey*), a ship which made transportations of convicts to Australia before the ownership changed hands in 1829.

The acquisition of scientific knowledge in the eighteenth and nineteenth centuries depended a great deal on maritime networks.[35] Not only did Mangles have shipping in his family background, but at age fourteen he entered the navy and fought in the Napoleonic Wars. He had reached the position of officer by the time he left in June 1815 with Napoleon's abdication. The next year, he travelled with his friend Captain Charles Leonard Irby, a messmate from his earliest years in the navy, to Egypt, Syria and Asia Minor, and they published a book on their travels in 1823.[36]

On his return from this journey, while in France, Mangles became friends with James Stirling, another naval captain. He invited Stirling to his uncle's estate in Woodbridge in Suffolk. There, Stirling met Mangles's cousin Ellen, with whom he fell in love. They married when Ellen came of age in 1823. Subsequently, Mangles was elected a fellow of the Royal Society in 1825, and in 1830 he was co-founder and one of the first fellows and members of council of the Royal Geographical Society. He had connections with John Lindley, the first professor of botany at University College, London; with the Loddiges nurserymen of Hackney; and with Joseph Paxton, gardener at Chatsworth and designer of the Crystal Palace for the 1851 Great Exhibition.

After an exploratory trip to Western Australia in 1827, Stirling returned to Britain and lobbied for a settlement at Swan River. When this was approved, he set sail with his family and established the colony in 1829. Two years later, Mangles visited his cousin and friend. By this stage he was a member of the Royal Society, and he was interested in plants,[37] the collection and dissemination of which depended on connections which could increase access to different objects from which new knowledge could be formed.[38] While at the colony, he made the acquaintance of James Drummond, George Fletcher Moore, Captain Richard Goldsmith Mears, Henry Ommaney and Richard Spencer, and requested them to collect seeds for him.[39] In 1837, Molloy was added to this network via Ellen Stirling, Mangles's cousin, with whom she was friends.

When Mangles received seeds from Western Australia, he distributed them to his botanical acquaintances as a way of cementing social relations and exchanging knowledge. Within British aristocratic circles, exotic plants became a currency that could buy prestige.[40] The exchange of plants could also create new social relations, while '"tributes" and "briberies" were paid in the forms of seeds and specimens; rewards were given by coining names; revenues were counted in terms of "new" specimens'.[41] In a letter to Joseph Paxton on 30 June 1840, Mangles included with Molloy's seeds a request for goldfish, which he wanted to grow in a fish pond in his garden in Cambridge Terrace, London. Paxton had no fish and answered in the negative.

Mangles had more luck in his exchanges with Stirling. David Don, professor of botany at King's College London from 1836 to 1841, and librarian at the Linnaean Society of London from 1822 to 1841, explained: 'This singularly beautiful species of Anigozanthos was raised in the garden at Whitmore Lodge, Berks., the seat of Robert Mangles, Esq. from seeds brought from Swan River by Sir James Stirling, the enterprising governor of that colony, by whom they had been presented to Mr. Mangles.'[42] The friendship between Mangles and Stirling was cemented by the gift of seeds and their growth in the soil of Robert Mangles's Berkshire estate. Don further celebrated the family by naming the plant, *Anigozanthos manglesii*, in their honour, thus overwriting the Noongar name for the plant, *Kurulbrang*. The plant, the common name of which is the 'red-and-green kangaroo paw' or 'Mangles kangaroo paw', is also now the floral emblem of Western Australia.

While also detailing the networks of wealthy white men, these exchanges demonstrate the translation of Australian plant life into British soil. Mangles's acquaintances were enamoured of Australian plants and chronicled their growth in letters to each other. George Wailes of Newcastle updated Mangles on his lack of success, writing on 25 March 1841, 'in my eager desire to oblige a friend I lost a large portion of the "Acacias", and Kennedias by taking them out of the seed Boxes in November.'[43] Others were so successful at growing the specimens that they cultivated them for public purchase and entered them in shows. *Lechenaultia biloba* caused great excitement when it appeared in Britain in 1841. It was raised from seeds collected by Molloy's contemporary James Drummond, and won a Silver Knightian Medal from the Horticultural Society that year.[44]

These processes of 'biological translation', as Bewell has noted, meant that local natures were transformed through their integration 'within a globalised system of trade and knowledge exchange'.[45] He draws on Paul Carter's research on cartography and naming to illuminate how '[i]n the same way that early explorers claimed ownership of territory through maps and landscape studies, scientific naming and describing were inherently a claim of ownership, based on the idea that the British were the first people to truly understand this nature'.[46] Although she participated in the colonial project of possessing through collecting and classification, Molloy did not have the capacity to name plants[47] and did not benefit financially from her efforts (Mangles sent her gifts of green silk and books instead). This exclusion, while it led to a lack of recognition for her efforts, still radically altered Molloy's relationship to the spaces of her natural surroundings, as well as her sense of self.

Precision and poetry

Molloy's familiarity with collecting stemmed from her education as a young woman of leisure in Carlisle. Botany was a polite activity in the lives of English girls and women of the late eighteenth and early nineteenth centuries, being 'both a fashionable form of leisure and . . . an intellectual pursuit'.[48] Molloy sailed to Australia with intentions of collecting, for she packed a *hortus siccus*, a book into which specimens were fastened for identification purposes. Her brother George had asked her to collect seeds, but she could not find time to satisfy this request,[49] although she did send seeds to her sister Elizabeth. When she received Mangles's first letter, Molloy explained her shortness of time, but added that she had 'already collected some seeds', with his box arriving 'just at the proper season'.[50] After the death of her son, however, she went into the bush daily to take her mind from her grief.

As Molloy began to collect flowers, her perception of her surroundings began to shift. Where before she had referred to the bush as an indistinguishable mass of vegetation, unable to relate it to dramatic rocky outcrops or the still water of lochs, now she focused upon individual flowers and came to adore them. Part of the reason for this was the intense focus needed to observe and collect the flowers in this area. The soil of south-west Western Australia is poor in nutrients and many of the flowers are no bigger than a fingernail. Molloy lamented in a letter to Mangles, 'I long to see again a large flower.'[51]

As she had no knowledge of Australian flora, Molloy needed to carefully observe the tiny flowers to distinguish between them, collect their seeds and mount the dried specimens into a *hortus siccus*. Her careful attention to the plants supports Bernard Smith's observations in *European Vision and the South Pacific* that the precision needed to illustrate new (to British eyes) flora and fauna altered the prevailing mode of perception, neoclassicism. Where neoclassicism 'stressed the extreme importance of the unity of mood and expression', the analytical observation of the New World 'tended towards the disruption of such unity, forcing the artist to look at the world as a world of disparate things'.[52]

Another reason for Molloy's attentiveness to the plants was her belief that she did not have the authority to name them. Although she collected and grew plants in Britain, like many of her female contemporaries she did not have a scholarly understanding of botany as it was impossible for women to participate in the institutions which formalized botanical science. They could not be 'members of the Royal Society or the Linnaean Society, could not attend meetings, read papers, or (with very rare exceptions) see their findings published in journals of those societies'.[53] Latin was not part of their education, which meant they did not always have the means of understanding the classes and orders through which these plants were classified. Restrictions such as these led Molloy to write to Mangles on 8 July 1840, 'I send two flowers of the . . . I dare not say what, Dr Lindley must determine.'[54] Dr Lindley was, ironically, behind the movement to make botany more scientific, by engineering a gendered demarcation between what he called 'amusement for ladies' and botanical science, 'that occupation for the serious thoughts of man'.[55]

Desperate for knowledge, Molloy developed her own system, whereby she gave each flower and its seed a number. She then asked Mangles, to 'oblige me by sending me the names of the different flowers according to their numbers; I have kept the numbers of each, and the duplicates of most of the Specimens that I might have the satisfaction of hearing some name attached to them'.[56] In this way, Molloy was able to avoid the frustration created by using the Linnaean system, which plagued others new to Australian flora, such as James Edward Smith, founder of the Linnaean Society.

In *A Specimen of the Botany of New Holland* (1793), Smith described his attempts to fit the flora into a language not designed for it:

> Whole tribes of plants, which at first sight seem familiar to his acquaintance, as occupying links in Nature's chain . . . prove, on a nearer examination, total strangers, with other configurations, other oeconomy [sic], and other qualities; not only the species that present themselves are new, but most of the genera, and even natural orders.[57]

As indicated by his words 'points', 'links', 'configurations' and 'orders', Smith found himself frustrated by a lack of correspondence. For Molloy, however, the absence of a classification system prompted a more poetic means of describing plants. She wrote to Mangles: 'No 67 is very elegant, of uncommon foliage, the color [sic] of its blossoms a bright reddish lilac and very viscous; the plant with small white pendulous blossoms tipt with red is particularly beautiful and more like the flower of a dream.'[58] By referring to the plant only by number, not by name, Molloy was free to associate with it in a poetic way, with the reference to the 'dream' shifting it to a symbolic rather than scientific realm.

She also, once she learned the scientific names of the plants from Mangles, began to use them liberally in her letters to show Mangles that she was learning her science. The effect of this was a combination of precision and fancy:

> you ought to be interested in the *Isopogon*, and *Petrophila*; – they are beautiful beyond description, such flowers of imagination; I am now in raptures when I think on them, in searching to come suddenly on such gems, and be surrounded by them, makes you for a time think you are in Fairy Land.[59]

Where, on her 1828 trip to Inverary, Molloy's mental distress alloyed her descriptions of scenery, here her imagination – now liberated by her scientific attention to plants – makes a joyous association. This underscores Richard Gray's observation that:

> Perhaps it is significant that enlightened reason and Romantic imagination, despite their differences, at least share one central metaphorical and perceptual 'prejudice': an insistence on the importance of sight, vision and 'image' as the proper domain of human thought and creativity.[60]

Molloy's intense visual focus on the tiny flora of south-west Western Australia gave rise to her rapturous reimagining of the world.

Shaping a self

Molloy used writing not only to express her reception of her new natural surroundings but also to convey its ripening into an obsession. In a letter begun in June 1840, she wrote to Mangles, 'scarcely a day passes I am not thinking what I can do or how in any way I could promote your cause.'[61] Earlier that year, she gushed, 'I never met with any one who so perfectly called forth and could sympathise with me in my prevailing passion for Flowers.'[62] While Molloy used these lines to charm Mangles,[63] they belied a more serious motive.

Anne Mellor has outlined how the traditional canon of male romantic writers (Blake, Wordsworth, Coleridge, Byron, Shelley and Keats) 'prompted a "masculine Romanticism" that celebrated the development of an automous self' which has 'free will, agency, independence'.[64] Women of the romantic period, by contrast, existed under the legal doctrine of couverture. Under this law, 'females were virtual non-persons: they could not make contracts, initiate lawsuits, or bear witness in court; they could not own property, keep the wages they earned, or possess custody of their children.'[65] Middle-class women such as Molloy were educated 'solely to attract and please husbands with their accomplishments', and they were taught few useful skills.[66]

Yet through these skills, Molloy found her freedom. By using her accomplishments in botany, she was able to practise science.[67] She made empirical observations on the plants she collected and assessed what they needed to survive:

> I have no hesitation in declaring that were I to accompany the box of Seeds to England, knowing as I do, their situation, time of flowering, soil and degree of moisture required with the fresh powers of fructification they each possess – I should have a very extensive conservatory or conservatories of none but plants from Augusta.[68]

This is a clear assertion of the importance of collecting and classifying for Molloy, but there are other statements in her writing that point to her understanding of her work as a vocation. On 22 June 1840 she wrote, 'when I sally forth either on foot or Horseback, I feel quite elastic in mind and Step; I feel I am quite at my own work, the real cause that enticed me out to Swan River.' Her mention of 'my work' indicates how integral the project was to Molloy's sense of taking on a vocation. Yet there is another phrase which gestures towards the freedom she found in her environment: 'being in the bush is to me one of the most delightful states of existence free from every household care, my husband & Children and all I possess on Earth about me.'[69] Completely untrammelled, Molloy was able to experience a freedom which was usually confined to male romantic poets.

In this sense, Molloy continued engaging with and finding inspiration in science at a time when, in Britain, women's scientific authority was under threat. As Melissa Bailes outlines in *Questioning Nature*, female writers such as Anna Barbauld, Charlotte Smith, Helen Maria Williams and Mary Shelley 'exerted cultural authority through the natural sciences, particularly natural history' at a time when women 'did not possess political power'.[70] However, by the 1820s, the increasing secularization of science, the professionalization of disciplines such as literature and natural history, as well as Victorian ideals of feminine propriety, made it 'more difficult for women to participate in serious scientific discussion, let alone to posit new scientific thoughts, observations, or discoveries through imaginative literature'.[71] Molloy, because of her isolation in Australia, and because she was using the medium of private letters rather than poetry, did not face the same set of circumstances as these writers.

She was mindful of managing the boundaries of propriety, and being careful in her assertion of her botanical knowledge. When she noted that she would have 'a very extensive conservatory or conservatories of none but plants from Augusta', she hastened to add, 'I do not say this vauntingly, but to inspire you with that ardour and interest with which the collection leaves me.'[72] Molloy modifies her confident statement about the acquisition of scientific knowledge about plants and their conditions for growth with a denial of her 'vaunting', as well as an acknowledgement of her gratitude to Mangles. In her next breath, she refers to her 'ardour and interest', which echoes her mention of the 'warm and ardent temperament' which prompted her vivid descriptions of the lochs. Where Molloy's romantic attitude to landscape occasioned those early literary renditions, here the unique flora of south-west Western Australia precipitated another 20,000 words to Mangles, signifying the remarkable way in which botany ignited her imagination over the course of the following seven years until her untimely death from puerperal fever in 1843.

Extinction and erasure

In her tour of the lochs in 1828, Molloy reacted strongly to the incursions of industrialization when she visited the site of Shaws Water Works, a reservoir created in 1827 to supply water to the town and power to local industries such as a grain and paper mill and a sugar refinery. At the time that she visited, a cotton mill was planned, and her response to the destruction of the environment was vehement: 'what Goths and sordid beings men are!'[73] She wished that the ground allocated to the mills 'belonged to me and I would save it from such profanation',[74] signalling an impulse for conservation, one of the hallmarks of environmentalism. Onno Oerlemans asserts that 'romanticism is an important origin for environmental thought',[75] and Molloy's intense attention to, and delight in, the flora of south-west Western Australia provides a template for understanding the importance of the natural world for emotional, intellectual and imaginative nourishment.

However, her enduring joy in botany was not without repercussions. Although her gender prevented her participation in the more violent expressions of colonization (such as the 1843 massacre of Wardandi Noongar people instigated by her husband, who was government resident, after a white colonist, George Layman, was speared),[76] her collecting project meant that she remained implicated. Colonizers continued to arrive after the Molloys, and

European land management methods had a terrible impact on this unique area. Clearing land for wheat within south-west Western Australia, for example, 'has given rise to the largest single extirpation event in Australia'.[77] As a consequence of these pressures, in 2000, south-west Western Australia was recognized as a biodiversity hotspot, a biologically rich area which has lost at least 70 per cent of its original habitat and which is highly threatened. It is one of thirty-six such regions worldwide, only two of which are in Australia, drawing attention to the need to care for this precious and precarious environment.

Perhaps turning back to the romantics helps us to understand not only the roots of the threat to our natural world, but also the possibility for shifting our perception from disinterestedness to wonder. Resilient, perceptive and curious, Georgiana Molloy is just one of many female figures[78] whose lead we might follow to understand how science transformed her vision of Australian nature from one of incomprehension to one of love.

Notes

1. Georgiana Molloy, 'Notebook Diary in the Handwriting of Georgiana Molloy', ACC4730A/18, Battye Library. Transcribed by H. Margaret Wilson, updated by Patrick Richardson-Bunbury and Mr Graham Hopner.
2. Alan Bewell, *Natures in Translation: Romanticism and Colonial Natural History* (Baltimore: Johns Hopkins University Press, 2017), 28.
3. Bernice Barry, *Georgiana Molly: The Mind that Shines* (Sydney: Picador, 2016), 35.
4. Bernice Barry, *Georgiana Molly*, 43.
5. Sara Hutchinson to Mary Hutchinson, 19 November 1812, in *The Letters of Sarah Hutchinson*, ed. Kathleen Coburn (Toronto: University of Toronto Press, 2017), 50.
6. Barry, *Georgiana Molloy*, 34.
7. Kirsten Sandrock, 'Robert Burns, Selected Poetry (1791-1795)', in *Handbook of British Romanticism*, ed. Ralf Kaekel (Berlin and New York: De Gruyter Mouton, 2017), 261.
8. Fiona Stafford, 'Burns and Romantic Writing', in *The Edinburgh Companion to Robert Burns*, ed. Gerard Carruthers (Edinburgh: Edinburgh University Press, 2009), 109.
9. Stafford, 'Burns and Romantic Writing', 109.
10. Stafford, 'Burns and Romantic Writing', 109.
11. Yann Tholoniat, 'Robert Burns: Nature's Bard and Nature's Powers', in *Environmental and Ecological Readings: Nature, Human and Posthuman Dimensions in Scottish Literature & Arts*, ed. Philippe Laplace (Besançon: Presses Universitaires de Franche-Comté, 2015), 76.

12 Onno Oerlemans, *Romanticism and the Materiality of Nature* (Toronto: University of Toronto Press, 2003), 3.
13 Nicola Trott, 'The Picturesque, the Beautiful and the Sublime', in *A Companion to Romanticism*, ed. Duncan Wu (Oxford: Blackwell Publishers, 1998), 81.
14 Trott, 'Picturesque', 82.
15 Trott, 'Picturesque', 82.
16 Molloy, 'Notebook Diary'.
17 Molloy, 'Notebook Diary'.
18 Molloy, 'Notebook Diary'.
19 Molloy, 'Notebook Diary'.
20 Molloy, 'Notebook Diary'.
21 Danielle Clode, *Voyages to the South Seas: In Search of Terra Australes* (Carlton: The Miegunyah Press, 2007), xx.
22 John West-Sooby, 'Introduction', in *Discovery and Empire: The French in the South Seas*, ed. John West-Sooby (Adelaide: University of Adelaide, 2013), 8.
23 W. B. Kimberly, *History of West Australia: A Narrative of her Past Together with Biographies of her Leading Men* (Melbourne: F.W. Niven, 1897), 31.
24 Georgiana Molloy to Elizabeth Kennedy, (no day) November 1830, DKEN 3/28/9, Cumbria Archive Centre.
25 Georgiana Molloy to Helen Story, 1 October 1833, ACC3278A, Battye Library.
26 Georgiana Molloy to Helen Story, 1 October 1833, ACC3278A, Battye Library.
27 Georgiana Molloy to Elizabeth Besley, 9 November 1832, WAA501, Battye Library.
28 Molloy, 'Notebook Diary'.
29 Cited in Bernard Smith, *European Vision and the South Pacific* (New Haven: Yale University Press, 1985), 14.
30 Molloy, 'Notebook Diary'.
31 Richard T. Gray, *Inventions of the Imagination: Romanticism and Beyond* (Seattle: University of Washington Press, 2011), 4.
32 Gray, *Inventions of the Imagination*, 6.
33 Georgiana Molloy to James Mangles, (no day) September 1838, James Mangles's Letter Books, ACC 479A, Battye Library.
34 *The History of Parliament: The House of Commons 1820-1832*, ed. D. R. Fisher (2009), https://www.historyofparliamentonline.org/volume/1820-1832/member/mangles-james-1762-1838.
35 See Sarah Easterby-Smith, *Cultivating Commerce: Cultures of Botany in Britain and France, 1760–1815* (Cambridge: Cambridge University Press, 2017).
36 James Mangles and Leonard Charles Irby, *Travels in Egypt and Nubia, Syria, and Asia Minor: During the years 1817 and 1818* (London: T. White and Co, 1823).
37 Mangles was chiefly interested in the cultivation of plants and their aesthetics. In 1839 he published *The Floral Calendar*, a guide for cultivating plants for window boxes and other small spaces in town and city gardens.

38 Easterby-Smith, *Cultivating Commerce*, 14.
39 See James Mangles's Letter Books.
40 Beth Fowkes Tobin, *Colonizing Nature: The Tropics in British Arts and Letters, 1760-1820* (Philadelphia: University of Pennsylvania Press, 2005), 181.
41 Staffan Müller-Wille, 'Walnuts at Hudson Bay, Coral Reefs in Gotland: The Colonialism of Linnaean Botany', in *Colonial Botany: Science, Commerce and Politics in the Early Modern World*, ed. Londa Schiebinger and Claudia Swan (Philadelphia: University of Pennsylvania Press, 2005), 47–8.
42 Robert Sweet, *The British Flower Garden (Series the Second): Containing Coloured Figures & Descriptions of the Most Ornamental and Curious Hardy Flowering Plants; or Those That Are Somewhat Tender* (London: J. Ridgeway, 1835), 265.
43 George Wailes to James Mangles, Letter Books, 25 March 1841.
44 David Morrison and Alex George, 'The Genus Lechenaultia', *Curtis's Botanical Magazine* 21, no. 2 (2004): 165.
45 Bewell, *Natures in Translation*, 137.
46 Bewell, *Natures in Translation*, 138.
47 Although Molloy sent hundreds of seeds and specimens to Mangles, only one plant, *Boronia molloyae*, was belatedly named for her in the 1970s. Drummond's name, by contrast, is attached to hundreds of specimens.
48 Ann B. Shteir, *Cultivating Women, Cultivating Science: Flora's Daughters and Botany in England, 1760-1860* (Baltimore: Johns Hopkins University Press, 1996), 36.
49 Georgiana Molloy to James Mangles, 31 March 1837, Letter Books.
50 Georgiana Molloy to James Mangles, 31 March 1837, Letter Books.
51 Georgiana Molloy to James Mangles, 25 January 1838, Letter Books.
52 Smith, *European Vision and the South Pacific*, 3.
53 Shteir, *Cultivating Women*, 37.
54 Georgiana Molloy to James Mangles, Letter Books, 8 July 1840.
55 Cited in Shteir, *Cultivating Women*, 5.
56 Georgiana Molloy to James Mangles, Letter Books, 25 January 1838.
57 James Edward Smith, *A Specimen of the Botany of New Holland* (London: J. Davis, 1793), 9.
58 Georgiana Molloy to James Mangles, Letter Books, 22 June 1840.
59 Georgiana Molloy to James Mangles, Letter Books, 21 November 1838.
60 Gray, *Inventions of the Imagination*, 5.
61 Georgiana Molloy to James Mangles, (no day) June1840.
62 Georgiana Molloy to James Mangles, 31 January 1840.
63 For further detail of Molloy's literary techniques, see Jessica White, 'Efflorescence: The Letters of Georgiana Molloy', *Hecate* 28, no. 2 (2002): 176–90.
64 Anne K. Mellor, 'Gender Boundaries', in *The Oxford Handbook of British Romanticism*, edn David Duff (Oxford: Oxford University Press, 2018), 206.

65 Mellor, 'Gender Boundaries', 205.
66 Mellor, 'Gender Boundaries', 205.
67 In this Molloy was not alone. Artists such as Francois Basseporte and Marianne North, writers such as Priscilla Wakefield and Jane Marcet, collectors such as Jeanne Baret and even patrons of botanical collections like Josephine Bonaparte worked around the peripheries of professional sciences from which they were progressively excluded.
68 Georgiana Molloy to James Mangles, Letter Books, 25 January 1838.
69 Georgiana Molloy to James Mangles, Letter Books, 31 January 1840.
70 Melissa Bailes, *Questioning Nature: British Women's Scientific Writing and Literary Originality 1750-1830* (Charlottesville and London: University of Virginia Press, 2017), 2.
71 Bailes, *Questioning Nature*, 19.
72 Georgiana Molloy to James Mangles, Letter Books, 25 January 1838.
73 Molloy, 'Notebook Diary'.
74 Molloy, 'Notebook Diary'.
75 Oerlemans, *Romanticism and the Materiality of Nature*, 3.
76 Jessica White, '"Paper Talk": Testimony and Forgetting in South-West Western Australia', *Journal of the Association for the Study of Australian Literature* 17, no. 1 (2017): 1–13.
77 Nigel D. Swarts and Kingsley W. Dixon, 'Terrestrial Orchid Conservation in the Age of Extinction', *Annals of Botany* 104, no. 3 (2009): 545.
78 See also Michelle Scott Tucker, *Elizabeth Macarthur: A Life at the Edge of the World* (Melbourne: Text Publishing, 2019); Danielle Clode, *The Wasp and the Orchid* (Sydney: Picador, 2018); and Melissa Ashley, *The Birdman's Wife* (South Melbourne: Affirm Press, 2016).

Bibliography

Ashley, Melissa. *The Birdman's Wife*. South Melbourne: Affirm Press, 2016.
Bailes, Melissa. *Questioning Nature: British Women's Scientific Writing and Literary Originality, 1750–1830*. Charlottesville and London: University of Virginia Press, 2017.
Barry, Bernice. *Georgiana Molloy: The Mind that Shines*. Sydney: Picador, 2016.
Bewell, Alan. *Natures in Translation: Romanticism and Colonial Natural History*. Baltimore: Johns Hopkins University Press, 2017.
Clode, Danielle. *Voyages to the South Seas: In Search of Terra Australes*. Melbourne: The Miegunyah Press, 2007.
Clode, Danielle. *The Wasp and the Orchid: The Remarkable Life of Australian Naturalist Edith Coleman*. Sydney: Picador, 2018.

Easterby-Smith, Sarah. *Cultivating Commerce: Cultures of Botany in Britain and France, 1760–1815*. Cambridge: Cambridge University Press, 2017.

Gray, Richard T. *Inventions of the Imagination Romanticism and Beyond*. Seattle: University of Washington Press, 2011.

Hutchinson, Sara. *The Letters of Sara Hutchinson from 1800 to 1835*. Edited by Kathleen Coburn. London: Routledge and Kegan Paul, 1954.

Kimberly, Warren Bert. *History of West Australia: A Narrative of her Past Together with Biographies of Her Leading Men*. Melbourne: F.W. Niven, 1897.

Mangles, James. *The Floral Calendar, Monthly and Daily*. London: F.W. Calder, 1839.

Mangles, James. Letter Books. ACC 479A, Battye Library.

Mangles, James and Leonard Charles Irby. *Travels in Egypt and Nubia, Syria, and Asia Minor: During the Years 1817 and 1818*. London: T. White and Co, 1823.

Mellor, Anne K. 'Gender Boundaries'. In *The Oxford Handbook of British Romanticism*, edited by David Duff, 204–16. Oxford: Oxford University Press, 2018.

Molloy, Georgiana. Letter to Elizabeth Besley, 9 November 1832, WAA501, Battye Library.

Molloy, Georgiana. Letter to Elizabeth Kennedy, (no day) November 1830, DKEN 3/28/9, Cumbria Archive Centre.

Molloy, Georgiana. Letter to Helen Story, 1 October 1833, ACC3278A, Battye Library.

Molloy, Georgiana. 'Notebook Diary in the Handwriting of Georgiana Molloy'. ACC4730A/18. Transcribed by H. Margaret Wilson, updated by Patrick Richardson-Bunbury and Mr Graham Hopner.

Morrison, David and Alex George. 'The Genus Lechenaultia'. *Curtis's Botanical Magazine* 21, no. 2 (2004): 106–10.

Müller-Wille, Staffan. 'Walnuts at Hudson Bay, Coral Reefs in Gotland: The Colonialism of Linnaean Botany'. In *Colonial Botany: Science, Commerce and Politics in the Early Modern World*, edited by Londa Schiebinger and Claudia Swan, 34–48. Philadelphia: University of Pennsylvania Press, 2005.

Oerlemans, Onno. *Romanticism and the Materiality of Nature*. Toronto: University of Toronto Press, 2003.

Sandrock, Kirsten. 'Robert Burns, Selected Poetry (1791–1795)'. In *Handbook of British Romanticism*, edited by Ralf Kaekel, 259–76. Berlin and New York: De Gruyter Mouton, 2017.

Shteir, Ann B. *Cultivating Women, Cultivating Science: Flora's Daughters and Botany in England, 1760–1860*. Baltimore: Johns Hopkins University Press, 1996.

Smith, Bernard. *European Vision and the South Pacific*. New Haven: Yale University Press, 1985.

Smith, James. *A Specimen of the Botany of New Holland*. London: J. Davis, 1793.

Stafford, Fiona. 'Burns and Romantic Writing'. In *The Edinburgh Companion to Robert Burns*, edited by Gerard Carruthers, 97–109. Edinburgh: Edinburgh University Press, 2009.

Swarts, Nigel D. and Kingsley W. Dixon. 'Terrestrial Orchid Conservation in the Age of Extinction'. *Annals of Botany* 104, no. 3 (2009): 543–56.

Sweet, Robert. *The British Flower Garden (Series the Second): Containing Coloured Figures & Descriptions of the Most Ornamental and Curious Hardy Flowering Plants; or Those That Are Somewhat Tender*. London: J. Ridgeway, 1835.

Tholoniat, Yann. 'Robert Burns: Nature's Bard and Nature's Powers'. In *Environmental and Ecological Readings: Nature, Human and Posthuman Dimensions in Scottish Literature & Arts*, edited by Phillipe Laplace, 75–92. Besançon: Presses universitaires de Franche-Comté, 2015.

Tobin, Beth Fowkes. *Colonizing Nature: The Tropics in British Arts and Letters, 1760–1820*. Philadelphia: University of Pennsylvania Press, 2005.

Trott, Nicola. 'The Picturesque, the Beautiful and the Sublime'. In *A Companion to Romanticism*, edited by Duncan Wu, 79–98. Oxford: Blackwell Publishers, 1998.

Tucker, Michelle Scott. *Elizabeth Macarthur: A Life at the Edge of the World*. Melbourne: Text Publishing, 2019.

West-Sooby, John. *Discovery and Empire: The French in the South Seas*. Adelaide: University of Adelaide Press, 2013.

White, Jessica. 'Efflorescence: The Letters of Georgiana Molloy'. *Hecate* 28, no. 2 (2002): 176–90.

White, Jessica. '"Paper Talk": Testimony and Forgetting in South-West Western Australia'. *Journal of the Association for the Study of Australian Literature* 17, no. 1 (2017): 1–13.

Part III

Decolonial poetics

10

Transcultural ecopoetics and decoloniality in *meenamatta lena narla puellakanny*

Meenamatta Water Country Discussion

Peter Minter

A transcultural ecopoetic event

On a 2004 excursion on Country with friends, plangermairreenner (turbuna-meenamatta) elder, renowned poet, playwright and essayist puralia meenamatta (Jim Everett) chanced upon a man 'painting on a small island in the middle of the river'.[1] They were camping in the pristine Blue Tier region of northeast Tasmania, an escarpment and headwater of four major rivers, known to the plangermairreenner clan of the Ben Lomond people as meenamatta Country.[2] The painter happened to be Jonathan Kimberley, an eighth-generation Anglo-Australian visual artist who has for many years been developing transcultural collaborative art practice with Aboriginal artists such as Warmun elder and painter Patrick Mung Mung (Gija), as well as other artists from the Warmun (Gija) and Patjarr (Ngaanyatjarra) communities in Western Australia. Standing by the flowing water and talking together about the paintings and meenamatta Country, puralia and jonathan found something in common. As a political leader and writer, puralia had for many years interrogated the impacts and legacy of the English invasion of Tasmania, a task which (perhaps necessarily for a poet) included questioning 'the full implications of . . . linguistic colonisation . . . [for while] colonising the land may have been the main game . . . colonising the culture, the soul and spirit of the people, was [also deliberate]'.[3] From Kimberley's perspective, he had been radically rethinking Western landscape painting traditions, questioning their usefulness in the Australian context and the compositional and theoretical problem of how 'the (Western) landscape paradigm in Australia [might] reconfigure itself in collaboration with . . . the "fact-reality" of Aboriginal Country'.[4] What they shared from the outset was not only this common intellectual and creative interest in liberating their own histories, cultures and imaginations from the chains of coloniality, but also a desire to encourage the emergence of a transcultural third space that might positively incorporate, as puralia says, 'different ways of seeing the world', a project of reparative and restorative decoloniality in which 'the world' might be profoundly transformed.[5]

And so began one of the most compelling transcultural collaborations in contemporary Australian literature and art which after 'about twenty field trips over a period of two years'[6] resulted in *meenamatta lena narla puellakanny: Meenamatta Water Country Discussion*, a suite of 'painting-writings' exhibited at the Bett Gallery Hobart in 2006 and the Devonport Regional Gallery in 2007.[7] *Meenamatta Water Country Discussion* is a paradigmatic moment in the expression of a transcultural ecopoetics that is uniquely Australian, not only for its creative synthesis of an Aboriginal cosmology and poetic language with a Western 'countermodern' mode of landscape painting (which Kimberley defines in his practice variously as 'Postlandscape', 'Unlandscape' and 'Working Exmodern'),[8] but also for its particularly situated, Australian expression of decoloniality grounded in a worldly Aboriginal eco-philosophy of Country. As puralia writes:

> Jonathan and I discussed the diversity of concepts of *worldliness* as a means to understand that which is the 'fact-reality' worldliness of 'all-life' Country as compared with that which has been created inside of the *colonial-dome of thinking*. This dome is what I call the West's conditioned thinking that this is the way the world should be, rather than thinking outside of its parameters to redefine the world in its natural state. Through our collaboration we have been able to create a discussion to explore concepts without the limitations of the West's angst for [imagined] Paradise. Our discussion has opened our minds to redefined concepts of a Paradise unwritten, embracing all-life in its fact-reality. It takes us beyond the written, or imagined Paradise to understand that as humans we are but one small component of the ONE 'paradise' in its fact-reality of all-life. Thus our art collaboration produces ONE painting-writing immersion with all-life; our shared identity within it, and of it.[9]

In essence, this chapter seeks to join the conversation by addressing how the 'fact-reality' of the 'all-life' of Country might help disenthrall us from the 'colonial-dome of thinking'. I wish to draw attention to the extraordinary liberatory potential of puralia and jonathan's collaboration, how deliberately working together as 'ONE' they develop a structurally unique 'in-between' third space which not only produces 'painting-writings' from the artists' 'shared identity' as One, but also therefore functions to displace the coloniality of Western modes of modernism and postmodernism as they appear in Australia. Rather than hinging, for instance, upon dialectical progressions between 'intercultural juxtapositions' and quotative appropriations, puralia and jonathan say their 'collaborative use of text and image as One is the absolute opposite of appropriation': 'our work together is One, both the painting and the writing.'[10] Working together as One, the artists challenge contemporary thinking about transcultural conversations and collaborations in Australia, and in doing so contribute to the development of antipodean modes of transcultural and ecopoetic expression that can be decolonizing for everybody. So, while gladly sharing what I think are a remarkable group of painting-writings that are a positive and very compelling instance of a decolonizing Australian transcultural ecopoetics, I also hope to advance a more general sense of how a positively constituted transcultural ecopoetics in Australia might best be defined, particularly when any such category is, for us, striated necessarily by milieu of settlement and coloniality. In part my analysis will rely on what I think of as *the transcultural ecopoetic event* understood across two generic types – a 'nourishing transcultural ecopoetics' and a 'damaging transcultural ecopoetics' – and that *Meenamatta Water Country Discussion* is an exemplary case of the former. I suggest that *Meenamatta Water Country Discussion* produces a uniquely Australian transcultural ecopoetic event that has much to offer planetary-wide conversations about solving important ecopolitical issues such as anthropogenic climate change, especially as we intimately know how deeply ecologies, as much as poetries, can be affected by coloniality in all its guises.

Transcultural ecopoetics and decoloniality

Before moving on to discuss *Meenamatta Water Country Discussion* and its promise as a model for understanding the transcultural ecopoetic event, I first wish to briefly suggest a theoretical framework that describes what I mean by a transcultural ecopoetics and how it can be applied within a broader framework of decoloniality in Australia. An Australian transcultural ecopoetics can best be understood as a regional expression of a broader, planetary formation which is always transformatively imbricating wide-scale molar configurations with localized (and localizing) molecular 'archipelagos of sense'.[11] As I've suggested earlier, an Australian transcultural ecopoetics is necessarily entangled with complex histories of settlement and colonial violence, and so (as is the case almost everywhere) a workable, ethically anchored Australian transcultural ecopoetics can only be properly conceived through its relation to coloniality and decoloniality. A central goal of this chapter is to help realign the transcultural and the ecopoetic according to contemporary Australian historical and cultural specificities.[12] While much important work has been done internationally at the intersection of ecocriticism and postcolonial theory,[13] in Australian criticism there is still a need for work that regionally complicates such narratives in ways that respond to local expressions of transcultural ecopoetic events. In this section I will outline what I think might be central terms for such a framework.

I begin by proposing that 'transcultural ecopoetics' can be a general term in the analysis of environmental literature that emerges where cultures meet, interact and are mutually transformed into a third space, something new.[14] 'Cultures' in this context denotes not only human socio-aesthetic formations, but also non-human species and materialities that are to varying degrees implicated in the formation and expression of meaning from time to time. A 'transcultural ecopoetics' offers a particularly adaptable set of critical tools in which contemporary ecopoetic theory can be productively entangled with special types of transcultural events, particularly those that emerge at the intersection of mutually receptive creative entities or systems in which new onto-poetic pathways and substances are materialized at points of human and non-human confluence and convergence. Essentially a decolonizing transcultural ecopoetics in Australia addresses the appearance of local, transformative transcultural ecopoetic events that, in a movement that reaches beyond the postcolonial, perform a liberatory function in which (i) poiesis in the event is positively delinked from modes of 'coloniality', (ii) all actors in the event (human and non-human: 'cultures' are everywhere) similarly undergo a transformative reframing (that includes delinking from 'coloniality') and (iii) novel, decolonizing onto-poetic spaces emerge. Such transformations can be further historicized by addressing how such events demonstrate emergent types of form, mode and genre in literary and, in this case, visual artworks. The field should be understood as 'transcultural' rather than 'transnational'; its incorporation of both human and non-human species and materialities within local but multiply appearing (transcultural) contact zones suggests how local subjectivities, entities and gestures, for example, can produce meaning that is opaque or resistant to a bordered and/or borderless 'transnational', which in contrast reifies late-Western sociopolitical, economic and aesthetic modernity and globalization. Indeed, the transcultural can contribute to a resistant decolonizing of the transnational. The field is 'ecopoetic' in that it contributes to a field of contemporary literary enquiry that variously problematizes relationships between, very broadly speaking, 'the literary' and, very broadly speaking, 'nature'.[15] I align my work with what Simon Estok describes as one of the 'distinguishing birthmarks of ecocriticism: its activist visions' and how 'the radical appeal of ecocriticism [can be found in] its gestures toward activist possibilities, like other "political" theories before it – feminism, queer theory, postcolonial theory, and versions of cultural materialism'.[16] To this list we can add a decolonizing activist ecopoetics aligned and emergent with planetary Aboriginal eco-philosophies, where the study of poetics and 'nature' is critically informed by First Nations' cultural standpoints and specific interrogations of eco-coloniality and eco-decoloniality.

In broad terms I also propose at least two types of transcultural ecopoetics, a 'nourishing transcultural ecopoetics' and a 'damaging transcultural ecopoetics', in which the event's transformative reframing of constituents bends towards either positive or negative vectors through fields such as the ecological, the aesthetic, the transcultural or the decolonial. Obviously, terms such as 'positive' and 'negative' are (perhaps necessarily) vague, but here, again following ecocriticism's 'activist vision', my discourse is explicitly politicized. On social, cultural and environmentalist grounds, I emphasize an ethical as well as an aesthetic demarcation between generic types of transcultural events that are either peaceful and nourishing ('positive') or warlike and extractive ('negative'). In the case of the negative, a 'damaging transcultural ecopoetics' typically appears in literary and other aesthetic objects that are imbued with 'the colonial matrix of power', a term that has emerged in recent work by prominent Latin American theorists of decoloniality such as Aníbal Quijano and Walter Mignolo.[17] In this milieu, for example, Australian nativist-settler literary formations such as the Jindyworobaks can be appreciated as a damaging regional expression of a 'colonial matrix of power', in which Aboriginal sources are situated as passive repositories for an imperialist extraction of aesthetic value. In the case of a nourishing transcultural ecopoetics, on the other hand, and again in a specifically Australian context, my use of 'nourishing' signals a methodological alignment with Deborah Bird Rose's decolonizing 'Nourishing Terrains'[18] and an Aboriginal eco-philosophy of Country represented in the work of Aboriginal theorists such as Bill Neidjie (1989), David Mowaljarlai (1993), Ambelin Kwaymullina (2005), Vicki Grieves (2008) and Marcia Langton (2017), among many others.[19] A transcultural 'nourishing terrain' suggests both a 'negative ecopoetics', a withdrawal, peeling back or refiguring of settler modes of eco-coloniality – a walking back out of Country – and a coincident liberation of otherwise tyrannized Aboriginal material, philosophical and aesthetic systems.[20]

Writing on the centrality of spirituality in Aboriginal knowledge systems, Grieves (Worimi) writes of 'a philosophy that establishes the wholistic notion of the interconnectedness of the elements of the earth and the universe, animate and inanimate, whereby people, the plants and animals, landforms and celestial bodies are interrelated'.[21] A 'nourishing terrain' is positively multidimensional, embracing all human and non-human entities in generative systems of co-relation constituted by networks of life, law, kinship and narrative.[22] Kwaymullina (Palyku) underscores how '[f]or Aboriginal peoples, country is much more than a place. Rock, tree, river, hill, animal, human – all were formed of the same substance by the Ancestors who continue to live in land, water, sky. Country is filled with relations speaking language and following Law, no matter whether the shape of that relation is human, rock, crow, wattle.'[23] Such systems of relation embody what Mowaljarlai (Ngarinyin) describes as 'the gift of *pattern thinking* . . . the culture which is the blood of this country, of Aboriginal groups, of the ecology, of the land itself',[24] which Kwaymullina addresses when she asks us to:

> Imagine a pattern. This pattern is stable, but not fixed. Think of it in as many dimensions as you like – but it has more than three. This pattern has many threads of many colours, and every thread is connected to, and has a relationship with, all of the others. The individual threads are every shape of life. Some – like human, kangaroo, paperbark – are known to western science as 'alive'; others, like rock, would be called 'non-living'. But rock is there, just the same. Human is there, too, though it is neither the most nor the least important thread – it is one among many; equal with the others. The pattern made by the whole is in each thread, and all the threads together make the whole. Stand close to the pattern and you can focus on a single thread; stand a little further back and you can see how that thread connects to others; stand further back still and you can see it all – and it is only once you see it all that you can recognise the pattern of the whole in every individual thread. The whole is more than its parts, and the whole is in all its parts. This is the pattern that the Ancestors made. It is life, creation, spirit, and it exists in country. . . . [pattern thinking is a] web of relationships established by the Ancestors . . . [which] formed the pattern that was life itself. This pattern – being life – is everywhere.[25]

Unlike transcultural ecopoetic events that reify the 'colonial matrix of power' in cultural and aesthetic formations that are categorically damaging, *Meenamatta Water Country Discussion* constitutes a 'nourishing transcultural ecopoetics' in which onto-poetic ecologies of Aboriginal pattern thinking and enriching relationality are embodied together with an explicitly decolonizing and reparative approach to how Country is represented. Before discussing the collaboration in finer detail, I should finally emphasize that the project of decoloniality is always unfinished and open-ended. I haven't, for example, entitled this section 'A *Decolonised* Transcultural Ecopoetics' because (apart from in utopian imaginings) I don't believe that anything can ever be completely or finally decolonized. All transcultural interactions leave historicized and historicizing ideological traces, just as corporeal interactions between humans always leave imprints and marks such as fingerprints, handprints and sweat, on and through the Other. Put simply, the question can never be one of complete substantive decolonization, but rather the asymptotic imbrication of a built-in ethos in which the character or nature of the imprint and interaction is structurally imbued with varying trajectories of decoloniality and delinking. *Meenamatta Water Country Discussion* is such an event.

meenamatta lena narla puellakanny: *Meenamatta Water Country Discussion*

Returning to a small island in a river in meenamatta Country, we can perhaps listen-in on a conversation between puralia and Kimberley. Puralia says,

> the writing and the painting are the same work. It's not my writing and Jonathan's painting, it's one. . . . The writing and discussion shifted the meaning and form of the painting and vice versa. It was a seamless process. In some respects it was one of the easiest things I have ever done. There was no procrastination. It just flowed.[26]

Kimberley says, 'making work collaboratively is, I suggest, the most effective "way" through the intercultural "between-space" . . . unlimiting "in-between" cultures [by] activating collaborative potential.'[27] Elsewhere Kimberley cites the Cuban art theorist and curator Gerardo Mosquera, who suggests that '[i]ntercultural involvement consists not only of accepting the Other in an attempt to understand him or her and to enrich myself with his or her diversity. It also implies that the Other does the same with me, problematizing my self-awareness', neatly encapsulating a double movement at work in the transcultural, whereby each active node in the event is changed while catalysing change in others.[28] As noted earlier, alongside these changes the transcultural event also produces a completely novel artefact from within the 'in-between' – as puralia says, 'the writing and the painting are the same work. It's not my writing and Jonathan's painting, it's one.'

The 'one' in this case is the work, the exhibition itself, as well as puralia and jonathan's situational Oneness. Without access to the exhibition in situ, we can only rely upon another 'one' that exists as perhaps an archival analogue or register of the physical exhibitions of 2006 and 2007, namely the artists' book published by the Bett Gallery Hobart in 2006. The first page of the book includes two reverberant parallel titles, 'meenamatta walantanalinany (meenamatta country all around)' and 'beyond the colonial construct: meenamatta map of unlandscape'.[29] In a letter to Kimberley dated 16 March 2007, puralia correlates the concept of 'country all around' with the 'fact-reality of being': 'my viewpoint is that I deal with the simple fact-reality, eg. water country connection, that water flows over and through all-life, and the inanimate world . . . I call [this] the simple, fact-reality of being.' Alongside the 'fact-reality of being' in puralia's meenamatta Country, its irrevocable embodiment of an 'all-life' in which 'all living things, including the land, are interconnected and exist simultaneously in the here and now, and in all time, ever-present',[30] Kimberley's overall project is framed by an explicitly decolonizing approach which reaches 'beyond the colonial construct' for an 'unlandscaping' methodology in which Western landscape painting traditions are simultaneously interrogated and radically transformed. As Kimberley says, his collaborations with Aboriginal artists are always initiated through collaborative discussion and as such are

> guided expertly as to the appropriate way to . . . approach Country . . . my role [is] as a student of Country itself . . . primarily in the role as 'listener'; and specifically as a non-initiated whitefella who claims no traditional knowledge or 'ownership' of Country – but rather, one who is open to whatever finds its way into the work and myself, from Country.

Kimberley respectfully understands how 'this is [representative of] the main impediment to be overcome by the Western *Landscape Paradigm* when it comes to relating more reciprocally with Aboriginal Country.'[31]

The transcultural force of *Meenamatta Water Country Discussion* can be felt from the very first image in the catalogue, the monumental painting *beyond the colonial construct: meenamatta map of unlandscape*, sister work to *meenamatta lena walantanalinany (meenamatta water country)* (Figure 10.1). These paintings, both individually and presented together as a diptych, actualize a nourishing transcultural ecopoetic by materially substantiating the 'in-between' discussion between puralia and jonathan as it appears between them and

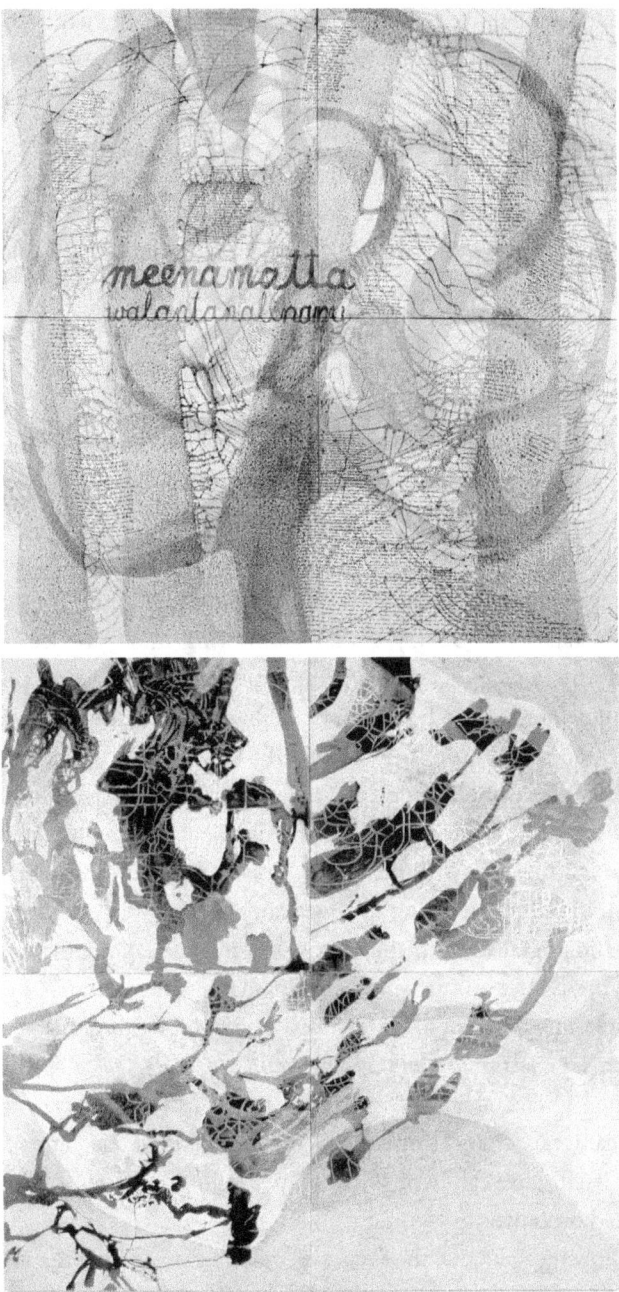

Figure 10.1 Jonathan Kimberley and puralia meenamatta (Jim Everett), *beyond the colonial construct: meenamatta map of unlandscape* [2006, synthetic polymer, charcoal and text on linen, 240 x 240 cm (four panels)] and *meenamatta lena walantanalinany (meenamatta water country)* (2006, synthetic polymer and charcoal on linen, 240 x 240 cm (four panels)). Reproduced with permission of the artists.[32]

meenamatta Country itself. Kimberley writes that they expand 'the spatiality "in-between" Landscape meeting Country. One half of the work contains all of the writing for the project, both in Tasmanian Aboriginal languages and in English, while the other half deliberately contains no written text at all, demonstrating that Aboriginal oral tradition is an implicit part of meenamatta Country and of the collaboration.'[33] As jonathan and puralia related to art critic Helen Vivian, 'in recognition of Aboriginal oral culture ... [t]he sister painting *meenamatta lena walantanalinany (meenamatta water country)* is the one that declares that the map isn't needed, the words and stories always already exist in-Country.'[34] Kimberley puts it perfectly when he writes, 'Country unwritten obliterates the horizon text of landscape.'[35]

beyond the colonial construct: meenamatta map of unlandscape is particularly compelling as it incorporates all thirteen poems into the body of the painting – puralia and jonathan working as One. Overlaying a globular, brain-like orb of interconnected fluid contours, the painting is structured by four vertical columns (representing both large forest trees and the four real/mythical major rivers of meenamatta Country and those flowing into Paradise in medieval maps) and the intermingled texturing of their handwritten poems amid capillaries of driplines. Two translucent red shapes hover like anatomical organs, one overwritten with the word 'ANTIPODES'. This One artwork, together with the exhibition as a whole, is a pivotal moment in the progression of a nascent decolonizing transcultural ecopoetics in Australia. It demonstrates how, in a positive, nourishing transcultural space, poetry and painting can be made to recast and redistribute meaning in ways that are liberatory and transformative. In a sense hinging at first on the words 'beyond the colonial construct', from the title of the first painting, we see 'meenamatta water country' in discussion with the 'unlandscaping' of Country in painting and writing. In the sister work *meenamatta lena walantanalinany (meenamatta water country)*, the absence of the written poems articulates what the artists call 'Country Unwritten'; the painting's calligraphic inscription and embodiment of meenamatta Country is fluidity itself, through which tributaries and capillaries of meaning are substantiated on canvas.

Viewed together as One, the works also demonstrate how the collaboration is striated by matrices of coloniality and decoloniality. The presentation and absenting of the artists' words across the two paintings reflects the productive tension of an emergent transcultural 'in-between' space that speaks of an entanglement between Western language systems and modes of representation with a sovereign Aboriginal onto-poetics. In this way the paintings recast and redefine the modern through a countermodern, transcultural third space that emerges from 'in-between' puralia and Kimberley's measured discussion. As I've mentioned earlier, contemporary modernist and postmodernist frameworks are further displaced by what Kimberley describes as 'a deliberate counterpoint to neo/postmodern appropriation . . . our collaborative use of text and image as One is the absolute opposite of appropriation . . . intended as a clear counterpoint to modernism's perpetual *collage* of appropriation . . . working as One rather than in intercultural juxtaposition'. The artists are 'unwriting as much as they are unpainting'.[36] Thus, in keeping with their sense of how 'the writing and discussion shifted the meaning and form of the painting and vice versa', the artists produce unique patterns of meaning that are mutually transfiguring across the human and non-human:

> The work has gone beyond Country – Meenamatta – it's about 'all-life'. Water is the theme because it connects everything. It is in us and we are part of one big eco-system. Identity and connection to place is the beginning, an important part of it. There is no separateness. Everything is connected, even the rocks and the stones which are washed by water, the clouds that travel water through the sky. What happens when we die is that the water inside us continues on its journey. Humans aren't outside, they are inside.[37]

Without separateness, working together as One clearly raises some interesting questions about Western categories of authorship that rely upon Enlightenment and Romantic formulations of the individual and individual genius. In *Meenamatta Water Country Discussion* we are inside a relational onto-poetics that decolonizes the contours and boundaries of identity and the imprimatur of both literary and painterly authorship. It's important to underline here that while puralia meenamatta was initially identified as the author of the text laid out typographically as free-verse poetry in the first edition of the artists' book, the artists jointly consider the works as 'painting-writings' or 'writing-paintings' produced together as One. I'll refer to them as poems below, because to my mind 'The Poem' can be understood as an aesthetic object that incorporates all such categories, both writerly and painterly, and musically and so on. Insight into this key, central metaphysic is amply provided in the book's long and profoundly affective opening poem, 'water'. An epic creation, abyssal 'middle passage' and renewal poem that enunciates an Aboriginal eco-philosophy of Country against the backdrop of the 'colonial matrix of power', 'water' marks out a set of central terms in puralia's philosophy of 'all-life', how such a philosophy responds to various kinds of coloniality, and how despite coloniality meenamatta Country is nevertheless sustained in ways that enrich both meenamatta sovereignty and a common ground for a nourishing transcultural ecopoetics. The poem begins with a creation story:

> moinie knew that to create life
> would mean that life would need
> a common thread to life
> with country and place so that
> each life would have a role
> yet even though life would be
> many different kinds they all
> would need the 'blood' of life
> itself a thing across everything
> it touches like a fluid
> that would be life
> this all clear fluid 'blood' was created
> and moinie created everything
> with it so that life's blood
> was made 'water' so to travel
> through everything and bond it
> as 'life' that lived with life[38]

The artists then enunciate an eco-philosophy in which the 'all-life' of Country is sustained by water as a 'clear fluid "blood"' that permeates everything:

> so that the trees could drink
> and the possums and birds
> and humans also lived with life
> that connected with all-life
> from the skies to the subterranean
> awash with life's blood as one
> big family that sustained life itself
> ... country was
> home for all-life in a water world
> with a water flow in their blood veins[39]

In cycles of co-substantiation and replenishment, which they remarkably term the 'blood juice cloud', we see a matrix of water as blood, the sustenance of 'all-life' that includes Country, all animals and plants, arteries of kinship in family and clan, and boundless capillaries of kinship between the human and the non-human.

In a radically contrasting middle section of the poem the impact of the 'colonial matrix of power' is laid bare:

> meenamatta being clear-felled for money
> until only the money we cannot drink
> must barter for life from a water controller
> yet it is my blood country from a time before people
> would want to take it all heeding nothing
> that it does when trees are gone and life is still
> in the taking of country from family custodians
> while a society will care not that water will cry
> with dry tears of drought destruction despair
> from the cutting of connections to the death of
> an all-clear water to an all-clear country
> of the all-life that we are family through
> our old world where all-life was with family
> meenamatta country is blood country for clans
> almost lost in the colonial nation of people
> to forget the memory of our first-nations
> where all-life were citizens of the greater family
> to take a place for life for to sustain it with all
> family members who would look after you
> and the life is all-life of family to one and all[40]

In this section of the poem, puralia and jonathan narrate an abyssal 'middle passage' about the destruction caused by extractive, profit-driven industries such as logging and agricultural water control. Uncannily, their 'middle passage' neatly echoes Mignolo's description of the 'four interrelated domains' of 'the colonial matrix of power' (economy; state; corporeality; subjectivity; see endnote 17) in a conflagration that maps the impact of coloniality and modernity upon the meenamatta 'all-life'. Put simply, the artists' discourse makes a clear demarcation between life and death, the nourishing and the damaging.

The impact of 'the colonial matrix of power' is desperately intense but essentially short lived, as with a stroke of cultural confidence and integrity they reassert the vitality and fecundity of water-blood saturated meenamatta Country and the restorative function of cultural and kinship memory:

> in meenamatta country with the clans
> who belong as one under the spiritual-all of life
> with our connector in water through water and blood

> in common theme as family of our blood country
> thus we celebrate our life in connection with all
> we live on in our meenamatta country with its life
> for all things where the magic of truth in water
> keeps our journeys alive in the true essence of life
> ... as with ochre it is with our tomatoes and peppers or man-ferns
> the fullness of life as blood juice red yet with ashes
> or blue yet grey is life we see in blood juice cloud
> ... country is place and space with the all-life
> where king-ferns stand over man-ferns
> on winifred river's steep banks in native forest
> that cups big boulders on rocky floors
> until water falls from cloudy skies
> to journey down in rising cascade
> to cover the big boulders in their cups
> as the king-ferns look over the creek-veins[41]

In an extraordinary enunciation of trans-species kinship networks that are at the heart of Aboriginal eco-philosophies of Country, puralia tropes humans as ferns that grow in cascades of forest and river, waterways and arteries making moisture and blood for living, 'creek veins' feeding 'man-ferns' with 'an invisible spirit of all-life / the clear water is all-clear forever'.[42]

Following 'water', the artists' poems elaborate a nourishing and decolonizing ethics of Country in which clan and kinship are always saturated by water and blood. 'In the time of living origin' they contemplate temporal scale, noting that 'time is endless for water' despite the coloniality of church and state. puralia's natal, living origins are underlined in the following poems 'birthing water' and 'water spirits', which are embedded in the painting *pura-lia lena retena aya–aya: paperbark water-heart rebirth*, in which puralia's birth and totem are substantiated in a complex network of relation and nourishing, generative collaborative poiesis. Vivian conveys how this painting is essentially a 'portrait of Jim [puralia], in that Jim's identity and his country are inseparable, and also in terms of the re-birth into country that arose through the process of creating these works', noting how, like Oodgeroo Noonuccal, puralia's name means 'paperbark'.[43] The painting and words function as an onto-poetic substantiation of puralia's 'all-life' in Country, and in keeping with our discussion of a positive, nourishing transcultural ecopoetics, puralia's 'rebirth into Country' is paralleled by jonathan being 'welcomed into the country also'.[44]

Paired with the arterial painting *drakurringer legana tagarilia: breathe my family water*, these connections are intensified in the magnificent poem 'planegarrartoothenar'. In a dreaming story of creation, water and the corporealization of family and language, corpuscles of sensation and cognition live in the arterial flow of filial sustenance and a-temporal kinship in-with Country:

> planegarrartoothenar grew up in meenamatta country.
> ... wherever planegarrartoothenar's family journey there is water. the family
> always respect water because it gives life to all living things that nurtures
> them, and other living things. water is the connector across all clans,
> people, birds, animals, plants, and even the rocks and grounds.[45]

'planegarrartoothenar' enunciates an Aboriginal eco-philosophy in which the 'all-life' of family, clan and kinship networks, embedded across human and non-human networks of relation, is poetically mapped and activated across millennia:

> ... when i camp on meenamatta country i think
> about the many families that live in this place. for more than 35,000 years
>
> ... we talk about our old people when we camp here, remembering the past with
> our present ...
>
> ... this place is where i visit planegarrartoothenar and his family,
> finding memories of our connection that go beyond time and space. here,
> i find my grandfather and grandmother, my parents, and my brothers and
> sisters. meenamatta country is me as i am it, living in the natural world
>
> ... we are connected through our bloodline, our all-life waterline ...
> ... we are one family
> in the all-life, with waterlines that journey in our arteries and veins, the cycle
> of recycle in timeless space of no space, where there exists no past, present or
> future. our today is forever, yet in time i am with planegarrartoothenar forever.[46]

As in the poem 'water', the artists actualize a decolonizing, liberatory power in poetry, writing, as puralia relates, 'meenamatta country takes me beyond the colonial construct, beyond landscapes and development, it takes me to freedom.' Perhaps it's little wonder that in the following poem, 'this place is outside of the bible', the artists focus on the demarcation between 'nourishing' and 'damaging' onto-poetics by returning to figures of environmental destruction, where colonized Country is

> powerless to prevent its death throes
> from saws and axes of the followers

of god's rules where it has been given
to all men to tame.[47]

Following the 'all-life' poem 'some call me water' ('my form journey's inside the veins and arteries / to be pumped by living/hearts that carry me / as their blood-water'), the penultimate set of poems, 'turbana', 'antipodes', 'europa', 'asia', 'africa', turn outward from Ben Lomond country to view the wider world itself, inflecting the arterial circuitry of meenamatta blood Country through the darker prisms of 'the colonial matrix of power', modernity, the transnational and trans-Indigenous.[48] The ethical centre and anchor of this movement is 'turbana', or Ben Lomond mountain:

> across meenamatta in turbuna and all neminah
> as the lore of our lands are laid down for all
> timelessness and spaciousness of blood country
> of us who belong here forever home with family
> to hold the law of our lands in respect and trust
> or it is who we are that is meenamatta blood[49]

The artists promptly contrast such figures of the nourishing integrity of Country by returning to the damage caused by 'the colonial matrix of power'. In 'antipodes', they write of

> white sails explore country
> the white sails come
> with owners in their blood
> money for the monarch
> and everything of all-life
> is taken to another place
> where no heaven can be
> and trees become logs
> of woodchip planks
> ... water will sicken
> ... all-life cannot drink money[50]

In 'europa', the artists drive a final stake into the heart of (to again reference Mignolo) the darker sides of Western, post-Renaissance modernity. This short poem is worth quoting here in full:

> colonies established post-colonialism
> which became neo-colonialism
> in the new nation of people exclusively

under the controlling marketplace
until all-life dies and neo-colonialism
reaches its final regression
in broken water dead[51]

They leave us in no doubt that an engagement with transcultural ecopoetics in Australia, overdetermined as it is by the imperialism of 'europa' and local forms of settler coloniality, always hinges on either 'nourishing' or 'damaging' onto-poetic vectors. In a very interesting gesture, the artists broaden this rubric in the poems 'asia' and 'africa' by pivoting back to a positive sense of a countermodern, decolonial planetarity in which the water-life-blood-kinship matrix can be mapped transculturally across other colonized spaces, such that 'water spirits live in all time touching people culture' everywhere.[52]

The final poem of the collaboration, 'blue tears in manalargenna country', is a coda that returns us to water flowing through and across meenamatta Country in gestures of healing and lament. The book closes with an almost Taoist figure of silence and warbling water interacting a-temporally like ying and yang:

warbling water moving fast in a creek-bed journey
... small rapids
... caught on the walls of green moss where they gather
in the stillness of silent life over the warbling water[53]

Here, puralia and jonathan underline the central ethical dimension of Aboriginal eco-philosophy and its continuance in Country. The endless, nourishing warbling of water and the rich circulation of 'the blood juice cloud' through networks of kinship, ecology and language underpin the 'all-life' and its expression in poiesis and poetic utterance. In keeping with what I have argued elsewhere, an Aboriginal relation to Country is inescapably a relation to ethos, because a relation to Country always emerges from within a system of law aimed at the sustenance of Country, clan and culture, such that Country, ethos and expression are always interconnected and concurrent with one another.[54] When they write of 'spiritual memories ... / reminding those who can hear its song in new worlds / to bring back shared journeys on a land of blue tears', the artists reach back into the 'pattern thinking' embedded in Country while spatializing ethos to embrace both human and non-human kinship networks and transcultural possibilities.

Jonathan and puralia's pictorial works materialize a similar but very particular set of propositions. We have already noted how in *Country Unwrapping Landscape* Kimberley queries the status of the Western landscape painting tradition in contemporary Australian art practice. Kimberley and meenamatta's answer is to seek a liberatory, transcultural model 'for true artistic emancipation from the "Western Landscape Paradigm" or the "Australian Landscape Tradition"... [because] [w]ithout this clear understanding of Aboriginal Country and its distinct differences from the imported (Western) Landscape Paradigm, we simply perpetuate the idea of *terra incognita* in Australia'.[55] The artists' exquisite paintings in *meenamatta lena narla puellakanny: Meenamatta Water Country Discussion* offer a case study for how we might understand a nourishing transcultural ecopoetics from perspectives in which traditions in settler-colonial landscape representation might be positively decolonized and transformed.

The artists' methodological and compositional solution to the 'Western Landscape Paradigm' is an approach that Kimberley has very usefully termed, in *Country Unwrapping Landscape*, as 'unlandscape' and 'unlandscaping'. Drawing on and critiquing the work of landscape theorists Robin Kelsey, Kenneth R. Olwig and W. J. T. Mitchell, among others, Kimberley seeks to peel back imperialist trajectories of the Western landscape painting tradition to help encourage a positive transcultural practice that can undo 'the colonial matrix of power' and open new possibilities beyond the delimitation of 'Australian landscape' that are in dialogue with and responsive to Aboriginal Country.[56] Essentially 'unlandscape' and 'unlandscaping' permit ways to think about 'a conceptual and real discussion between the origins of Western mapping and Aboriginal stories of country' by seeking new representational paradigms that are delinked from the coloniality of, for instance, the cartographic lens through which Western landscape painting traditions have overwritten, obscured and disenfranchised Country.[57] In *Meenamatta Water Country Discussion*, the artists' approach is to seek 'a more reciprocal and meaningful discussion with Country' by 'unlandscaping' colonial representations of meenamatta Country in ways that reach back past the development of imperial modes of mapping and representing landscape, to the pre-imperial, precolonial distance when the antipodes were perceived only obscurely. Just as Mignolo in *The Darker Side of the Renaissance* (1995) identifies the emergence of Western modernity and coloniality from around 1500, jonathan and puralia look to a pre-Renaissance 'landscape' sensibility that might offer potential vectors for 'unlandscaping' in ways that decolonize contemporary painterly representations of Country.

What would such 'unlandscaped' landscapes look like? Vivian writes that for decades 'Kimberley has been interested in medieval maps as a way of understanding early Western interpretations of our world, when Australia existed for Europeans only on the fringes of their imagination',[58] and in *Meenamatta Water Country Discussion*, we see this interrogation draw upon medieval map-making conventions, the Macrobian or Zonal, Tripartite, Quadripartite and Complex 'mappa mundi' produced before the beginning of the Renaissance between about 700 and 1500. Distinguished by their orb-like, globular representation of 'the world' (see, for instance, Mappa Mundi in *La Fleur des Histoires*. 1459–63[59]) 'mappa mundi' foreground the schematization of mythological, historical and narratorial elements across speculative geographies, creating complexes of information that emphasize *cultural* rather than purely cartographic mapping in ways that are resistant to the post-Renaissance imperium's Euclidean spatial, economic and martial projections. But rather than simply looking backwards to a kind of pre-Renaissance Western primitivism, which would negatively reinscribe the logic of coloniality, Kimberley and meenamatta instead help bring an Aboriginal ontology forward by aligning the spatialization of myth, story and narrative in the architecture of an unlandscaped mappa mundi with the shape and substance of puralia's 'all-life'. I am reminded here of Howard Morphy's description of Aboriginal art as a mode of mapping mythological rather than topographical geographies:

> Aboriginal paintings are maps of land. It is necessary, however, to define precisely what is meant by a 'map' in this context. . . . [F]rom an Aboriginal perspective the land itself is a sign system. . . . Aboriginal paintings can only be fully understood as maps once it is realised that the criterion for inclusion is not topographical but mythological and conceptual; paintings are thus representations of the totemic geography.[60]

What we see when looking at *Meenamatta Water Country Discussion*, once we allow our eyes to adjust and take in the multidimensionality of the artists' painting-writings, are transcultural, decolonizing 'mappa mundi' of meenamatta Country that function not as 'landscapes' in the traditional Western sense, but rather as *encultured* painterly and poetic narratives in dialogue with Country (Figure 10.2). Western projections of scale and space, vanishing point and volume, are rejected in favour of organic, living planetary spheres or corpuscles of water-blood, hearts beating through rivers, Country, corporeality, all forms of embodiment and capillaries of painting language, mythos and poetry. By withdrawing from the coloniality of Western landscape painting traditions, while in dialogue with Country itself, the paintings simultaneously liberate new ways in which nourishing transcultural events can emerge. To return to the collaborative One work 'beyond the colonial construct: meenamatta a map of unlandscape' and 'meenamatta lena walantanalinany (meenamatta water country)', we can therefore underscore how they function onto-poetically as

Figure 10.2 Jonathan Kimberley and puralia meenamatta (Jim Everett), *balouina miengalina bagota: blood juice cloud (meenamatta tomato)* (2006, synthetic polymer, charcoal and text on linen, 182 x 182 cm (four panels)). Reproduced with permission of the artists.[61]

figurative mechanisms that allow a positive transcultural ecopoetics of Country to emerge through a process of 'unlandscaping' that takes us 'beyond the colonial construct'. If we look at them together, and keeping in mind the artists' poetic invocations of water-blood Country in the 'all-life', the nourishing arterial networks of filial kinship between humans and non-humans in Country, and keeping in mind their echoing of the trope of the mappa mundi, we can perceive in the works an intense projection of the living corporeality and meaningfulness of Country through a transcultural ecopoetic matrix of sensation, relation, language and image.

'the blood juice cloud': A 'Key to writing'

The transcultural significance of the collaboration is finally underwritten by the last image in the artists' book, 'Key to writing: beyond the colonial construct: meenamatta a map of unlandscape'.

In Figure 10.3 we can observe how as a transcultural ecopoetic event the collaboration works to corporealize poetry and painting language in an image that decolonizes the representation of meenamatta country as both mappa mundi and, like a heart pumping the water-blood of the 'all-life' and language itself, as a meaningful corpuscle of being which fervently and meaningfully nourishes and enriches the 'blood juice cloud'. The term 'key to writing' echoes Deborah Bird Rose's reading of William Stanner, where she writes,

> Stanner's definition . . . of Dreaming as a 'poetic key to Reality' hints at the dynamism of Dreaming in the present . . . Dreaming beings generate the Law by which life is sustained. Law is about relationships . . . what may best be termed meta-rules: rules about relationships.[62]

In this case, perhaps like Stanner's 'poetic key to reality', puralia and Kimberley's 'Key to writing' substantiates how, in a nourishing transcultural ecopoetic event, relationships between the 'all-life' of human and non-human kinship, the embodiment of language, law and culture in Country, and the sustenance of an Aboriginal cosmology and eco-philosophy, can be inscribed 'beyond the colonial construct' in ways that decolonize the meta-rules of Western aesthetic traditions in landscape painting and poetics.

When meenamatta and Kimberley say 'it's about "all life" . . . we are part of one big eco-system . . . [t]here is no separateness . . . [h]umans aren't outside, they are inside', they are describing a 'nourishing terrain' that multidimensionally incorporates all entities at every scale, a transcultural weaving of human and non-human interiorities and exteriorities which can be implicated in naturally emerging, human-made forms such as poems and paintings. In meenamatta Country, the 'blood juice cloud' connects everything in arterial tributaries of networked kinship and reciprocity, the 'gift of *pattern thinking*' (Mowaljarlai)[63] which underpins Grieves sense of an Aboriginal philosophy of human and non-human 'interconnectedness . . . whereby people, the plants and animals, landforms and celestial bodies are interrelated'.[64] puralia and jonathan's 'blood juice cloud' similarly tropes a non-dualistic, non-Cartesian philosophical tradition in which 'poetry', among other things, emerges from nature as a natural substance that materially embodies culture, language and law while substantiating living Country. The work simultaneously asserts a sovereign Aboriginal imagination that is confidently responsive to dialogue with non-Aboriginal creators as One work, and so can positively mark out a space that makes possible a nourishing transcultural ecopoetic event.

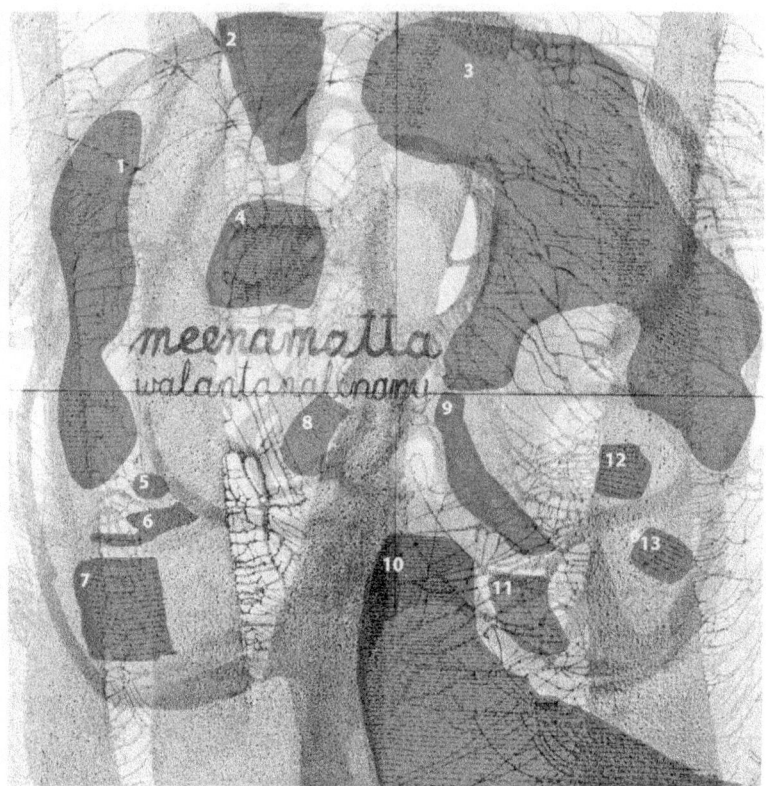

Figure 10.3 Jonathan Kimberley and puralia meenamatta (Jim Everett), *Key to writing: beyond the colonial construct: meenamatta map of unlandscape* (2006, from Puralia (Jim Everett) Meenamatta and Jonathan Kimberley, *Meenamatta Lena Narla Puellakanny: Meenamatta Water Country Discussion. A Writing and Painting Collaboration* (Hobart: Bett Gallery and Devonport Gallery, 2006), p. 41). Reproduced with permission of the artists.

An Aboriginal eco-philosophy of Country has much to offer contemporary planet-wide thought about how we might understand and creatively respond to climate change and, among other things, its liability to regimes of coloniality. In *Meenamatta Water Country Discussion*, puralia meenamatta and Jonathan Kimberley produce an exemplary collaborative transcultural event which delinks from 'the colonial matrix of power' by producing radical and liberatory aesthetic value via an 'in-between' in which puralia's eco-philosophy of meenamatta Country meets Kimberley's decolonizing and reparative 'unlandscaping' interrogations of Western landscape painting traditions. The collaboration is mutually transformative, while also producing an emergent third space in which the peeling away of damaging, settler modes of coloniality coincides with the liberation of tyrannized Aboriginal thought and expression. At the very least, local nourishing transcultural events such as *meenamatta lena narla puellakanny: Meenamatta Water Country Discussion* show us a way forward not only for their local reinvigoration of positive and embodied transcultural dimensions in meenamatta Country, but also for how puralia meenamatta and Jonathan Kimberley's One work is representative of modes of co-inspired transcultural discourse that could be key to how a future ecopoetics might free an 'all-life' future itself.

Notes

1 Helen Vivian, 'An Unlandscape of Words and Paintings: From Meenamatta to Paradise', *Artlink* 29, no. 2 (2009): 66–70. Being 'on Country' is widely used by Australian Aboriginal peoples to express being on one's ancestral, traditional lands.

2 Throughout this chapter, I followed advice from puralia meenamatta (Jim Everett) noted in Jonathan Kimberley, 'Country Unwrapping Landscape: Kuluntjarra World Map (the Nine Collaborations)' (MFA (Research), University of Western Australia, 2010): words from Tasmanian Aboriginal languages will 'be written in lowercase only' (n. 9, p. 7). The artists also use lowercase when named in their collaboration as One. Capitalized surnames and given names may also be used where the context allows.

3 Vivian, 'An Unlandscape of Words and Paintings: From Meenamatta to Paradise', 67.

4 Kimberley, 'Country Unwrapping Landscape: Kuluntjarra World Map (The Nine Collaborations)', 6.

5 puralia in Vivian, 'An Unlandscape of Words and Paintings: From Meenamatta to Paradise', 70. On the in-between 'third space', see Charmaine Papertalk Green,

'Third Space', in Charmaine Papertalk Green and John Kinsella, *False Claims of Colonial Thieves* (Perth: Magabala Books, 2018), 100–1.
6 Vivian, 'An Unlandscape of Words and Paintings: From Meenamatta to Paradise', 68. Green and Kinsella, *False Claims of Colonial Thieves* (2018) is another significant example.
7 Pura-lia (Jim Everett) Meenamatta and Jonathan Kimberley, *Meenamatta lena narla puellakanny: Meenamatta Water Country Discussion. A Writing and Painting Collaboration* (Hobart: Bett Gallery; Devonport: Devonport Regional Gallery). At the time of writing the artists' book is still available to download from http://www.devonportgallery.com/uploadFiles/documents/meenamatta_lena_narla_puellakanny_catalogue.pdf. The term 'painting-writing' is suggested by the artists to denote the 'together as ONE' onto-poetic foundation of the work.
8 See Kimberley, 'Country Unwrapping Landscape: Kuluntjarra World Map (The Nine Collaborations)'.
9 puralia meenamatta (Jim Everett) and Jonathan Kimberley, 'Paradise: Working Exmodern' (2nd International Imagined Australia Forum, University of Bari, Italy), in Kimberley, 'Country Unwrapping Landscape: Kuluntjarra World Map (The Nine Collaborations)', 54–5.
10 Personal correspondence, 24 and 29 June 2020. I am especially grateful for the correspondence with puralia and jonathan in which my thinking about key ideas in this chapter benefited greatly from their generous advice and clarifications. I am also grateful for their permission to reproduce images from the artists' book.
11 Peter Minter, 'Archipelagos of Sense: Thinking About a Decolonised Australian Poetics', in 'The Political Imagination: Postcolonialism and Diaspora in Contemporary Australian Poetry', Ann Vickery and Ali Alizadeh (eds), *Southerly* 73, no. 1 (2013): 155–69. My use of 'molar' and 'molecular' here points to a possible Deleuzian account of emergent onto-poetic substance in transcultural events.
12 It's important to note that I don't wish to homogenize the category 'settler' as an undifferentiated mass that makes no account of the many different kinds of settler communities and subjectivities in Australia, which can be observed across multiple and various intersections of culture, race, gender, sexuality and so on.
13 A vast body of work has emerged at the intersection of these areas, more than I can possibly cite here. Starting points include Bob and Vijay Mishra Hodge, *Dark Side of the Dream* (Sydney: Allen & Unwin); Deborah Bird Rose, *Dingo Makes Us Human: Life and Land in an Aboriginal Australian Culture* (Cambridge and Melbourne: Cambridge University Press); Graham Huggan and Helen Tiffin, *Postcolonial Ecocriticism: Literature, Animals, Environment* (New York: Routledge); Elizabeth M. DeLoughrey and George B. Handley, *Postcolonial Ecologies Literatures of the Environment* (New York and Oxford: Oxford University Press); Elizabeth M. DeLoughrey, Jill Didur and Anthony Carrigan, *Global Ecologies and the*

Environmental Humanities: Postcolonial Approaches, Routledge Interdisciplinary Perspectives on Literature 41 (New York: Routledge); Stuart Cooke, 'Indigenous Poetics and Transcultural Ecologies', *Interdisciplinary Literary Studies* 20, no. 1 (2018): 1–32.

14 I first used the term 'transcultural ecopoetics' in my paper 'Phenomenal Australian Poetics: Jean-Luc Nancy's "Same time/Same place" and signs of Co-appearance in TGH Strehlow's "Songs of Central Australia"' (Contemporary Environmental Poetics, Brunel University London, Friday, 9 July 2004). Subsequent papers in which I develop the term's conceptual framework include 'Writing Country: Composition, Law and Indigenous Ecopoetics' (2012) and 'Kath Walker (Oodgeroo Noonuccal), Judith Wright and Decolonised Transcultural Ecopoetics in Frank Heimans' Shadow Sister' (2015). This chapter has been developed from a paper presented at the *Literary Environments: Place, Planet and Translation* conference, convened by Stuart Cooke and Peter Denney at Griffith University in July 2017, and I am grateful for their hospitality then and now.

15 See Cheryll Glotfelty and Harold Fromm, eds, *The Ecocriticism Reader: Landmarks in Literary Ecology* (Athens: University of Georgia Press), xix.

16 Simon C. Estok, *Ecocriticism and Shakespeare: Reading Ecophobia*. Literatures, Cultures, and the Environment (New York: Palgrave Macmillan), 2.

17 For example, see Aníbal Quijano, 'Coloniality and Modernity/Rationality', Article, *Cultural Studies* 21, no. 2/3, https://doi.org/10.1080/09502380601164353, and Walter Mignolo, *The Darker Side of Western Modernity: Global Futures, Decolonial Options* (Duke University: Duke University Press). Mignolo describes the 'four interrelated domains' of 'the colonial matrix of power' as 'control of economy (land appropriation, exploitation of labor, control of natural resources); control of authority (institution, army); control of gender and sexuality (family, education) and control of subjectivity and knowledge (epistemology, education and formation of subjectivity)'. In Walter Mignolo and Arturo Escobar, *Globalization and the Decolonial Option* (London: Routledge), 3. To 'gender and sexuality' above we might add 'race'.

18 Deborah Bird Rose, *Nourishing Terrains: Australian Aboriginal Views of Landscape and Wilderness* (Canberra: Australian Heritage Commission, 1996). https://webarchive.nla.gov.au/awa/20170226002424/https://www.environment.gov.au/system/files/resources/62db1069-b7ec-4d63-b9a9-991f4b931a60/files/nourishing-terrains.pdf. Rose developed 'a definition of country which starts with the idea that country, to use the philosopher's term, is a nourishing terrain. Country is a place that gives and receives life. Not just imagined or represented, it is lived in and lived with' (7). And '[n]ourishing terrains are the active manifestation of creation' (23). Her 'philosopher' here is Emmanuel Lévinas, whose '*espace vital*' is underscored as a 'nourishing terrain [in] which the land, in the geographical sense of the term . . . draws out its spiritual

meaning'. See Emmanuel Lévinas and Seán Hand, *The Levinas Reader* (Oxford and Cambridge, MA: B. Blackwell), at 192, and 210 at note 2.

19 Bill Neidjie, *Story About Feeling* (Broome: Magabala Books). David Mowaljarlai and Jutta Malnic, *Yorro Yorro: Everything Standing Up Alive: Rock Art and Stories from the Australian Kimberley* (Broome: Magabala Books, 2001). Ambelin Kwaymullina, 'Seeing the Light: Aboriginal Law, Learning and Sustainable Living in Country', *Indigenous Law Bulletin* 6, no. 11 (May–June): 12–15. Vicki Grieves, 'Aboriginal Spirituality: A Baseline for Indigenous Knowledges Development in Australia', *The Canadian Journal of Native Studies* 28, no. 2 (2018): 363–98. Marcia Langton, 'Sacred Geographies', in *Aboriginal Religions in Australia: An Anthology of Recent Writings*, ed. Howard Morphy Françoise Dussart (London: Routledge).

20 In a recent paper, 'Walking with Louise Crisp' (Unsettling Ecological Poetics, University of Sydney, 25 October 2019) I proposed a 'negative ecopoetics' in which decolonizing settler poets 'peel back coloniality' by writing themselves *out* of Country. Also see my comments on Judith Wright's alignment of environmentalism and Aboriginal land rights in 'Kath Walker (Oodgeroo Noonuccal), Judith Wright and Decolonised Transcultural Ecopoetics in Frank Heimans' Shadow Sister'.

21 Grieves, 'Aboriginal Spirituality: A Baseline for Indigenous Knowledges Development in Australia', 364.

22 Rose, *Nourishing Terrains: Australian Aboriginal Views of Landscape and Wilderness*, 8.

23 Kwaymullina, 'Seeing the Light: Aboriginal Law, Learning and Sustainable Living in Country', 12.

24 Mowaljarlai, ABC Radio 1995, in Grieves, 'Aboriginal Spirituality: A Baseline for Indigenous Knowledges Development in Australia', 364.

25 Kwaymullina, 'Seeing the Light: Aboriginal Law, Learning and Sustainable Living in Country', 13.

26 puralia in Vivian, 'An Unlandscape of Words and Paintings: From Meenamatta to Paradise', 68.

27 Kimberley, 'Country Unwrapping Landscape: Kuluntjarra World Map (The Nine Collaborations)', 56, 59.

28 Gerardo Mosquera, 'The Marco Polo Syndrome', in *The Third Text Reader – on Art, Culture and Theory*, ed. Sean Cubitt and Ziauddin Sardar Rasheed Araeen (London: Bloomsbury Academic), 273, cited in Kimberley, 'Country Unwrapping Landscape: Kuluntjarra World Map (The Nine Collaborations)', 30.

29 Meenamatta and Kimberley, *Meenamatta lena narla puellakanny: Meenamatta Water Country Discussion. A Writing and Painting Collaboration*, 4.

30 Kimberley, 'Country Unwrapping Landscape: Kuluntjarra World Map (The Nine Collaborations)', 7.

31 Kimberley, 'Country Unwrapping Landscape: Kuluntjarra World Map (The Nine Collaborations). MFA (Research) – Exegesis: Exhibition / Creative Component' (MFA (Research) University of Western Australia), 13–14.

32 See Meenamatta and Kimberley, *Meenamatta lena narla puellakanny: Meenamatta Water Country Discussion. A Writing and Painting Collaboration*, 5, 29.
33 Kimberley, 'Country Unwrapping Landscape: Kuluntjarra World Map (The Nine Collaborations)', 28.
34 Vivian, 'An Unlandscape of Words and Paintings: From Meenamatta to Paradise', 70.
35 Jonathan Kimberley, PhD, Australian National University (forthcoming), in correspondence with the author, 29 June 2020.
36 Kimberley, in correspondence with the author, 29 June 2020.
37 puralia in Vivian, 'An Unlandscape of Words and Paintings: From Meenamatta to Paradise', 70.
38 Meenamatta and Kimberley, *Meenamatta lena narla puellakanny: Meenamatta Water Country Discussion. A Writing and Painting Collaboration*, 6.
39 Meenamatta and Kimberley, *Meenamatta lena narla puellakanny: Meenamatta Water Country Discussion. A Writing and Painting Collaboration*, 6.
40 Meenamatta and Kimberley, *Meenamatta lena narla puellakanny: Meenamatta Water Country Discussion. A Writing and Painting Collaboration*, 6–7.
41 Meenamatta and Kimberley, *Meenamatta lena narla puellakanny: Meenamatta Water Country Discussion. A Writing and Painting Collaboration*, 7–8.
42 Meenamatta and Kimberley, *Meenamatta lena narla puellakanny: Meenamatta Water Country Discussion. A Writing and Painting Collaboration*, 8.
43 Vivian, 'An Unlandscape of Words and Paintings: From Meenamatta to Paradise', 68–9.
44 Kimberley in Vivian, 'An Unlandscape of Words and Paintings: From Meenamatta to Paradise', 69.
45 Meenamatta and Kimberley, *Meenamatta lena narla puellakanny: Meenamatta Water Country Discussion. A Writing and Painting Collaboration*, 14.
46 Meenamatta and Kimberley, *Meenamatta lena narla puellakanny: Meenamatta Water Country Discussion. A Writing and Painting Collaboration*, 15.
47 Meenamatta and Kimberley, *Meenamatta lena narla puellakanny: Meenamatta Water Country Discussion. A Writing and Painting Collaboration*, 18.
48 'Trans-Indigenous' here is indebted to the ground-breaking work of Native American (Chickasaw) scholar Chadwick Allen. See Chadwick Allen, *Trans-Indigenous Methodologies for Global Native Literary Studies* (University of Minnesota Press, 2012).
49 Meenamatta and Kimberley, *Meenamatta lena narla puellakanny: Meenamatta Water Country Discussion. A Writing and Painting Collaboration*, 24.
50 Meenamatta and Kimberley, *Meenamatta lena narla puellakanny: Meenamatta Water Country Discussion. A Writing and Painting Collaboration*, 26.
51 Meenamatta and Kimberley, *Meenamatta lena narla puellakanny: Meenamatta Water Country Discussion. A Writing and Painting Collaboration*, 26.

52 Meenamatta and Kimberley, *Meenamatta lena narla puellakanny: Meenamatta Water Country Discussion. A Writing and Painting Collaboration*, 28.
53 Meenamatta and Kimberley, *Meenamatta lena narla puellakanny: Meenamatta Water Country Discussion. A Writing and Painting Collaboration*, 30.
54 Peter Minter, 'Writing Country: Composition, Law and Indigenous Ecopoetics', *Journal of the Association for the Study of Australian Literature* 12, no. 1 (2012).
55 Kimberley, 'Country Unwrapping Landscape: Kuluntjarra World Map (The Nine Collaborations)'.
56 Kimberley, 'Country Unwrapping Landscape: Kuluntjarra World Map (The Nine Collaborations)', 14.
57 Kimberley in Vivian, 'An Unlandscape of Words and Paintings: From Meenamatta to Paradise', 70.
58 Vivian, 'An Unlandscape of Words and Paintings: From Meenamatta to Paradise', 70.
59 'Mappa Mundi in La Fleur des Histoires. 1459-1463'. https://commons.wikimedia.org/wiki/File:T-O_Mappa_mundi.jpg.
60 Howard Morphy, *Aboriginal Art* (London: Phaidon Press), 103, 106.
61 See Meenamatta and Kimberley, *Meenamatta lena narla puellakanny: Meenamatta Water Country Discussion. A Writing and Painting Collaboration*, 23.
62 Rose, *Dingo Makes Us Human: Life and Land in an Aboriginal Australian Culture*, 44.
63 Mowaljarlai, ABC Radio 1995, in Grieves, 'Aboriginal Spirituality: A Baseline for Indigenous Knowledges Development in Australia', 364.
64 Grieves, 'Aboriginal Spirituality: A Baseline for Indigenous Knowledges Development in Australia', 364.

Bibliography

Allen, Chadwick. *Trans-Indigenous Methodologies for Global Native Literary Studies*. Minneapolis: University of Minnesota Press, 2012.

Cooke, Stuart. 'Indigenous Poetics and Transcultural Ecologies'. *Interdisciplinary Literary Studies* 20, no. 1 (2018): 1–32.

DeLoughrey, Elizabeth M. and George B. Handley. *Postcolonial Ecologies Literatures of the Environment*. New York and Oxford: Oxford University Press, 2011.

DeLoughrey, Elizabeth M., Jill Didur and Anthony Carrigan. *Global Ecologies and the Environmental Humanities: Postcolonial Approaches*. Routledge Interdisciplinary Perspectives on Literature 41. New York: Routledge, 2015.

Estok, Simon C. *Ecocriticism and Shakespeare: Reading Ecophobia*. Literatures, Cultures, and the Environment. New York: Palgrave Macmillan, 2011.

Glotfelty, Cheryll and Harold Fromm, eds. *The Ecocriticism Reader: Landmarks in Literary Ecology*. Athens: University of Georgia Press, 1996.

Green, Charmaine Papertalk and John Kinsella. *False Claims of Colonial Thieves*. Perth: Magabala Books, 2018.

Grieves, Vicki. 'Aboriginal Spirituality: A Baseline for Indigenous Knowledges Development in Australia'. *The Canadian Journal of Native Studies* 28, no. 2 (2008): 363–98.

Hodge, Bob and Vijay Mishra. *Dark Side of the Dream*. Sydney: Allen & Unwin, 1991.

Huggan, Graham and Helen Tiffin. *Postcolonial Ecocriticism: Literature, Animals, Environment*. New York: Routledge, 2010.

Kimberley, Jonathan. 'Country Unwrapping Landscape: Kuluntjarra World Map (the Nine Collaborations)'. MFA (Research), University of Western Australia, 2010.

Kimberley, Jonathan and puralia meenamatta (Jim Everett). 'Paradise: Working Exmodern'. 2nd International Imagined Australia Forum, University of Bari, Italy, 2009.

Kwaymullina, Ambelin. 'Seeing the Light: Aboriginal Law, Learning and Sustainable Living in Country'. *Indigenous Law Bulletin* 6, no. 11 (May–June 2005): 12–15.

Langton, Marcia. 'Sacred Geographies'. In *Aboriginal Religions in Australia: An Anthology of Recent Writings*, edited by Howard Morphy Françoise Dussart, 131–39. London: Routledge, 2017.

Lévinas, Emmanuel and Seán Hand. *The Levinas Reader*. Oxford and Cambridge, MA: B. Blackwell, 1989.

'Mappa Mundi in La Fleur Des Histoires. 1459–1463'. https://commons.wikimedia.org/wiki/File:T-O_Mappa_mundi.jpg

Meenamatta, Puralia (Jim Everett) and Jonathan Kimberley. *Meenamatta Lena Narla Puellakanny: Meenamatta Water Country Discussion. A Writing and Painting Collaboration*. Hobart: Bett Gallery; Devonport: Devonport Regional Gallery, 2006.

Mignolo, Walter. *The Darker Side of Western Modernity: Global Futures, Decolonial Options*. Durham: Duke University Press, 2011.

Mignolo, Walter and Arturo Escobar. *Globalization and the Decolonial Option*. London: Routledge, 2010.

Minter, Peter. 'Archipelagos of Sense: Thinking About a Decolonised Australian Poetics'. in 'The Political Imagination: Postcolonialism and Diaspora in Contemporary Australian Poetry'. Ann Vickery and Ali Alizadeh (eds), *Southerly* 73, no. 1 (2013): 155–69.

Minter, Peter. 'Decoloniality and Geopoethics in Meenamatta Lena Narla Puellakanny: Meenamatta Water Country Discussion'. *Literary Environments: Place, Planet and Translation*, Griffith University, 17 July 2017.

Minter, Peter. 'Kath Walker (Oodgeroo Noonuccal), Judith Wright and Decolonised Transcultural Ecopoetics in Frank Heimans' Shadow Sister'. *Sydney Studies in English* 41 (2015). http://openjournals.library.usyd.edu.au/index.php/SSE/article/view/10048/9937

Minter, Peter. 'Phenomenal Australian Poetics: Jean-Luc Nancy's 'Same Time/Same Place' and Signs of Co-Appearance in TGH Strehlow's "Songs of Central Australia"'. *Contemporary Environmental Poetics*, Brunel University London, Friday, 9 July 2004.

Minter, Peter. 'Settlement Defiled: Pollution, Ventriloquy and Transnational Ecopoetics in Eliza Hamilton Dunlop's "the Aboriginal Mother"'. In *Text, Translation, Transnationalism: World Literature in 21st Century Australia*, edited by Peter Morgan. North Melbourne: Australian Scholarly Publishing Pty Ltd, 2016.

Minter, Peter. 'Walking with Louise Crisp'. *Unsettling Ecological Poetics*, University of Sydney, 25 October 2019.

Minter, Peter. 'Writing Country: Composition, Law and Indigenous Ecopoetics'. *Journal of the Association for the Study of Australian Literature* 12, no. 1 (2012). https://openjournals.library.sydney.edu.au/index.php/JASAL/article/view/10173

Morphy, Howard. *Aboriginal Art*. London: Phaidon Press, 1998.

Mosquera, Gerardo. 'The Marco Polo Syndrome'. In *The Third Text Reader – on Art, Culture and Theory*, edited by Sean Cubitt and Ziauddin Sardar Rasheed Araeen, 267–73. London: Bloomsbury Academic, 2002.

Mowaljarlai, David and Jutta Malnic. *Yorro Yorro: Everything Standing Up Alive: Rock Art and Stories from the Australian Kimberley*. Broome: Magabala Books, 2001.

Neidjie, Bill. *Story About Feeling*. Broome: Magabala Books, 1989.

Quijano, Aníbal. 'Coloniality and Modernity/Rationality'. Article. *Cultural Studies* 21, no. 2/3 (2007): 168–78. https://doi.org/10.1080/09502380601164353

Rose, Deborah Bird. *Dingo Makes Us Human: Life and Land in an Aboriginal Australian Culture*. Cambridge and Melbourne: Cambridge University Press, 1992.

Rose, Deborah Bird. *Nourishing Terrains: Australian Aboriginal Views of Landscape and Wilderness*. Canberra: Australian Heritage Commission, 1996. https://webarchive.nla.gov.au/awa/20170226002424/https://www.environment.gov.au/system/files/resources/62db1069-b7ec-4d63-b9a9-991f4b931a60/files/nourishing-terrains.pdf

Vivian, Helen. 'An Unlandscape of Words and Paintings: From Meenamatta to Paradise'. *Artlink* 29, no. 2 (2009): 66–70.

11

Theorizing decolonized literary environments

Stephen Muecke

Rather than theorize from the start, this chapter aims to *describe* a particular transcultural literary environment in north-west Australia with which the author was intimately involved, and only then bring theoretical, and even political, considerations to bear where necessary.[1] I have, for many years, been writing with Paddy Roe, an Australian Aboriginal man, an elder from the Nyigina traditional nation. The work we did clearly was and is 'transcultural' in a number of dimensions, not just from the important fact that Paddy Roe did not write in English, so I was translating from the oral to the written, and I had to decide what kind of writing that would be. But what we discovered, in the process of our long collaboration, was that all the categories pertaining to literary production, in the European-derived model, ended up being defamiliarized if not 'provincialized'.[2] The ongoing work of transcultural translation that we carried out reminded me that these categories are not necessarily universal. They include the idea that writing is more permanent than speech; that the 'functions of authorship' can indeed be very diverse;[3] that genres are culturally specific; that a fully formed grammatical sentence is a 'natural' form for language to take and so on.

Building on Bruno Latour's 'compositionist' approach to cultural networks that helps to break down the familiar, linear writer-text-reader model for literary communication, I want to think of literary production as the reproduction of sets of relations that are not in themselves purely literary, but which are the compost (if you like) for the reproduction of a culture.[4] What makes literature possible, it seems obvious to state, is not just the artist's genius or training, but also the networks of devotion that keep the very possibility of literature alive in a reproductive kind of way,[5] the kinds of normative networks that Keri Glastonbury points out the fragility of with her 'questioning of the currency of artistic tradition in a local contemporary context'. She reproduces, while challenging, a familiar and almost violent (Australian) 'anti-attitude' to poetry: 'Shut Up, Nobody Wants to Hear Your Poems!'[6]

Extensions of the human

These networks are reproduced as *extensions* with no clear central node, and they connect different kinds of living beings and objects. Spoken words can obviously end up being connected, through a complicated process, to books as objects. Imagine a literary world without books! But this is precisely the world I came to explore under the tutelage of Paddy Roe, a man whose artful words were not considered to be part of the self-supporting network that was Australian literature at the time, in the early 1980s. He and his people, his countrymen and women all across the continent who had been producing oral literatures for thousands of years, had been collectively told (up until about 1970) to 'shut up, what you are talking about is not literature!', an attitude that, of course, had the effect of bringing about the opposite reaction, among those, like myself, who had been primed to listen again, and start describing again, as I am doing in this chapter.

What kinds of extensions can a literature have? Words can extend into books, clearly, but what part does the body play? What about mountains, rivers, printing presses and other technologies? What about muses or spirits of the dead?[7] I don't think there is any limit to the heterogeneity of any possible literary network which is defined by the kinds of extensions it engenders. But because we can only know the network by *following* its extensions, they cannot all be perceived immediately by an observer. The observer has to move forward, making connections that *realize* the network (make the network real) through a process of tracking and surprise discovery. This moving forward is especially evident in narrative structure, so let's exemplify in that mode.

Imagine you are reading by the fire in an isolated farmhouse, with only your dog for company. She is lying on the rug at your feet, perhaps sleeping, then she growls softly and you say to yourself, 'Ah, must be a car coming up the drive.' Then she gets up, goes to the window and starts barking urgently, and you speak to her: 'Jackie, who is it? A car you don't recognize?' Then you start to hear the sound of the motor, something she had heard a good minute earlier. You part the curtains, and see headlights flashing against the dark trees. You start to wonder, who could be visiting this late at night? We're not expecting anyone.

Even though the conditions for a horror story are being set up here, what interests me is a particular multispecies configuration that is enacted. The human capacity to hear is extended by the dog's sharper hearing, and in this case by her acute capacity to distinguish familiar sounds from strange ones. By enlisting the help of animals and plants, humans extend their capacities to hear, see, smell, even think. A walk in the bush with a dog is more enjoyable because of what she might notice, and it is safer because she could easily find her way home should you lose your way.[8]

There are large numbers of examples of animals' specific capacities being used to extend the envelope of the human sensorium: canaries' greater sensitivity to poisonous gas; sniffer dogs in discos or minefields; flocks of finches telling Walmajarri people in the Western Desert where water lies; falconry for hunting; the famous *Kluge Hans* (Clever Hans); Paul the octopus who could predict the results of the football world cup; and so on. The field of animal studies has lately been busy reviving such stories of multispecies and intersubjective co-existence, including the whole history of domestication, where words like 'harnessing' and 'husbandry' add metaphorical depth to their basic functionality.[9] Humans, therefore, were never on their own, even as they strived to deny their animality.

But the history of modernization is also a story of machine versus animal: people in an early motor car laughing at the farmer in a cart when his horse bolts after the car backfires. And the counter-story, as the farmer deigns to stop and help, a few miles down the road after the car had broken down. Modernization was an enthusiastic effort to strengthen the culture-nature division (the great bifurcation of Nature, as Whitehead had it), so that humans could do everything on their own, or so they thought. So when it is a case of seeing better, telescopes and microscopes, rather than hawks and falcons, are developed as extensions of the eye. And they work. The results have been those breathtaking achievements that are 'the very pinnacle of Western civilisation', as they say.

I want to stress that these achievements are not just the result of a process of *extraction* from Nature, from the raw materials that are refined, machined and recomposed to produce a beautiful telescope, so that the telescope can sit there on its pinnacle and tell us about our position in the universe for evermore. If you shift your attention from what the object *is* to the *process of maintaining it as it is*, then its apparent autonomy begins to falter. Its continued existence as an object is dependent on its immediate and extended environment. And the continued existence of the facts that it demonstrates is also dependent on its immediate and extended environment. Climate scientists have found this out the hard way over the last few years, and have taken to the streets to defend their institutions that have seen their funding, trust and prestige eroded in the context of the politics of the climate crisis. In other words, the most simple and the most complex things are embedded in ecologies, which can enhance their life trajectories, or not. A telescope, in this sense, is not all that unlike a rabbit or a tree: its existential logic is *reproductive*. It wants to keep going, with the help of its friends. It is the precondition for giving birth to better telescopes, and it can't do this by itself.

You may be wondering what all this has to do with literature. Well, literary forms are not exceptional in the ecological framework I am developing, just as humans are not exceptionally masterful, or central, as a form of life on Earth. All are subject to reproductive logic, and nothing can reproduce on its own. So, what does it take to create a good story, and send it on its way through the world, gathering listeners?

I want to develop a contrast between what I will call by way of shorthand, 'traditional' and 'modern' societies and their modes of aesthetic production, focusing here on verbal art. The ethno-psychiatrist Tobie Nathan usefully calls these two types of societies 'one universe societies' (the Modern) and 'multiple universe societies' (traditional ones).[10] This was modernist orthodoxy: disdainfully reject all mumbo-jumbo and superstition, spells and chants (except at the football); stop using formulaic language like proverbs. They began to insist that there was only *one* world, the 'real' environment surrounding them, and it suited them to stand outside of this natural world, in their cultures, distant and somewhat omniscient (like their one god above them) and free to roam globally.

Traditional peoples, on the other hand, are tied to their sacred lands, refusing to budge, and no wonder: they have a pagan[11] god in every river and mountain, they have a vitalist and totemic extended kinship system that links humans to an array of animals and plants. Ancestors and spirits inhabit parallel universes to their own, and they use special techniques to interface with these other parts of their worlds. Among all the complex things that inhabit this ('multiple universe') world, you can't pick and choose: you can't suddenly decide you are not going to 'believe' in *balangan* – spirits of the dead – any longer, or stop protecting a special species of tree whose wood is used in a man-making ceremony. All of these things are tied together in a heterogeneous network with two fundamental concepts at its centre: territory, called 'Country', and *bugarrigarra*, the law and culture of the Dreaming.[12]

Oral poetics

I'll come back to some of these categories later. But I want to start with a bit of textual analysis to try to show how this schema plays out all the way down to the structure of the text. I refer to a text Paddy Roe, Krim Benterrak and I worked on in the early 1980s, *Reading the Country*. After Paddy and I had collaborated on *Gularabulu*, I proposed to him an idea for a book he wanted to make about the Country[13] where he was born, Roebuck Plains (near Broome, Western Australia). Country would be the constant focus around which we would elicit, describe or produce various readings, without privileging one over the other, except historically: Paddy's reading, which was his heritage, would be prioritized out of respect, and as part of a literary decolonization, in our small way. Krim Benterrak is a landscape painter, so his reading of Roebuck Plains was in paint, responding both to his Moroccan heritage and his responses to Australian landscape art. We also found economic readings of the Country, historical ones, and we even asked a geologist for his reading. Paddy taught us about the importance of the songs for Country, and how they brought life to Country or performed magic, like rain-making.

The book evolved, in the field, as we went along (we used Deleuze and Guattari's 'nomadology' as a philosophical guide, embracing fluidity rather than fixity, lines rather than boundaries, becomings rather than beings). As it began to take shape as a collective creation, I kept up a correspondence with Ray Coffey, the editor at Fremantle Arts Centre Press. For such an experimental work, I saw that his support was crucial. He was happy with the way Paddy's first book, *Gularabulu*, had been received, and had agreed in principle to publish *Reading the Country*.

Coffey liked the verbatim mode of transcription I used, inspired by the prominent pioneer in ethnopoetics, Denis Tedlock.[14] Tedlock and I had both been trained in linguistics, so we were conscious of what values were associated with accurate transcription (that there are language varieties, that these variations have meaning, that forcing non-standard varieties into the National Standard means much is lost). And because of a sense of meaningful linguistic variation, that is, poetics, we were aware that while people often didn't talk in sentences, verbal arts used different formulae to everyday speech. Let me give you a sample from a story called 'Making Rain':

> We call this one *nilababa* –
> *nilababa* belong him –
> that's his *nilababa* –
> *nilababa* means his earhole (laughter) you know –
> yeah, *nilababa* –
> earhole that's his earhole –

Roe's technique here is to alternate pause and speech. He breathes in the pause and each line of speech is a breath group. It is a corporeal technique, the same is used in songs in the region. Rather than being rendered in standard English as something like, 'The name of this spring is *nilababa* and it means "earhole"', I have retained the rhythm of repetition, elaboration and chiasmus, or cross-parallelism. The first two lines have *nilababa* first at the end of the line, then the beginning, with the sense of 'we call this one' elaborated with the extended meaning of 'belong him'. These repetitions and elaborations slow down the count of morphemes/minute, and the listener accordingly has more chance of remembering the name and its meaning, repeated five times and three times respectively. The rhythm is engaging – it helps you remember, right? – as is the collective laughter. After all, this is a culture where nearly all information was transferred orally; they couldn't rely on it being in a book somewhere.

You might be interested to follow how the story develops:

Me an' my old people used to go before –
you know- -
'Ooh poorfella sheep all dead' –
you know? –
too dry country can't get –
dry –
too dry –
sheep can't eat you know - -

'Ooh' my oldfella say, 'Oh' –
'No matter, *yunmi* go get rain –
Look 'round try –
see if we can get some rain for –
make a bit of grass for sheep' –
(Laugh) –
too many dying everywhere –
lil' lil' lambs kicking hungry (Laugh) –
big sheep too - -

So –
he bring me here - - -
all right –
that's my oldman too –
my old father's brother –
young man –
old man died before - -
'All right' he say –
'We must get rain'" - - -[15]

If you want to know how they made rain that day, you will have to read the book! But even that text, for all its attempts at verbatim authenticity, is a reduced written version of the oral performance, and it looks, at least for some readers, like poetry, simply because of the lines. But the radical standardizing I had suggested was typical of other ethnographic transcriptions ('The name of this spring is *nilababa* and it means 'earhole') would have taken away the first person and hence Paddy Roe's authorship. This kind of radical textual violence was not unusual in the rewriting of Indigenous stories. But, even more violently, it removes the possibility of multiple universes, as the new third-person narrator looks down on the *one real world*.

I wasn't aware of it at the time that I was coming from an environment where literary production was conceived of in relation to one world, to arrive in an environment where literary production saw its job as linking different worlds. In the cities, writers were happy to invent other worlds imaginatively; they were called fiction, they were not real. But in Paddy Roe's country, there is no such thing as 'fiction', only true stories, 'liar' stories (where you trick people) and *Bugarrigarra*, Dreaming stories. It is to this last category that magical portals to other universes are kept open through the arts of performance.

Now I could have listened to Paddy Roe over and over (as his extended family did) and become more attuned to the glimpses to these other universes that his performances afforded. But I was a young man in a hurry; I thought I had to get a book out quickly. So I extended my capacity to listen with a clever piece of technology that was fairly new at the time, the cassette tape recorder, something I brought forward from my training in linguistics. The original recording of us at *nilababa*, on Roebuck Plains, was made as we were walking around. You can hear feet tramping the grass, wind in the microphone. What else was in the literary environment in which I got busy with my tape recorder? There were often other people present, interjecting, laughing, being consulted. These laughs and noises and interruptions all got transcribed, and I worked also with pen and notebook, sometimes doing interlinear translations of songs in the Nyigina, Ngumbal or Jabirr Jabirr languages. The occasional Malay word might pop up. Back at camp, Paddy used to write with his finger in the sand, carefully smoothing a space, making his icons while telling his story; erasing it at the end with his hand, again carefully, and finishing by saying *mabu*, good. His story stayed where it was.

Mine was captured by the alphabet, then by the notebook, to be taken away. And it was captured by the magnetized ferrous particles in the cassette tape. Then the technologies multiplied themselves. Imagine: back at my desk, I had my notebook, the cassette was now in a dictaphone machine, audio output to headphones, with a stop-start foot-pedal for transcription, my fingers flying over the keyboard of an electric typewriter, at the time. What a complex apparatus, and yet all the time I had imagined that Paddy was telling a story to me, one human to another, along a line of communication! How wrong I was; it was a network already, heterogeneously composed of humans, machines, concepts, habits and feelings. All this just to make a book.

It was a book being nurtured by Ray Coffey at Fremantle, another enabling network, and a few months later the pages were flying through machines that had descended from Gutenberg, at Koon Wah Printing Pte. Ltd., Singapore, typeset in 11/12 pt. IBM Press Roman, printed on 135 grams per square metre Matt Artpaper paper stock. It was published with the financial assistance of the Literature Board of the Australia Council and the West Australian Arts Council. Later, Ray Coffey was to reveal that publishing *Reading the Country* was an 'economic risk'. It was subsidized by the success of an earlier Fremantle book, A. B. Facey's *A Fortunate Life*. The latter book was a success

> that almost killed us. Pre-publication sales were such that by the release date we had had to press the reprint button, and this run too had effectively sold on release, so a loan was required for another printing. And still it went on. The problem of success like this for a small organisation with no capital is that print bills were due at thirty days, but bookshops paid at sixty or ninety days.[16]

but, he goes on:

> the great success of *A Fortunate Life* was such that Penguin were quickly back negotiating an extension of the lease. As part of that extension agreement, we negotiated a national distribution arrangement with Penguin for all our books.... Thus, *Reading the Country* was among the first of our books to benefit from this arrangement, increasing national distribution and sales considerably above what might have been expected for a 'difficult' book produced by what was, at the time, a tiny publishing house on the wrong side of the country.[17]

The view from inside the publishing house adds to the actor-network description of the literary environment, and has the further effect of decentring the human. Such a focus on the literary ecology as an enabling composition, or even compost, debunks any remnants of the old Weaver and Shannon 'line of communication' model for literary ontology.[18]

Specifying all the mediations and heterogeneous network chains that go into literary composition helps describe these two vastly differing literary environments. Maybe the Sony tape recorder was the most important actor in my literary environment with Paddy. Maybe, to paraphrase Debbie Bird Rose, 'tape recorder makes us human', because being a work in progress, the human is not given in advance.[19] The human has no capacity for *generalized* expansion. It can grow and extend its capacities, and this is of utmost importance, but it can only do so with *specific technologies*, with specific kinds of *craft*, including by creating new *percepts* and inventing new *concepts*, to borrow from Deleuze and Guattari. To the extent that the tape recorder can make us listen really carefully, like we never could before, in a superhuman way, then yes, 'tape recorder makes us human' because it enables us to reproduce ourselves in a new and risky way, with a leap into a way of being human with a bit more than we thought we had going for us.

So yes, we make 'bouquets of words' as I said somewhere else about poems,[20] compositions offered in love – for those with an interest in reproduction we also need to keep engendering interest – and of course this reproduction is not 'straight down the line' but cross-species kin-making with techniques and technologies. You can't reduce reproduction simply to biochemistry, to DNA or RNA, all the other environmental conditions have to be right. In the case of animals: seasons, scents, courtship rituals (see Stuart Cooke's analysis of the Albert's Lyrebird's operatic performance);[21] in the case of human animals, bouquets of words. In the case of things, networks of interest, otherwise the Model T Ford would never have evolved into a more sustainable vehicle.

So, to summarize and extend the argument: literary environments consist of networked relations that are the 'compost' with the right 'culture' for something to germinate. Even a book burgeoning in a printing press required a lot of people to say 'yes' to its potential, they weren't just responding to 'it', they were responding to a network of concepts, hunches and institutional structures. For instance, one hunch that Ray Coffey had in the early 1980s was that it was the right time to start publishing Aboriginal literature in Western Australia. To this I added the point that the literary experiments are about extensions of the human, without making much of a distinction between living and non-living things. An animal capacity, like a dog's sense of smell, is networked to human capacities, and the tape recorder's capacity to listen is not essentially any different, except that the idea of purely technological extensions is a science fiction that has been particularly damaging to the living world: the hawk's eye is replaced by binoculars; the horse by a motorcycle; healing by medicine – these are all great steps for mankind, are they not? – and before long unique forms of life, each with its *umwelt*, become extinct. We never needed the Thylacines, the modernization script told us they were just wild animals killing sheep.

Now, it is very important that you don't hear an argument for the preservation of pure natural forms, because that is just the kind of philosophy that underpins the science fiction fantasy of a realm of nature dominated by and separated from the cultures that humans reserve for themselves. A singular nature is a denial of the *multinaturalism* (as elaborated by anthropologist Vivieros de Castro,[22] not distinct in any important way from Nathan's 'multiple universes') necessary for sustaining different kinds of existence. What I have discussed as extensions of the human is not at all the expansion of human capacities to understand more and more of the natural world, summarizing its laws scientifically, or finding ways to be 'open' to it; rather it is a way of forging specific relationships.

In order to elaborate on this, I want to take you back to north-west Australia and my research with the Goolarabooloo mob, Paddy Roe's descendants. Over the last few years they have had a battle with a mining company, Woodside Energy, and associated companies, that wanted to build a huge factory to liquefy coal seam gas. Fine: shareholders would make a bit of money as the gas is exported, and Broome folk would continue to cook their fish with expensive bottled gas transported from Perth. This kind of extraction colonialism sees Nature as 'out there' and as a smooth undifferentiated space with resources reducible to material, like CH_4, the methane molecule. This will be accumulated and distributed in a market to turn it into money. Now, the important thing about this modern configuration co-ordinating science, technology, finance and government is that its proponents think not only it is real ('how the real world works') but *more realistic* than other ways of being in the world. Their economists will tell you that they are the 'adults in the room'.[23]

These adults, in the business of creating monetary value, are maintaining a network that hinged on the radical separation of nature and culture. For them, the 'environment' is either a benign resource, or composed of 'externalities'. They tend to call them externalities if they are surprising contingencies that can interrupt their network: a cyclone, a technological breakdown, recalcitrant animals or humans withdrawing support. An extractive network (one that removes value to a remote market) is thus deliberately constructed to 'get away with it', things extracted cheaply in one place to be sold at a profit in another. If a damaged environment is left behind, then that is an unaccounted-for externality, something else one has 'gotten away with'. Environmentalists, on the other hand, generally embrace a principle of connection or attachment. The idea is not to get away, but to embrace multispecies entanglements and to acknowledge the responsibility of keeping things alive in their places.

Literary formations, too, can be more or less extractive, more or less embedded in territories. Those imperial literary formations much critiqued over decades of postcolonial criticism are made legible and given value by virtue of their kinds of geopolitical networks centred on the publishing industries of London, Paris and New York. Anything too self-referentially parochial is rejected – it is literally incomprehensible – unless it expands its referential spheres to include that broader readership. This is what Paddy Roe does in the first story of his *Gularabulu* collection, 'Mirdinan':

> Yeah - - - - -
> well these people bin camping in Fisherman Bend him and his missus you know - -
> Fisherman Bend in Broome, *karnun* - -
> we call-im *karnun* - - -[24]

You can see that the precise place, 'Fisherman Bend', is repeated and then expanded to the regional location, Broome. That reference is destined for the listener outside of the region. The narrator includes this broader audience, as if he knows his story will become a book and be read in faraway places. But it is then translated back again into another world, the world of the Indigenous collective, the locals ('we') who know it by another name, *karnun*. Place-names like *karnun* label 'camps' or places the Goolarabooloo locals would call their *buru*. Perhaps the referential trick was learnt by the next gas company that came after Woodside (with an English-sounding name) was blocked in its attempt to industrialize the Country. The new fracking company has called itself Buru Energy, thus embedding itself if only in a nominal way.

The autonomy of the aesthetic

So, finally, I can come back to literature with a riposte to the offensive rhetoric of the economists, or certain sorts of scientists as well, who think they are the only adults in the room, who tell us that in the Humanities we are not particularly 'realistic', being involved with imaginative departures from the (one) real world. Being more realistic isn't achieved by universal scalability: as in, what worked in Peru or Ghana will work here. That, in fact, is a reduction, a normalizing tendency. Being more realistic means, I think, *adding more* to what we think is there. This is, in part, what I have called extensions of the human. It is also what societies with multiple universes live with all the time. The reality of spirit worlds is a given, but doesn't dominate the other modes of existence.

The reality of the literary domain, or the aesthetic more generally, can be given a more forceful existence with some of the strategies I have suggested. I think seeing a literary form as being in a *symbolic* relationship with its environment is a weaker link than the so-called totemic one that reinforces nature-culture continuities. Example: if you are chatting in an art gallery with a Nyangumarda artist and she says of her work, 'this one is the yam dreaming, from my country, that's my dreaming', she is not saying that this art work *represents* her dreaming; she is saying the same life flows through the country, her body and the painting. There remains, of course, much to be understood about Indigenous Australian aesthetic modes of existence.

Yet we can still propose more of a compositionist aesthetic, following Bruno Latour. The art work – painting, poem, song – is not a 'mere' construction, a reflection of some other reality that is more solid. It is a *well-constructed* object that comes into being as a heterogeneous array of elements flowing together in a satisfying composition. What are some of these elements? There is the artist, with craft skills and a devotion to the art work she is anticipating, hoping to see, fearful that it may not 'work'. It is, says Étienne Souriau, 'A form accompanied by a halo of hope and wonder, the reflection of which is like an iridescence for us'.[25] The poet, he continues, needs to 'love the poem a little before having written it'. And the readers are an essential part of the literary mode of existence, for they realize its form also, each time it is reproduced in a book, at a reading, in a classroom: their devotion extends to a network that has the potential to suspend the artwork forever in a web of immortal existence. Hamlet or Emma or Ginger Meggs live beyond their existence on the page or in language. You will say the same can be said for a historical character, like Napoleon, but I would argue that he has emerged from a historical factual existence and taken form, with various tropes and figures, as a fictional being, who, like all the others, has a palpable influence on our lives. The coming into being, or instauration, of the work of art is remarkable in one respect, and in this is quite unlike historical facts that can be made and then unmade, falsified. The instauration of the work of art is one-way, it cannot go backwards. That is why the poet's waste basket is full of failed attempts, and the artist's canvasses are painted over. The artist and the audience feel a responsibility for the instauration of the work. We are not detached from our literary environments, reflecting on them, or extracting material from them. Rather we are implicated in worlds brimming with possible becomings, and we feel the responsibility to help other beings on their existential journeys of fulfilment. These existences of humans, of technologies and of other living beings precede and extend each other, they overlap and reinforce each other in generative helixes, and when they have an aesthetic form, there is also the forward-moving force and autonomy of that aesthetic mode of existence.

The global dimension

In the second half of the twentieth century, traditional decolonization took place in the context of human struggles within national formations, and literary works expressing these kinds of struggles often deployed a vocabulary of *liberation* from the colonial yoke, and possibly also Bandung-like principles of 'non-aggression, cooperation and mutual benefit' as these new nations expelled foreign administrations and (re-)instituted 'native' government. India, in 1947, is a paradigmatic case. But in many other administrations there was, as Partha Chatterjee argues, a fairly rapid shift away from a decolonizing, 'third way' of development, towards high-growth capitalist development in the authoritarian style of Singapore and Taiwan.[26]

Other countries, notably on the African continent, succumbed to neocolonialism and *comprador* collaboration with extractive industries, while others, like Australia, retained colonial sovereignty and are yet to formally acknowledge any meaningful form of Indigenous sovereignty or treaty, while also promoting extractive industries. So while decolonization debates still take place within certain nations and among small groups of intellectuals, the late-twentieth-century movement to globalized capital formations and neoliberal ideology makes it all the harder to imagine in what contexts the now older idea of 'liberation' could take place. Cooke argues that 'ecological poetics needs to be able to deal better with the unavoidably powerful shift towards a "global" imagination'[27] as he moves towards solutions based in those 'transcultural' localities where valuable ecological knowledge is retained, along with valuably conserved means to express it. Let me stress that ecological knowledge is neither fixed nor in place, its value emerges through transcultural or translocal work, which is another kind of emancipatory network. Peter Minter also stresses the value of the kind of dialogue that Oodgeroo Noonuccal and Judith Wright pioneered, as he writes of their 'transcultural environmentalism' which he tellingly defines as 'an idiosyncratic mode of decolonisation, one in which a burgeoning western environmental movement intersects with the local Aboriginal land rights movement and a political agenda that is anti-colonial, anti-capitalist, ecocentric and pro-human rights'.[28] Aware of the limits of globalization, and the plurality of possible ways of being modern, Minter sees the potential for international Indigenous collaborations in the context of environmental emergency.

The current climate crisis shows the globalizing imaginary of 'modernization for all' is now impossible, and there is a now a 're-terrestrialization' movement that Bruno Latour claims is 'massive'.[29] It often takes its cue from burgeoning Indigenous initiatives around the planet, the focus of which is less one of liberation and more one of sustaining modes of belonging to territories, and caring for them in the most fundamental ways. These modes of belonging are encoded in Indigenous literatures, not just as content, but as practices of production. They have the important effect of reinforcing nature-culture continuities, making those brought up in modernist, 'Western' literary environments a little more aware of the specific way their own literary environments have distanced them from their 'environment'. That environment, I have argued, is neither natural nor given. Literary environmental networks are realized (made more real) as they are progressively uncovered. And while the Indigenous literary formations and networks we have explored in this chapter have, I hope, been instructive, they do not have the privilege of being in any way closer to any kinds of natural harmonies. Rather, it is in transcultural and translocal collaborations, of all kinds, that greater awareness of literary environments is cultivated.

Notes

1 A companion piece to this chapter, 'Literary Worlds: Indigenous and Western Network Ethnography', is forthcoming in Elisabeth Bloomfield and Claire C. Lyu, eds, *Nonmodern Practices: Latour and Literary Studies* (London: Bloomsbury, 2020).

2 Dipesh Chakrabarty, *Provincializing Europe: Postcolonial Thought and Historical Difference* (Princeton: Princeton University Press, 2000).

3 Michel Foucault, 'What Is an Author', in *Language, Counter-Memory, Practice: Selected Essays and Interviews*, ed. Donald F. Bouchard (Ithaca: Cornell University Press, 1977), 113–38.

4 Bruno Latour, 'An Attempt at a "Compositionist Manifesto"', *New Literary History* 41 (2010): 471–90.

5 Stephen Muecke, 'Reproductive Aesthetics: Multiple Realities in a Seamus Heaney Poem', in *The Mother's Day Protest and Other Fictocritical Essays* (London: Rowman and Littlefield International, 2016), 63–75.

6 Keri Glastonbury, 'Shut Up, Nobody Wants to Hear Your Poems!: Painter Versus Poet', *Cultural Studies Review* 12, no. 1 (2006): 153–72, 3.

7 Chakrabarty, *Provincializing Europe* (2000), has aptly noted that the secular academy has 'problems in handling practices in which gods, spirits, or the supernatural have agency in the world' (72).
8 There is an extensive literature on technological extensions of the human, for instance Marshall McLuhan, *Understanding Media: The Extensions of Man* (New York: McGraw-Hill. Paperback edition, 1966).
9 On the collaboration of farm animals, see Vinciane Despret and Jocelyne Porcher, 'The Pragmatics of Expertise', *Angelaki: Journal of the Theoretical Humanities* 20, no. 2 (2015): 91–9.
10 See Part 1 of Tobie Nathan and Isabelle Stengers, *Doctors and Healers* (Cambridge: Polity Press, 2018).
11 The etymology of *pagan* is Late Latin, *pagus*, 'country'.
12 In the West Kimberley, '*bugarrigarra*' is the term for the Dreaming, the ancestral law and culture for a number of different language groups and communities in the region.
13 To make this distinction, 'Country' will be capitalized in this text. Deborah Bird Rose writes about it as follows:

> Country in Aboriginal English is not only a common noun but also a proper noun. People talk about country in the same way that they would talk about a person: they speak to country, sing to country, visit country, worry about country, feel sorry for country, and long for country. People say that country knows, hears, smells, takes notice, takes care, is sorry or happy. Country is not a generalized or undifferentiated type of place, such as one might indicate with terms like 'spending a day in the country' or 'going up the country'. Rather, country is a living entity with a yesterday, today and tomorrow, with a consciousness, and a will towards life. Because of this richness, country is home, and peace; nourishment for body, mind and spirit; heart's ease. (Deborah Bird Rose, *Nourishing Terrains: Australian Aboriginal Views of Landscape and Wilderness* (Canberra: Australian Heritage Comm., 1996), 7)

14 'Lines were broken and turned to the next line at pauses, with the varying lengths of the pauses represented by dashes at the ends of lines. As with the earlier book, with the new stories this radically new form of presenting such material worked brilliantly.' Ray Coffey, 'A Ute, Not a Land Cruiser: Publishing *Reading the Country*', in *Reading the Country: 30 Years On*, ed. Philip Morrissey (Ultimo: UTS ePress, 2018), 52; Dennis Tedlock, *Finding the Center: Narrative Poetry of the Zuni Indians* (Lincoln: University of Nebraska Press, 1978).
15 Krim Benterrak with Stephen Muecke and Paddy Roe, *Reading the Country: Introduction to Nomadology* (Fremantle: Fremantle Arts Centre Press, 1984), 74–5.
16 Coffey, 'A Ute, Not a Land Cruiser', 53.

17 Coffey, 'A Ute, Not a Land Cruiser', 54.
18 C. E. Shannon and W. Weaver, *The Mathematical Theory of Communication* (Urbana: The University of Illinois Press, 1949).
19 Deborah Bird Rose, *Dingo Makes Us Human: Life and Land in Aboriginal Australian Culture* (Melbourne: Cambridge University Press, 1992).
20 Muecke, 'Reproductive Aesthetics', 64.
21 Stuart Cooke, 'Towards an Ethological Poetics: The Transgression of Genre and the Poetry of the Albert's Lyrebird', *Environmental Humanities* 11, no. 2 (2019): 302–23.
22 Eduardo Vivieros de Castro, *Cannibal Metaphysics,* ed. and trans. Peter Skafish (Minneapolis: Univocal, 2013).
23 Yanis Varoufakis, *Adults In The Room: My Battle With Europe's Deep Establishment* (London: Vintage, 2018).
24 Paddy Roe, *Gularabulu: Stories from the West Kimberley* (Fremantle: Fremantle Arts Centre Press, 1983), 24.
25 Étienne Souriau, *The Different Modes of Existence,* trans. Erik Beranek and Tim Howles, intro. Isabelle Stengers and Bruno Latour (Minneapolis: Univocal, 2015), 230.
26 Partha Chatterjee, 'Empire and Nation Revisited: 50 Years after Bandung', *Inter-Asia Cultural Studies* 6, no. 4 (2005): 488.
27 Stuart Cooke, 'Indigenous Poetics and Transcultural Ecologies', *Interdisciplinary Literary Studies* 20, no. 1 (2018): 2.
28 Peter Minter, 'Kath Walker (Oodgeroo Noonuccal), Judith Wright and Decolonised Transcultural Ecopoetics in Frank Heimans' "Shadow Sister"', *Sydney Studies in English* 41 (2015): 64.
29 Bruno Latour, interviewed by Carolina Miranda, 'Trouble dans l'engendrement', *Revue le Crieur* 14 (October 2019): 8.

Bibliography

Benterrak, Krim with Stephen Muecke and Paddy Roe. *Reading the Country: Introduction to Nomadology*. Fremantle: Fremantle Arts Centre Press, 1984.
Chakrabarty, Dipesh. *Provincializing Europe: Postcolonial Thought and Historical Difference*. Princeton: Princeton University Press, 2000.
Chatterjee, Partha. 'Empire and Nation Revisited: 50 Years after Bandung'. *Inter-Asia Cultural Studies* 6, no. 4 (2005): 487–96.
Coffey, Ray. 'A Ute, Not a Land Cruiser: Publishing *Reading the Country*'. In *Reading the Country: 30 Years On*, edited by Philip Morrissey and Chris Healy, 44–57. Ultimo: UTS ePress, 2018.
Cooke, Stuart. 'Indigenous Poetics and Transcultural Ecologies'. *Interdisciplinary Literary Studies* 20, no. 1 (2018): 1–32.

Cooke, Stuart. 'Towards an Ethological Poetics: The Transgression of Genre and the Poetry of the Albert's Lyrebird'. *Environmental Humanities* 11, no. 2 (2019): 302–23.

de Castro, Eduardo Vivieros. *Cannibal Metaphysics*. Edited and translated by Peter Skafish. Minneapolis: Univocal, 2013.

Despret, Vinciane and Jocelyne Porcher. 'The Pragmatics of Expertise'. *Angelaki: Journal of the Theoretical Humanities* 20, no. 2 (2015): 91–9.

Foucault, Michel. 'What Is an Author'. In *Language, Counter-Memory, Practice: Selected Essays and Interviews*, edited by Donald F. Bouchard, 113–38. Ithaca: Cornell University Press, 1977.

Glastonbury, Keri. 'Shut Up, Nobody Wants to Hear Your Poems!: Painter Versus Poet'. *Cultural Studies Review* 12, no. 1 (2006): 153–72.

Latour, Bruno. 'An Attempt at a "Compositionist Manifesto"'. *New Literary History* 41 (2010): 471–90.

Latour, Bruno interviewed by Carolina Miranda. 'Trouble dans l'engendrement'. *Revue le Crieur* 14 (October 2019).

McLuhan, Marshall. *Understanding Media: The Extensions of Man*. New York: McGraw-Hill. Paperback edition, 1966.

Minter, Peter. 'Kath Walker (Oodgeroo Noonuccal), Judith Wright and Decolonised Transcultural Ecopoetics in Frank Heimans' "Shadow Sister"'. *Sydney Studies in English* 41 (2015): 61–74.

Muecke, Stephen. 'Reproductive Aesthetics: Multiple Realities in a Seamus Heaney Poem'. In *The Mother's Day Protest and Other Fictocritical Essays*, 63–76. London: Rowman and Littlefield International, 2016.

Nathan, Tobie and Isabelle Stengers. *Doctors and Healers*. Cambridge: Polity Press, 2018.

Roe, Paddy. *Gularabulu: Stories from the West Kimberley*. Fremantle: Fremantle Arts Centre Press, 1983.

Rose, Deborah Bird. *Dingo Makes us Human: Life and Land in Aboriginal Australian Culture*. Melbourne: Cambridge University Press, 1992.

Rose, Deborah Bird. *Nourishing Terrains: Australian Aboriginal Views of Landscape and Wilderness*. Canberra: Australian Heritage Comm., 1996.

Shannon, Claude E. and W. Weaver. *The Mathematical Theory of Communication*. Urbana: University of Illinois Press, 1949.

Tedlock, Dennis. *Finding the Center: Narrative Poetry of the Zuni Indians*. Lincoln: University of Nebraska Press, 1978.

Varoufakis, Yanis. *Adults In The Room: My Battle With Europe's Deep Establishment*. London: Vintage, 2018.

12

Placing invisible women

Environment, space and power in two works by Ana Patricia Martínez Huchim

Maia Gunn Watkinson

This chapter begins by providing a historical, political and cultural context for the representation of space and place in the work of Maya women writers. It discusses the principal ways that Maya women writers have negotiated the contradictions between representations of Maya culture and their lived realities. Then, I provide a survey of the forest as cultural and social space in Yucatán, addressing the history of the chicle (chewing gum) industry and the forest in anthropological discourses of Maya culture. Finally, I examine how Ana Patricia Martínez Huchim, through her depiction of the forest and how women move in and relate to the natural environment, challenges these discourses and depictions. Her work is attracting significant attention among scholars, however, the role of the natural environment in her construction of gendered identities has been overlooked. Martínez Huchim seeks to give a voice to women silenced in Maya literature and to challenge community discourses, and the natural environment plays a key role in this subversive project. Conventional female subjectivities in Maya writing emphasize ancestral knowledge specific to women, traditional spaces and gender roles. Martínez Huchim disrupts these traditions in Maya literature by writing the forest, a traditionally male domain, as a place where women belong.

The Yucatán Peninsula is marked by a history of contact between cultures and languages that extends long before the arrival of the Spanish to the region in the early sixteenth century. The historical, social and cultural significance of colonization, however, cannot be underestimated. Indeed, the Spanish and Maya languages and cultures are firmly contrasted in the social consciousness of the Peninsula. There are two aspects to the Yucatecan postcolonial condition that are important to address here to understand the position of Maya women writers: the relationship between class and ethnicity in distinguishing Maya from Spanish identities, and the global fame of Mesoamerican cultures. Archaeologists, intellectuals and anthropologists have long promoted Maya history and culture in their studies, travel accounts and popular histories. The appropriation and valorization of Maya culture presents both challenges and benefits for contemporary Maya writers. This valorization contrasts with the association, in the Yucatecan social consciousness, of being Maya with being poor.

Women are placed, and place themselves, within these narratives of culture and history in distinct ways. In this chapter I use a postcolonial feminist approach to my analyses of the representation of the forest as gendered space in Martínez Huchim's texts. I find Gloria Anzaldúa's notion of the borderlands helpful in understanding how borders are not just geographic but cultural and intersect with material realities of gender, language and class. The borderland is a 'vague and undetermined place created by the emotional residue of an unnatural boundary' where new identities are formed.[1] In addition, I am informed by feminist geographer Doreen Massey's critique of the definition of space as empty and *a priori*, and of place as 'fixed'.[2] Massey shows that the notion of place as static is linked to Western categories of gender as bounded, and instead defines place as multiple, shifting and open. Social relations make a place. I also draw upon studies in history, anthropology, linguistics and literary studies to analyse depictions of the natural environment in the work of Maya writers.

Martínez Huchim's texts can be contextualized within the historical emergence of contemporary Maya-Spanish literature, what distinguished Maya writer and intellectual Jorge Miguel Cocom Pech calls 'the rebirth of the Maya voice'.[3] In the 1980s and 1990s, poets, school teachers and cultural promoters from the Yucatán Peninsula in southern Mexico, which comprises the three states of Yucatán, Quintana Roo and Campeche, began to write bilingual texts in their native language, Maya and in Spanish.[4] There was indeed a relative silence of Maya voices in Yucatecan literature before the Maya literary revival. For almost forty years, few texts written in the Maya language circulated in the Peninsula. The number of speakers of the Maya language was not the cause of this absence: in the 1970s, for example, almost half the population of the state of Yucatán spoke both Maya and Spanish.[5] Rather, the lack of texts reflected the low levels of literacy in Maya, the weakening public use and status of the language, the minimum social mobility of Maya speakers, and the decline in parents transmitting the language to younger generations.[6]

Before her death in 2018, ethnographer Ana Patricia Martínez Huchim had an influential role in the Maya cultural and linguistic literary revival in Yucatán.[7] Attesting to her significance within the state of Yucatán, six months after her death the *Revista Yucateca de Estudios Literarios* dedicated a special edition to her life and work.[8] In diverse ways, Martínez Huchim established paths for new Maya authors to follow. She recorded, transcribed and collated oral literatures in the Maya language, opened spaces for writers and storytellers to disseminate Maya-Spanish bilingual texts through establishing and organizing a cultural centre and bilingual magazine and sought to create a culture of reading and writing in rural Yucatán by producing low-cost bilingual texts and distributing them free of charge.[9] While her professional career focused on the transcription, compilation and dissemination of Maya oral traditions, in 2005 Martínez Huchim began to create her own tales.[10] In numerous interviews she has remarked that she turned to writing fiction to redress the silences of the collective tradition and community discourses.[11] In this chapter I focus on these fictional works.

Indigenous literature in Latin America is a growing area within literary studies, cultural studies and linguistic anthropology.[12] Scholars from these disciplines, including Gloria Chacón, María Luz Lepe Lira, Alicia Salinas, Paul Worley and Margaret Shrimpton Masson, are addressing the innovation of Martínez Huchim's work. In particular, they show how Martínez Huchim's narratives challenge dominant representations of both the rural Yucatecan canon and the emerging corpus of Maya texts that are forming a separate canon.[13] Amid this attention, however, the role of the natural environment in the construction of gendered identities has been overlooked.

Thus, in this chapter I analyse the collection of stories *U ka'ajsajil u ts'u' noj káax / Recuerdos del corazón de la montaña* (*Memories from the Heart of the Forest*) because it is a good example of how environment informs representations of what it means to be a Maya woman.[14] *Recuerdos del corazón de la montaña* recounts the memories of a dying elderly woman who worked as a cook in the forest for *chicleros*, men who extract resin from *sapodilla* or *zapote* trees to make chicle (chewing gum).[15] I also address one story, 'xsaataj óol / Divagación' ('The Wanderer'), from the collection *U yóol xkaambal jaw xíiw / Contrayerba* (*Antidote*). I chose 'xsaataj óol / Divagación' because of the importance of natural environment to the protagonist's sense of belonging. The tales in *Contrayerba* focus on women stigmatized by the people of their communities because of their role or employment within their village. Their subject matter is notable because it differs from other contemporary bilingual Maya-Spanish literature. For almost all Maya writers, space is closely linked to an affirmative view of tradition and culture. The work of Martínez Huchim, on the other hand, reflects a new tendency among Maya women writers to explore social marginality as liberating for women.

I argue that the writings of Martínez Huchim challenge ethnocentric and essentialist ideas of what it means to be a Maya woman by depicting the protagonists of her tales belonging to locations, such as the forest, that anthropologists and other Maya writers consider to be culturally and socially male rather than female. She writes about the forest through an Indigenous feminist lens. My analysis of the sociopolitical history of the chicle industry and how the forest is situated within anthropological discourses of Maya culture aids our understanding of the ways Maya women writers use the environment to confront and shape their place in history and culture.

Historical, political and cultural contexts

Sociologist Rosalva Aída Hernández Castillo argues that Indigenous women in Mexico are caught between, on the one hand, ethnocentric hegemonic feminisms of mostly urban and middle-class orientation that tend to victimize Indigenous women and, on the other hand, the ethnic essentialism of Indigenous movements themselves that argue that gender inequality does not exist.[16] The ethnic essentialist position is that social relations in Maya communities are based on ideas of complementarity and interdependence between women and men, a balance of sexes that recognizes differences in a non-hierarchical way and is distinct from Western binaristic conceptions of gender. For example, Maya sociologist Rosa Pu Tzunux contends that this alternative view of gender is reflected in the cosmology, the organization of agricultural modes of production and the structure of Mayan languages themselves.[17] Gloria Chacón, however, outlines the diverse Maya perspectives on gender, highlighting that not all Maya feminists share this essentialist perspective. Some argue that cosmology and the structure of languages are not the same as everyday reality, and others ask whether gender complementarity ever existed outside of cultural representations.[18] In turn, Aymara intellectual Julieta Paredes views colonization as the historical moment when two patriarchal systems met and benefited from one another.[19] Martínez Huchim's work aligns closely with these critiques of ethnic essentialism. It challenges both the neocolonial discourse of Indigenous women as victims and the ethnic essentialist discourse of gender in Maya society and culture as harmonious.

Both non-Indigenous and Indigenous women writers from Latin America have represented traditional spaces of womanhood, such as the kitchen, as spaces where they realize their potential or identity as women. Indigenous women, however, have different struggles and social realities that inform their representations of space. The distinction can be seen by comparing the kitchen in Rosario Castellanos's short story 'Lección de cocina' ('Cooking Lesson') with the *fogón* (hearth) in Briceida Cuevas Cob's poem 'Yann a bin xook / Irás a la escuela' ('You will go to School'). In Castellanos's story, a recently married woman returns from her honeymoon to cook a meal for her husband but subverts social expectations by breaking the rules of cooking. The protagonist realizes she can exercise control.[20] In Cuevas Cob's poem a mother authoritatively instructs her daughter that she will go to school and get an education in the Western system but will also return home to her stool by the *fogón*.[21] That is, she will not forget her village and Indigenous roots. The kitchen is where the young woman realizes her Maya identity.

Unlike more traditional examples of Maya writing that represent the places and sacred acts associated with traditional female roles in Maya culture, the work of Martínez Huchim depicts women who are stigmatized for their labour and role in their communities. The protagonists' stigmatization informs where they go, how they move in space and how the other inhabitants of the village perceive and interact with them. Her representation of women occupying the village, street and forest, traditionally male domains in Maya writing, alone distinguishes her work from other Maya writers.

Similar to many other writers publishing in Maya and Spanish, Martínez Huchim is concerned with revitalizing and validating *in writing* Maya genres and forms of communicating from the oral tradition. Literary scholar María Luz Lepe Lira categorizes Martínez Huchim's work as one of three main types of Indigenous literature, 'recreational literature of the tradition . . . , which links the tradition and testimonial experience with a new creation'.[22] That is, rather than transcriptions of oral traditions that reflect a desire to rescue culture, or a hybrid literature primarily based on Western forms, Martínez Huchim develops and modifies oral traditions. Lepe Lira explains that the recreation of tradition has been particularly important for women writers as they negotiate their roles as Indigenous authors: 'writers try to be loyal translators of their communities, while also resisting sexist or discriminatory discourses recounted by narrators as spokespeople for the tradition.'[23] The storyteller as spokesperson for Maya culture is indeed central to Martínez Huchim's narratives. Two of her texts begin and close with a device to frame narratives common in the Maya language, '*Ku tsikabta'al'* ('they say') and *'ka'aj maanen'* ('when I passed by'). With this device, the storyteller opens the narrative by addressing common knowledge and closes the tale by interjecting as a witness to the events narrated.²⁴ In his analysis of Martínez Huchim's short story 'Chen konel / Es por demás', anthropologist Paul Worley argues that she uses these formulae to play on 'assumed knowledge' and to emphasize the importance of performance to Maya oral literatures.²⁵ Moreover, her works foreground the oral traditions of daily life by including songs and epigraphs of popular sayings. She validates both the more formal and the everyday ways of communicating in Maya in her works.

When Indigenous women depict natural environments *and* write in their native language, they are informed by the multiple oppressions of ethnicity and gender that shape meaning and material reality. A context to the chicle industry, the main topic of Martínez Huchim's collection, highlights how natural environments are implicated in narratives of cultural and social development in postcolonial contexts and of what it means to be Indigenous. The extraction of resin of *sapodilla* trees to make chewing gum began in the Yucatán Peninsula in the mid to late nineteenth century and increased rapidly, reaching its height in the 1940s and ending in the 1960s. In literature, the chicle industry was popular as a topic in the 1930s and 1940s, the period following the Mexican Revolution of 1910–19. Driven by socialist ideals, non-Indigenous writers from the Peninsula and elsewhere in Mexico wrote novels, poems and histories on chicle production with the often explicit aim to reduce the influence of foreign companies, and the national private contractors whom they controlled, in the industry.²⁶ Owing to federal policies under the presidency of Porfirio Díaz, North American companies were allowed to have significant control over its production. The United States was also the primary consumer, with 95 per cent of chicle produced in Mexico exported there.²⁷ *Sicté* became chewing gum, an emblematic product of North American culture.

As a subject, chicle production has enabled non-Indigenous Yucatecan intellectuals and politicians to explore in their literature issues of regional identity, politics, changing labour relations and the capitalist mode of production. In particular, the topic was a way that these writers challenged unequal power relations. Industries in the south-eastern region of Mexico rarely served to improve the living conditions of people who lived in those areas but instead profited North American companies.²⁸ Yet the importance of the industry for locals cannot be underestimated. In 1945, Claudio Vadillo López notes that 8,000 families in Campeche depended on chicle production.²⁹ The industry fell with the rise of synthetics and, as Wolfgang Gabbert states, 'excessive exploitation'.³⁰ It was also a period when intellectuals raised questions about the political status of the territory that became the state of Quintana Roo in 1934.

Luis Rosado Vega wrote about chicle production for the greatest amount of times. A critical voice of *indigenismo yucateco*, literature written about Maya culture and history by non-Maya Yucatecan writers, Rosado Vega wrote what continues to be some of the most popular collections of Maya oral traditions. The chicle industry is the main topic of his collection of epic poems, *Poema de la selva trágica* (1937) and the novel *Claudio Martín: vida de un chiclero* (1938). In addition, he wrote a history of Quintana Roo, *Un pueblo y un hombre* (1940), focusing on the environmental and labour policies of the first governor of Quintana Roo, socialist Rafael E. Melgar (1935–8). *Un pueblo y un hombre* especially dealt with the creation of cooperatives for *chicleros*. According to Rosado Vega, the tragedy of the forest is the unequal relations of production. His creative works emphasize the ancestral Maya knowledge of *chicle* tapping, the exploitation of labour by the federal Mexican government and foreign companies and the physical danger that the work entailed.

The labour, which involves climbing the tree, cutting into it and collecting the sap, is indeed strenuous and dangerous as it must occur during the rainy season. The work is also precarious because of the animals and insects of the forest, which include jaguars, snakes, vultures, armadillos, mosquitoes, fleas and termites.

For the *chicleros*, the labour and social conditions were favourable in comparison with the henequen plantation, the site of the dominant industry in the Peninsula that preceded the chicle epoch. In the nineteenth century, Yucatán's economy was reliant on the production of henequen, a plant native to the state of Yucatán that was used to make fibres for twine. Henequen was produced on large estates that were based on debt peonage, a system that kept landless peasants attached to the estate.[31] Henequen plantations and chicle camps were two vastly different social spaces in distinct natural environments. Working as a *chiclero* offered mobility unlike the confinement of henequen plantations. Life on plantations was highly controlled and demarcated. Yucatán's larger henequen plantations, or *haciendas*, were, as historian Ben Fallaw puts it, 'a world unto themselves, boasting their own chapels, stores, and schools; residents rarely interacted with neighbouring towns and villages'.[32] For women, the henequen plantations were often more restrictive than the villages. Piedad Peniche Rivero in her chapter 'Gender, Bridewealth, and Marriage in Yucatan' shows that marriage and 'exchanging women' was a way that the peons maintained a stable labour population and kept men in debt but that this system depended on the 'traditional Mayan customs, so in this case one could say that ethnicity actually reinforced oppression'.[33] Further, the *hacendados*, owners of the *haciendas*, exploited women's labour by forcing them to do unpaid 'agricultural chores' and domestic service.

In contrast to the *hacienda*, the chicle camp was a vast and unplanned space and work in the chicle industry unpredictable and nomadic. The recovery period of the *sapodilla* tree is four and a half years so *chicleros* must constantly establish new camps as they wait for the old trees to regrow. Testimonies recorded in Campeche by ethnographer Martha Patricia Ponce Jiménez reveal that *chicleros* regarded the camps as peaceful and free.[34] It was common for women and children to come with the men to the camps and to work there as cooks. *Chicleros* respected women accompanied by their husbands. And when women were unmarried, according to testimony recorded by Ponce Jiménez, the captain would tell them to 'choose' the *chiclero* they would settle with so as to not create problems between the men in the camp.[35] Prostitutes also occasionally visited the camps.

Although chicle production has not been the focus of the work of male Maya writers, the forest and the bush are two critical sites of cultural resilience in their texts. They are spaces of male self-realization similar to the *fogón* in the work of women writers. In the collection of tales *Muk'ul T'an In Nool / Secretos del abuelo* by Jorge Miguel Cocom Pech, the forest and bush are where Maya boys learn the knowledge of their male ancestors and attain pride in being Maya.[36] Wildernain Villegas in his collection of poems *Áak'abe' ku ya'alik táan u k'áaxal ja' / Lluvia que la noche dicta* contrasts the noises, smells and inhabitants of the city with the trees, air, nights and animals of his village.[37] His verses mimic prayers with few breaks for pausing. For these writers, Maya identity is formed or realized through the performance of agricultural rites and ceremonies to honour the ancestors and gods. The imagery is of flowers, incense, drinks and food used in ritual such as *balché*, a fermented drink made from the bark of the *balché* tree. Men speak an esoteric Maya language. As Cocom Pech recalls in his testimony of his initiation into manhood, his grandfather spoke 'surely an ancient Maya' that sounded as if it came 'from the depths of a cave'.[38] In these narratives, the gaze on the environment is overtly poetic and implicitly political. The gaze is about valuing and transmitting a cultural education not derived from the colonial system of the school but the teachings of their ancestors.

In almost all of the foregoing narratives the forest is a male social and cultural space. The protagonists of cultural transmission, resistance and continuity in these tales are male and the forest and bush are depicted as socially and culturally significant for men but not women. In Maya texts, women rarely venture into the forest. In non-Maya Yucatecan literary representations, especially narratives of chicle in the post-revolutionary era, the forest tends to be a space controlled by men. Governments and companies imposed the use of a space, and male *chicleros* sought to resist this dominance.

Between anthropological discourse and ethnocentric agendas: Forest as Maya space

In the Yucatán Peninsula's cultural and symbolic landscape, the forest has a paramount place in demarcating differences between Maya and Spanish cultures. The Peninsula is a densely forested region, and the forest has not solely been occupied by Maya or significant only to Maya speakers. Yet in the social consciousness of Yucatán it is chiefly associated with the maintenance of Maya culture, including environmental practices and beliefs, such as the *Yuumilk'aax* or *Yuntsiloob,* deities who guard the forest and enforce respectful behaviour. Maya narratives emphasize a reciprocal, and at times volatile, relationship between humans, animals, trees, plants and spirits in the forest. In the Maya language, the forest (*kaax*) is defined as 'uncultivated' in comparison with 'cultivated' or 'settled' areas. In collections of oral traditions, the forest has an important place in the stories that Maya writers tell each other, and others, about their culture. In these narratives, the forest is many things: dangerous, where misbehaving children disappear and alcoholic men are supposedly trapped by a beautiful woman in the branches of a ceiba tree; spiritual, where gods reside and Maya ancestors performed ceremonies; and it is associated with hunting and the cultural beliefs surrounding interaction with and maintenance of the natural environment.

In dominant anthropological conceptions of what it means to be Maya, the forest is a pristine and authentic cultural space, and untouched by Spanish or Western cultures. This can be seen in *The Folk Culture of Yucatán*, a work by anthropologist Robert Redfield that has had a profound impact on anthropological and popular discourses of Maya culture and identity. Redfield placed the forest at the end of his 'folk-urban continuum', a social scale that marked where tradition began and modernity ended. He stated: 'Yucatan, considered as one moves from Mérida, southeastward into the forest hinterland, presents a sort of social gradient in which the Spanish, modern, and urban gives way to the Maya, archaic and primitive.'[39] In this model, the forest exists in a different temporality from the modern city. Despite being published half a century later, Macduff Everton, American photographer and essayist, expresses similar ideas in *The Modern Maya: Incidents of Travel and Friendship in Yucatán*. In his chapter on a family of *chicleros*, the topic of Martínez Huchim's book, as I will discuss later, he asserts that 'the forest belongs to the Maya. It's their home, where they are most comfortable.'[40] Later in the same section, he adds that not all Maya share this perspective, including women in his list. Everton presents the predominant view among non-Yucatecan anthropologists that 'the Maya' have progress forced upon them, mostly by North America, and thus have to abandon tradition. In dominant anthropological discourses of Maya identity, then, the forest is authentically Maya, marking them as traditional and primitive, unlike the ordered and modern Spanish.

The forest has important symbolic weight in contemporary Maya literature, and not all Maya writers challenge anthropological discourses in which the forest and rural village are considered more Maya than the city. The agenda of Maya writers to emphasize the resilience of the Maya language and culture, however, produces a different discourse of the forest as space of self-realization. It is where elders passed on traditional rituals and teachings to their grandchildren and one could speak Maya without discrimination. Indeed, in chicle camps in the forest, the Maya language was often the only language spoken.[41] The production of chicle also helped Maya resist non-Maya regional and federal armed forces. Profits from the production of chicle in the Yucatán Peninsula were used to support Maya rebels in the Caste War (1847–1901), an event that had significantly shaped Maya and non-Maya relations in the region.[42] In the work of Maya writers the relationship to the forest is more intimate than that of Redfield and other anthropologists.

The collection of songs and tales *Recuerdos del corazón de la montaña* by Martínez Huchim is a good example of the forest as a historically significant site of Maya resistance and cultural continuity. The book is based on the memories of xTuux, an elderly and dying female relative of Martínez Huchim, having spent most of her life working as a cook in chicle camps. Through recounting her memories, the book weaves an unofficial history of chicle workers, or *chicleros*, men who extract resin from *sapodilla* trees. Chicle production involves tapping *sapodilla* trees, collecting the resin (*sicté*, in Maya), heating it over a fire so it coagulates and then fitting it into moulds for export.

Martínez Huchim's decision in *Recuerdos del corazón de la montaña* to focus on the memories of a female cook during the chicle epoch revives the topic in Yucatecan literature and breaks the cycle of its predominately male narratives. The chicle industry is an outdated topic in Yucatecan literature. Although chicle is still produced by small cooperatives for specialist markets, it is no longer a dominant industry in Yucatán. In addition, the chicle industry was predominantly controlled, and the work undertaken, by men. Yet chicle production was important for women, too, because it enabled them some freedom from the restrictions of the village. Chicle is a topic implicated in anthropological discourses of Maya culture surrounding imperialism, and the loss of tradition and imposition of modernity. In her collection, Martínez Huchim has an agenda to preserve culture, critique modernization and recover silenced regional histories. She does so through a feminist lens that depicts the forest as a place where Maya women belonged.

Recuerdos del corazón de la montaña: Forest as female space

Recuerdos del corazón de la montaña provides an unofficial history of the chicle era by focusing on a female cook named xTuux rather than the male *chicleros*. The book includes three songs and eight tales; the collection is neither an epic nor heroic narrative but rather intimate and disjointed. The tales are based on the testimony of a family relative. They are short in length, with most being two to six pages long, and recount xTuux's scattered memories. The narrator introduces xTuux as the granddaughter of 'scribes' and 'runaway Maya' and as a 'faithful speaker' of the Maya language, although the inhabitants of her village view her as a 'dejada'. XTuux is noble but faces the challenges of a harsh environment, the labour of cooking and working in an all-male camp.

The forest in *Recuerdos del corazón de la montaña* is represented as dangerous, consuming and imposing, at the same time as musical and life-sustaining. The forest has its own laws of cosmology and reciprocity based on prayer and song. The first of the three songs in the collection, 'song of the heart of the forest', depicts the forest as a powerful environment that gives and takes life, 'provee para vivir / provee para morir' ('it provides for life / it provides for death'), attracts animals and invokes fear in men and pumps its own white and red blood, the colours of the resin of the *sapodilla* tree.[43] This song and other parts of the collection capture the remarkable physical appearance of the tree when it is cut in which the different colours of the resins appear indeed as red and white blood.

Martínez Huchim inscribes her feminist vision in these songs by accentuating the relations between women. The second song locates Maya memory and belonging specifically in the *sapodilla* tree: 'única nuestra memoria, nuestra estirpe, una sola de grueso tronco de raíces profundas' ('our only memory, our lineage, a single, thick trunk with deep roots').[44] The *sapodilla* tree, the origin of Maya identity and metaphor of lineage, is also 'una sola'. The feminine quality is more potent in the Spanish translation than in the Maya original as both the words for resin and blood are feminine:

> La resina del zapote rojo es su escasez.
> La resina del zapote blanco es su medida.
> La resina del zapote morado es su abundancia.
> La blanca resina es su sangre.[45]

> (The resin of the red zapote is its scarcity.
> The resin of the white zapote is its measure.
> The resin of the purple zapote is its abundance.
> The white resin is its blood.)

The frequent descriptions of the resin as the blood of the *sapodilla* tree bring to mind networks, ancestry and lineage. Indeed, the final stanza of the second song lists the familial relations of women: grandmother, mother, older sister, younger sister, twin sister and (female) friend.[46] Only women are included in these networks.

There is an ecological ethics in Martínez Huchim's text. She critiques the commercial exploitation of the environment. Similar to writers of the post-revolutionary era, the history of the chicle industry offers Martínez Huchim a way to comment on the socio-economic issues of the present. To do this she uses a device from storytelling in Maya, the coda 'Ka'aj máanen' or 'Cuando pasé'. In her thesis on oral narratives in Xocén, a town in Valladolid, Yucatán, Martínez Huchim explains that this coda is when, in telling a story, 'the narrator participates subjectively like a character witness in order to give veracity to the narrated'.[47] Here, it serves to relate the history of exploitation of the *sapodilla* tree to modernization in rural Yucatán. The narrator comments that while passing the town where xTuux lived, a 'big black road' brought 'new things': 'Cuando pasé el otro día por el rumbo donde vivió la difunta doña xTuux, habían tapado el pozo público y un amplio camino negro era tránsito de cosas nuevas. Destacaba un *xtokoy* solar donde leñaban el grueso tronco de un zapote seco' (The other day when I passed by the place where the late doña xTuux lived, they'd filled the public well and a wide black road was bringing new things. An open *xtokoy* stood out, where they were chopping up the thick trunk of a dry zapote).[48] The *sapodilla* tree, known for its longevity and resistance to drought, was dry and only its base remained. The final lines of the story conflate the blood of xTuux and all the others who have died with that of the *sapodilla* tree: 'ch'aaj, cayó la última gota de resina' (ch'aaj, the last drop of resin fell).

The exploitation of the female body and the forest are inextricably linked in the tales. XTuux has an affinity with the *sapodilla* tree in life and death. Within the story, the *sapodilla* tree is referred to as xTuux's protector and 'unconditional friend'. In the final story, she hugs the tree and then dies, her body fusing with the tree and, matching it, becoming rigid, 'llegó al árbol y jalando aire se abrazó al tronco, quedando su cuerpo rígido y fundido con él' (she went to the tree and squashing the air she hugged the trunk, keeping her body rigid and fusing with it).[49] A return to the tree represents her freedom and it is only in death, as 'culebra que se despoja de la piel' (snake that sheds its skin), that she is finally free from the burdens of an arduous life.

Historian Jennifer Mathews notes that a Maya word for the *sapodilla* tree is *tzicte' ya'*, which she translates as 'wounded noble tree'.[50] The image of the wounded tree with noble lineage links the depictions of gender relations and the constructions of the environment in *Recuerdos del corazón de la montaña*: there are many possible meanings of who is noble and wounded in the context of bilingual Maya-Spanish literature: women, *sapodilla* tree, forest or Maya language.

In addition to the tree itself, fauna are prominent in *Recuerdos del corazón de la montaña*. The closest animal xTuux represents is the deer. The frequent references to the deer as pleading, captive and watched mirrors xTuux's own experience as trapped and exploited in a male-dominated and volatile environment. 'El mentado Janamás', the fourth story in the collection, begins by describing, through the metaphor of the deer and the hunter, the difficulties xTuux faces working in an all-male camp; the *chicleros* watched her as a hunter spies deer.[51]

Both the chicle camp and xTuux's village and home are under constant surveillance from men in the camp; xTuux had to urinate standing to avoid the attention of men and to wait until night time to defecate in the forest, crouched between the trees. The habit of directing her eyes to the floor to evade their 'malos entendidos' stayed with her even when she was not in the camp. The book emphasizes the challenges of her sex: 'Los días de menstruación le resultaban de los más incómodos' (The days of menstruation were to become the most uncomfortable).[52] Similar to the work of *indigenista* writers, the chicle camp is portrayed as isolating and dangerous, and the work there arduous, but instead from a Maya female perspective.

The machete is a symbol of protection, violence and resourcefulness. In the final story xTuux hangs up the machete signifying the end of the chicle epoch, a complex enterprise that afforded women freedom from the restrictions of village, despite the challenges of working in a male-dominated social space. This act denotes her symbolic discarding of patriarchal constraints. In an earlier story, the reader learns that the machete belonged to her father and that she began to carry it with her when her partner left her; 'el machete chiclero al cinto formó parte del atuendo de xTuux y no se separaba de él, ni cuando dormía' (the *chiclero* machete on the belt formed part of xTuux's outfit and was never separated from her, not even when she slept).[53]

The foremost agenda of Maya writers is to make the Maya language the core of their literature. A dominant perspective among Maya writers and cultural promoters in Yucatán is that Maya writers should eliminate the traces of the Spanish language and of the *mestizo* culture in their literature. Feliciano Sánchez Chan is the most vociferous Maya writer with this perspective. In his poetry he aims to rescue the specialized and ritualistic ways of speaking Maya, especially the discourses of the *jmeen* [Maya priest]. Sánchez Chan argues that the older generation of Maya writers practised *milpa* agriculture, especially ceremonies, and thus had 'comprehensive contact with the full essence of Maya language'.[54] The importance of these ceremonies and rites, according to writers such as Sánchez Chan, is the knowledge of the cultural referents that underpin them.

Martínez Huchim's decision to include paratextual elements that aim to educate the reader on linguistic and cultural mixing in the Peninsula, vernacular expressions and customs is politicized in this context. She portrays what Anzaldúa in the essay 'How to Tame a Wild Tongue' calls a language that is a 'border' or 'forked tongue'.[55] The 'traces' of Spanish are not hidden from the Maya version. In notes, Martínez Huchim explains terms, plants and other details specific to the local cultural and social context. More importantly, and unlike most other Maya authors, she incorporates a Maya-Spanish glossary in both her collections including 'español yucateco', 'hibridismos maya-castellanos', 'onomatopeyas', 'préstamos de castellano' and 'préstamos del maya'. These categories highlight not only the regional difference of the Spanish spoken in Yucatán but also the contact and borrowings between Maya and Spanish. Indeed, Martínez Huchim emphasizes the vitality of the Maya language in the book's dedication: 'Al vivo recuerdo de los muertos del corazón de la montaña, / esta ofrenda / del palpitar de la lengua maya' (To the living memory of the dead in the heart of the forest, / this offering / of the palpitation of the Maya language).[56] There are two notable aspects to this statement. One is that recording memory is described as an offering. The second is that the Maya language is 'living' and 'beats', resembling a heart. In her dissertation, Alicia Marie Salinas discusses the glossary, mentioning that it 'suggests that she anticipates that readers will be unfamiliar with the Yucatecan vocabulary and word usage she employs' and that regardless of how someone reads the text 'they experience the Maya character of both the original text and its translation'.[57] The glossary, hybridisms and fragmented structure of the tales do not anticipate nor invite identification with a universal subject. At the same time, Martínez Huchim makes reading the translation more laborious. This is important in a regional context where Maya tales sell but are often promoted and perceived of as 'easy reading'. In contrast, Martínez Huchim in her tales makes the non-Maya reader aware of the potential limits of knowledge.

Similar themes of linguistic and cultural diversion surface in the sixth tale 'xsaataj óol / Divagación' published in the collection *U yóol xkaambal jaw xíiw / Contrayerba (Antidote). Contrayerba* comprises a series of nine tales each about a different woman. The women are defined by their roles in the local community. These include the herbalist, midwife, prostitute and deaf wood-bearer. I focus on the tale 'xsaataj óol / Divagación' because of the role of the environment in the protagonist's sense of belonging. In the Maya language, her name, *xsaataj óol*, suggests a female soul or being who has digressed from her path. The prefix 'x' means female in Maya. The verb *sa'at* means 'to lose' and *óol* has a host of meanings including animated state, life, intention, being, capacity, centre and heart. According to linguist Gabriel L. Bourdieu,[58] *óol* can both refer to the central region of the body and the 'spirit' or 'soul'. As for other Mayan languages, the material and immaterial are not easily separable. In Maya and in Spanish her name evokes a diversion from the course, path or centre.

The borders that Divagación transgresses in this tale mirror the two linguistic and cultural worlds that Martínez Huchim as a Maya writer operates in and between. Divagación transgresses physical, social and cultural boundaries: she wears men's clothing; she wanders the town, occasionally entering a house: 'algunas veces entra a una casa, escudriña cosas y luego se retira' (a few times she enters a house, scrutinizes things and then leaves).[59] For this reason I translate her name as the Wanderer rather than the Rambler. Irrespective, her name suggests an aimless passage and the untranslatable or incomprehensible. According to town gossip, she was led to madness by her ex-boyfriend who left her, and she assimilated the abandonment by wearing his clothes and 'se volvió marimacho' (she became a tomboy).[60]

The narrative is focalized, however, through the perspective of a young girl named Mercedes who is fascinated by Divagación. Although other children scatter and hide when Divagación approaches, Mercedes stays to continue to watch from the back wall of her house and is fixated and perplexed at seeing Divagación so close; her thick lips and grey hair reminds her of her grandmother called 'Benigna', who speaks to her plants. Early in the tale, an opposition is established between Mercedes, who is confined, and the freedom of Divagación, who wanders the streets and bathes in public. The freedom of Divagación is in stark contrast to the socialization and the indoctrination of women into gendered roles reflected in the young Mercedes. In the final story of the collection, 'Otra senda', the narrator refers to Mercedes as 'la abandonada con cinco hijos' (the abandoned woman with five children).[61] Indeed, we come to the conclusion in Martínez Huchim's work that gendered roles provide Maya women in villages with few opportunities.

The natural environment is critical to Divagación's creation of her own sacred space. During the afternoons of the dry season, Divagación collects water from the well, places it in a wooden keg and has a 'dip'.[62] Divagación has a sacred aura: 'Del altillo oriente, cual pétalos arrojados por alguna mano invisible para honrar a una reina, cientos de mariposas de variados colores descendieron hacia la rehoyada' (From the eastern mezzanine, like petals thrown by some invisible hand to honour a queen, hundreds of butterflies descended towards *la rehoyada*).[63] In Maya culture, the east is the quintessentially sacred direction because of the position of the rising sun; it is emblematic of God's successful emergence from the underworld.[64] In this moment, Divagación becomes part of her surroundings. Butterflies spin around her, a moment described as a celebration: 'Así inicia una fiesta, el revolotear de mariposas en torno suyo y el perfume embriagador de flores' (Thus begins a party, the fluttering of butterflies around her and the heady perfume of flowers).[65] Divagación's whistle camouflages with the song of the birds, allowing her to meld with the natural environment, similar to xTuux in *Recuerdos del corazón de la montaña*. For the female protagonists of *Recuerdos del corazón de la montaña* and 'Divagación', the experience of the environment is one of belonging.

Maya women writers, as other writers in Indigenous languages, negotiate competing discourses that either victimize, romanticize or altogether silence their place in culture and history. In her literature, Martínez Huchim critiques anthropological discourses of Maya culture, and ethnocentric discourses promoted by other Maya writers, by inscribing the forest with a female identity, representing multiple and shifting ways of belonging in the forest, and drawing affinities between women and nature. An analysis of the forest as female space in Martínez Huchim's work helps to think through what makes a place in postcolonial literary environments. Analysing and elucidating the contested literary representations of a particular geographic area and ecosystem, such as the forest, is one way we can gain a greater understanding of how histories of language, culture and ethnicity influence the identities of places in postcolonial contexts. Analysing literary environments in Indigenous bilingual literatures, however, poses challenges that are not present in the examination of literatures written in a hegemonic language. Undoubtedly, there is the significant practical difficulty concerning the analysis of literatures written and published bilingually in Spanish and Indigenous languages. There are also little-known ways that the natural environment is implicated in the social histories of conflict between hegemonic and counter-hegemonic languages and cultures in postcolonial contexts. The agenda of contemporary Maya writers to recuperate and revitalize Indigenous languages and cultures through literature informs the depiction of natural environments. Writers challenge the relationship between space, gender and tradition in dominant discourses of what it means to be Maya by rewriting sites of cultural struggle as places where new identities are constantly formed.

Notes

1 Gloria Anzaldúa, *Borderlands: The New Mestiza = La Frontera* (San Francisco: Aunt Lute Books, 2012), 25.
2 Doreen Massey, *Space, Place, and Gender* (Minneapolis: University of Minnesota Press, 1994), 5–7.
3 Jorge Miguel Cocom Pech, 'Renacimiento de la palabra de los mayas de hoy: ká síjil u t'an mayao'ob bejlae', *Tierra Adentro* 78 (February–March 1996). For additional studies and examinations of the Maya literary revival, see Miguel May May and Santiago Dominguez Aké, 'Taller de Literatura Indígena: Unidad Regional Yucatán', in *Testimonios de Culturas Populares,* ed. Dirección General de Culturas Populares (Mexico City: Dirección General de Culturas Populares, 1988), 132; and Carlos Montemayor, *La literatura actual de las lenguas indígenas de México* (Mexico City: Universidad Iberoamericana Departamento de Historia, 2001), 24–5.
4 There is a considerable body of research on Maya identity and ethnicity from the Yucatán Peninsula. In this chapter I use 'Maya' to refer to the language spoken in the Peninsula, parts of northern Belize, and the places where migrants from the region have travelled. Anthropologist Quetzil Castañeda in the blog 'Maya or Mayans? Comment on Correct Terminology and Spellings', notes that 'Mayan' is not the way to refer to persons who identify as Maya in the plural but that Maya is both the singular and plural and also an adjective. I avoid the phrase 'the Maya' which is not only redundant but awkward in English. Castañeda, 'Maya or Mayans?

Comment on Correct Terminology and Spellings', blog for the Open School of Ethnography and Anthropology. Accessed 1 May 2014. http://www.oseacite.org/program/maya_or_mayans.php. On the distinction between self-identification and external constructions of 'the Maya', see: Quetzil E. Castañeda's *In the Museum of Maya Culture: Touring Chichén Itzá* (1996); Juan Castillo Cocom's dissertation 'Vulnerable Identities: Maya Yucatec Identities in a Postmodern World' (2000); and Wolfgang Gabbert's *Becoming Maya: Ethnicity and Social Inequality in Yucatán Since 1500* (Tucson: University of Arizona Press, 2004).

5   Barbara Pfeiler and Lenka Zámišová, 'Bilingual Education: Strategy for Language Maintenance or Shift of Yucatec Maya?', in *Mexican Indigenous Languages and the Dawn of the Twenty-First Century*, ed. Margarita Hidalgo (Berlin: Mouton de Gruyer, 2008), 284.

6   There is significant research on language use and intergenerational transmission of the Maya language and other Indigenous languages in southern Mexico. Wolfgang Gabbert provides an overview of the use of Maya in his chapter 'Education and Language Policies' (Tucson: University of Arizona Press, 2004), 107–13. He notes the rise of an educated middle class who value the Maya language, which includes contemporary Maya authors. For an overview of the political and social concerns of writers in Indigenous languages in Latin America and the critical but contested place of bilingualism in this literature, see María Luz Lepe Lira, *Lluvia y viento, puentes de sonido: Literatura indígena y crítica literaria* (Monterrey: Universidad Autónoma de Nuevo León; Consejo para la Cultura y las Artes de Nuevo León, 2010), and Gloria Chacón, *Indigenous Cosmolectics: Kab'awil and the Making of Maya and Zapotec Literatures* (Chapel Hill: University of North Carolina, 2018).

7   Martínez Huchim was born in Tizimín, a city in eastern Yucatán. Formally educated in Spanish, she studied anthropology with a specialization in linguistics and literature at the Universidad Autónoma de Yucatán, and as part of her studies she has written a thesis on oral storytelling in Xocén, a municipality in Valladolid.

8   *Revista Yucateca de Estudios Literarios*, year 7 no. 8 (January–February 2019), special edition ed. Silvia Cristina Leirana Alcocer.

9   Martínez Huchim created and edited the bilingual Maya-Spanish magazine, *K'aaylay / Canto de la memoria* (2006–10), which she circulated electronically.

10 Martínez Huchim began to write fictional tales in 2005 and won prizes for them in the same year. It was not until eight years later that state and federal government institutions published them. The main publishers of bilingual Maya-Spanish texts are federal government institutions, Mexican universities and independent Yucatecan presses.

11 Lepe Lira, *Lluvia y viento, puentes de sonido*, 58. Martínez Huchim expressed similar sentiments in our interview in March 2015, in Mérida, Yucatán. She said that there had to be more stories to tell than what is represented in collections of

Maya oral literature. The protagonists of her tales are predominately women. At the time of our conversation, she was writing tales about male musicians.

12 There are few readers of Maya literature, and almost all are foreign academics. Throughout Mexico, literary critics of the Mexican cultural establishment have tended to view literatures published in Indigenous languages and written from the regions of Mexico as inferior to literature published solely in Spanish and from Mexico City.

13 Chacón, *Indigenous Cosmolectics*, 63–6; Paul M. Worley, *Telling and Being Told: Storytelling and Cultural Control in Contemporary Yucatec Maya Literatures* (Tucson: University of Arizona Press, 2013), 145–53; Margaret Shrimpton Masson, 'Islas de tierra firme: ¿un modelo para el Caribe continental? El caso de Yucatán', *Memorias: Revista digital de historia y arqueología desde el caribe colombiano* 25 (January–April 2015): 202–4, http://dx.doi.org/10.14482/memor.25.1.6856; Alicia Marie Salinas, '"Tu táan yich in kaajal" [On the Face of My People]: Contemporary Maya-Spanish Bilingual Literature and Cultural Production from the Yucatán Peninsula' (PhD diss., University of Virginia, 2018), 106–18; Lepe Lira, *Lluvia y viento, puentes de sonido*, 56–61.

14 In Maya, *noj káax* refers to high forest or high mountains. *Zapote* trees are located in the forest rather than the mountains. Thus, 'Memories from the Heart of the Forest' is a more appropriate English translation.

15 The scientific name of the *sapodilla* tree, also referred to as *chicozapote* or *zapote* tree, is *Manilkara zapota*. *Sapodilla* trees are common in the southern part of the Yucatán Peninsula, northern Belize and Petén, Guatemala.

16 Aída Hernández Castillo, 'Entre el etnocentrismo feminista y el esencialismo étnico. Las mujeres indígenas y sus demandas de género', *Debate Feminista* 24 (October 2001): 206–29.

17 Rosa Pu Tzunux, *Representaciones sociales mayas y teoría feminista: crítica de la aplicación literal de modelos teóricos en la interpretación de la realidad de las mujeres mayas* (Guatemala City: Iximulew, 2007).

18 Gloria Chacón, 'Poetizas mayas: subjetividades contra la corriente', *Cuadernos de Literatura Bogotá (Colombia)* 11, no. 22 (2007): 96.

19 Julieta Paredes and Comunidad Mujeres Creando Comunidad, *Hilando Fino Desde el Feminismo Comunitario*, 2008, http://mujeresdelmundobabel.org/files/2013/11/Julieta-Paredes-Hilando-Fino-desde-el-Fem-Comunitario.pdf.

20 Rosario Castellanos, 'Lección de cocina', *Diálogos: Artes, Letras, Ciencias humanas* 4, no. 5 (September–October 1968): 4–8. For a discussion of the discourse of the kitchen as subversive space in the work of Latin American women writers and an analysis of 'Lección de cocina', see *Chicanas and Latin American Women Writers Exploring the Realm of the Kitchen as a Self-empowering Site*, ed. María Claudia André (Lewiston: Edwin Mellen Press, 2001).

21 Briceida Cuevas Cob, *Ti' u billil in nook' / Del dobladillo de mi ropa* (Mexico City: Comisión Nacional para el Desarollo de los Pueblos Indígenas, 2008).
22 Lepe Lira, *Lluvia y viento, puentes de sonido*, 61. All translations from the Spanish are by Stuart Cooke.
23 Lepe Lira, *Lluvia y viento, puentes de sonido*, 56.
24 Ana Patricia Martínez Huchim, 'K-maaya tsikbal. Jaajil t'aan: Estudio del género cuento de la tradición oral en Maya-Yukateko (El caso de Xocén, municipio de Valladolid, Yucatán, México)' (bachelor's thesis, Universidad Autónoma de Yucatán, 1996), 103.
25 Worley, *Telling and Being Told*, 147.
26 For example, *México integro* (1939) by Moisés Sáenz and *Tierra del chicle* (1951) by Ramón Beteta.
27 Martha Patricia Ponce Jiménez, *La montaña chiclera: Campeche: vida cotidiana y trabajo (1900–1950)* (Mexico City: Centro de Investigaciones y Estudios Superiores en Antropología Social, 1990), 8.
28 Ponce Jiménez, *La montaña chiclera*, 5.
29 Claudio Vadillo López, 'Una historia regional en tres tiempos: Campeche siglos XVIII–XX', *Península* 3, no. 2 (Autumn 2008): 49–50.
30 Gabbert, *Becoming Maya*, 84.
31 Edward Moseley and Helen Delpar, 'Yucatán's Prelude to Globalization', in *Yucatán in an Era of Globalization*, ed. Eric N. Baklanoff and Edward H. Moseley (Tuscaloosa: University of Alabama Press, 2008), 28. The juice of the plant is now used to make liquor and the fibres to make works for tourists.
32 Ben W. Fallaw, *Cárdenas Compromised: The Failure of Reform in Postrevolutionary Yucatán* (Durham: Duke University Press, 2001), 10.
33 Piedad Peniche Rivero, 'Women, Bridewealth and Marriage: Social Reproduction of Peons on Henequen Haciendas in Yucatán', in *Women of the Mexican Countryside, 1860–1990*, ed. Heather Fowler-Salamini and Mary K. Vaughn (Tucson: University of Arizona Press, 1994), 86.
34 Ponce Jiménez, *La montaña chiclera*.
35 Ponce Jiménez, *La montaña chiclera*, 56.
36 Jorge Miguel Cocom Pech, *Muk'ul T'an In Nool / Secretos del abuelo* (Mexico City: Universidad Nacional Autónoma de México, 2001).
37 Wildernain Villegas, *Áak'abe' ku ya'alik táan u k'áaxal ja' / Lluvia que la noche dicta* (Mérida: Secretaría de la Cultura y las Artes, 2012).
38 Cocom Pech, *Muk'ul T'an In Nool / Secretos del abuelo*, 39.
39 Robert Redfield, *The Folk Culture of Yucatán* (Chicago: University of Chicago Press, 1941), 13.
40 Macduff Everton, *The Modern Maya: Incidents of Travel and Friendship in Yucatán* (Austin: University of Texas, 2012), 158.

41 For a background to the *chicle* industry in Mexico, see Ponce Jiménez, *La montaña chiclera*, 5.
42 Oscar A. Forero and Michael R. Redclift, 'The Role of the Mexican State in the Development of Chicle Extraction in Yucatán, and the Continuing Importance of Coyotaje', *Journal of Latin American Studies* 38, no. 1 (2006): 68.
43 Ana Patricia Martínez Huchim, *U kàajsajil u ts'u' noj kaax / Recuerdos del corazón de la montaña* (Mérida: Consejo Nacional para la Cultura y las Artes; Secretaría de la Cultura y las Artes, 2013a), 61.
44 Martínez Huchim, *U kàajsajil u ts'u' noj kaax*, 62.
45 Martínez Huchim, *U kàajsajil u ts'u' noj kaax*, 62.
46 Martínez Huchim, *U kàajsajil u ts'u' noj kaax*, 62.
47 Martínez Huchim, 'K-maaya tsikbal. Jaajil t'aan: Estudio del género cuento de la tradición oral en Maya-Yukateko', 120.
48 Martínez Huchim, *U kàajsajil u ts'u' noj kaax*, 91. In the glossary, Martínez Huchim explains that *Xtokoy* refers to 'solar abandonado', 96.
49 Martínez Huchim, *U kàajsajil u ts'u' noj kaax*, 88.
50 Jennifer P. Mathews, *Chicle: The Chewing Gum of the Americas from the Ancient Maya to William Wrigley* (Tucson: University of Arizona Press, 2009), 6.
51 Martínez Huchim, *U kàajsajil u ts'u' noj kaax*, 76.
52 Martínez Huchim, *U kàajsajil u ts'u' noj kaax*, 84.
53 Martínez Huchim, *U kàajsajil u ts'u' noj kaax*, 85.
54 Emir del Jesús Barbosa Kú, 'Poemas e identidad maya, Gerardo Can Pat: Creaciones y recopilaciones' (Bachelor's thesis, Universidad Autónoma de Yucatán, 2013), 162.
55 Anzaldúa, *Borderlands*, 77.
56 Anzaldúa, *Borderlands*, 51.
57 Salinas, '"Tu táan yich in kaajal" [On the Face of My People]', 224–5.
58 Gabriel L. Bourdin, *El cuerpo humano entre los mayas: una aproximación lingüística* (Mérida: Universidad Autónoma de Yucatán, 2007), 130.
59 Ana Patricia Martínez Huchim, *U yóol xkaambal jaw xíiw / Contrayerba* (Mérida: Comisión Nacional para el Desarrollo de los Pueblos Indígenas, 2013), 106.
60 Martínez Huchim, *U yóol xkaambal jaw xíiw*, 105.
61 Martínez Huchim, *U yóol xkaambal jaw xíiw*, 117.
62 Martínez Huchim, *U yóol xkaambal jaw xíiw*, 106.
63 Martínez Huchim, *U yóol xkaambal jaw xíiw*, 103. '*Rehoyada*' is a Yucatecan word for a large cavity in the ground created by the wall of a cenote or cave sinking. Some use the word when referring to the place where people filled the cavity.
64 Mario Humberto Ruz, 'La familia divina. Imaginario hagiográfico en el mundo maya', in *De la Mano de lo Sacro: santos y demonios en el mundo maya*, ed. Mario Humberto Ruz (Mexico City: Universidad Autónoma de México, 2006), 57.
65 Martínez Huchim, *U yóol xkaambal jaw xíiw*, 106.

Bibliography

Anzaldúa, Gloria. *Borderlands: The New Mestiza = La Frontera*. 25th Anniversary edn. San Francisco: Aunt Lute Books, 2012.

Barbosa Kú, Emir del Jesús. 'Poemas e identidad maya, Gerardo Can Pat: Creaciones y recopilaciones'. Bachelor's thesis, Universidad Autónoma de Yucatán, 2013.

Bourdin, Gabriel L. *El cuerpo humano entre los mayas: una aproximación lingüística*. Mérida: Universidad Autónoma de Yucatán, 2007.

Castañeda, Quetzil E. 'Maya or Mayans? Comment on Correct Terminology and Spellings'. The Open School of Ethnography and Anthropology. Accessed 1 May 2014. http://www.oseacite.org/program/maya_or_mayans.php

Castellanos, Rosario. 'Lección de cocina'. *Diálogos: Artes, Letras, Ciencias Humanas* 4, no. 5 (September–October 1968): 4–8.

Chacón, Gloria. *Indigenous Cosmolectics: Kab'awil and the Making of Maya and Zapotec Literatures*. Chapel Hill: University of North Carolina, 2018.

Chacón, Gloria. 'Poetizas mayas: subjetividades contra la corriente'. *Cuadernos de Literatura Bogotá (Colombia)* 11, no. 22 (2007): 94–106. https://revistas.javeriana.edu.co/index.php/cualit/article/view/6636

Chavarrea Chim, María Elisa. 'Túumben ko'olel / Mujer de hoy'. Accessed 14 November 2016. http://acervo.bibliotecavirtualdeyucatan.com.mx/janium/AP4/PDF/84943.pdf

Claudia André, María, ed. 2001. *Chicanas and Latin American Women Writers Exploring the Realm of the Kitchen as a Self-Empowering Site*. Lewiston: Edwin Mellon.

Cocom Pech, Jorge Miguel. *Muk'ul T'an In Nool / Secretos del abuelo*. Mexico City: Universidad Nacional Autónoma de México, 2001.

Cocom Pech, Jorge Miguel. 'Renacimiento de la palabra de los mayas de hoy: ká síjil u t'an mayao'ob bejlae'. *Tierra Adentro* 78 (February–March 1996): 53–8.

Cuevas Cob, Briceida. *Ti' u billil in nook' / Del dobladillo de mi ropa*. Mexico City: Comisión Nacional para el Desarollo de los Pueblos Indígenas, 2008.

Everton, Macduff. *The Modern Maya: Incidents of Travel and Friendship in Yucatán*. Austin: University of Texas, 2012.

Fallaw, Ben. *Cárdenas Compromised: The Failure of Reform in Postrevolutionary Yucatán*. Durham: Duke University Press, 2001.

Forero, Oscar A. and Michael R. Redclift. 'The Role of the Mexican State in the Development of Chicle Extraction in Yucatán, and the Continuing Importance of Coyotaje'. *Journal of Latin American Studies* 38, no. 1 (2006): 65–93. https://doi.org/10.1017/S0022216X05000295

Gabbert, Wolfgang. *Becoming Maya: Ethnicity and Social Inequality in Yucatán Since 1500*. Tucson: University of Arizona Press, 2004.

Hernández Castillo, Aída. 'Entre el etnocentrismo feminista y el esencialismo étnico. Las mujeres indígenas y sus demandas de género'. *Debate Feminista* 24 (October

2001): 206-29. http://www.debatefeminista.cieg.unam.mx/wpcontent/uploads/20 16/03/articulos/024_13.pdf

Humberto Ruz, Mario. 'La familia divina. Imaginario hagiográfico en el mundo maya'. In *De la Mano de lo Sacro: santos y demonios en el mundo maya*, edited by Mario Humberto Ruz, 21-66. Mexico City: Universidad Autónoma de México, 2006.

Lepe Lira, Luz María. *Lluvia y viento, puentes de sonido: Literatura indígena y crítica literaria*. Monterrey: Universidad Autónoma de Nuevo León; Consejo para la Cultura y las Artes de Nuevo León, 2010.

Martínez Huchim, Ana Patricia. 'K-maaya tsikbal. Jaajil t'aan: Estudio del género cuento de la tradición oral en Maya-Yukateko (El caso de Xocén, municipio de Valladolid, Yucatán, México)'. Bachelor's thesis, Universidad Autónoma de Yucatán, 1996.

Martínez Huchim, Ana Patricia. *U k'a'ajsajil u ts'u' noj k'áax / Recuerdos del corazón de la montaña*. Mérida: Consejo Nacional para la Cultura y las Artes; Secretaría de la Cultura y las Artes, 2013a.

Martínez Huchim, Ana Patricia. *U yóol xkaambal jaw xíiw / Contrayerba*. Mérida: Comisión Nacional para el Desarrollo de los Pueblos Indígenas, 2013b.

Massey, Doreen. *Space, Place, and Gender*. Minneapolis: University of Minnesota Press, 1994.

Mathews, Jennifer P. *Chicle: The Chewing Gum of the Americas from the Ancient Maya to William Wrigley*. Tucson: University of Arizona Press, 2009.

May May, Miguel and Santiago Dominguez Aké. 'Taller de Literatura Indígena: Unidad Regional Yucatán'. In *Testimonios de Culturas Populares*, edited by the Dirección General de Culturas Populares, 129-34. Mexico City: Dirección General de Culturas Populares, 1988.

Montemayor, Carlos. *La literatura actual de las lenguas indígenas de México*. Mexico City: Universidad Iberoamericana Departamento de Historia, 2001.

Moseley, Edward H. and Helen Delpar. 'Yucatán's Prelude to Globalization'. In *Yucatán in an Era of Globalization* edited by Eric N. Baklanoff and Edward H. Moseley, 19-41. Tuscaloosa: University of Alabama Press, 2008.

Paredes, Julieta and Comunidad Mujeres Creando Comunidad. *Hilando Fino Desde el Feminismo Comunitario*, 2008. http://mujeresdelmundobabel.org/files/2013/11/Julieta-Paredes-Hilando-Fino-desde-el-Fem-Comunitario.pdf

Peniche Rivero, Piedad. 'Women, Bridewealth and Marriage: Social Reproduction of Peons on Henequen Haciendas in Yucatán'. In *Women of the Mexican Countryside, 1860-1990*, edited by Heather Fowler-Salamini and Mary K. Vaughn, 74-92. Tucson: University of Arizona Press, 1994.

Pfeiler, Barbara and Lenka Zámišová. 'Bilingual Education: Strategy for Language Maintenance or Shift of Yucatec Maya?' In *Mexican Indigenous Languages at the Dawn of the Twenty-First Century*, edited by Margarita Hidalgo, 281-300. Berlin: Mouton de Gruyer, 2008.

Ponce Jiménez, Martha Patricia. *La montaña chiclera: Campeche: vida cotidiana y trabajo (1900-1950)*. Mexico City: Centro de Investigaciones y Estudios Superiores en Antropología Social, 1990.

Pu Tzunux, Rosa. *Representaciones sociales mayas y teoría feminista: crítica de la aplicación literal de modelos teóricos en la interpretación de la realidad de las mujeres mayas*. Guatemala City: Iximulew, 2007.

Redfield, Robert. *The Folk Culture of Yucatán*. Chicago: University of Chicago Press, 1941.

Rosado Vega, Luis. *Claudio Martín: vida de un chiclero*. Mexico City: SCOP, 1938.

Rosado Vega, Luis. *Poema de la selva trágica*. Chetumal, Quintana Roo: SCOP, 1937.

Rosado Vega, Luis. *Un pueblo y un hombre*. Mexico City: Bucareli, 1940.

Salinas, Alicia Marie. "'Tu táan yich in kaajal" [On the Face of My People]: Contemporary Maya-Spanish Bilingual Literature and Cultural Production from the Yucatán Peninsula'. PhD diss., University of Virginia, 2018.

Shrimpton Masson, Margaret. 'Islas de tierra firme: ¿un modelo para el Caribe continental? El caso de Yucatán'. *Memorias: Revista digital de historia y arqueología desde el caribe colombiano* 25 (January–April 2015): 179–208. DOI: http://dx.doi.org/10.14482/memor.25.1.6856

Vadillo López, Claudio. 'Una historia regional en tres tiempos: Campeche siglos XVIII–XX'. *Península* 3, no. 2 (Autumn 2008): 45–56. SciELO.

Villegas, Wildernain. *Áak'abe' ku ya'alik táan u káaxal ja' / Lluvia que la noche dicta*. Mérida: Secretaría de la Cultura y las Artes, 2012.

Worley, Paul M. *Telling and Being Told: Storytelling and Cultural Control in Contemporary Yucatec Maya Literatures*. Tucson: University of Arizona Press, 2013.

Wubbold, Manya. 'Language and Symbolic Representation in Contemporary Mayan Poetry: A Linguistic and Literary Analysis of "Yaan a bin xook" by Briceida Cuevas Cob (2005)'. *Estudios de Cultura Maya* 47 (2016): 181–216. http://dx.doi.org/10.19130/iifl.ecm.2016.47.747

13

Geoterritorial island poetics, or transcultural composition with a wetland in southern Chile

Stuart Cooke, with Juan Paulo Huirimilla Oyarzo

Introducing a wetland

This chapter has one overarching objective: to communicate something of the importance of a small wetland on the outskirts of a southern Chilean city. As part of an ongoing collaboration with leading Mapuche-Huilliche poet and activist Juan Paulo Huirimilla Oyarzo, I seek here to document the cultural and ecological significance of the Humedal Antiñir.[1] I will begin by introducing the Humedal as a site of Indigenous and ecological significance, and by situating it with relation to Huirimilla's own theory of poetics. I will also draw parallels between Huirimilla's poetics and other theory, particularly from and of the southern hemisphere, a region in which he is very interested. As a collaboration between Australian and Chilean, and non-Indigenous and Indigenous perspectives, Huirimilla and I want to explore how we can make the Humedal 'move' to other places. Furthermore, as both poets and scholars, we hope to use poetry as the cohering mechanism for the variety of divergent perspectives which, according to Huirimilla, form the 'geoterritory' of the Humedal. While prose explications (such as this chapter) are important, our project is based on the premise that it is through the flexible structures of poetry that different ways of seeing and understanding the Humedal can best correlate. Integral to our research, therefore, is open, exploratory poetic composition. Our compositional methods are not directed inwards in order to explore our interiorities; similarly, our methods are not geared towards describing the Humedal with static, timeless details, as if it were an inanimate, uninhabited natural landscape. At heart, our research is motivated by the following questions: (a) How can we understand the Humedal in local *and* global contexts? (b) How, through poetry, is important knowledge about the Humedal protected and shared? (c) How might such knowledge 'move' transculturally, or be translated for non-Huilliche and/or international readers? I introduce our approach to these questions in this chapter, and will elaborate on them in further publications. In the third section I include three of our poems, by way of conclusion.

Humedal Antiñir is located on the outskirts of Puerto Montt, a small, harbourside city and the last outpost of state bureaucracy before the lands of Patagonia to the south. The Humedal is surrounded on all sides by apartment buildings, highways and vast, new suburbs of near-identical homes; to a developer's eyes it might look like wasteland, or untapped capital. Central to the wetlands is a large lagoon, approximately 500 metres in diameter. Currently the lagoon is being drained by nearby industrial and residential developments, despite the fact that it contains a number of federally protected species. But the Humedal is not only an important site of biodiversity on the edges of a rapidly growing city; it is also a vital repository of traditional medicine for the local Huilliche-Mapuche community.[2] Furthermore, the Humedal is home to many local spirits, who guard different parts of it, transform into different creatures and provide the Huilliche with messages and guidance from their ancestors. As a video by a local Indigenous film maker asserts, 'OUR ANCESTORS inhabited this place; this memory cannot be severed.'[3] Indeed, Macarena Gómez-Barris points out that 'Indigenous peoples are often at the forefront of defending lands in regions that are continually extracted for their biodiversity'.[4] In Puerto Montt it is no different: a coalition of concerned Indigenous and non-Indigenous locals has formed to respond to these environmental pressures and to protect the Humedal from further exploitation. However, the sociopolitical context of the region adds a level of intensity to such advocacy: the ongoing efforts of the coalition take place in the context of a region where historically the environment has been represented as cleansed of human presence, Indigenous or otherwise. Home to extraordinary national parks with sublime lakes, forests and snow-capped volcanoes, southern Chile is invariably represented as unpeopled in governmental, environmental and commercial discourses.[5] To advocate for the Humedal as a site of ecological importance *and* vital Indigenous knowledge is therefore a pointed critique of what Gómez-Barris might call an 'extractive' understanding of this remarkable landscape.

In fighting to protect a remnant wetland on the periphery of a small city, this coalition is occupying, in a very literal sense, what Pierre Joris has termed 'the nomadic margins of the polis'. But in using this phrase Joris is referring specifically to the role of the *poet*; in particular, to the crucial capacity (and responsibility) of the poet to critique, roam and 'trample on' the 'well-manicured gardens' of 'the imperial City of Capital'.[6] It is perhaps no coincidence, then, that a leader of this coalition is a poet: Paulo Huirimilla. One of the most original and compelling of contemporary Mapuche poets, Huirimilla is the author of a number of well-received collections of poetry, as well as a perceptive critic and a keen cultural theorist.[7] In terms of the broader milieu of Mapuche poetry, his work might sit somewhere between the two groups described by Joanna Crow, the most prominent and widely read of which – found in the work of poets like Elicura Chihuailaf and Leonel Lienlaf – 're-projects a glorious Mapuche past and a utopian rural community'. The second of Crow's groupings, in contrast, is more 'distinctly politicized, urban and mainly [writes in] Spanish'. Openly critical of state-sponsored neoliberalism, poets in this grouping – often based in Santiago and without access to their ancestral territory – are much less likely to be deemed 'authentically' Mapuche by the conservative literary establishment.[8] Similarly, in one of Huirimilla's most well-known poems, 'Warrior Song', we encounter an 'urbanite of jacket and leather / Combed with hair gel / born in shit' who has lost his 'identity card' and 'stammers' in Spanish.[9] While based in a much smaller city than Santiago, Huirimilla is outspoken in his critique of neoliberal politics, and frequently his poems depict what Crow (via Charles Hale) would call the 'dysfunctional' lives of urban Mapuches,[10] many of whom are born into severe poverty and suffer life-long discrimination. As I have said elsewhere, '[i]n a technologically complex urban environment, the sacred spaces of ritual and song are problematised in [Huirimilla's] work by a recognition that Mapuche culture can never return to what it once was.'[11]

However, while Huirimilla is no purist, while he would never equate fluency in the native tongue (*Mapudungun*) with 'being Mapuche', for example, he nevertheless argues that it is vital for Mapuches to learn as best they can their native language, and to have connection to their ancestral territory. Huirimilla returns regularly to his childhood home in order to help his father with the cultivation of various traditional and non-traditional vegetables, and increasingly seems to locate the source of his identity in that land. To the Humedal, to which he does not have an immediate, familial connection, he imagines a more communal, transcultural responsibility. Part of this responsibility is enacted by introducing it to groups of children during school excursions, during which he teaches them about the plants, animals and spirits that live there. Another part of this responsibility is enacted in the time he spends with me, in the hope that the value of the Humedal, and the forces that threaten it, might be translated for other communities in other places. Importantly, for Huirimilla the Humedal is not just the site for an environmental or political struggle; it also forms the locus for his theory of poetics. In this sense it is a localized instance of a broader feature of Mapuche poetry – similar to much Aboriginal Australian poetry, for example – where nature is not 'a background or mere decorative element', to use Eva Palma's words, but is rather a generative nexus of all human and non-human life.[12] However, terms like 'nature' risk reducing the complexity of this nexus: this is no idyll emptied of historical or cultural context; rather, as a witness to ongoing imperialist violence and territorial dispossession, the natural world is a potent sign of cultural resistance, providing both the ground *for* and testimony *of* events otherwise concealed by official history.[13]

As the source of all meaning and sentience, the earth is inextricable from Mapuche poetics. As Huirimilla himself says, 'when Mapuche poets try to poeticise the world, we *are* the world. The world is inside of us ... our blood is intimately related to the ocean ... to the colours of flowers.'[14] There is no artificial separation of 'nature' and 'culture' in Mapuche poetics; the poet is inextricable from the world:

> You are the world, invisible rivers, air, clouds, falling comets flow through you. This extends to the depths of your dreams, and then you try and carry it to that white page with black type [...] that vibration that produces the world is what I think Mapuche poets capture and try to locate on the page.[15]

One of the objectives of our collaboration is to articulate the relationship between this more traditional Mapuche formulation and other, non-Mapuche knowledges, and to do so according to a particular locus that Huirimilla calls the 'geoterritory' of the Humedal. For Huirimilla, geoterritory refers to the multidimensionality of place, or the way in which, to use Bruno Latour's language, place is a collusion of multiple modes of existence. Where Latourian analysis might ascribe different things, such as a flower, a human and a poem, different modes of existence, in Mapuche philosophy each such thing is part of a universe of other, similar things. For example, Huirimilla explains, 'the universe of birds has the signs, sounds and forms of every bird', along with the universe for herbal medicine, for the ocean and so on. 'But ultimately everything makes up one single universe', he says, 'where every thing has relations with other things'.[16] Within this cosmology, Huirimilla's geoterritory synergizes deep time – containing what he calls its 'archives' of palaeontological and biological information – with the ecological and cultural diversity of landscape as it is experienced in the present.[17]

Next to this temporal scale, geoterritory also has a spatial component: in Spanish as in English 'geo' refers to the earth and, usually, to an imagination of an earth larger than the place of one's immediate location. In conceiving of the Humedal as part of a geoterritory, therefore, Huirimilla is acknowledging its embeddedness in a larger whole. That said, the Humedal is *not* accordingly subsumed into an endless, uniform space known as 'the environment' or 'the world'; as he says in 'Külme Energy', though drawing on a larger geoterritory of ancestral presence, he is focused on protecting 'this little woodland' (see the third section). Indeed, the Humedal engages with a broader network only through particular, concrete relations: Antiñir is actually connected to another wetland system higher up in the mountains by subterranean rivers which 'communicate with one another'.[18] The rivers' connection and communication is for Huirimilla a characteristic of a much more complex semiotic system, with powerful decolonial implications:

> it's as if the word were part of this: if the rivers communicate with each other in the tributaries, in the springs . . . this means that the unearthed word, and memory, time, discourse, poetry, philosophy and everything, thought, everything is connected. What science does is separate this idea of territory, categorise everything, organise according to the interests of each scientist . . . [on the other hand] geo-territory is the binding of all the sites of importance, of relevance, in this great territory, which communicate and speak with one another, so that people might comprehend and feel this connection. Because there are spirit beings in all of these places, and these spirits demand respect and they demand understanding.[19]

The reference to the 'unearthing' of language in the previous quote is significant because it signals Huirimilla's interest in the geoterritorial imagination as a form of cultural and linguistic recovery. Part of the geoterritorial assemblage is a geo*language* – specifically, Mapudungun (meaning, literally, 'language of the earth'). Mapudungun, says Huirimilla, is learned in relation to the natural world; thus, when people speak it, they are literally articulating the world, or reclaiming contact with the world in order to illuminate it. Linguistic recovery is, therefore,

> like unearthing the DNA of our people, strengthening our own DNA. One can learn the grammar and pronunciation, but one can also learn in contact with nature, which is a kind of fire that is present throughout the world. . . . This immaterial fire calls you . . . the birds [for example] will also teach you the language of our people, of our earth.[20]

Finally, though no less importantly, Huirimilla's geoterritory also refers to the different epistemologies, ontologies and discursive practices that are bound to our experience of the earth. This has implications for who one must speak to in order to learn about a place – be they elders, Machi ('medicine women'), archaeologists, biologists and so on – and implications for the language that one might use to describe and/or imagine that place. This *also* has implications for the particular kinds of discursive forms that a place might require: writing, even writing poetry, is but one form of articulation; the complexity of place requires a similarly complex response composed of writing (in various languages and genres), painting, song and so on. For Huirimilla, then, the book that might result from this project would be at once 'a history, a story, an essay mixed with narrative poetry, and analytical essay as well'.[21] It is telling that a precedent for this project, the multi-authored *Reading the Country*, also aimed to elucidate the different 'layers' – Indigenous, non-Indigenous and otherwise – that composed a particular region in Australia's West Kimberley: any serious attempt to evoke a geoterritory requires a diversity of descriptive and expressive modes.[22]

It is vital to acknowledge here that the basis of Huirimilla's thinking lies in the spatio-temporal flexibility of the Mapuche landscape. The spatial and temporal axes of geoterritory are grounded on the topography of *Wallmapu* (from Mapudungun, referring to the totality of time and space). Corresponding to the four points of a western compass, the spatial representation of Wallmapu denotes the peoples of the north, south, east and west. At the same time, this flat, spatial plane can become the mid-section of a sphere: 'underneath' is the land of below (*Miñche mapu*), while 'above' is the sky, or *Wenu mapu*. Huirimilla's synthesis of deep time and contemporary ecologies echoes this three-dimensional complex. However, these spatial representations can also become the surface upon which cycles of time recur: the four sections of the compass also denote the four seasons; the lines between them thus become something like a four-handed clock. In geoterritory as in Wallmapu, space and time shimmer between one and the other. Time clusters around space, waiting for a tremor to crack open the ground and reveal the endless cycles of history clustered beneath. But space, too, will wait in the wings: if one attempts to walk into time, soon one discovers that she is in fact walking across country, that all time has been condensed into the ground upon which movement can take place.

Because of its syncretic possibilities, we can make links between Huirimilla's geoterritory and more familiar accounts from Anglo-Western scholarship. Surprisingly, given that he knows little of their work, part of Huirimilla's conceptual structure overlaps with Gilles Deleuze and Félix Guattari's geo*philosophy*. For Huirimilla as for Deleuze and Guattari, 'thinking takes place in the relationship of territory and the earth'.[23] Though Deleuze and Guattari place more importance on the distinction between the key terms of this phrase (territory and Earth) than would Huirimilla, their geophilosophical apparatus is a useful way of thinking transculturally about the Humedal. The earth, according to Deleuze and Guattari, is constantly deterritorializing territory (where 'territory' is akin to region or place): the earth provides the space for those who wish to leave their territory to move elsewhere, or the condition for which any single territory cannot be hermitically sealed off from others. At the same time, the earth is itself fundamentally deterritorialized, or without territory; territories are produced or recovered by (re)territorializing the earth. Territory and Earth are therefore inseparable from one another:

> Movements of deterritorialization are inseparable from territories that open onto an elsewhere; and the process of territorialisation is inseparable from the earth, which restores territories.[24]

Similarly, it is possible to conceive of the Humedal as a form of territorial 'eruption' upon the earth, where the earth might be, depending on the scale and mode, the Chilean state, capitalism, and/or the spiritually populated universe of Wallmapu. Territorialized by particular forces of glaciation and sedimentation, and by particular ancestors and creation spirits, the Humedal is composed by the larger forces of the earth. In a more contemporary milieu, these forces are under threat of being unravelled by the *de*territorializing suction of extractive capitalism; at the same time, the coalition is trying to petition capitalism's beneficiaries – namely, the local government – to use some of its earnings to protect the territory of the Humedal. The key point here is that territorialization and deterritorialization are entangled on the same plane, with the same forces.

It is also the case that Huirimilla's geoterritory resonates with Aboriginal Australian understandings of 'country', particularly in the terms of Deborah Bird Rose's definitive explications of country in northern Australia. As territorialization produces locality, it also produces difference. In Aboriginal Australia, differentiated continuities are constructed between the past and the present through matrices that are located in specific, particular countries. A country is therefore 'politically autonomous in respect of other, structurally equivalent countries'. At the same time, however, country is 'interdependent with other countries'.[25] In addition to its relationality, country contains elements similar to those encompassed by Huirimilla's geoterritory:

> Country is multidimensional: it consists of people, animals, plants, Dreamings, underground, earth, soils, minerals and waters, surface water and air. There is sea country and land country; in some areas people talk about sky country. Country has origins and a future; it exists both in and through time.[26]

Just as country possesses the meta-sentience that Rose is describing here, it is also entirely dependent upon the good custodianship of those who inhabit it: '[a]ll living things are held to have an interest in the life of the country because their own life is dependent on the life of their country.' This entanglement results in what for Rose is a 'fundamental proposition: those who destroy their country destroy themselves'.[27] Like Huirimilla, for whom 'nature' is not to be figured at a distance, but to be understood on the basis that its very forces flow through human bodies, respect for country in Aboriginal Australia also implies an understanding of (a) a country's relationship with other countries, (b) an appreciation of country's deep, temporal dimension and (c) an onto-ecology, or an understanding of how one's being is embedded in ecological relations.

Next to these transcultural correlations, the details of Huirimilla's own understanding of relationality are best elaborated with attention to his interest in island geography. Similar to the conceptual qualities of the geoterritory, Huirimilla's island has multiple layers and can operate at various scales. On the one hand, like many Huilliches, he identifies as a man born of the islands: Huirimilla grew up on Calbuco, one of various islands scattered to the south of Puerto Montt. However, he also understands humans in general as islands, and locales or places as islands. More grandly, he distinguishes the southern hemisphere from the north because the south is, he says, a hemisphere of islands, of fragmented and isolated cultures and languages that, together, resist the homogenizing forces flowing from the north.[28] In our project, islands function as metaphorical vehicles with which to understand transcultural and trans-Pacific relations. Each island requires a site-specific ethnography, but each island is necessarily connected, by the ocean in which it sits, to many other islands. Thus, islands are far from isolated entities, or atoms lost in an unchartable vacuum, but rather are enmeshed, related. But to travel from one island to another requires multiple acts of translation – moving from land to sea to land, the traveller encounters multiple cultures, languages and ecosystems. It is therefore entirely possible to cross from one island to another, but there are different permissions to obtain, and different rules and protocols to follow, on each one. For Huirimilla and I, the Humedal is one such island; as much as we are interested in documenting its many unique qualities, we are also concerned with showing how the discussion that develops around it might be taken elsewhere.

It is through his conceptualization of an archipelago of island cultures that Huirimilla imagines a vital, transcultural relationship with all the Indigenous cultures of the Pacific. In his major long poem, 'Rivers of Swans', for example, he flies across to the 'desert' island of Australia, where he searches for 'Koori swans' in the island's 'inland sea'.²⁹ Indeed, Huirimilla travelled to Australia in 2007, where he was hosted by Peter Minter. Minter's own theorization of 'archipelagos' of Australian poetics provides a resonant, trans-Pacific analogue to Huirimilla's island-based ontology. Drawing on other poet-critics such as Édouard Glissant and John Mateer, Minter imagines an island as an 'archipelagic locus', or an outcrop of intensities. Less interested than Huirimilla in defining the global North or South, he proposes that 'the whole world [and, indeed, planet Earth itself] is an archipelago'.³⁰ The image can be scaled, however, down to the level of Australia itself: as Mateer argues, Australia is actually 'an archipelago, culturally porous and edgeless . . . a handful of islands – Melbourne, Sydney, Brisbane [etc.]'.³¹ For Minter, an archipelagic model is useful for unsettling normative ideas about cultural and national homogeneity. The advantage is that islands keep 'things local' and resist the colonialist imperative to group enormous amounts of space under a single, imperial banner; at the same time, islands are always, nevertheless, 'nodes in constantly evolving networks'.³²

As a metageography, therefore, archipelagic thought encourages repetition (of intensities and of rest) and multiplicity, unstable condensations and turbulences, and constant disruptions (of land and sea formations).³³ Like Huirimilla's, Minter's archipelagic imaginary consists of more than pieces of land risen from the oceans with great stretches of water between them. Rather, the concept has a profound metaphorical flexibility:

> it can be applied to any part of the surface of the planet to describe a set of relations between outcrops or nodes of intensity. Imagine an archipelago of psycho-geographic concentration, ballooning and emergent in related and unrelated physical and psychic and ecological relationships, in areas of Country in Dreaming and story and law, or cohering as various kinds of habitus in cities and towns and across regions.³⁴

Here we see that Minter's 'psychogeographic concentration' is clearly indicative of the same spatial and temporal diversity as Huirimilla's geoterritory. Most strikingly, those 'areas of Country in Dreaming and story and law' indicate similar, resurgent inscriptions of Indigenous culture and poetics to those that underpin the structure of Huirimilla's own archipelagic theory. Through Mateer's fragmentation of Australia into an archipelago – and, with it, the need to imagine 'Australia' as a uniform cultural space – and Glissant's archipelagic constellation of essence and difference – or the extent to which islands are irreducible singularities in much larger, oceanic webs – Minter arrives at 'a vigorous and fecund archipelagic *antipodean* poetic'.³⁵ In other words, this is no longer an Australian poetic, but one which readily coheres with Huirimilla's own, Southern induction towards a totality beyond local sites/sight.

Poetics and ethnography: Theory

From the foregoing contextualization of the Humedal and of Huirimilla's poetics, I'd like to turn to outline briefly the nature of our ethnographic method, or to outline *how* we are attempting to work with the Humedal, and with each other, in order to produce poetic compositions. One objective of our project is to conduct a kind of ethnography that avoids the mono-directionality of the traditional anthropological investigation. Yet we are not satisfied with what is a commonly proposed solution to this paradigm, either: for us, self-reflexive forms of analysis such as autoethnography are similarly mono-directional in their excessive focus on the author as the subject of composition.[36] Instead, we propose to work with a different investigative method, based on the exploratory, poetic composition of two subjects/objects and their relations to a generative locale. This involves a triangular relationship between the Humedal, Huirimilla and I, in which each member of the relationship responds to, and is responsible for, the others:

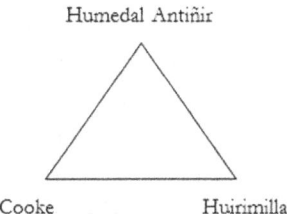

Figure 13.1

In other words, rather than a dialogical relationship – whether between the investigator and his Indigenous subject (classical anthropology), or between the investigator and the Humedal (romantic poetry and/or nature writing) – we are interested in establishing a *tri*alogical relationship of unsettled, moving parts. Here, each of the two human subjects might at any moment become objects. For example, I might follow Huirimilla around the Humedal and record his observations and stories. However, he will also use *me* as what he terms 'an object of study' by bringing me into his classes, where his students might ask me about my own culture and background. Alternatively, when we take students on excursions through the Humedal, he might direct their questions and queries to me instead. Similarly, while examples of his poems are here translated into

English at the end of this chapter, at other times I have translated my own poems into Spanish so that Huirimilla can consider them alongside his own. At all times, too, the third subject/object – the Humedal itself – controls and contours the parameters of our discussions and relations, in that our excursions are defined by its topography and inhabitants, and our poetic compositions are inextricable from what it reveals to us. In 'Mountain Grape', for example, Huirimilla writes from the perspective of a plant commonly found in the Humedal; in turn, in translating the poem I temporarily assumed the same perspective (see the third section). With the Humedal as our guide, we tend towards the alternative, 'ecologically-inflected historiography' outlined by Rose, which is directed

> toward the Earth itself, toward country, in Aboriginal English, and thus toward a living world that has its sources in the past and in place, that is in process of becoming, that works towards interspecies relationships that are 'always coming'.[37]

Within this practice of mutual, ecologically oriented exchange and translation, we are interested in aspects of what Melisa Stocco would call 'self translation'. Stocco's term refers primarily to Mapuche poets who 'self-translate', or write and translate their own poems in both Mapudungun and Spanish; for her, 'translation' refers not only to the movement between languages but also to the material transformation of bodies and subjectivities as they journey between Indigenous and non-Indigenous, urban and rural, traditional and contested cultural spaces.[38] While we accord with Stocco's theorization of translation, for us, 'the self' in self-translation can be somewhat more porous: where Huirimilla writes of the Humedal, for example, he is translating expressions that are articulated by the region of a 'super-self', or an entity composed of more than one sentient organism. Our interest, then, is in what Rose would call 'an expanded concept of self', which includes a dialogical openness to place and its history and, therefore, 'an expanded concept of self-interest'.[39] At any rate, for Huirimilla and I as for Stocco's self-translators, composition produces a 'transitory territory', which dissolves subjects and objects and establishes 'a mobile poetics between cultures and languages'.[40] In this fluid territory we find echoes of Homi Bhabha's 'third space', where hybrid, transcultural forms might emerge. Following Edward Soja's 'ontology of the third space', Stocco proposes a 'spatial trialectics', where territory is not the synthesis of dialectical opposites into a uniform or static field, but rather is the production of possibilities and alternatives by means of disordered, tentative reconstructions.[41] This same, trialectical relation is illustrated in Figure 13.1: in our compositions, both Huirimilla and I respond to a three-part relation of Indigenous, foreign and non-human subjectivities; in other words, there can be no single point of focus for either of our gazes. There is of course a 'middle ground' within this triangulation, but it's indeterminate and dynamic rather than crossed by the line between two, opposed coordinates.

In sum, our aim is to provide what Clayton Eshleman might call a 'fuller reading' of the Humedal.[42] Similar also to collaborative, multilayered texts like the aforementioned *Reading the Country*, our project is not based on one kind of method, be it anthropological, archaeological, literary analytical or otherwise, but seeks to collaborate with all of these modes of enquiry, exploiting our poetry as a site for a mobile, dynamic bricolage. Here we are interested in the poet as a particular kind of intellectual nomad: in Joris's terms, poets 'may be the last of the least-affiliated, the least "specialized", thus those with the free-est hands to think'. Like these nomad poets, Huirimilla and I are 'general practitioner[s]' of a richly 'variegated space' – our poetic method attempts to chart those 'non-Euclidean geometries of mind and imagination needed [for] the complexities of [the Humedal's] multiverse'.[43] But poetry, like everything else, isn't free from critique, or from qualification by other forms of understanding (I, for one, don't want to write a-historical poems that remove the Humedal, via a typically romantic transcendence, from its context). In this chapter, for instance, poems are brought into conversation with academic prose, but elsewhere we are in conversation with artists, archaeologists and ecologists. Our approach is different because, instead of *solely* employing the rational documentation of facts and observations, we are, to paraphrase Eshleman, approaching this 'inseparable mix' of Huilliche and non-Indigenous knowledges by 'using poetic imagination as well as thorough fieldwork and research'.[44]

Importantly, such epistemological bricolage is not meant to result, whether in the form of a poem or otherwise, in some kind of idealized, uniform synthesis of all knowledges and all perspectives. Rather, this is a research method born of an Einsteinian, relativistic universe, where different subject positions produce necessarily different forms of articulation. In the writing of this chapter, for example, there is no pretence that Huirimilla and I are equal partners; though it relies on his guidance, the chapter is authored by me. Huirimilla, however, is a much more prolific poet than I; the book that results from this project will therefore contain much more of his poetry. Similarly, while the Humedal did not write this chapter or write our poems, it produced, and continues to produce, its own, myriad articulations. These might be in the forms of *ngen*, or guardian spirits, or as *külme*, an earth-based, generative energy; articulations might also occur through animals and plants, whose sudden, dramatic or unusual movements can constitute apparitions of significance for Huirimilla's interpretation. Indeed, the traditional basis of Huirimilla's own poetics, the structures of Mapudungun, involve the conceptualization of language as being *of* Earth (remembering that 'Mapudungun' is the 'language of the earth'). There is no categorical distinction, in other words, between the inflections of birds, ngen or human language: all can be catalysed by the Humedal. Instead, there are what Stocco would call the 'copulative disjunctions' of a Mapuche poet as he recovers and repairs the torn links between his being and country. Such disjunctions are 'a manifestation of the body's immanent connection with an environment configured by human and non-human worlds', which are marked everywhere by colonialist violence and suppression.[45]

To explicate the nature of our compositional method in some more detail, it is necessary to point out its two most central features. First, our compositions begin not based on particular, interior states, such as personal moods or preoccupations, but are directed 'outwards', towards the Humedal. The Humedal, in other words, is prioritized as the basis for our poetry. This is not to ignore or downplay the significance of cognition, but rather to acknowledge its entanglement with the body's location. Here, the territory of the mind is constantly deterritorialized by the flux of the Humedal, as much as the mind constantly reterritorializes itself in an attempt to take control. Secondly, in privileging the world beyond our bodies, we are not interested in a representational or pictorial poetics, the outcome of which might be the depiction of static landscapes and environments akin to old-fashioned landscape paintings. Here, my own interest in the dynamic environmental systems described by contemporary ecological theory aligns with Huirimilla's commitment to the articulation of Huilliche reality: geoterritory is the profusion of selves from the productive wellsprings of cosmic and ancestral creation. Our poems, therefore, tend to focus on moving figures and forms, rather than their careful description, and on the elaboration of articulations, dialogues and messages. What Huirimilla is clearly interested in, and what I am hoping to produce myself, aren't idealized representations of some kind of timeless 'Other', whose beauty, wisdom and/or difference transcends the material conditions that threaten it. What we find in Huirimilla's two poems in particular is something like a shared proximity, in which discrete selves are at least partially blended or dissolved within an open space of relation. To be sure, 'an open space' is not a blank or apolitical space, but the very onto-ecological terrain of the Humedal, whose rules and signs we follow as Huirimilla guides me along its paths, which provide the context for our discussions and the structure of our outings. The aim, then, is a form of respectful relation, or a conscious, ethical cohabitation.

As a result, our poems are contributions to the Humedal's broader geoterritory; of course, they are not necessarily *of* the Humedal per se, but they contribute to the array of forces that populate it and bind it to the earth: after oxygen, carbon, hydrogen; after spirits; after flora and fauna, there are also poems.

Finally, I'd like to make some brief comments about my own role as a poet-translator-investigator. Despite the neatness of the triangular graphic (Figure 13.1) that I provided earlier, it is false to suggest that our roles in this investigation are equal, or that my responsibilities for, and rights to, the Humedal are the same as Huirimilla's. I am, essentially, a tourist, albeit an especially interested one. Unlike Huirimilla, if the Humedal is eventually destroyed then I will be able to leave and find yet other places of interest. Still, in the hope that this does not happen, my detachment has advantages as a critical model: a certain placelessness or 'non-fixity' is necessary for the island researcher, for whom there can be no continental centre; I am perennially 'at sea', away from home.[46] So, while I need Huirimilla to help me read the Humedal, Huirimilla has no need for me in this regard; rather, both he and the Humedal need me so that they can *be read* – that is, be translated, disseminated, taken on journeys beyond the worlds of Puerto Montt, Chile and Spanish. I am akin to Jean-François Lyotard's translator, 'moving between the absolute difference and particularity of each island' with no island of my own, 'only a milieu or field, which is the sea'.[47] If I am rootless, I am also without a detailed schema or itinerary; dependent on the inclinations of the other parties involved, my use is precisely in my ability to leave, to note echoes elsewhere, encourage relations. Thus, the island accretes multiple potentials: it is both object, destination, desire and locale, locus, source. Like 'a tunnel generating its own light' or a 'crown of flame', the island is

> grounded in both absence and appearance, a convexcavatious abyss. When it rests for a moment in contraction, some of us experience it as a cave or pit. When it expands beyond what the mind can contemplate, some call it the void.[48]

Poetics and ethnography: Practice

– Juan Paulo Huirimilla

Uva del monte

Aquí estoy en los ojos de tu abuelo
Curándolo de su ceguera
Dos de mis hojas se han puesto en su mirada

Los cometas se devuelven a las galaxias
Oscuro está el ser en las sombras
Con miedo de no ver la memoria
Y el paisaje
Una anciana que conversa conmigo
Me ha venido a pedir ayuda para él
Me ha traído otra sabía con agua
Y harina tostada
Yo me he inclinado en la luna menguante
Antes que salga el sol
Me ha pedido por tu abuelo cuando niño
Ahora que está oscuro por un momento
Y sienta las estrellas que vuelve en su mirada
Que tome mi sabia tibia y lentamente
El suelo se lo he dado a la anciana
Ya amanece la isla está ahí de nuevo
Ahora que le bruñan con ceniza tibia
Un poquito los ojos
Y que vuelva a mirar el mundo
Con sus cuatro direcciones

Mountain Grape

Here I am in the eyes of your grandfather
Treating his blindness
Two of my leaves have been placed on his gaze
The comets return to the galaxies
Dark is the being in the shadows
With fear of not seeing the memory
And the landscape
An old lady I know
Has come to ask that I help him
Has brought me more sap with water
And toasted flour
I have leaned on the waning moon
Before the sun breaks out
She asked me to help him when I was a child
Now that it's dark for a moment
Feel the stars returning to his gaze
Take my wisdom slowly and tepidly
I have given the soil to the old woman

The island is rising there it is again
Now to burnish him with tepid ash
A little on the eyes
And may he look upon the world again
With its four directions

Energía külme

He andado de mañana oliendo
Y mirando la laguna hundida
En la lluvia y rayos de sol
Entre las nubes cortadas
De plomo, café y celeste.
Me vienen a ver y yo te veo primero
Crees que soy una pequeña gaviota
Anclada en la laguna
Que vuela ahora brillante
Una llama flotando en una isla de poñpoñ
Y encima del agua.
Te he arañado mitras caminas
En el tibio líquido
Que ha guardado las hojas
En forma de un pie de caballo
Y si te da sueño después
De tu entrada al humedal
Es para que sientas mi cansancio
Porque cuidas este bosquecito
Que guardo para todos.

Külme Energy

I have walked since morning smelling
And gazing at the lagoon sunken
In rain and rays of sun
Between chopped clouds
Of lead, coffee and cerulean.
They come to see me and I see you first
You think I'm a small seagull
Anchored in the lagoon
Taking off now brilliant
A flame floating on an island of poñpoñ[49]

Upon the water.
I've scraped together your different paths
In the tepid liquid
That has preserved the leaves
In the form of a horse's foot
And if it makes you sleepy after
Your entrance to the wetland
It's so you might feel my fatigue
Because you take care of this little woodland
That I protect for everyone.

– **Stuart Cooke**

On the Humedal

after the welcome
ceremony the rain arrives; we huddle
for shelter under the arms of the maqui[50] –
muddled islands, unmoored, swept up
in a current that converges upon you

following you, the sense
is of knowledge returning, of communities
emerging, the birds and the medicines
no sense in description, the place
is too busy with the provision of seeds
for thoughts

every few steps we pause for a story
this is what
your grandfather told you
this is how
sight is returned
further on, giant leaves used for baking
for wrapping up potatoes like babies
in the way of your mothers

the poetry begins beneath glaciers, grows to weave
between the boulders strewn in their wake
protected by dreams, you search the volcanoes
when your wife falls ill you dream
of her medicine; the next day it calls to you
from the scrub beside the lake; rivers

talking with other rivers, the language
of water, of errant geology
a geolanguage in a geoterritory
swampy archives and erratic blocks of ice

now the plants have to talk, you say
the islands have to talk, the way
to fight for the earth is to follow its pathways
illuminating the roots of one place
in another, transforming ecology
into responsibility, islands of memories
atop the world of below – the source
of events, of futures and their residues

the way to fight is to learn the languages
and discover their knots
at moments where the eye catches
the way to fight is to recover the articulation
the meaning of a word in a phrase
the meaning of a place in a territory, and
the duration of its structure
the rhythm of its terrain, stutters
cluttering the heads of restless children, what
you say to them now, as we reach the height of the day
and the bad spirits begin to thaw
take this leaf, rub it between your fingers
and in the decades that follow
feel it spin you into a slow spiral
back to the source of your unfolding

Notes

1 *Humedal* is Spanish for 'wetland'. Hereafter I will use the Spanish term only.
2 The Huilliche are the southern-most collective of the Mapuche people, the Indigenous inhabitants of south-central Chile and south-west Argentina.
3 Esteban Alejandro Urriaga Astudillo, 'RIÑITNA LADEMUH', https://youtu.be/7ZBsy225gFk. (my translation) A variety of videos about Humedal Antiñir can be found on YouTube.
4 Macarena Gómez-Barris, *The Extractive Zone: Social Ecologies and Decolonial Perspectives* (Durham and London: Duke University Press, 2017), xix.

5. Gómez-Barris, *The Extractive Zone*, 85.
6. Pierre Joris, *A Nomad Poetics* (Middletown: Wesleyan University Press, 2003), 12–13.
7. For extended analysis of Huirimilla's poetry, see Chapter 7 of Stuart Cooke, *Speaking the Earth's Languages: A Theory for Australian-Chilean Postcolonial Poetics* (Amsterdam and New York: Rodopi, 2013).
8. Joanna Crow, 'Mapuche Poetry in Post-Dictatorship Chile: Confronting the Dilemmas of Neoliberal Multiculturalism', *Journal of Latin American Cultural Studies* 17, no. 2 (2008): 223.
9. Juan Paulo Huirimilla, *Palimpsesto* (Santiago: LOM Ediciones, 2005), 101 (my translation).
10. Crow, 'Mapuche Poetry in Post-Dictatorship Chile', 237.
11. Cooke, *Speaking the Earth's Languages: A Theory for Australian-Chilean Postcolonial Poetics*, 231.
12. Eva Palma, 'What if the Land Could Speak? Mapuche Poetry and Ecocriticism', *Interdisciplinary Studies in Literature and Environment* 23, no. 1 (2016): 139.
13. Melisa Stocco, 'La autotraducción en la poesía mapuche como territorio de tránsitos, tensiones y resistencias', *Estudios Filológicos*, no. 59 (2017): 190.
14. Personal communication, 23 January 2017. This chapter draws on information from interviews conducted in Spanish with Huirimilla in January and November of 2017. All translations into English are by the author.
15. Personal communication, 23 January 2017.
16. Personal communication, 23 January 2017.
17. Personal communication, 15 November 2017.
18. Personal communication, 15 November 2017.
19. Personal communication, 15 November 2017.
20. Personal communication, 15 November 2017.
21. Personal communication, 15 November 2017.
22. Krim Benterrak, Stephen Muecke and Paddy Roe, *Reading the Country: Introduction to Nomadology* (Fremantle: Fremantle Arts Centre Press, 1984).
23. Gilles Deleuze and Félix Guattari, *What Is Philosophy?*, trans. Hugh Tomlinson and Graham Burchell (New York: Columbia University Press, 1994), 85.
24. Deleuze and Guattari, *What Is Philosophy?*, 85–6.
25. Deborah Bird Rose, *Reports from a Wild Country: Ethics for Decolonisation* (Sydney: University of New South Wales Press, 2004), 153.
26. *Reports from a Wild Country*, 153.
27. *Reports from a Wild Country*, 154.
28. Personal communication, 18 November 2017.
29. See Chapter 7 of Cooke, *Speaking the Earth's Languages: A Theory for Australian-Chilean Postcolonial Poetics*. 'Koori' is a name that Aboriginal people from New South Wales and Victoria commonly use to refer to themselves.

30   Peter Minter, 'Archipelagos of Sense: Thinking about a Decolonised Australian Poetics', *Southerly* 73, no. 1 (2013): 156.
31   In Minter, 'Archipelagos of Sense', 164.
32   Minter, 'Archipelagos of Sense', 160.
33   Elaine Stratford et al., 'Envisioning the Archipelago', *Island Studies Journal* 6, no. 2 (2011): 117.
34   Minter, 'Archipelagos of Sense', 163. Note that 'Country' is capitalized by Minter, according to a developing convention which seeks to emphasize Country's subjecthood. Similarly, I refer to the Humedal as a proper name, rather than to 'the wetland'.
35   Minter, 'Archipelagos of Sense', 165 (my emphasis).
36   For an introduction to the legacies of classical and 'postmodern' ethnography, see, for example, Orin Starn, 'Writing Culture at 25: Special Editor's Introduction', *Cultural Anthropology* 27, no. 3 (2012): 411–16.
37   Deborah Bird Rose, 'On History, Trees and Ethical Proximity', *Postcolonial Studies* 11, no. 2 (2008): 157. Quoting Gershom Scholem.
38   Stocco, 'La autotraducción en la poesía mapuche', 197.
39   Deborah Bird Rose, 'Dialogue with Place: Toward an Ecological Body', *Journal of Narrative Theory* 32, no. 3 (2002): 322.
40   Stocco, 'La autotraducción en la poesía mapuche', 186 (my translation).
41   Stocco, 'La autotraducción en la poesía mapuche', 187.
42   Clayton Eshleman, *Juniper Fuse: Upper Paleolithic Imagination & the Construction of the Underworld* (Middletown: Wesleyan University Press, 2003), xii.
43   Paraphrasing Joris, *A Nomad Poetics*, 12.
44   Eshleman, *Juniper Fuse*, xv.
45   Stocco, 'La autotraducción en la poesía mapuche', 197 (my translation).
46   Stratford et al., 'Envisioning the Archipelago', 125.
47   Stratford et al., Envisioning the Archipelago', 125.
48   Paraphrasing Eshleman, *Juniper Fuse*, 236. Eshleman is referring to the archetypal significance of the hole, and its relationship to caves, souls and the number zero.
49   Huirimilla: '[From the Mapugundun,] poñpoñ is a species of highly absorbent moss. It's used in the making of nappies, and also to mop up petroleum after an oil spill.'
50   Maqui: *Aristotelia chilensis*, also known as Chilean wineberry.

Bibliography

Astudillo, Esteban Alejandro Urriaga. 'RIÑITNA LADEMUH', 2017.
Benterrak, Krim, Stephen Muecke and Paddy Roe. *Reading the Country: introduction to nomadology*. Fremantle: Fremantle Arts Centre Press, 1984.

Cooke, Stuart. *Speaking the Earth's Languages: A Theory for Australian-Chilean Postcolonial Poetics*. Amsterdam and New York: Rodopi, 2013.

Crow, Joanna. 'Mapuche Poetry in Post-Dictatorship Chile: Confronting the Dilemmas of Neoliberal Multiculturalism'. *Journal of Latin American Cultural Studies* 17, no. 2 (2008): 221–40.

Deleuze, Gilles and Félix Guattari. *What Is Philosophy?* Translated by Hugh Tomlinson and Graham Burchell. New York: Columbia University Press, 1994.

Eshleman, Clayton. *Juniper Fuse: Upper Paleolithic Imagination & the Construction of the Underworld*. Middletown: Wesleyan University Press, 2003.

Gómez-Barris, Macarena. *The Extractive Zone: Social Ecologies and Decolonial Perspectives*. Durham and London: Duke University Press, 2017.

Huirimilla, Juan Paulo. *Palimpsesto*. Santiago: LOM Ediciones, 2005.

Joris, Pierre. *A Nomad Poetics*. Middletown: Wesleyan University Press, 2003.

Minter, Peter. 'Archipelagos of Sense: Thinking about a Decolonised Australian Poetics'. *Southerly* 73, no. 1 (2013): 155–69.

Palma, Eva. 'What If the Land Could Speak? Mapuche Poetry and Ecocriticism'. *Interdisciplinary Studies in Literature and Environment* 23, no. 1 (2016): 138–48.

Rose, Deborah Bird. 'Dialogue with Place: Toward an Ecological Body'. *Journal of Narrative Theory* 32, no. 3 (2002): 311–25.

Rose, Deborah Bird. 'On History, Trees and Ethical Proximity'. *Postcolonial Studies* 11, no. 2 (2008): 157–67.

Rose, Deborah Bird. *Reports from a Wild Country: Ethics for Decolonisation*. Sydney: University of New South Wales Press, 2004.

Starn, Orin. 'Writing Culture at 25: Special Editor's Introduction'. *Cultural Anthropology* 27, no. 3 (2012): 411–16.

Stocco, Melisa. 'La autotraducción en la poesía mapuche como territorio de tránsitos, tensiones y resistencias'. *Estudios Filológicos*, no. 59 (2017): 185–99.

Stratford, Elaine, Godfrey Baldacchino, Elizabeth McMahon, Carol Farbotko and Andrew Harwood. 'Envisioning the Archipelago'. *Island Studies Journal* 6, no. 2 (2011): 113–30.

Index

2312 (Robinson) 28

Áak'abe' ku ya'alik táan u k'áaxal ja'/ Lluvia que la noche dicta (Villegas) 245
Aboriginal
  Australia 268–9
  eco-philosophies 192, 195, 201, 204–13
  knowledge systems 196
  pattern thinking 196–7
  people 114, 116, 191–8
  oral culture 200–201
Adorno, Theodor 4
aesthetic 71, 124–41
  autonomy of 231–3
  fashion 137
  planetary 9
Afghanistan 137–8
African Anthropocene 8–9, 63–74
After the Dreaming (Stanner) 114
Aggarwal, Mayank 159
Agra 131–2
Alberta 109
Alex & Me (Pepperberg) 52, 60 n.38
alien self 94–5
Allahabad 126, 130, 157
Allora, Jennifer 51
American Revolution 107–9
Anderson, John 172
Anigozanthos 176
Anigozanthos manglesii 176
Anthropocene 7–8, 24, 41–8
  African 8–9, 63–74
  as Glissant anticipates 71
  human perspective 41–8
  non-human perspective 48–50
  scale effects 7–8, 41–8
  urbanization and 21–3
anthropomorphism 51, 153
Anzaldúa, Gloria 239
Araluen, Evelyn 5, 118

Arctic Zoology (Pennant) 103–4, 107, 109
Arrival 51
art work 232
Ashcroft, Bill 70
Australia 3, 6, 10, 114–16, 270
  Aboriginal 268–9
  into archipelago 270
  Indigenous names 114–15
  Kangooroo 114–16
  robins 116
  south-west Western 12, 170–82
  transcultural ecopoetics 193–213
  transcultural literary environment in 221–34
avant-garde poetics 1–2

Bacigalupi, Paolo 26
Bahuguna, Sunderlal 158
Bahunguna, Vimla 165 n.68
Bailes, Melissa 180
balangan 224
balché tree 245
Ballard, J. G. 27
Banks, Joseph 114, 124
Barbauld, Anna 180
Basel Convention 87
Bassnett, Susan 113
Baudin, Nicholas 172–3
Bauman, Zygmunt 86, 88
Baxter, Stephen 27
Beijing 82–3
Bell, Andrew 171
Bengal 126–8, 130–5, 141
Bennett, Jane 74
Benterrak, Krim 224–5
Berlin Alexanderplatz (Döblin) 32
Berman, Morris 63
Bewell, Alan 10, 170, 176
Bhabha, Homi 272
Bhagalpur 132
Bhatt, Chandi Prasad 158

Bhutan   124–5
Bihar   131
Blake, William   11, 149–52
'Bleeding Heart' (Ivanchenko)   159, 161
'blood juice cloud'   202, 210–12
Bloom, Dan   24
Bombay   137, 141
Botany Bay Eclogue (Southey)   114
Bourdieu, Gabriel L.   252
Brandão, Ignacio de Loyola   26
British India   10–11, 126–41
British Zoology (Pennant)   107
Buchanan, Francis   136
bugarrigarra   224, 227, 235 n.12
Burke, Edmund   134
Burns, Robert   169, 171

Calbuco   269
Calcutta   139
Calthorpe, Peter   23
Calvert, Mary   170
Calvert, Richard   170
Calzadilla, Guillermo   51
cannibalism   92
caribou   107
Carter, Paul   176
Castellano, Katey   149
Castellanos, Rosario   242
Caste War (1847–1901)   247
Castillo, Rosalva Aída Hernández   241
Catesby, Mark   108
CAVAT (Capital Asset Value for Amenity Trees)   148, 152
censorship   113–15
Chacón, Gloria   240, 241
Chakrabarty, Dipesh   8, 41–8
Chamoli   157
Chan, Sánchez   251
Chatterjee, Partha   233
'Chen konel/Es por demás' (Huchim)   243
Chen Qiufan   9, 83–9
Chiang, Ted   8, 50–7
chicleros   240, 244–5, 247
Chihuailaf, Elicura   264
China
   Chen Qiufan   83–9
   ecological problems of   82–3
   e-waste problem   84–9
   Han Song   83, 89–94

hukou system   85
modernization   95
pollution in   82–3
science fiction   9, 82–95
waste, global cycle of   83–9
Chipko movement   157–9
Chrulew, Matthew   45
Cigarini, Chiara   89
Clark, Timothy   24, 42–3
Claudio Martín: vida de un chiclero (Vega)   244
climate change   6–8, 21–38, 42–8, 193, 213
   drowning cities   24–8
   human perspective   41–8
   non-human perspective   48–50
   submarine surrealism   28–32
   urban amphibiguity   32–8
   urbanization and   23
climate fiction   7–8, 24
   New York 2140   7, 23, 32–8
   Nước 2030 (*Water 2030*)   7, 23, 28–32
Climatopolis (Kahn)   23
Cob, Briceida Cuevas   242
Cocom Pech, Jorge Miguel   239
Coffey, Ray   225, 228
Colebrooke, Henry Thomas   135
Coleridge, Samuel Taylor   103
colonialism   29, 103–20, 230
colonial matrix of power   195–6, 201, 203, 206–8, 213, 215 n.17
colonial natural history   108–20
Common Agricultural Policy   148
composition   68
comprador collaboration   233
connectedness   4, 117
Cook, Captain   114, 127
Cooke, Stuart   14, 215 n.13, 218, 229, 233
   'On the Humedal'   278
Corvus olivaceus   115
Countdown (Weisman)   22
country   225, 227–8, 231, 235 n.13, 268–9
Country Land and Business Association (CLA)   148
Country Unwrapping Landscape (Kimberley)   207–8
Couto, Mia   8–9, 63–74, 74 n.4
   Under the Frangipani   67–70, 72–3
   Last Flight of the Flamingo, The   67–70, 72

on Mozambique   63–74
re-enchanting fiction   68–9
River Called Time, A   72
Sleepwalking Land   66–7
Tuner of Silences, The   69
Voices Made Night   66
Woman of the Ashes   66, 72–3
COVID-19   6–7
Crow, Joanna   264
Crutzen, Paul   21, 41

Danta, Chris   8
Darker Side of the Renaissance, The (Mignolo)   208
Darug people   114
Darwin, Charles   46
Davies, Jeremy   48
Davis, Mike   21
Davis, Wade   154
Dawson, Ashley   23
Day After Tomorrow, The (Emmerich) 25, 27
Dazagon Hill   140
de Barros, João   72
de Castro, Vivieros   230
Deleuze, Gilles   267–8
dendrophilia, romantic   11, 148–61
Denney, Peter   10–11
Derrida, Jacques   56
Der Schwarm (*The Swarm*, Schätzing)   27
Devi, Amrita   158
Díaz, Porfirio   243
disenchantment   63, 67
Ditie (*The Subway*, Han)   9, 89–90, 94
Djou   115
Döblin, Alfred   32
Domus et Animae   160
Don, David   176
Dos Passos, John   32
Drowned World, The (Ballard)   27
drowning cities   24–8
Dudley, Paul   108
Duke of Richmond's First Bull Moose, The (Stubbs)   104–5
Dunbartonshire   169, 173–4
Durand, Marcella   2
Dürer, Albrecht   103–4
Durham, John   47

earth   41, 47–55, 71–4, 268
Earth Liberation Front (ELF)   155–6
Eastern Whipbird   115
East India Company   124, 126–8, 133, 136
'Ecchoing Green, The' (Blake)   149–50
Eco, Umberto   51
ecocriticism   2–3
  nature poems in   3
  romantic   10
  tenacity of romanticism in   2–3
  transcultural   1–7
ecosystems   4–5, 7–8, 22, 269
Ehrlich, Paul   22
Eistau (Trojanow)   26
elk   104–13
  American   108–10
  European   107–8
  kinds   108
  vs. moose   108
Elk Island National Park   109
Emmerich, Roland   25
End We Start From, The (Hunter)   26, 27
England, nature in   106–17
environmental degradation   9, 73–4
environmental justice   1, 9, 23, 87–8
Eolian   103
Erickson, Bruce   45
Erithacus rubecula; see redbreast
Eshleman, Clayton   273
Estipah-skikikini-kots   109
Estok, Simon   195
ethnography   271–9
Euphorbia tirucalli   136
European elk   107–8
European Vision and the South Pacific (Smith)   177
Everett, Jim   191, 197–210, 212
Everton, Macduff   247
e-waste   9, 84–9
extinction   44–6
Extinction Studies   45–8
Extreme Cities (Dawson)   23

fables   49–50, 52–6
Facey, A. B.   228
Fallaw, Ben   244
Fall of Needwood, The (Mundy)   154–6
Flood (Baxter)   27

Folk Culture of Yucatán, The (Redfield) 246
folkloric exoticism 65
folk-urban continuum 246
Forbes, James 140
forests 11, 148–61
  conservation 156–7
  as cradle of freedom 154–5
  etymology of 156
  as female space 248–54
  in Indian subcontinent 156–61
  management, imperial model of 157
  in Maya language 246
  as Maya space 246–8
  in *Recuerdos del corazón de la montaña* 248–54
  Uttarakhand 157–8
  in Yucatán, cultural and social space 238–54
Forster, George 126, 132–3, 137
Fortunate Life, A (Facey) 228
fox 107
Freudenburg, William R. 22

Gabbert, Wolfgang 243–4
gadi 116
Ganges 130, 134
Garuba, Harry 74
geoterritory 14, 266–8
Ghosh, Amitav 24, 42, 46, 49
Gilpin, William 125, 127, 129–30, 133
Glastonbury, Keri 221
Glissant, Édouard 71, 270
globalization 9–10, 43, 86–9, 149, 194
global warming 25–6, 42
Gómez-Barris, Macarena 263
Goodell, Jeff 23
Gopal, Priyamvada 158
Gray, Richard 179
Great Derangement, The (Ghosh) 49
'Great Silence, The' (Chiang) 8, 46, 50–7
Greenock 169
Grieves, Vicki 195
Griffin, Carl 157–8
Guattari, Félix 267–8
Guha, Ramachandra 157–8
guiyi 89

Guiyu 9, 84–9
Gularabulu (Roe) 225, 231
Guugu Yimithirr 114

haciendas 245
Haida nation 118–20
Han Song 9, 83, 89–94
Haraway, Donna 66
Harjo, Joy 5
Hartigan, John 49–50
Hastings, Warren 126–8, 134
Head-Smashed-In 109
Hecht, Gabrielle 71–2
Heidegger, Martin 4
Heise, Ursula 4, 7–8, 44, 49, 53–4
henequen 244
Hindoostan 134
Hindutva 159
History of Four-Footed Beasts (Topsell) 106
Hodges, William 126–33
Hongse Haiyong (*The Red Sea*, Han) 9, 89–94
Hood, Robin 154
Horkheimer, Max 4
hortus siccus 177
Howarth, Richard B. 22
Huang Chao (*The Waste Tide*, Chen) 9, 83–9
Huilliche-Mapuche people 14, 263, 269, 274, 279 n.2
Huirimilla Oyarzo, Juan Paulo 14, 262–75
  Humedal Antiñir and 262–75
  Külme Energy 277
  'Mountain Grape' 276
  poetics and ethnography
    practice 275–9
    theory 271–5
  'Warrior Song' 264
human 8, 41–8, 92–4
  and animals relationship 106–7
  extensions of 222–4
Humedal Antiñir 14, 262–75; *see also* wetland, southern Chile
Hunter, Megan 26
Hybers 137

If a Tree Falls: A Story of the Earth Liberation Front 155
Imagining Extinction (Heise) 44–5

Indian Horse (Wagamese)   119
Indigenous ecological knowledge   3–5, 12, 113–14, 196–8, 233, 243–5, 262–7
Indigenous peoples   3, 10, 12, 107–11, 113–20, 263
Indigenous sounds   115
Indigenous women   241–3
informal urbanization   21–2
intertidal property pricing index (IPPI)   35
Irby, Charles Leonard   175
Ivanchenko, Andriy   159
Ives, Edward   137

Jamaica   116
Jefferson, Thomas   108
Jensen, Liz   25
Jia Liyuan   89
Jindyworobaks   195
Johnson, James   140
Jones, William   138
Joris, Pierre   263–4
Joyce, James   32

Kafka, Franz   54–5
Kahn, Matthew E.   23
Kaizong, Chen   85
Kangooroo   114–16
Kashmir valley   131
Keller, Lynn   2–3
Kennedy, Elizabeth   170
Khejri trees   158
Kimberley, Jonathan   12, 191, 197–210
Kindersley, Jemima   130
King's Square; *see* Soho Square
kinship system   13
Kirby, Vicky   6
Kluge Hans (Clever Hans)   223
Knight, Richard Payne   129
koala   114
Külme Energy   266, 277–8
Kurulbrang   176
Kwaymullina, Ambelin   195
Kwenda, Chirevo   70

Langton, Marcia   195
Last Flight of the Flamingo, The (Couto)   67–70, 72
Latham, John   115

Latour, Bruno   43, 68, 89, 234
Lawrence, Henry W.   151
'Lección de cocina' ('Cooking Lession'; Castellanos)   242
Lechenaultia biloba   176
Lee, Kai N.   22
Lehtinen, Tapani   26
Li Daoyuan   93–4
Lienlaf, Leonel   264
Li Guangyi   89
Lira, María Luz Lepe   240, 242
literary communication   13, 221
López, Claudio Vadillo   243
Lost in Translation   111
Lyotard, Jean-François   275

McGurl, Mark   43, 50
machine *vs.* animal   223
Mackintosh, William   134, 137–9
'Making Rain'   225
Mangles, James   170, 174–5
Manhattan   32–8
Manhattan Transfer (Passos)   32
Mapuche poetry   12, 264–5
Mapudungun   264, 266–7, 272, 274
Martínez Huchim, Ana Patricia   13, 238–54, 255 nn.7, 9, 10
   'Chen konel/Es por demás'   243
   feminist vision   248–54
   professional career   240
   Recuerdos del corazón de la montaña   240, 247–54
   role in Maya cultural and linguistic literary revival in Yucatán   240–54
   U yóol xkaambal jaw xíiw/Contrayerba (Antidote)   240, 252
   work of   241–54
masculine Romanticism   179–80
Massey, Doreen   239
Masson, Margaret Shrimpton   240
Mateer, John   270
Mathews, Jennifer   250
Maya culture   238–54
Maya identity   254 n.4
Maya language   239, 246, 251, 255 n.6
Maya oral literatures   243–4
Maya woman   238–54
Maya writing   12–13, 238–54

meenamatta water country   192, 197–210
Mekong Delta   28–9
Melgar, Rafael E.   244
Mellor, Anne   179
Mignolo, Walter   195
Minter, Peter   5–6, 12–14, 233, 270
Mitchison, John   170
modernization   223–4
Modern Maya: Incidents of Travel and Friendship in Yucatán, The (Everton)   247
Molloy, Georgiana   12, 169–82
  attentiveness to plants   177–9
  in Australia   170–82
  Australian flora, knowledge of   177
  erasure   181–2
  extinction   181–2
  poetry   177–9
  precision   177–9
  romantic visions   170–2
  seeds and   174–7
  self shaping   179–81
  shipping and   174–7
  translocation   172–4
  vision   173–4
moose   104–8
Morton, Timothy   1
Mosquera, Gerardo   197
Mowaljarlai, David   195
Mozambique   8–9, 63–74
  Couto on   63–74
  culture   70–1
  disenchantment   67
  geohistory   64–6
  'harvest of death'   66–71
  'sacred web'   66–71
  war   64, 66–70
  weather   65
Mrs. Dalloway (Woolf)   32
Muecke, Stephen   13
Mughal empire   126–8, 132
Muk'ul T'an In Nool/ ecretos del abuelo (Pech)   245
multinaturalism   13, 230
Mundy, Francis Noel Clarke   149, 152–6, 159
Mung, Patrick Mung   191
Mysore   130, 133–6

'nan xia'   85
Não Verás País Nenhum (Brandão)   26
Nathan, Tobie   224, 230
'National Sword' policy   88
'Nature Attacks' film   24–5
natures   124–5
  colonial translation of   103–20
  India   126–30
  notion of   10
  poems   3
Natures in Translation (Bewell)   10, 170
Needwood   152–5
Needwood Forest (Mundy)   152, 156, 160
Neidjie, Bill   195
'Neither above nor Below' (Stanford)   28
neo-colonialism   233
New York   7, 23, 32–8
New York 2140 (Robinson)   7, 23, 32–8
New Zealand   110–11
Nghiêm-Minh, Nguyễn-Võ   23, 28–32
Nicol, C. W.   148
nilababa   226–7
Nixon, Rob   64
noj k'áax   256 n.14
Noonuccal, Oodgeroo   233
normative networks   221–2
North America   105–11, 116, 119, 243, 247
nourishing terrain   195–6, 211
Nước 2030 (*Water 2030*)   7, 23, 28–32
Nurpur   138
'Nurses Song' (Blake)   151–2

Odds against Tomorrow (Rich)   25, 27–8
Oerlemans, Onno   172, 181
omnipoetics   2
Oneness   198
óol   252
opossum   107
optopia   37
oral poetics   224–31
Origin of Species (Darwin)   46

Palar River   134
Paradisaea apoda; see Eolian
Parantaja (*The Healer*, Tuomainen)   26

Paredes, Julieta   241
parrot communication   52–7
parrots   131
Paul (octopus)   223
Pennant, Thomas   103–7
Pepperberg, Irene M.   52, 60 n.38
Permanent Settlement of Bengal   126, 135
Peter, Red   54
Phillip, Arthur   174–5
picturesque
   India, representation of   129–41
   principles   129
   scenery   129
   as sense of vision   129–30
   taste   10–11, 125–6, 129–41, 171–2
   tourism   129–41
planetary aesthetic   9, 22, 32, 42–3, 63–8, 71–4
plangermairreenner clan   191
Platypus anatinus   103–4
Poema de la selva trágica (Vega)   244
poetics   1–2, 271–9
pollution   82–3
Ponce Jiménez, Martha Patricia   245
Population Bomb, The (Ehrlich)   22
Predators   92
Protester (Watt)   156
Psophodes olivaceus; see Whipcoach bird
Puerto Montt   263
Punjab   132

Questioning Nature (Bailes)   180
Quijano, Aníbal   195

raccoon   37, 107
Rajmahal, Bengal   134
Rapture, The (Jensen)   25, 27
Reading the Country (Benterrak, Muecke and Roe)   224–5, 228, 267
re-animated planet   71–4
recomposition   68
Recuerdos del corazón de la montaña   240, 247–54
redbreast   116
red deer   108–11
Red Deer River   109
Redfield, Robert   246
re-enchantment   8, 63, 65
Reid, Bill   118–20

Rennell, James   131, 134
Revista Yucateca de Estudios Literarios   240
Reynolds, Kevin   27
Rich, Nathaniel   25
Rigby, Kate   3–4
River Called Time, A (Couto)   72
Rivero, Piedad Peniche   244–5
Robinson, Kim Stanley   23, 28, 32–7
Roe, Paddy   221–2, 224–8
Rohilla War   134
Rojas, Carlos   89
romantic dendrophilia   148–61
romanticism   2–4, 181
Romanticism and the Materiality of Nature (Oerlemans)   172
Rose, Deborah Bird   45, 195, 211, 215 n.18, 228–9, 268, 272
Rothenberg, Jerome   1–2
Rothman, Joshua   51

sa'at   252
Saigon   23, 28–32
Salinas, Alicia   240, 251–2
Samuelson, Meg   8
sapodilla trees   13, 243, 247–50, 256 n.15
Saul Indian Horse   119
Saunders, Robert   124
scale effects   41–8
Schätzing, Frank   27
Schilthuizen, Menno   22–3
science fictions   9, 50, 95
Sea and Summer, The (Turner)   26, 27
"Search for the Perfect Language, The" (Eco)   51
self translation   272
Sense of Place and Sense of Planet (Heise)   4
Seward, Anna   153, 155
Shaw, George   103
Shaws Water Works   181
Shelley, Mary   180
Sherwood Forest   153–6
Sherwood Forest (Williams)   152
Shuijing Zhu (*Commentary on the Water Classics*, Li)   93
skunk   107
Sleepwalking Land (Couto)   66–7
Smith, Bernard   177

Smith, Charlotte   180
Smith, James Edward   178
Smith, John   159
social marginality   241
Soho Square   151–2
Soja, Edward   272
Songs Chiefly in the Scottish Dialect (Burns)   171
Songs of Experience (Blake)   151–2
Songs of Innocence (Blake)   150–2
'Sonnet LXIII. To Colebrooke Dale' (Seward)   155
Souriau, Étienne   232
Southey, Robert   114, 170
south-west Western Australia   170–82
space   239
Spanish language   238–9
spatial trialectics   272–3
species fictions   53–4
Specimen of the Botany of New Holland, A (Smith)   178
Spirit of Haida Gwaii, the Black Canoe, The (Reid)   118
spirituality   56, 196, 246
stag   108
Stanford, Claire Miye   28
Stanner, W. E. H.   114
Stengers, Isabelle   71
Stirling, James   173, 175–6
Stocco, Melisa   272, 274
Stoermer, Eugene   21, 41
Storey, Helen   173
'Story of Your Life' (Chiang)   51
Stott, Philip   152
Stubbs, George   104
submarine surrealism   28–32
Sun, Mengtian   9
Surry   175
Suvin, Darko   95
Swan River   173
SWILCAR Oak   153, 159–60
Swilcar Oak (Smith)   159

Tasmania   191
Tedlock, Denis   225
Tee, Ve-Yin   11
Tehri   157
terra nullias   113
territory   268

'Tianxia Zhi Shui' ('All the Water in the World')   93
Tibet   124–5
tombstones   150
Topsell, Edward   106
transcultural ecocriticism   1–6, 215 n.14
 Australian   193–213
 cultures   194–5
 damaging   195
 and decoloniality   193–7
 event   12, 191–3
 nourishing   195–6
 theoretical framework   193–4
transcultural literary environment   221–34
 aesthetic, autonomy of   231–3
 globalization   233–4
 human, extensions of   222–4
 oral poetics   224–31
translation   108–13, 263, 272
Travels in India (Hodges)   127–8
travel writing   10, 125–7, 140
 about India   126–41
 British   126–41
trees
 balché   245
 Khejri   158
 love for   148–61
 sapodilla   13, 243, 247–50, 256 n.15
 Zapote   256 n.14
Trexler, Adam   24
Trojanow, Ilija   26
Tsering, Dechen   83
Tuner of Silences, The (Couto)   69
Tuomainen, Antti   26
Turner, George   26
Tzunux, Rosa Pu   241

U ka'ajsajil u ts'u' noj k'áax / Recuerdos del corazón de la montaña (*Memories from the Heart of the Forest*)   240
Ulysses (Joyce)   32
Under the Frangipani (Couto)   67–70, 72–3
Uninhabitable Earth, The (Wallace-Wells)   23
Un pueblo y un hombre (Vega)   244

Urbanism in an Age of Climate Change
(Calthorpe)   23
urbanization   7
   Anthropocene and   21–3
   challenges   22–3
   cities   21–2
   climate change and   23–32
   drowning cities   24–8
   environmental justice   23
   environment and   22–3, 263
   European   21–2
   informal   21–2
   political ecology   23
   populations   21–2
USA trilogy (Passos)   32
Uttarakhand   157–8
U yóol xkaambal jaw xíiw/Contrayerba
(Antidote)   240, 252

Valentia, Viscount   130, 133, 141
van Dooren, Thom   45
Vega, Luis Rosado   244
Villegas, Wildernain   245
Villeneuve, Denis   51
Vint, Sherryl   53
Vivian, Helen   200
Voices Made Night (Couto)   66
von Mossner, Alexa Weik   24

Wagamese, Richard   119
Wailes, George   176
Wallace-Wells, David   23
Wallmapu   267
Walmajarri people   223
Wang Yao   89
Wapiti   110
War of the Worlds, The (Wells)   50
Waskasoo Seepee   109
waste, global cycle of   83–9
Water Will Come, The (Goodell)   23
Waterworld   27
Watkinson, Maia Gunn   13
Watling, Thomas   174
Watt, T. J.   155
Weber, Max   63
Webster, Robert M.   45
Weisman, Alan   22
Wells, H. G.   50
wetland, southern Chile   262–71

Whipcoach bird   115
White, Gilbert   103, 149–51
White, Jessica   12
Williams, Helen Maria   180
Williams, Raymond   153
Williams, Sarah Johanna   149, 152–3
Wilson, Edward O.   48
Windup Girl, The (Bacigalupi)   26, 27
Woman of the Ashes (Couto)   66, 72–3
women   12, 92
   exchange   244–5
   exploitation   244–5, 250
   henequen plantations for   244
   Maya   238–54
   roles   252
   vs. sea   92–3
woodland   152–3
Woolf, Virginia   32
Wordsworth, William   169
Worley, Paul   240, 243
Wright, Judith   233

Xanthorrhoea   116
xsaataj óol   252
'xsaataj óol/Divagación' ('The Wanderer')   240, 252
Xuuaji   119

'Yann a bin xook/Irás a la escuela' ('You'll go to School'; Cob)   242
Yucatán Peninsula   238–49
   anthropological discourse *vs.* ethnocentric agendas   246–8
   forests as female space   248–54
   forests as Maya space   246–8
   henequen production in   244
   historical, political and cultural contexts   241–6
   literature   238–54
   postcolonial condition   238–9
   Recuerdos del corazón de la montaña   240, 247–54
   sapodilla trees   13, 243
Yuumilk'aax/Yuntsiloob   246

Zapote trees   256 n.14
Zheng He   93
Zoology of North America   107

www.ingramcontent.com/pod-product-compliance
Lightning Source LLC
Chambersburg PA
CBHW072125290426
44111CB00012B/1779